ROYAL INSTITUTE OF PHILOSOPHY LECTURES
VOLUME EIGHT · 1973–1974

NATURE AND CONDUCT

ROYAL INSTITUTE OF PHILOSOPHY LECTURES
VOLUME EIGHT · 1973–1974

NATURE AND CONDUCT

Edited by

R. S. PETERS

ST. MARTIN'S PRESS NEW YORK

CONTENTS

FOREWORD

MOST British philosophers would regard G. E. Moore's *Principia Ethica* as a turning-point in ethics, though they would now disagree about whether the turn was in a desirable direction. Firstly Moore's concentration on the meaning of 'good' initiated a long period of concentration on the meaning of ethical terms. Seemingly his exposure of the alleged naturalistic fallacy made it difficult for philosophers to outline moral systems in which close connections were made between human conduct and features of human nature or of the natural world.

The climate of opinion in philosophy, however, is now less restrictive. Queries are constantly raised not just about the activity of 'conceptual analysis' but also about its importance in philosophy. The possibility is challenged of strictly delimiting philosophical enquiries from other enquiries – e.g. in psychology or the social services. And in ethics itself many are bored with minute questions of meaning and wish to raise again larger issues which were considered by past philosophers such as Hume, Kant, Mill and Bradley. There is also a growing conviction, exemplified by the journal *Philosophy and Public Affairs*, that philosophy has an important contribution to make to the discussion of substantive issues such as euthanasia, abortion, the use of violence, academic freedom, and the pollution of the environment.

The time therefore seems opportune to raise again some of the general questions about the relationship between nature and conduct. And this is the theme of the series of lectures delivered at the Royal Institute of Philosophy in 1973–4. 'Nature' was not restricted to human nature and no particular pattern was laid down into which contributors to the series were asked to fit. The general theme of the series was explained to them and they were asked if they had some ideas which they wished to explore which were consonant with it.

In spite of this lack of plan the lectures which were given fall roughly into four groups. The first and largest group deals with the most general questions about the nature of man and the role of empirical assumptions in morality. The second group is concerned with how more specific notions such as 'needs', 'happiness', 'conscience', and 'playing a role' enter into morality. In the third group wider questions are raised about man's relationship and attitudes to the natural and animal world. In the final and smallest group there are two papers which raise ethical issues about environmental planning and cost-benefit analysis.

THE ROLE OF EMPIRICAL ASSUMPTIONS IN MORALITY

In the first lecture, which was also the H. B. Acton Lecture, Renford Bambrough, Fellow of St John's College, Cambridge, uses the title 'Essay on Man' to ask whether the general question 'what is the nature of man?' can be legitimately raised. He distinguishes the logical constraints on what can count as a man from the causal constraints connected with human existence, and the moral constraints to which a being is subject if he is to be worthy of being called human. But, he argues, the question 'what is man?' is still one question in its own right. The unity of the question must not be forgotten in following up different aspects of the answer.

A more specific and historically hallowed version of this question is raised by Anthony Quinton, Fellow of New College, Oxford, in his paper on 'Has Man an Essence?' He has sympathy for the general move away from the formalism of recent moral philosophy and for a return to the attempt to base principles of right conduct on human nature. But he does not think that this return is helped by any attempt to revive doctrines about the essence of man. For, he argues, even if it can be shown that man has an essence, it cannot be shown that this has any ethical implications. He illustrates this theme by exploring the theories of Aristotle, Marx, and Sartre.

G. J. Warnock, Principal of Hertford College, Oxford, is interested in a looser connection between morality and human nature than that suggested by the doctrine of man's essence. He wants to know 'what, and how much empirical information is required for, or relevant to, moral philosophy?' His starting-point for this enquiry is Kant's work in 'practical anthropology'. So he calls his paper 'Kant and Anthropology'. He examines the situation of persons hypothetically placed behind 'the veil of ignorance' in John Rawls's treatment of the principle of justice, but objects that the liberal allowance of information granted to them is due to Rawls's assimilation of moral philosophy to legislation. On the other hand he argues that Kant's more stringent exclusion of the empirical is difficult to defend because he does not consider carefully enough why principles are wanted, and what they are supposed to do for us.

It is the obverse of the type of question raised by Warnock that interests Ted Honderich, Reader in Philosophy at University College, University of London, namely, why certain facts are not taken notice of by philosophers, and why some sorts of palpable facts arouse a less ready response than others. In his paper 'On Inequality and Violence, and differences we make between them' he catalogues facts about inequality and violence. He then notes and tries to explain the difference in quietness which characterises our responses to these two types of facts. He discusses and rejects considerations which might justify the psychological supremacy of our responses to violence and argues for the relevance of facts about distress in interpreting the principle of equality.

Another kind of connection between human nature and morality is examined by Christopher Cherry, Senior Lecturer in Philosophy at the University of Kent, in his paper on 'Agreement, Objectivity, and the Sentiment of Humanity in Morals'. He wishes to rebut the suggestion that human consciousness and moral consciousness are completely distinct – that the absence of the latter would only affect the former in minimal respects. His question, in other words, is about the relationship between being aware and being morally aware. He shows, first of all, that our concern about certain matters in human life, which is evidenced by the concepts which we have developed, cannot be separated from our adoption of a 'moral point of view'. He also indicates directions in which he would have to travel to sustain the stronger and more interesting thesis that conceptualising creatures must be creatures with moral interests.

In the last paper of the first group Ian Gregory, Lecturer in Philosophy and Education at the University of York, approaches the problem of the relationship between human nature and conduct by comparing and contrasting three theories of human nature within the psycho-analytic tradition, those of Freud, Klein, and the neo-Freudians. In his paper 'Psycho-analysis, Human Nature and Human Conduct' he argues that the differences between these theories are only in part rooted in empirical considerations. They also reflect deep-seated presuppositions that inform our conception of the kind of creature man is. These differing images of man affect fundamentally the conception – of man as a moral agent – that emerges from each of the theories.

MORALITY AND SPECIFIC ASPECTS OF HUMAN NATURE

With the second group of papers attention is directed away from general issues about the relationship of conduct to human nature towards more specific ways in which they might be related. The most obviously moral aspect of human nature is a man's conscience, which Justin Gosling, Fellow of St Edmund Hall, Oxford, interprets as being connected with what upon reflection a person thinks it right to do. In his paper on 'The Natural Supremacy of Conscience' he asks what importance in morality should be given to this type of reflection. His answer is that this emphasis goes easily only with certain moral positions. There are other moral views – e.g. Platonic, consequentialist, on which it becomes a puzzle why anyone should have any enthusiasm at all about the development or exercise of conscience.

Happiness, too, is a state of mind whose relationship to morality has been a matter of controversy amongst philosophers. Roger Scruton, Lecturer in Philosophy at Birkbeck College, University of London, is interested in happiness because he thinks that it affords some basis for the objectivity of moral judgements. In his paper 'Reason and Happiness' he explains, first of all, the 'path of truth' to the objectivity of moral judgements, by examining whether it makes sense to apply the concept of truth to them and whether their truth conditions can be described. This path peters out in a bewildering series of questions. So he turns to the 'path of reason', which construes the categorical imperative as an expression of attitude and looks for reasons acceptable to any man for acquiring moral attitudes, which are reasons independent of his particular desires. His case is that the appeal to happiness provides reasons which are not relative to desire, but which are practical and acceptable to any man. It is important, however, to realise that happiness does not provide a *further* end for action any more than friendship provides a further end for actions done out of friendship. Morality is a part of happiness, not a means to it. 'In happiness what one is, is what one thinks it a good thing to be.'

Another state of mind which has often been closely connected with morality is that of 'need'. Human needs have been cited to support demands for rights and as a relevant ground for applying the principle of distributive justice. It is not, however, this type of connection between human nature and morality that is the main focus of interest in the paper by Richard Wollheim, Grote Professor of Mind and Logic at University College, University of London, in his paper on 'Needs, Desires and Moral Turpitude'. He is worried about the confusion between needs and desires both in philosophy and in life itself. This bears upon morality because 'moral turpitude' consists in representing to ourselves and to others our pressing desires in language appropriated from 'need'. To set the stage for the exposure of this strategy Wollheim examines the phenomenon of need in simple and complex forms and contrasts it with that of desire. He emphasises that 'need' involves a departure from a norm and that the object of need constitutes a remedy.

Martin Hollis, Senior Lecturer in Philosophy in the University of East Anglia, tackles issues surrounding the long-standing assertion that man is a social animal. In his paper on 'My Role and its Duties', which is a modern variant of Bradley's famous essay on 'My Station & its Duties', he argues that, though the old doctrine that man has an essence may be rejected, presuppositions about human nature are still crucial to social theory and to the explanation of behaviour. He takes the modern explanatory notion of 'role-playing' as a case study and shows how this behaves differently in social theories depending on whether they work with a presupposition of man as plastic or as autonomous. He also sketches his own theory of the free social individual who creates his own social identity by acting rationally within a consistent role-set of his own choosing and who becomes what he has chosen by accepting his 'duties' as his duties.

MAN'S RELATIONSHIP TO THE NATURAL WORLD

The conviction that man is a free agent raises wider questions about the position of man within the natural world with which the third group of papers is concerned. John Watkins, Professor of Logic and Scientific Method at the London School of Economics and Political Science, in his paper on 'Three views concerning Human Freedom', addresses himself to these wider issues of free-will and determinism. He considers the empiricist view of Hobbes and Hume and the a priorist view of Spinoza and Kant and finds them both inadequate. The fact that both theories were developed within a deterministic framework gives a common explanation of some of their inadequacies. Watkins then proceeds to outline a third conception of autonomy which reflects the shift from Kantian determinism and a priorism to Popperian indeterminism and conjecturalism.

The question 'How is man related to the universe?' is regarded by Shirley Letwin as the ghost in modern philosophy. In her paper 'Nature, History and Morality' she sets out carefully the Greek view of this relationship as represented by Plato and Aristotle, who were impressed by the fact that although everything changes, there appears to be a limit and order to these changes. To explain this they postulated an eternal ordering spiritual principle, which men are both subject to and incorporate. She then explains how man became a stranger in the universe once, with the rise of modern science, teleological explanations were abandoned. She examines evolutionary and structural patterns discerned in the human world by Popper and Lévi-Strauss which she regards as attempts to save eternal truth by dispensing with human freedom, and Sartre's existentialism which saves human freedom by eliminating any reason for exercising it.

In her view these attempts to deal with the void left by rejection of the Greek view are unsatisfactory because of their repudiation of historical orders which consist of contingent connections between contingent ideas made by man. She then explains how such historical orders can be objective by taking the example of language, and passes to a consideration of other historical objectivities such as science and art. She denies the superior objectivity often accorded to science. 'If there is no rational cosmic order, the variety cannot be arranged in a hierarchy.' She ends by examining the features of morality as one such historical objectivity.

The importance of the question 'How is man related to the universe?' which, in Shirley Letwin's view, most emancipated modern philosophers refuse to hear, is high-lighted by modern debates about conservation. For objections to the despoliation of the natural world are seldom based just on some view about the harm which it does to human beings. More deep-seated pre-suppositions about man's place in nature lurk beneath. It is these which John Passmore, Professor of Philosophy in the Australian National University, discusses in his paper on 'Attitudes to Nature'.

He deals, first of all, with the two leading traditions in modern Western thought, the Cartesian view that matter is inert and that man's relationship to it is that of a despot who can legitimately re-shape it in accordance with his desires and the Hegelian view that 'nature exists only *in potentia*, as something which it is man's task to help to actualise through art, science, philosophy, technology, converting it into something human, something in which he can feel thoroughly "at home", in no sense alien or strange to him, a mirror in which he can see his own face'. He proceeds to ask what general conditions any philosophy of nature must fulfil if it is to do justice to the scientific themes of the ecological movement as distinct from its mystical overtones, without being tempted by forms of reductionism that deny the important differences between natural and human dealings.

Passmore then examines the contention that the West now needs a new ethic, with responsibility for nature lying at its centre. He argues that, to a considerable degree, very familiar ethical principles are strong enough to deal with despoilers but that, in addition, the Augustinian doctrine has to be dropped that in his dealings with nature man is simply not subject to moral censure, except where specifically human interests arise. Cruelty to animals, for instance, is wrong, and vandalism is as applicable to those who damage or destroy the natural world as it is to those who damage or destroy artefacts. If we can bring ourselves to admit fully the independence of nature, the fact that things go on in their own complex ways, we are likely to feel more respect for the ways in which they go on. In brief the emergence of new moral attitudes to nature is bound up with the emergence of a more realistic philosophy of nature.

John Benson, Professor of Philosophy in the University of Lancaster, has a very different kind of interest in the natural world. In his paper 'Hog in Sloth, Fox in Stealth: Man and Beast in Moral Thinking' he examines the ways in which other species enter our moral thinking. An obvious way is in the use of animal personages in children's stories, which permits some undidactic pointing of morals. Then there is the way in which species of animals have entered our moral vocabulary as a shorthand way of referring to human character-types, e.g. the wolf, worm, and lamb. They help understanding as well as evaluation. Indeed Benson is particularly interested in this aspect of our reference to animals; for he thinks that they provide overtly observable paradigms for understanding certain explanatory notions such as greed, for which we cannot give a list of characteristic types of behaviour. The behaviour of the fox, for instance, provides a simple paradigm on which we can build our understanding of 'cunning'. There is, however, a danger in pushing surface similarities too far and taking metaphors too literally as, for instance, when the behaviour of people in libraries is explained in terms of the territory-defending behaviour of some species of animals.

ETHICAL ASPECTS OF ENVIRONMENTAL PLANNING

The last two papers in the series deal with the ethical aspects of environmental planning. In the first paper on 'Contrasting Methods of Environmental Planning' Richard Hare, White's Professor of Moral Philosophy in the University of Oxford, discusses two methods

of approach to problems of planning. In the first, which he calls the
means-end model, goals have to be decided upon first and then
means looked for to attain them. In the second, the trial design
model, the designer produces more or less detailed particular designs
and the client chooses which he prefers. An illustration of the former
method is given by Roger Creighton's book *Urban Transportation
Planning* and of the second by Sir Colin Buchanan's books *Alternatives for Edinburgh* and *Edinburgh: the Recommended Plan*. One
of the deficiencies of the former method is shown to be the tendency
to omit goals that are not measurable in terms of money, as was seen
in the majority report on the third London airport. This vitiates
attempts to 'prove' that one plan is better than another. In the latter
method, however, there is no attempt to 'prove' an evaluative conclusion – only to make as well-informed a choice as is possible in the
circumstances. Hare then discusses different ways of ensuring that
the interests of all are taken into account and sets out the case for his
own approach in which 'ought to be adopted' goes along with 'prepared to prescribe' for 'universal adoption in cases just like this' as
against that of the 'ideal observer' or 'rational contractor' theories.

In the final paper Peter Self, Professor of Public Administration
at the London School of Economics and Political Science, in his
paper 'Techniques and Values in Policy Decisions' deals with difficulties in the fashionable technique of cost-benefit analysis. He
explains it first as a form of economic populism, as an attempt to
apply the concept of consumer choice to a much broader range of
political decisions and compares it with political methods of assessing
interests. He thinks that the best case for cost-benefit analysis is as a
check upon interest group claims within a general policy framework.
He then demonstrates the intractability for the cost-benefit analysis
approach of claims based on respect for rights and 'basic needs'.
There is also the problem of 'welfare', the most neglected subject of
welfare economics, and the difficulties of quantifying any assessment
of it. Considerations such as these justify scepticism about the possibility of translating political issues into the more precise language of
economics; for it is based on the mistaken assumption that economics
possesses a single normative yardstick (such as consumers' welfare)
which is lacking in politics.

Self ends by comparing the cost-benefit analysis approach with
that of 'consensus planning', which works through goals by political
leaders and other spokesmen for interest groups, and which is
guided by a large number of social norms and beliefs about 'the
common good'. An example of this was the classic Ebenezer Howard
case for new towns. He points out that these two approaches pre-

suppose different views of man in society, the 'consensus-planning'
approach tending to see the needs of man and society in much more
integrated terms. His conclusion is that, at best, a modified version of
cost-benefit analysis can be used as an instrument of policy criticism,
not as a positive instrument for decision or arbitration.

R. S. PETERS

Acting Honorary Director
The Royal Institute of Philosophy

Professor of the Philosophy of Education
University of London Institute of Education

1

ESSAY ON MAN

Renford Bambrough

The H. B. Acton Lecture

I AM grateful for the honour that is done to me by the invitation to give the first H. B. Acton Lecture. We are all grateful for an occasion to honour Professor Acton. It is disappointing, however understandable, and fitting to his modesty, that he has not felt able to be here to receive our gratitude.

It is fitting, too, that the first lecture to bear his name should be an Essay on Man and should open a series on *Nature and Conduct*. Harry Acton is a man of letters, a reader and writer of those *literae* which are *humaniores* than the human sciences, more sociable than sociology, but at least as difficult and disciplined for writer and reader when they flow from the right pen. Marx and Mill, *The Morals of Markets*; Crime and Punishment, *The Idea of a Spiritual Power*: his themes have had to do with man and his nature and conduct. He has had regard in the treatment of them to the human value of tradition and to a tradition of humane values: no generation is an island; even the youngest of us is involved in Mankinde.

By today's conventions he is therefore unconventional, and accordingly accustomed to misrepresentation and misunderstanding, and even – in some of the comments on *The Right to Strike* and *The Morals of Markets* – to the hysteria that shrieks from outraged conformity. This is not the least of the reasons for doing him honour.*

*   *   *

* This lecture was delivered on 19 October 1973. Professor Acton died on 16 June 1974. The text was prepared for publication before his death, and has not been altered.

Socrates called down philosophy from the heavens and placed it in towns and markets and in the houses and the hearts of men. He stayed in Athens because the object of his study lived there, and he did not care for mythical beings when there were human beings to talk to.[1]

In France the English-speaking visitor is sometimes baffled in bookshops by the category of *sciences humaines*, where Aristotle and Wittgenstein rub shoulders with Freud and Frazer, Evans-Pritchard and Lévi-Strauss. We forget how recent and local is the attempt to undo what Socrates did – to return philosophy to the skies of the abstract, or to empirical enquirers who are no less φυσικόι for giving the name of language or mind to the mythical constructs on which they fix their Cyclopean eyes. At most times and in most places philosophy is and has been a study of man, issuing in a *Treatise of Human Nature* or an *Essay concerning Human Understanding*, a set of *Principles of Human Knowledge* or *Essays on the Intellectual Powers of Man* as often as in a *Discourse on Method* or a *Begriffschrift*. In our own lifetime we have seen *Human Knowledge: Its Scope and Limits* and *Human Society in Ethics and Politics*. The Moral Sciences whose Newton Russell was still aspiring to be are the very humanities from which we continue to distinguish the natural and social sciences.

Kant and Hegel and the Idealists who Anglicised and Anglicanised them are the latest generation of anthropocentric philosophers in the tradition that runs from Socrates to the twentieth-century 'revolution in philosophy', and hence it is against them that the revolution is primarily directed. (It is the sins of the fathers and not of the great-grandfathers that set the children's teeth on edge.) The first step was the de-psychologisation of logic: we have been taught to think of the logic of propositions instead of the psychology of judgement or the rhetorical tactics of assertion and denial. It was not a long second step to the de-psychologisation and de-historicisation of philosophy: a process helped by using the term *logic* in a sense wide enough to include all or most of philosophy. Unless we resist, firmly and very soon, the de-psychologisation of psychology will follow. Already John Wisdom has felt it necessary, even thirty years ago, to remark that Dr Waddington is very severe on those of us who persist in being anthropomorphic about men.[2]

The reactions have already happened in impressive number and variety, but reactionaries are not always the best respondents to the excesses of revolutionaries. Too often they share the either/or

---

[1] Plato, *Phaedrus*, 229e–230b.
[2] *Philosophy and Psycho-Analysis*, p. 103.

premises that led to the excesses in the first place. Phenomenologists, Existentialists, and various more or less modish forms of Marxism and Wittgensteinism have threatened to preserve too much of the bath water with the baby. Moore and Russell were not infallible, but that is a poor reason for expecting to achieve salvation or dignity or anything else worthwhile by standing them on their heads. Here again we need long memories and a wide purview. When Wittgenstein calls his work a species of natural history (even if he has the grace to notice that some of it is fictitious natural history),[3] he is in touch not only with Socrates, but with Protagoras and the idea of man as the measure of truth and falsehood, of the things that are that they are, and of the things that are not that they are not. When he says that mathematicians are inventors not discoverers he is travelling the beaten track of the *physis/nomos* controversy on to which most epistemology at most times has been shunted.[4] Nominalism and Realism about universals, Conventionalism and Platonism about necessity, Subjectivism and Naturalism about ethics – these are the poles between which philosophers continue to oscillate even when they are or think they are unattached to the apron strings or coat tails of any old wives or Dutch uncles.

It is in the nature of the philosophical case that the necessary reaction against a revolution should need reacting against. Correctives always go too far and in some wrong directions.

All the strands whose ends I am tugging at here are involved in a tangled skein of issues on which I have for many years carried on a dialogue with various members of a group of philosophers whom you will recognise – even though the title is doubtless not very welcome to them – if I call them the Swansea Wittgensteinians. The most sustained and public episode of this dialogue was the symposium on 'Unanswerable Questions' between Rush Rhees and myself in 1966.[5] But it began some years before that and has certainly continued since, not only with Rhees but also and increasingly with Peter Winch, Ilham Dilman, D. Z. Phillips and their colleagues at Swansea and elsewhere. Winch on Rationality, Phillips on Prayer, Phillips and Mounce and Beardsmore on Morality, are some of the documents on the other side of the case. In an aside to Peter Winch during my lecture here last year I promised to return to these disagreements, and this is a suitable occasion for fulfilling that promise.

The discussion of these differences has been helpful to me, and may be helpful to others, particularly because they are differences

---

[3] *Philosophical Investigations*, §415 and p. 230e.
[4] *Remarks on the Foundations of Mathematics*, p. 47e.
[5] *Proceedings of the Aristotelian Society, Supplementary Volume*, 1966.

between allies. It is not just that I share with these philosophers a generally 'Wittgensteinian' origin and orientation, though that is connected with what I have in mind. What is more specific and substantial is that we all regard some things in philosophy as having been definitively altered by the work of Wittgenstein, but there remains a difference between us about what has *not* been altered by the new perspective we have achieved, with Wittgenstein's help, on the nature and history of philosophical investigation.

One central issue in this peaceable conflict has had to do with unity and variety, and this can usefully be illustrated from my exchanges with Rhees in 1966. He did not understand what I meant by talking about *all* questions at once, and saying that they all have answers. He reminded me how different question is from question (interview, inquisitive neighbour, disappointed child, examining one's conscience, etc.). And his list could have been much longer. There is an indefinitely wide range of kinds of questions, of contexts and sets of circumstances in which something occurs which qualifies as the asking of a question, and there is no one element which is present in all of them.

But not just *anything* is a question. The infinite internal variety of the class of questions is quite compatible with the unity that makes us call them all questions, and justifies us in calling them all questions. (There is an infinite number of numbers between the number 1 and the number 2, but not just anything, not just any number, is a number between 1 and 2.)

Rhees is rightly anxious that nobody should suppose that the class of questions has a kind of unity that it does not have. But I suggest that when he goes so far as to suggest or imply that the class of questions has *no* unity, that nothing sensible can be said about it, he is himself making a mistake that he shares with those whose misrepresentation he is most concerned to warn us against. For those who try to impose on questions (or games, or assertions, or cases of reading, expecting, understanding) the simple-minded single-common-element kind of unity do so because they recognize that there is a unity in the class and do not recognize that there can be any other kind of unity than that simple kind. Rhees recognises that there is no unity of that simple kind in the class of questions, and then, because he too thinks that in the absence of that simple kind of unity there is no unity, he suggests that the class lacks unity and cannot be talked of *as* a class.

We can contrast asking with asserting, describing with explaining, tragedy with comedy, men with women, without necessarily losing that grasp of the internal variety of each class, and that awareness of the overlappings and criss-crossings and continuities between them, that Rhees is rightly determined to preserve.

Of course what is said about the unity of such a class is liable to be platitudinous, but in a philosophical discussion a platitude may turn out to be highly contentious, as I found when I suggested that all games are games. In philosophy people often deny platitudes, that is to say they often make remarks that deserve to be denied and can be denied only by the assertion of platitudes.

But there is a time and a season for asserting platitudes and for denying them. Professor Ayer remarks in the first chapter of *The Problem of Knowledge* that it is true but unenlightening to say that all games are games and all instances of knowledge are instances of knowledge. In the last chapter and in a different tone of voice he says that the relation between the states that are the states of the same person is one of which perhaps nothing more illuminating can be said than that it is the relation that holds between states that are states of the same consciousness.[6]

In my general remarks about questions I went round in circles, as one inevitably does when one tries to speak of the unity of such infinitely internally varied classes. To say that all questions have answers, or that they all express or evince puzzlement, ignorance, or perplexity, or a need for information or knowledge or understanding or enlightenment, is to use a set of terms (*answer, ignorance, understanding*, etc.) each of which is in turn amenable only to the kind of treatment that *question* itself calls for. Each of them is one whose range of instances we can only come to grasp satisfactorily by being presented with many and varied instances from the range.

But let us not always put them 'so scattered' that we do not see the ways in which they are linked together, the ways in which they cluster and cohere. They do not indeed cohere and cluster round a single core, and they are not linked by a single link or a single chain. But that just means that we have to attend to the different kind of unity that they do have, and which is best found and presented by the very same procedure of setting one instance beside another that is also best calculated to exhibit their vast internal variety.

In recent treatments of the ancient problem of 'the one and the many' the important and long-overdue attention to the many has obscured the visibility of the one. It is time to re-redress the balance.

On that occasion in 1966 my general discussion with Rhees about unity was specifically designed to help us to grasp the unity of questions and answers, the unity of reason and of understanding, the unity of truth and knowledge, in spite of the impressive variety

[6] Pp. 11–12, 199.

that we were once, before Wittgenstein, in greater danger of con-
cealing or allowing to remain concealed. Today my interest is in the
unity of mankind, the singleness of humanity and its nature. But
there is a double connection between what concerned us then and
what concerns me now. It is not just that my general plea for the
recognition of the unity of the kind as well as the variety of the
instances applies directly to what it is to be a man as much as to what
it is to be a game or a question or a reason. Our common nature is
also the basis of our common understanding, and it is that community of understanding that unifies reason, truth and knowledge,
enquiry and the means of its pursuit, perplexity and the modes of its
resolution.

Some of what I have in mind here is expressed in Peter Winch's
well-known paper 'Nature and Convention'.[7] But in other and later
writings I have understood or misunderstood Winch as wishing to
maintain some propositions that I wish firmly to repudiate. He has
sometimes given the impression, and not only to me, that he is denying the unity and authority of reason, and coming at least too close
to those who over-emphasise the differences between facts and values,
facts and interpretations, and who base on them the conclusion that
what is most fundamental in our pictures of the world and life and
man is fashioned and not found, created not discovered. The in-
fection of scepticism has spread in recent years to debates in the
philosophy of science. The view that conflicting scientific theories
are incommensurable is only a special case of a general scepticism
to which there are general answers, some of which I have helped to
formulate elsewhere.[8]

Here I use Pope's title to suggest a way of unifying these themes.
What is man? What is a man? There is a plurality and variety of
men, but also a plurality and variety of questions about man. 'What
is man?' is itself many questions, and questions of different kinds.
Three main divisions suggest themselves when we attempt to describe
the order that can be seen through the bewildering multiplicity.

To ask what a man is, is in the first place to ask for a definition or
explanation of what it means to be a man, what use the word 'man'
has; to ask what are the *logical* constraints on what can count as a
man. Here human nature is conceived as the *essence* of man.

But we are still seeking a description of human nature when we
turn from the philosopher and logician to the historian or biologist
or anthropologist, or to any other enquirer who is primarily con-

---

[7] *Proceedings of the Aristotelian Society*, 1959–60. Reprinted in *Ethics and Action*.

[8] E.g. in *Conflict and the Scope of Reason*, University of Hull Press, 1974.

cerned with the *existence* of man and hence with the causal constraints beyond which, though there might have been men, there cannot in fact be any men.

And we are not ceasing to seek a description of human nature when we ask what is fitting to the *dignity* of man, when we explore the *moral* constraints to which a being is subject if he is to be worthy of the noble title of manhood or humanity. When Socrates said that an unexamined life was οὐ βιωτὸς ἀνθρώπῳ he did not mean that an animal living such a life would die, but that such an animal's life would not be human.

Essence, existence, dignity: these three, and each is many; but the question 'What is man?' is still *one* question.

Somebody who asks 'Can machines think?' is liable to be pressed by brisk philosophers to say whether his question is about meanings or about the present or future state of technology. But his question is about both if, as is likely, the curiosity or puzzlement that he expresses cannot be satisfied or resolved without a judicious mingling of reflection and information. Yet his puzzlement has its unity as well as its duality or multiplicity.

'Does God exist?' That this is not a single, simple question does not mean that it is not a single question. It cannot be answered without answering many questions, and some at least of these other questions may be parts or aspects of the question 'Does God exist?', and it could for all that be a unitary question.

In the question 'What is man?', we can distinguish parts or aspects and some or most or all of them may be questions in their own right, and the question 'What is man?' still be a question in *its* own right; the expression of a unitary need for explanation and understanding.

When you read *War and Peace* or *Middlemarch* or *Antony and Cleopatra*, is it so clear to you that you can separate for all purposes the essence and the existence and the dignity, the logical and the causal and the moral?

When we strive to fulfil the unitary need by making the distinctions and examining the details that are essential to its fulfilment we need not and must not forget this unity. Analysis must precede synthesis, and synthesis must follow analysis.

Let us analyse, distinguish.

THE LOGICAL CONSTRAINTS

To abandon hope of finding a definition of man is not to give up exploring the scope and limits of the concept, but only to recognise

the necessity and possibility of other means of travel round its borders
and through the jungle of its interior. Comparison and contrast between men and apes, angels, gods, machines, Martians can be conducted in various ways which neither look nor sound like the search
for definitions, but which are still contributions to the description of
the region of logical space in which we are clustered and scattered.
The essence of man cannot be fully described, but it can be described, and it will be correctly described in so far as the comparisons
and contrasts that constitute the description make plain how close
is the cluster and how wide is the scatter. As usual, help may be
sought and gained from the efforts at definition, at complete statement of the essence, that have been so persistent but so inescapably
unsuccessful. They naturally refer to capacities (such as rationality)
or to incapacities and imperfections (such as fallibility and mortality) that have much to do with what makes a man a man, and
they help us to remember the cluster when Swift or Orwell or
Evans-Pritchard or Freud or Proust, by reference to objects of comparison either actual or merely possible, are tracing out the limits
of the scatter and the intricacies of the structure of the nucleus. A
species as much as an individual can have a nature of its own without having a simple or statable or simply statable nature. Locke's
comparison and contrast between person and man and thing is part
of the story of human as it is of personal identity.

THE CAUSAL CONSTRAINTS

The variety of beings who would be recognisable as men is much
greater than the variety of men we may hope or fear to meet in our
time and space, and much greater even than those who could be
plausibly predicted for other regions of space or time. If we think of
the inexhaustible scope for the existence of rational beings who
would not be men (some at least of whom can be envisaged as
evolving from the human species), it becomes clearer than ever that
very little of the logical space that is bound by what I called the
logical constraints is actually occupied. For some of the most controversial of the questions we have to deal with in an Essay on Man
this relative narrowness is a welcome lightening of the burden of
proof. Sceptics and relativists, whether about reason or goodness,
language-games or frames of reference, make much of the abstract
possibility of meeting a being or tribe which totally disagrees with us.
These imaginings do not do the *a priori* work that is expected of
them: there cannot coherently be said to be a dispute or difference
of opinion or a conflict between two people or tribes or species who

do not share a common consciousness or understanding.[9] Even if I am wrong about this more abstract issue, that will not alter a centrally important *fact* that is the focus of what I now want to insist on: that all the actual disputes we have ever heard of or conducted are disputes between *men*. The parties to every dispute in history have shared their humanity. Now nobody is a man who does not know some of the things that we know, feel some of the things that we feel.

In the myth of the *Phaedrus*, Plato paints a picture of this fact, this axis on which the human world rotates. When the souls of dead men and animals are joined to new bodies for new lives, the divine authorities impose a severe restriction. No soul is allowed to enter a *human* body unless it is one of the privileged souls to whom, in the procession of the gods, there has been granted a vision of the Forms. Every human soul τεθέαται τὰ ὄντα and would not otherwise have been a *human* soul: ἢ οὐκ ἂν ἦλθεν εἰς τόδε τὸ ζῷον.[10]

Plato embodies this requirement in his more prosaic essays on anthropology and psychology, and enacts it in the detail of the Socratic conversations. The *Gorgias* or the *Protagoras* or the *Republic* is not just a conflict of *logos* against *logos* but also (and therefore) a conflict of man against man. And since every man has the truth in him, if he is convicted of untruth or unreason he is also, with an emphasis that we do not always think of giving to the words, convicted of contradicting *himself*. The incoherence in his thoughts is seen as involving an analogous disharmony in his feelings, so that the examined life is to be prized not only as the only rational life or the only moral life, but also (and again therefore) because it is the only *happy* life *for a man*.

We arm ourselves against learning some of Plato's lessons if we make too promptly, and preserve too loyally, a distinction between thought and feeling, reason and emotion. Like Sartre in *A Sketch of a Theory of the Emotions*, Plato helps us to see the emotions themselves as or as involving apprehension or cognition. To be afraid of something is to *regard* it as a threat, and in most cases if I am satisfied that it does not in fact represent any danger to me I shall cease to be afraid of it. If I continue to *feel* afraid of it after I have recognised it not to be dangerous, I shall usually recognise that the feeling is misplaced and shall try to restore the unity of reason and feeling that has been temporarily broken.

The spider is either dangerous or it is not. I either recognise or fail to recognise that it is dangerous or that it is not. I either face it with

[9] The argument is given in *Conflict and the Scope of Reason*.
[10] *Phaedrus*, 249e–250a.

confidence or shrink from it in fear. Here there are possibilities of
confusion of thought and of feeling and between thought and feeling,
but also (and therefore) of coherence and harmony of thought and
of feeling and of thought with feeling.

THE MORAL CONSTRAINTS

It remains to be seen on another occasion whether the moral constraints are not just a species of the logical constraints, but here I will
preserve my tripartition and speak of them separately.

That there are and must be such constraints on what is a human
being and what is a human life is firmly underlined by tracing one
line of thought that has been believed by many to point in the opposite direction.

We live, it is said every day, in a period of rapid social change. We
must change our morals as well as our manners to fit our changed
and changing circumstances. For example: our marriage laws and
customs, the institution of the family, and all our thoughts and
feelings about men and women, parents and children, date from
times long past and must be radically re-thought and re-felt. Perhaps
we need to follow Plato and the young state of Israel into a new
world where parental responsibilities are corporate and not particular. Perhaps, alternatively or in addition, we need to adopt a
scheme of serial marriage, or polygamy. Sometimes all this is cast as
prediction rather than as policy: this is what is happening or is
bound to happen, and is to be welcomed as a necessary adjustment
of man to a changing state of society.

To reveal the importance of the continuities that this line of
thought threatens to obscure it is sufficient to ask in what terms such
developments could be predicted or explained or justified or criticised, or even described in more than the slogan and schema with
which too many reformers are content. The answer can only be:
in *human* terms. The implicit or explicit claim of the innovators for
their innovations is that children will be happier or parents more
free, fathers less tyrannical and mothers more independent. The
appeal is and must be to the values of love and care and help and
comfort that are also relied on in the Book of Common Prayer's
exposition of the rights and reasons of the honourable estate of holy
matrimony, where it is declared that marriage is ordained for the
procreation and nurture of children, for a remedy against sin, and
also 'for the mutual society, help and comfort, that the one ought
to have of the other, both in prosperity and adversity'.

Changes in marriage or the family or any other part of human life

can be justified if at all as making it more human, a more fitting life
for a man, and the question what a man is and what is fitting for
him is not one that waits for a decision but one that can be answered
by experience and reflection and reflection on experience.

This is one of the many junctures in current controversies in
morals and philosophy where we need Aristotle's help and guidance.
Perhaps he did not sufficiently recognise the variety of human
beings and hence of the life that is compatible with humanity. But
he did see clearly that man has a nature and that his nature is the
guide to what befits his conduct. He saw clearly, too, that the life of
man neither needs nor will allow of any grounding outside the scope
of human life and human nature. He does not stand in need of
Auden's rebuke:

> Writers can be guilty of every kind of human conceit but one,
> the conceit of the social worker: 'We are all here on earth to
> help others; what on earth the others are here for, I don't know.'[11]

For him, as for Blake, the human being, mankind and the individual, has his own worth, what Iris Murdoch[12] calls the for-nothing-
ness of art and thought and life and action, just as the Tyger's fear-
ful symmetry is to be prized and praised in and for itself: 'The apple
tree never asks the beech how he shall grow; nor the lion, the horse,
how he shall take his prey.' 'A horse is not more a lion for being a
bad horse.'[13] Aristotle certainly and Blake probably recognised that
man is not the greatest and most worthy of the things that are in
heaven and earth. They both knew that man and tiger, oak and
eagle, each has a *telos* that is not only its form but also its dignity.
To the child's innocent question: 'What is that gentleman *for?*' there
is the answer that he is for nothing; for nothing, that is, except himself and his natural kind.

'*What does your philosophy teach you?*' The layman's insistent
question needs two answers. First he must be told that the philosopher's prime task is the search for understanding and not for
guidance through the bogs and thickets of life and morals. But then
he may be told – and by reaction needs now to be told at greater
length – of what a philosopher can learn that is or may be of use to
those, including himself, who are more or less than philosophers.

My philosophy has taught me a respect for some things that are
not philosophy: for the inexplicit and inarticulate understanding of
life and death and good and evil and knowledge and ignorance that

---

11 *The Dyer's Hand*, p. 14.
12 *The Sovereignty of Good*, pp. 71, 92.
13 *The Marriage of Heaven and Hell.*

it may be the philosopher's aspiration to articulate but which too often he thinks it is his duty to deny or contradict or underwrite or overturn. If the articulation displays a contradiction we must consider the possibility that the contradiction is in the articulation rather than in the understanding, and even when we are satisfied that the common understanding has turned out to be confused, it is by preserving what is more deeply entrenched in it and abandoning what is nearer to the surface of it that we remove the contradiction.

Philosophers repeatedly forget what they and all of us know. They know that revenge is a kind of wild justice but rebel against the simple consequence that the administration of justice is a kind of cultivated revenge. They know that to be without desires is inhuman but they construct systems of ethics or ideal constitutions that could have application only, if at all, to a race of robots. To have desires and purposes is to be capable of being frustrated and hence of being in conflict with other men and other things, but they dream of a life that will still be human and will yet be free of all friction between men or between man and his environment.

In all these cases we have to do with the limits of human choice, the inescapability of fact and truth and reason; and it is by offering to human choice a role that it cannot fill that philosophers most often and most seriously misrepresent what life is like. The endlessness of humility is pictured for us in the facts that the philosophers forget: I do not choose to be human or rational and still less do I choose what is fitting or rational for one to do or believe who is rational or human – or, for that matter, for one who is male or English or who lives in an era of rapid social change. And even when an obligation is one that I do incur by choice, it is not for me to choose what are the scope and limits and nature of what I have incurred. That I need not have been a husband or a father or an ambassador or a ship's captain or Secretary-General of the United Nations does not make it a matter for me to decide what is fitting to such a role.

Men fear that reasons may become tyrants: that if they are allowed to be dominant they will be domineering; that if it is admitted that man has a nature his nature will have to be seen as a slave driver, with man, the species or the individual, as its slave. But the nature of man is man, not something different. A man's character is his destiny because it is himself. The mastery is, as Socrates and Spinoza show, self-mastery and not a thraldom to an alien king. Bacon rebuked those who held it bondage to fix a belief.[14]

[14] Essay 'Of Truth'.

He might have added a reprimand to those who think it tyrannical to suggest that some opinions are true and others false.

Part of this fear of acknowledging the rationality of reason has its source in a reasonable resistance to dogmatism and authoritarianism – to abuses and corruptions of the power of reason. But such abuses and corruptions are no better reasons for repudiating reason than the abuse of political power is a reason for preferring anarchy to a civil constitution. In any case, such perversions of the powers of the mind are found among the sceptics and relativists themselves. *Knowingness*, the smugness of one who is privy to secrets or to secret arts, fits ill with a formal denial of the role of reason or a declaration of narrow bounds to the scope of knowledge, but it commonly afflicts those whose conclusions are relativist or sceptical. Behind the scenes, they assure us, there is nothing but emotion or social or psychological conditioning or arbitrary presuppositions or choice of frame of reference: something that can be represented or plausibly misrepresented as not just explaining but explaining away our actions and beliefs and agreements and disputes.

Philosophy teaches that thinking things through to a conclusion is not only necessary but also possible. Hence it teaches philosophical self-respect. Popper has spoken of his excuses for being a philosopher.[15] Others have done philosophy in such a manner, or given the name of philosophy to such things, as to suggest that in their view, too, philosophers need excuses unless they can represent themselves as being something other than or in addition to philosophers. But thinking things through is an ancient and honourable profession. It was human of Tithonus to forget when he was asking for immortality to ask for perpetual youth as well. It was also human to realise the mistake as soon as it was made, and would have been human to avoid it. Odysseus was just as human when he bound himself to the mast and stopped the ears of his crew against the sirensong as when he wavered under Circe's wiles.

Professor Acton has not made excuses for philosophy, and has not felt that they needed to be made. In his most recent work, *The Idea of a Spiritual Power*, he has once again shown how much he prizes and how well he practises the dignity of thought and dignity of utterance that are central to the dignity of man. It is one of many and not the least of the reasons why we honour him today.

[15] In *The Listener*, 7 January, 1971.

2

HAS MAN AN ESSENCE?

Anthony Quinton

I. INTRODUCTORY

MUCH of recent ethics has been thoroughly formalistic in character.
In the first place it has confined itself to the investigation of the
general logical properties of moral discourse and has largely ignored
the broad psychological context of motives and purposes in which
that kind of discourse has its life. Secondly, it has sought to distinguish the field of discourse that it takes as its subject-matter in a
formalistic way, in terms of such properties as its universalisability, its
autonomy and its overridingness, without reference to the concrete
and specific human interests with which moral discourse is connected and which it might serve to promote.

For the formalist moral philosopher it is just brute, established
fact that people are in the habit of making utterances that contain
members of a set of logically interconnected evaluative terms, such
as *good*, *right*, *ought* and their opposites; that there is a particularly
noteworthy and formally distinguishable moral way of using these
terms; and that, in so using them, men are making universal prescriptions for conduct. The question why these terms should be used
in this way is not raised. It is, no doubt, ambiguous. It could mean:
what is the causal explanation of the fact of moral discourse? It
could also mean: what is the justification of the practice, what
valuable or desirable purpose does it serve? The formalist will remit
the question in its causal form to psychology and sociology. In its
justificatory form he will probably deny that it arises, unless in
what he might hold to be the trivially prudential form in which it
invites such answers as that honesty is the best policy.

The most immediately objectionable consequence of this kind of formalism is that it sets no limit to the content of what can be universally prescribed. Such a prescription is adequate or proper provided that it is sincerely affirmed. Sincerity is shown by the speaker's rigid adherence to the principles embodied in his own moral evaluations, his indignation at the deviations of others from them and, perhaps, by the guilt he feels about his own. Ineradicable conflicts of ultimate principle are not merely allowed for, they are positively welcomed. In so far as there is any sort of convergence towards a moral consensus it is, on this view, a happy accident of emotional similarity between moral agents.

It is understandable that dissatisfaction with this body of doctrine should send its critics back to a very different ethical tradition, that which seeks to base the principles of right conduct in human nature. I am entirely sympathetic to this move in general but there is a traditionally well-established conception of human nature, that of the essence of man, which I do not believe will serve for the purpose. It is this that I propose to consider today.

'Philosophical questions of the form . . . "what is the nature of x?" . . . are all requests for definitions,' Ayer has said (*Language, Truth and Logic*, p. 65). On this view if 'what is the nature of man' is a philosophical question it must be asking what are the defining, necessary or essential properties of man. If that is so, human nature is not an exclusively philosophical concept. Many things are true of human beings in general that are not logically constitutive of the concept of humanity. We should, then, distinguish between a strict interpretation of the phrase 'human nature' in which it refers to the essence of man and a wider interpretation in which it includes as well properties which are as a matter of fact true of men in general.

It is on the strict interpretation of human nature as human essence that two of the most noteworthy attempts to derive the principles of right conduct from human nature, those of Aristotle and Marx, have been founded and I shall begin by considering them. I shall go on to examine two very different ways in which it has been argued that man has no essence, those of Sartre and orthodox positivism. A curious, indeed paradoxical, feature of Sartre's position is that his claim that man has no essence is an abbreviated version of his account of the fundamental, one hardly likes to say logically, distinguishing characteristic of human existence, of *le pour-soi* or Heideggerian *Dasein*. Man is the being whose essential property is to have no essence. Furthermore Sartre goes on, much in the manner of Aristotle and Marx, to derive moral conclusions from his anti-essentialist account of human essence.

The orthodox positivist objection to human essence brings to light an important ambiguity in the question I have set myself: has man an essence? It can be taken to mean: are there certain properties everything that is a man must have just in virtue of being a man? But it could also mean: are there certain properties which every individual man has? In other words 'has man an essence' can amount either to: 'has humanity an essence?' or to 'have men essences?' The orthodox positivist will presumably regard it as fairly obvious that humanity has an essence. To admit this is to admit only that 'man' or 'is a man' is a significant predicative general term. He would probably go on to allow that the essence of humanity is verbally specifiable since the concept is not a Lockean simple idea or ineradicably ostensive, but could be introduced by a verbal definition, even if it is not usually so defined on its first introduction to language-learners. What he would resist is the idea that the essence of humanity is part of the essence of the individuals who are human. For, on his view, no individuals have essences at all, except relatively to the indefinitely numerous descriptions of which any one of them is susceptible.

In the traditional doctrine of essence these two versions of the question are not distinguished. Aristotle was primarily concerned with the distinction of the essential from the accidental properties of concrete individuals. Yet the ethically fruitful-seeming claims about essence that he makes are couched in general terms. Conclusions about how men in general ought ideally to live are drawn from premises about the essence of man in general. What seems to be involved is the view both that each concrete individual is essentially a thing of a specific kind, while everything else that it is, it is accidentally, and, further, that the essential, real or natural kind of which it is an instance can be defined or elucidated into some set of properties. Individual essence thus conceived will not of course include all the properties of an individual that has it since such individuals will, in general, have further, accidental properties. Furthermore it will not in general be sufficient to individuate the individual in question, to pick it out from other things of the same essential kind as the unique individual that it is.

I shall conclude by considering the defensibility of the notion of essence as applied to concrete individuals, which has been argued for as required for the identification of individual things and by asking whether, if it is defensible, it has any implications for ethics as far as men are concerned.

2. ARISTOTLE: MAN AS RATIONAL ANIMAL

Aristotle's theory of human essence is incorporated in that prime and exemplary specimen of definition *per genus et differentiam:* 'man' = 'rational animal'. As an animal man is, first, a living thing which takes nourishment and reproduces itself and, secondly, moves itself about and has emotions and desires. The specific difference of man is reason or the power to think, what Aristotle calls 'mind', which for him is only a part of the soul. The detailed working-out of this line of thought in the *De Anima* is not altogether clear about the dividing-line between men and non-human animals. The latter are credited with sensation (at least that of touch) and with imagination. The implication is that non-human animals do not have knowledge, which necessarily presupposes the power to think, or, for that matter, the power of judgement, of forming beliefs, true or false.

Aristotle's position is, at any rate, like that of sensible men in general, somewhere between the extremes of Descartes and Hume. For Descartes animals were complex mechanical contrivances, the possession of souls was proprietary to human beings and God. Hume, however, credited animals with the power of 'experimental inference', though with them, as with most human beings most of the time, he did not dignify this kind of inference by describing it as reasoning, seeing it as a matter of custom or habit. 'If there be in reality any arguments of this nature, they surely lie too abstruse for the observation of such imperfect understandings.' (*Enquiry Concerning Human Understanding*, p. 106.) The contrast of reasoning with custom and habit seems to imply that the former is a matter of consciously embracing and of applying in conscious processes of inference such general principles as that the unknown resembles the known.

Descartes's view that the distinguishing characteristic of men is consciousness implies that talk of the sensations, desires and emotions of animals is metaphorical. To speak of a cat's noticing a bird on a low branch or of a dog's anger must be analogous to speaking of a thermometer's noticing the increase in the heat of a room or of an old car's agony as it grinds up a steep hill in bottom gear. Why is this absurd? Presumably because of the systematic thoroughness of the analogy between a cat's perceptions and a man's. The cat has closely similar perceptual equipment in its eyes and their cerebral attachments. This equipment operates in the same sort of circumstances and under the same sorts of mistake-engendering hazards as our own. It connects opportunities to actions in the same sort of way as ours does.

There is a marginal imperfection about Aristotle's account of reason, mind or the power of thought as man's specific difference. This is his ascription of that power of thought to both 'man and possibly another order like man or superior to him'. (*De Anima*, 414b, 19–20.) Are these the 55 or 47 unmoved movers required to account for the movements of the planets? They are not animals exactly but they are not pure form, as God, the prime mover, is. The conceptual pigeon-hole hollowed out in the *De Anima* for the other possible order of rational beings was filled in due course by angels.

Apart from 'nature' and 'idea' there are few more elastic words in the philosophical vocabulary than 'reason'. But in taking it to be man's specific difference, Aristotle gives a fairly clear impression of what he means by it. It is the power of thought which is exercised in the attempt to acquire knowledge and whose success or perfection is the achievement of knowledge. To deny this to animals, Aristotle's account of the distinction between sensation and thought must be recruited. Sensation for him is a direct awareness of sensible objects and thought of intelligible objects, concepts or universals. He may be thought of as holding, with Locke and Geach, that 'brutes abstract not'.

There is no need to pursue this demarcation-dispute for the purpose in hand. For there are, fairly obviously, some powers of thought or kinds of rationality that men possess which non-human animals do not. A currently favoured way of marking them out is as those mental operations involved in the understanding of a language. This manœuvre makes the material in question more palpable, perhaps, but not all that more perspicuous. How is it to be decided that the systems of signalling or communication in use among animals are languages only in a metaphorical sense? The aspect of human communication that seems lacking from its animal correlates is not the conveying of factual information. Bees are not confined to the expression of their emotions and incitements to action. What is lacking is argument or critical discussion, the practice of deliberately attempting to correct beliefs, in other words reasoning in its most elevated sense. We may agree with Hume that animals infer but they do not construct or conduct inferences.

The protracted authority of Aristotle's idea that rationality is the specifically differentiating part of the essence of man is not un-deserved. Rationality is not possessed by all the beings we should describe as human but the exceptions are not of a kind calculated to undermine the principle. Babies are not rational in the way that an ordinary adult who is not reasoning at the moment is. But they are potentially rational in a way that dogs are not. It is, presumably, logically possible that a dog should learn to speak, make up stories, get some O levels. These are possible to a baby in a much stronger, more factual sense. If time and the normal opportunities are supplied it will acquire these accomplishments. What of a mental defective who has either lost or never acquired the status of a rational being? It is surely not too mechanical a defence of the principle to say that they are defective human beings, who look and are physically constructed like men, but are only marginally or by a sort of prudent and humane courtesy fully human beings.

On the other hand the only animals we know of, rather than think about, that are rational are human beings. But what would happen if some non-humanly embodied creature, such as the logically possible dog I mentioned a moment ago, were to exhibit rationality? I suggest that we take both rationality and being humanly embodied as essential properties of men. Confronted with a situation in which the two criteria conflict we should most probably disentangle the concepts of human being and of person which, as things are, we can apply to the very same things and in the same way. A contrasted incentive to the same step would be the discovery of a society of creatures that while physiologically not significantly different from ourselves had the intellectual powers, modes of communication and general style of social interaction that prevail amongst dogs.

There are, indeed, other characteristics than rationality which seem to be common and peculiar to human beings, or as much so as it is. Examples would be laughing and cooking. But universal as these largely are among men they do not seem to be *essential* to humanity in the way that rationality is. It would, no doubt, be depressing to come upon a society of man-shaped creatures who neither laughed nor cooked, who met all changes of circumstance with straight or tear-stained faces and nourished themselves exclusively on the nuts and berries of folklore. But it would not inspire the thought that the creatures in question were not really men. After all there are unquestionably human beings here and there, who, perhaps under the influence of Schopenhauer's philosophy or the macrobiotic ideology, neither laugh nor cook. Laughing and cooking, in other words, are factual not conceptual ingredients of human nature.

A further consideration is that laughing and cooking are, properly conceived, forms of rationality. To laugh is not just to go through a particular audible and visible physiological routine. The cachinnations of the hyena would be laughter only if they were the expression of an ability to see jokes. The nearest that non-human animals get to that is in the smiles of glee on the faces of dogs when they hear the paper crackle in a box of Milk Tray. Similarly a dog who dropped an antelope haunch in a bushfire over which he was jumping and eventually retrieved it in a cooked state and ate it would not on that account be regarded as a colleague of Escoffier. The critical appreciation of incongruity involved in laughter and the intention to transform foodstuffs by the application of heat can be credited only to beings whose activities generally testify to rationality in the fairly advanced, transperceptual sense in which I have taken it.

The crucial ethical inference Aristotle draws from his account of human essence is that the perfection of man lies in the maximisation of his specific differentiating feature. An ideal man is one who exhibits intellectual virtue to the highest degree. In doing so he approximates as closely as possible to God, or pure intelligence, whose proper or exclusive activity is to think about himself or pure thought or, to take the widest possible interpretation, matters of abstract theory.

It should be emphasised that Aristotle's prescription for man's realisation of the ideal does not connect it with the whole of man's essence but only with the differentiating part of it. Animality, that is to say self-locomotion and the life of the senses, and, even more, mere livingness, consisting in nourishment and reproduction, are to be played down and as far as possible transcended. Aristotle's human paradigm is not what might be called a well-rounded man. He shows, indeed, a suspiciously close resemblance to Aristotle himself: he is a clever, truth-loving, hard-working metaphysician.

No blanket condemnation of inferences from *is* to *ought* is needed to put in question this particular inference from what a thing essentially and differentiatingly is to what it ideally ought to be. Is the best rose inevitably the one whose roseate characteristics are so emphatic that it cannot be confused from a distance with an anemone or a peony? Is the best island the one separated by the longest and deepest tracts of water from other land-masses?

There is, indeed, one type of entities with regard to whose perfection such an inference can possibly be drawn: entities of functional kinds. A knife is an instrument designed or intended for cutting things with. Any properties it has that are unconnected with its ability to cut things are superfluous. It is, of course, undifferentiatingly, a material body but no one would suppose that the criteria of its perfection are to be sought in that fact. A knife's excellence does not increase with its magnitude and solidity.

But men are not items of intentional construction, although many of them are brought into existence intentionally. Those who bring them into existence exercise negligible control over their design. At best the expectant mother may hope to avoid certain defects in her offspring by avoiding certain habits and indulgences. Christian theism would assign the detailed planning of the human species to God but Aristotle, holding no theory of creation, did not.

Hobbes and Spinoza ascribed to all kinds of being a self-preservative impulse or *conatus*, a drive to maintain themselves in existence. If, with Hobbes, one assumes that going out of existence is the worst fate that can befall a thing then the primary good for a thing must be the continuation of existence, on any terms and overriding all other considerations. As far as men are concerned this assumption is built into the practice of supposing that anyone who commits suicide does so because the balance of his mind is disturbed. Unless things, or, at any rate, living things, to which alone it is literally intelligible to ascribe such characteristics, had some native impulse to stay alive and avoid destruction they would be replaced by other living things which did have the impulse or by the inanimate destructive forces to which the notion of self-preservative instinct does not literally apply.

But if self-preservation, as well as being characteristic of living things, were a prime value for them this would not entail that an ideal member of a species was one in which the specifically differentiating part of its essence was most developed. Aristotle's metaphysicians, his ideal leisure-class of theorists, notoriously required a social substructure of slaves and soldiers to keep them in existence. More generally, it is obvious that a man in whom theoretical rationality is emphasised at the expense of other characteristics is in a precarious situation.

Something of Aristotle's idea that rationality is the perfection as well as the essential differentiating property of man survives in the curious argument in Kant's *Groundwork* which concludes that since the satisfaction of desire would be better served by instinct than by reason it is incumbent on men, equipped as they are with reason, to exercise it in actions that have nothing to do with the satisfaction of desire. In Kant, of course, the exercise of reason, in its legitimate, practical form, is connected much more closely with what is conventionally regarded as moral than it is in Aristotle. But the general structure of the argument is the same: it is reason that essentially differentiates men from non-human animals, so human excellence consists in the domination of the non-rational aspect of man by his reason. The difference between them is that in one case reason is exercised in metaphysics and theology, while in the other it operates through the conforming of actions to rationally universal principles.

I conclude that there is no justification for the view that since reason is what essentially differentiates men from other things it is the criterion of human excellence. Man is not a functional kind. The metaphysics of self-preservation supports no partiality to the differentiating part of man's essence at the expense of the rest of it. The fact that men ought logically to be rational, in so far as they are not really men unless they are, does not imply that the more rational they are the more they are what they morally ought to be. Whatever may be thought of the fallaciousness of ethical naturalism, it is clear that ethical essentialism of this kind is a fallacy.

3. MARX: MAN AS PRODUCTIVE

The most explicit statement by Marx of his theory of human essence occurs early in *The German Ideology*. He says, 'Men can be distinguished from animals by consciousness, by religion or anything else you like. They themselves begin to distinguish themselves from animals as soon as they begin to *produce* their means of subsistence.' He goes on, 'By producing their means of subsistence men are indirectly producing their actual material life', and a little later, 'As individuals express their life, so they are. What they are, therefore, coincides with their production.'

Earlier, introducing the concept of alienated labour in the *Paris MS*, he had written, 'Productive life is species-life...The whole character of a species, its generic character, is contained in its manner of vital activity and free conscious activity is the species-characteristic of man.' 'Alienated labour...alienates from man his own body, nature exterior to him and his intellectual being, his human essence.'

For Marx, says Tucker, 'man is universally a being who produces things'. Animals, of course, are also productive in a marginal way, by their own vital activity they *secure* the means of their own subsistence. But they simply appropriate nourishment that is immediately available. Man's production is a matter of conscious will and design. Developing this point, Acton takes Marx's view to be that man is essentially a tool-maker and tool-user. The making and use of *instruments* of production is a crucial expression of the conscious forethought peculiar to human productive activities. It could be argued that the provision of the means of subsistence is production proper, and not merely acquisition, to the extent that the use of tools is involved in it.

This conception of human essence is Marx's materialist correction of Hegel's idealist and more or less Aristotelian notion of man as an essentially rational being. Man is, indeed, essentially rational for

To_____

Time_____Date_____

While You Were OUT

Mr._____

of_____

Phone No._____

☐ Telephoned   ☐ Please call him

☐ Called to see you   ☐ Will call again

☐ Left the following message :—

_____

_____

_____

_____

DiBasil

233-7244

apt 315

Marx but his reason is actualised in productive activity, first and foremost in nature, of course, but also in the realm of ideas, broadly conceived. Marx allows for the spiritual aspects of human nature, but he conceives these as a sophisticated and developed form of productive activity, and not, in the Aristotelian way, as an activity of contemplation. Aristotle had, in effect, taken the theoretical exercise of reason to be a kind of higher perception, an encounter with the abstract objects of pure thought that is only truly active as a kind of attention. For Marx theories and works of art are literally human productions. Where for Aristotle there is a sharp break between the practical activities by which men satisfy their desires and the sequestered, contemplative life of the mind, for Marx the two are both on a continuum. The two points of view correspond to two conceptions of society: one in which a leisured elite is liberated for its contemplative enjoyments by a labouring mass which provides for its tiresome animal needs, another in which all who do anything worth doing are engaged in some form of production.

Marx does say in *The Poverty of Philosophy*, in a variant of a familiar formula, that 'all history is nothing but a continual transformation of human nature'. But this is not a denial of the conception of a human essence. The human nature that changes in history is contingent human nature, the set of needs, habits and beliefs that men have at a particular stage of history. Marx holds that men make themselves in the sense that the historically transitory aspects of human nature are the outcome of the interaction between man, producing his own means of subsistence, and nature, and particularly of the modes of social organisation through which material production is carried on, both man and nature being radically altered in the process.

Marx's account of human essence has some plain superiorities to that of Aristotle. In the first place, it treats man, as Marx would say, as he actually is, that is to say as a natural object and not as a pure intelligence which happens for some unfathomable reason to be embodied. Secondly, his conception of the higher, more spiritually elevated activities of man as being a kind of production rather than a kind of perception at once detaches the acquisition of knowledge from an unacceptable epistemology, which sees it as actually being a kind of perception, rather than as resting, among other things, upon it in a crucial way (one might say that it treats the business of acquiring knowledge as a whole and does not concentrate on the final, gratified phase of luxuriating in its achievement), and also accords a juster place to art than the traditional remission of it to the status of a practical craft for the fashioning of objects of amusement and instruction. In treating art as he does, Marx, one might say, inverts the traditional status of the creator and the contemplator.

An interesting implication of Marx's account of human essence is that it provides the outlines of a criterion for determining the point at which men proper evolved from mere anthropoids. With the invention of agriculture man is undoubtedly on the scene: it involves tools and long-sighted planning. To go one stage further back to herding, it could be reasonably held that the herd itself is an instrument of production which is assembled, preserved and improved by conscious design. To go further back again to hunting, its human could be distinguished from its animal form, not, of course, by its social or co-operative nature, but by its use of deliberately fashioned weapons. Only at the most elementary stage of food-gathering is there nothing in the species' mode of securing the means of its subsistence which exhibits humanly essential productiveness. Thus Marx's doctrine would allow humanity to the aboriginal inhabitants of Australia, though this would be, in the Wellingtonian phrase, a close-run thing.

Marx does not draw as direct an ethically essentialist inference from his account of human essence as Aristotle. He does not conclude that since man is essentially productive the best man is the most productive man. Nevertheless his notion of the ideal life for man is expressed in terms of the character of his production. The good life is a life of free and creative productive activity, a life in which men's productive essence is actualised without alienation. The chief source of alienation, of course, is the institution of private property in the means of production. Under the system where the worker sells his labour he does not decide what is to be produced and he does not control the product of his labour. He is thus alienated both from his labour and its products. But two further forms of alienation do not seem wholly attributable to the phenomenon of wage-labour, namely alienation from other men and from nature. These would seem to result, in the first instance at any rate, from the fact of scarcity, from the fact that men's desires, including those imperious desires that correspond to vital needs, outrun the supply of freely available goods. Men are in consequence alienated from other men in that they are in competition with them for the things they want or need and from nature since it does not directly supply, but has to be compelled laboriously to yield, the things men are in pursuit of. It can be argued that scarcity is intensified and exacerbated in two ways by the property-system. The owners of property by exploiting the mass of wage-earners appropriate goods that go far beyond their needs and which could, otherwise distributed, satisfy the needs of the mass of labourers. Secondly, it is characteristic of capitalism to induce wants in the mass of consumers by advertising, which should be understood to embrace the kind of conspicuous display which excites impulses of emulation. But even in a simple subsistence economy, whose technical and organisational primitiveness does not turn differences in energy and ability into large differences of wealth, there would still be scarcity, competition between men for the goods that there are and a natural compulsion to labour caused by a shortage of freely appropriable goods.

Marx's answer to this is that capitalism, at great human cost, has solved the primary problem of material production, in principle at any rate, by its accumulation and development of a vast array of instruments of production. In due course automation will finally free men altogether from the drudgery of compelled labour for the satisfaction of material needs. Once this has been achieved men will be free to engage in purely self-expressive, non-material productive activities.

One shadow on this rosy picture is the Malthusian one. Excessive population requires a mobilisation of productive resources proportionately greater than itself, if only because the satisfaction of the most elemental needs requires the cultivation of ever more marginal resources. It also seems to embody an oversimple conception of the difference between material needs and immaterial ones. A lot of labour is locked up in a power boat or a piano, but boating and piano-playing are not the satisfactions of primordial, natural desires; they cannot be assimilated to eating as if they were a kind of larger helpings. Even the paradigm immaterial activities of creative art and theorising often have lavish material conditions: linear accelerators and vast chunks of marble, for example.

Marx's ethical essentialism differs from that of Aristotle in an important respect. Aristotle derived his notion of human perfection not from the whole essence of man but from the specifically differentiating part of it. For the specific difference to serve as a criterion of excellence it had to be susceptible of difference of degree. Otherwise all men, just because they have to satisfy the logically necessary conditions of being men, would have to be perfect. Marx's specific difference, productiveness, also differs in degree, but, as I said earlier, he does not make that his criterion of excellence. He is not an ethical Stakhanovist.

What he does in fact is to say that man approaches perfection to the extent that his specific difference is actualised in a particular way, that is freely. And this is to introduce something that is not intrinsic to his conception of human essence at all.

The ethical upshot of Marx's reflections on the ideal nature of man is what Sorel called an ethic of producers. His notion of happiness, fulfilment or self-realisation defined it in terms of activity and not of the self-indulgent, passive, consumption which is intimated as the ideal end by the traditional utilitarian concept of pleasure. This is an interesting idea but it is rather a large and perceptive empirical generalisation about the real conditions of long-lasting human satisfaction than a consequence of his account of the essential nature of man.

A threefold distinction between types of men is crucial to Marx's thinking. There are unproductive owners, compulsorily productive workers (the indispensable correlate of the owners), and the freely productive creators of the future. He does not in any way suggest that leisured and unproductive owners are not really men at all. It might be said that, in their alienating but nevertheless historically indispensable way, owners are productive after all. It is necessary to distinguish here between the managerial activities which bring capitalist undertakings into existence and direct their operations and the merely passive reception by pure, non-managerial owners of the bulk of the fruits of the labour of others. Exploitation is an offshoot of productive activity but it is not a productive activity itself. The purely exploitative owner is, then, wholly non-productive, or is so, at any rate, in so far as he does not do anything else but just luxuriously consumes his wealth. But he is still a man. Marx, no doubt, thinks of him as a morally inferior sort of man, but he does not take him to be totally dehumanised.

Whatever Marx's attitude to merely leisured owners of wealth may be it is plain that there are and always have been some and that they are unquestionably human. So productiveness is not a logically necessary condition of being human. This difficulty can easily be circumvented by interpreting the productiveness which for Marx is the essence of man as the capacity for, rather than actual engagement in, productive activity. But it could be said that, for all his remarks about how to distinguish men from animals, which suggests that it is logical essence he is concerned with, his real purpose here is something different.

Productiveness should be conceived, perhaps, more as man's real essence, in a Lockean sense, than in the Aristotelian way as a logical criterion for the classification of men as men. Essence, on this interpretation, is not the set of defining properties of a kind, but the set of properties that are fundamental, from an explanatory point of view, with regard to a given kind. It is in this sense that it is not essential to fishes that they live in water or to mammals that they do not. The methodological fruit of the materialistic interpretation of history is the injunction to examine men in their productive, indeed in their materially productive, activities if their general characteristics and behaviour are to be understood. It is in this sense that the view that human beings are in essence erotic might be attributed to Freud.

But here too no ethical consequences follow. In his last writings Freud committed no inconsistency in holding that civilisation involved a repressive transformation of essential instincts and for valuing it on just that account. If Marx had based his criterion of human excellence on productiveness pure and simple, and not on the particular free and creative form of production that he did, a corresponding position would have been both consistent and appropriate and it is, in effect, implied by what Marx says. The pursuit of ever more massive productive output, even if it maximises the specific difference of man, is not his highest aim.

As an account of man's logically specific difference, then, productiveness is not an improvement on Aristotle's rationality. Contrasted as it is with the mere instinctive appropriation of the means of subsistence to be found in animals it is a form in which rationality is applied and presupposes it. There can be men who are wholly unproductive. The fact that for Aristotle they are the truest and most perfect of men is not a good reason for turning his view on its head, particularly since, as Marx himself saw in admitting that there is such a thing as non-material production, it is only by misrepresenting abstract thinking as a more or less passive, quasi-perceptual contemplation, that Aristotle assimilated those engaged in the purest exercise of reason with the class of leisured consumers.

4. SARTRE: MAN HAS NO ESSENCE

The freedom, which Marx attaches to his view that productiveness is the specifically differentiating essence of man, to arrive at his criterion of human excellence, occupies an even more central place in the account of human nature given by Sartre. Sartre takes it to follow from the fact that men are free that they have no fixed characteristics which, together with the circumstances in which they find themselves, necessitate their acting in the way that they do. Men, in contrast to mere things, are self-determining beings.

A radical distinction between men and natural objects is the starting-point of Sartre's philosophy, as it had been for Heidegger's

Sein und Zeit. A natural object is a being in-itself *(en-soi)*, existing as a matter of brute and determinate fact, endowed with a set of properties which rigidly fix its behaviour. A man, on the other hand, is a being for-itself *(pour-soi)* which endows itself with such properties as it has by its own choice and which is not bound by its past choices in making future ones. The ability to choose involves both consciousness and will: consciousness of possible future self-determining choices and the will that can select one of these possibilities for action. At any moment, then, man's properties are the result of previous choices as manifested in action, a man is what he has done. But these past circumstances do not circumscribe the range of future choice. Since what I now am I may negate by my choice for the immediate future, I am what I am not and I am not what I am. These defiant formulae are, I suspect, rendered intelligible by those who come across them by the cryptic addition of 'going to be'. So amended they amount to the statement that man is a changing being. This is not necessarily true and is not even contingently true on a universal scale unless it is trivialised by being taken to refer to long tracts of time and to all, and not only radical or important, changes of character.

So, Sartre says, 'there is no human nature ... Man simply is ... he is what he wills ... Man is nothing else but that which he makes of himself.' What this comes to, in humdrum and intelligible terms, is that man is a changing being whose changes are the outcome of his own free and unnecessitated choices. What this is directed against, in the first instance, would appear to be the notion that each man has a fixed and definite type of character or personality, in other words to the old doctrine of humours, where these are conceived as intrinsic and invariable attributes of their possessors. But in defining men as self-determining beings, equipped with consciousness and the power of choice, and by so distinguishing them from everything else that exists it amounts to the assertion of a theory of human essence. It denies that any specific attributes of character are essential to any individual man, but it plainly asserts that men in general, to be men, must have certain abstract or even higher-order properties, which account for the varying concrete characteristics which it is of the essence of men to choose to take on. It is the abstract and essential nature of men to choose and vary the concrete and specific nature they each individually have.

I said that Sartre was setting himself in opposition to the idea that each man is of a fixed character-type in the first instance. The further aim he has in taking this stand is ethical: he wants to emphasise the scope of men's moral responsibility. I cannot escape responsibility for my choices and acts by saying that I could not help doing what I did because I am that sort of man. The sort of man I am is itself something I have chosen and for which I am responsible.

He goes on to draw a further ethical conclusion from his account of human essence, one that is strictly analogous to the ethical essentialism I have attributed to Aristotle and, in a more qualified way, to Marx. As a self-determining being I cannot devolve my responsibilities of choice on to some external provider of moral principles. There is an important ambiguity about this contention. It may mean that I cannot avoid choosing; it may also mean that in submitting my choices to externally supplied moral principles I do not free myself of responsibility.

To guide one's choices by the principles supplied by a church or a political party or, worst of all, the conventional, customary morality of one's social group is to be guilty of inauthenticity. At times he says that this is not, however, to avoid choice, but is, at best, to economise it, since the selection of some mentor or institution is itself a choice. Even if my principles have been formulated by something or someone external to myself they come to govern my actions only by a choice I have made. But this kind of inauthenticity could equally, and in many cases more realistically, be regarded as a failure to choose, as a supine conformity to the prevailing moral assumptions of the community within which I live. In this case, rather than positively choosing a body of externally supplied principles, I have failed to choose a morality of my own and contented myself with passive absorption of the conventional.

The difference between the two interpretations is brought out by considering the case of a man who, after full and searching reflection, positively chooses to embrace the fully-articulated moral system of some group or institution. Is his situation reprehensible because the content of his principles has been externally supplied? Or is he to be praised for authenticity in that his moral commitments have been entered into by a free and consciously reflective act of choice?

At any rate if a man's morality, however external in origin and however passively embraced, is necessarily the outcome of choice, it follows that whatever morality he winds up with is an expression of his essence as a freely choosing being. If, on the other hand, the element of choice in his adoption of a morality can vary in degree, if he can at one extreme positively choose it and at the other slide passively into accepting it, it might be concluded that the morally superior man is the one whose morality by being positively chosen most fully expresses his essence. If Sartre's theory of essence is to have any ethical implications it must be on the latter interpretation.

But, as I have said, one may positively choose a morality whose content is externally supplied.

The idea that man is in essence a self-determining being *can* have ethical implications, if his exercise of his capacity for choice can vary in degree. But that is to say that it can have ethical implications *only* under these conditions, not that it actually does have any. It is also true that only a being with the capacity for choice is properly conceivable as a moral agent, as responsible for what he does. But that does not imply that one ought to choose one's moral principles any more than it implies that one should individualistically choose one's beliefs about matters of scientific fact and that one is being somehow cognitively inauthentic if one more or less passively accepts the beliefs of the scientists of one's epoch. One should, no doubt, be able and, when one's experience provides an opportunity, be willing to criticise generally accepted opinions, both in science and morals. But to say that is not to endorse a general free-for-all, in science or morals.

If the essence of man is self-determination by choice, and its exercise can vary in degree, is its maximisation the criterion of human excellence? Here, as in the two previous cases, there seems to be no necessary connection between premise and conclusion. With this conception of man, as with others, there is no inconsistency in taking 'all-too-human' to be an unfavourable description. Aristotle's doctrine of the mean is at least as applicable here as his doctrine that each natural kind has its intrinsic and essential excellence. To acknowledge that there can be too much choice as well as too little is at least as reasonable as the idea that the unlimited maximisation of choice (of choosings, not things to choose from) defines the perfection of man.

Sartre's view that the essence of man is self-determining choice entails either that he cannot help but choose, in which case there can be no merit in his doing so, or that he can exercise his capacity for choice in varying degrees. If the latter is what he means, it is far from obvious that he *ought* to exercise it to the utmost possible extent. It is not clear whether such a maximisation of choice is compatible with the adoption of already established, institutional or conventional moral attitudes, but it is at any rate calculated in fact, if not in logic, to enhance moral idiosyncrasy, perversity and disagreement. While not denying that these can be valuable in periods of great moral stodginess, I cannot see that they are of absolute and unconditional value. Sartre's theory of human essence elevates a Bohemian prejudice of post-Nietzschean urban intellectuals to the whole truth about the ideal life of man.

5. DO INDIVIDUALS HAVE ESSENCES?

At the beginning I pointed out that the question, has man an essence, is ambiguous. It could mean: is there a set of defining properties associated with the concept of man? This would be answered negatively in one way by those, if there are any, who believe the concept to be simple and unanalysable and in another way by those, and there are certainly some of these, who believe that men are linked not by a common property or properties but rather by family resemblance. But it could also mean: is it essential to the individuals that are men *that* they are men? That this is so is clearly assumed by all three of the doctrines of essence I have considered.

For Aristotle, Marx and Sartre would not deny that the individuals who are men have other properties than the rationality, productiveness or self-determination which they respectively regard as essential to being a man. Certainly both Marx and Sartre suggest that some of men's properties are somehow conspicuously foreign to their essence. In Marx's case these are the properties forced on men by the more or less oppressive social systems in which men find themselves. In Sartre's case there is an emphasis on the spurious, play-acting character of many typical human roles, as in the example of the elaborately investigated waiter. But this disparagement can hardly be applied to non-essential properties in general. To be female or red-haired or a good swimmer or have absolute pitch is neither an oppressive social distortion nor a piece of theatrical make-believe, even if it may have oppressive social consequences, on the one hand, or be exploited in a theatrical manner, on the other.

They clearly believe, then, that for any individual who is, amongst indefinitely many other things, a human being, the fact of being human has some overriding importance. A particular Hungarian postman is essentially a man, but only contingently a Hungarian and an employee of the postal service. Presumably one who holds this to be true would adopt an analogous view about non-human things. A particular Red Admiral would be essentially an animal but only contingently red and a butterfly; a particular television set would be essentially a machine but only contingently dark brown and of 27 inches in screen-width.

It is this assumption that is challenged by what I have called 'orthodox positivism'. C. I. Lewis bluntly observes, 'It is, of course, meaningless to speak of the essence of a thing except relative to its being named by a particular term.' (*Analysis of Knowledge and Valuation*, p. 41.) It is plainly implied that things are always capable of being named by a host of non-equivalent terms, each bearing a different essence with it. Ayer denies that individuals have any necessary properties. 'We can significantly ask', he says, 'what properties it is necessary for something to possess in order to be a thing of such and such a kind, for that is a way of asking what properties enter into the definition of that kind of thing . . . On the other hand, there is no such definition of an individual.' (*Central Questions of Philosophy*, p. 197.)

This position would seem to be strengthened by the existence of non-connotative ways of referring to individuals. If ordinary proper names and the pure demonstratives like 'this', which Russell thought to be logically proper names, are non-connotative and imply nothing about the properties of the things to which they refer and yet serve to identify them it would seem to follow that no denial of a property to a thing thus named could yield a contradiction and thus that no property whatever was essential to such a thing. It is not, indeed, necessary to individuals having no essences that there should be wholly non-connotative ways of referring to them. For it might be the case that there was no common element to the sets of properties connoted by the identifying descriptions that referred to them. But, if there are non-connotative names, the thesis that none of an individual's properties are essential to it seems all the more evident.

It is, indeed, widely agreed that even if not strictly connotative, in the sense of logically implying the possession of certain properties by the things they refer to, proper names and pure demonstratives are associated in their standard identifying use with something connotative. Anyone who uses such a term to identify an individual thing must be able to fix or further determine the reference he is making with some descriptions of the individual in question. But, it is admitted, these associated descriptions are not logically tied to the terms whose use they support. A referring term can be used in communication between people whose sets of associated descriptions are different and perhaps even have no element in common.

There is, however, a problem about the determinacy of identity-statements which might serve to reinstate individual essence to some extent, by way of implying at least a minimal connotation for apparently non-connotative terms. Geach has argued that identity is relative, in the sense that 'a is the same as b' may be true if a and b are thought of in one applicable way, and false if they are thought of in another, and thus that it means different things in the two cases. 'Is a the same as b?' is, in Geach's view, an insufficiently determinate question as it stands. It must always be possible, even if it is not always, or even often, practically necessary, to secure understanding, for the questioner to answer the counter-question, 'same what?'

The sort of example that inspires this conclusion may be illustrated by the question put to a sculptor working on a large lump of clay 'is that what you were working on when I called last week?' It may properly receive the answer 'it is the same piece of clay but a different statue, last week I was doing the archbishop of Canterbury, but this week I'm doing David Bowie'. As defenders of the univocal purity of the concept of identity have been quick to point out, such a state of affairs does not require the admission that the concept of identity is indeterminate, or that it is ambiguous as between different sortal respects in which it may be applied. It would be enough to allow that the reference of the singular terms 'this' and 'what you were working on' is indeterminate.

But, if that is so, then pure demonstratives like the word 'this' and proper names of the ordinary non-connotative sort must implicitly carry some minimal element of connotation with them when they are used to make identifying references. Something of the sort seems to be admitted by Ayer, despite his rejection of individual essence, in his consideration of the question 'what makes a person the person that he is'. To that question, he says, 'we can, then, answer that certain properties are after all essential; the property of having some human characteristics, perhaps also the property of occupying some position or other in space or time'. (*The Problem of Knowledge*, p. 208.) The fact that these properties do not serve to individuate the things whose essence they are, that none of the properties which are uniquely satisfied by an individual are essential to it, may be admitted without prejudice to the conclusion that an individual has an essence, even if not a proprietary one.

One consideration leading Ayer to this conclusion is the apparent existence of logical limits to the changes we can intelligibly conceive an individual to undergo without forfeiture of its identity. I might have been, or he might change into, a female, a Bulgarian, a trapeze-artist, an epileptic. But there seems no sense to the supposition that I might have been or that he might change into an ashtray or a daffodil or a Jumbo jet. Certainly the stuff of which I am composed might be turned into fertiliser or the *pièce de résistance* of a dinner-party in New Guinea. But then I am not identical with the stuff of which I am composed, I am just made of it.

Individuals, then, do have at least a minimal essence if the determinacy of reference without which they cannot be identified is to be secured. And as far as the individuals who are human beings are concerned it appears that this reference-determining essence is their humanity. Any other properties they may possess they can be conceived as losing without loss of identity, provided, of course, that they are not, as Ayer's property of location in time and space may be, logically implied by being human. Or perhaps one should say, being a person. For, as horror films concretely show, it is intelligible that a person should change from being a man, that is from being embodied in the characteristically human way, into a wolf, provided that the wolf is, as actual wolves are not, a person.

In fact, by and large, only all things that have, or are, living human bodies are persons. But in so far as they can be conceptually distinguished it is the personality rather than the human embodiment that is essential to them. Keeping both options open, for the moment, let me raise the question: does the fact that being men, in either or both of these senses, which is essential to the individuals that are men, in a way that none of their other properties is, have any ethical implications?

It is clear that the concept of a person enters into the constitution of many of the central concepts of morality, including the concept of morality itself. Moral principles are logically confined in their application to persons in two distinct ways: they enjoin or forbid the actions and approve or condemn the characters only of persons and, secondly, they are concerned with the actions of persons (and the characters these actions express) in regard to their effect on persons.

But this does not make the concept of a person a moral, and so perhaps especially disputable, concept any more than the fact that the concepts of negation or implication or causation enter into the constitution of such concepts as poison or defeat in war or resentment makes them concepts of chemistry, history or psychology. They are not peculiar to these disciplines and the concept of a person is not peculiar to morality.

I have argued elsewhere ('Two Conceptions of Personality', *Revue Internationale de Philosophie*, 1968 and *The Nature of Things*, pp. 103–5) that we tend to operate with two different notions of personality, one of rational, responsible agency, as exemplified by adult, sane human beings, the other much less exigent and applicable to babies, the insane, the senile and, I would suggest, the higher animals. Both figure in the two modes in which the concept of a person enters into the constitution of the concept of morality that I mentioned. The persons to whom alone moral injunctions are addressed are persons in the narrower sense, rational and responsible agents. But the persons whose interests are relevant to the determination of the moral qualities of action are the wider class of sensitive beings, capable of enjoyment and suffering, and to whom alone the possession of interests can be intelligibly ascribed. In neither case, however, does the fact that personality is the individual essence of those endowed with it have ethical implications. The relation is the other way round: the concept of morality presupposes both conceptions of personality. But that, as I have argued, does not make it a moral concept itself, although it is logically indispensable to the concept of morality.

3

KANT AND ANTHROPOLOGY

G. J. Warnock

THE question that I want to debate a little in this paper could be put in this way: what, and how much, empirical information is required for, or relevant to, moral philosophy? That question may well strike one as somewhat vague and woolly. Rightly so. What is needed to get rather clearer about its answer or possible answers is chiefly, I believe, to get clearer about its sense.

It is not difficult to see why reflection on the case of Kant should raise this question; for a straightforward reading of his text suggests that he gave, explicitly and emphatically, a very striking answer to it. In the *Grundlegung*, he begins by saying that Ethics – like physics, he says, and unlike logic – does have 'an empirical part'; and he proposes that this empirical part, as an area of what he is willing to call 'empirical philosophy', should be entitled *practical anthropology*. We may note by the way that he appears to envisage rather curiously what the subject-matter of practical anthropology would be; it would address itself, he admittedly rather cursorily suggests, not to general enquiry about people and their societies, so far as that might be relevant to practical issues, but rather to the special question what it is about human wills that makes it the case that 'what ought to happen frequently does not'. This makes his notion of practical anthropology look like part of what we would, perhaps, more naturally call moral psychology. But it is more pertinent to our question to observe that he immediately proceeds, notoriously, to insist that this empirical part of Ethics, whatever it is and whatever it should be called, is in any case quite secondary, non-fundamental. For 'moral laws with their principles' are 'essentially distinguished from every other kind of practical knowledge in which there is anything empirical'; and 'all moral philosophy rests wholly on its pure part' that is, its *a priori*, non-empirical part. Even when we 'apply' moral philosophy to man, we do not need – do not, in Kant's phrase, 'borrow the least thing from' – empirical knowledge about humans, that is, from anthropology. For the 'metaphysic of morals' – for moral *philosophy*, as we might say, as distinct from the human sciences – we not only do not require, but must even carefully and on principle rule out and disregard, empirical information about people, their actual 'nature' and predicaments. For 'the basis of obligation must not be sought in the nature of man, or in the circumstances in the world in which he is placed, but *a priori* simply in the conceptions of pure reason'.

It is possible to name at once one group of thinkers by whom this answer of Kant's would be vigorously rejected – those, namely, who today rally under the banner of 'radical philosophy'. Kant's insistence that there is such a thing as *pure* moral philosophy, the *metaphysic* of morals, bears at least a family resemblance to more recent contentions to the effect that moral philosophy is, so to speak, a proper topic in its own right, and is rightly, indeed essentially, distinguishable from, say, psychology or sociology, anthropology or economics – from, in fact, the empirical or partly empirical social and human sciences; and this contention is certainly viewed by some, possibly all radical philosophers with hostility and withering scorn. I do not want to debate at length whether or not this scorn is well-founded, chiefly because I am by no means clear enough about what its foundations are believed to be; but it appears to me to rest at least in part on simple confusion, and this confusion at least we can, I think, get out of the way. S. Sayers, writing in the *Cambridge Review* (vol. 94, no. 2209), selected me as an example of the belief that 'philosophy ... is one thing; the sciences ... and practical thought and activity ... are another'. Well, I do believe that, I think; so did Kant; and it is a comfort of a sort that, according to Mr Sayers, most recent British philosophers agree with us. Now the belief might be false, or if expounded and construed in certain ways might be at least partly false, or perhaps misleading; but I am sure that Kant and I and the rest do not make one specific mistake with which Mr Sayers charges us. 'They have felt', he writes – rejoicing in their 'abstract and dead' professionalism – 'fully qualified to pronounce on questions of morals, politics, science, and religion without any serious knowledge or interest in these fields.' But that charge at least is an absurd one, even obviously absurd. For of course those who have said that philosophy is one thing, the sciences (etc.) another, have regularly recognised as a mere corollary of that that philosophy does not settle questions *in* (or of) the sciences (etc.) and that thence philosophers are *not* as such 'fully qualified', or specially qualified at all, to pronounce on those questions. To hold that we should bring in no empirical information in moral philosophy would not be to maintain, and indeed would naturally lead one carefully to reject, the obvious absurdity that moral judgements of cases can be made in a state of total ignorance about everything; just as to hold that the philosophy of science is not an experimental enquiry would not be to maintain, absurdly, that problems in, say, chemistry can be solved with no knowledge of or engagement in any experiment. One can scarcely call in question the familiar, and I dare say orthodox, distinction between 'first-order' and 'second-order' enquiries by thus simply disregarding it, still less by alleging that it has been disregarded by the very persons who are simultaneously alleged to have taken it too seriously.

There has of course been some disagreement among commentators as to where exactly Kant himself stands on this matter. There is no serious doubt that he invites us to eject all empirical information from 'pure' moral philosophy, from the 'metaphysic of morals'; but some at least have read him as maintaining, additionally to that, that ground-floor moral judgement is also 'pure', completely non-empirical – that all we need for moral judgement is rationally certifiable maxims, not knowledge of, for instance, the consequences that action of this sort or that is in fact likely to have. It may well be thought unlikely that Kant, who was neither stupid nor silly, should seriously and deliberately have held this; for it seems very plain that maxims, however 'pure' in themselves or in their origins, could only be applied in particular cases on the basis of information as to what those cases actually are. But let it suffice for present purposes to say that Kant in any case *need* not have held this. If you wish to maintain, as he clearly did, that what we call moral philosophy is a non-empirical enquiry, to be distinguished from any scientific, factual study of humans and human societies, you certainly need not maintain – and most of us do not – that no facts need be known when it comes to making moral judgements.

But how 'pure' *can* moral philosophy be? We can bring in, I believe, another important witness on this question by juggling it about a little. Kant's project of identifying 'the basis of obligation' is not different in substance, I think, from that of formulating the most general, most basic principles of morality; it would be possible to pose the issue of what those principles are by considering what sort of principles one would, if one had the choice, reasonably choose; and here it may strike us that there is or appears a certain kinship between Kant's insistence that we must eschew all empirical infor-

mation in considering that matter, and the recent Rawlsian proposition that, in 'choosing' or 'adopting' principles of justice, we must
place ourselves, or must imagine the situation of persons hypothetically placed, behind 'the veil of ignorance'.[1] The question: what
empirical information do we need, or can we properly make use of?
comes to about the same as the question: what if anything should
Rawlsian rational contractors, behind the veil of ignorance, be
allowed *not* to be ignorant of? (How thick is the veil?) And we may
bring the Kantian and Rawlsian projects even closer together by
observing that, while Rawls himself is characteristically careful to
limit his own argument to the particular topic of justice, he does
tentatively suggest that its scope might be extended to cover much
if not all of the territory of moral philosophy, and that such an
extension has in fact been very powerfully attempted by Dr D. A. J.
Richards, in his book *A Theory of Reasons for Action*.

But, now, if the questions are in substance much the same, the
answers offered appear to be completely different. Kant is willing
to let in no empirical information; the Rawlsian project lets in a
very great deal. It lets in, in fact, information of two very different
kinds. In the first place, Rawls holds, in squaring up to the problem
of choosing or formulating principles of justice, we can properly take
ourselves to be informed of those facts in virtue of which the practical issue arises at all. We can take ourselves to know, for instance,
that the earth we inhabit is of finite extent and of finite, often even
moderately scarce, resources, occupied by individuals, nowadays ever
more numerous, of more or less comparable powers and equal vulner-
ability, pursuing different ends and purposes and putting forward conflicting claims. If all that were not so, then justice would be not exactly
unimportant, but rather a non-issue; problems simply would not
arise as to which there would be occasion to look for a 'just'
resolution; we do not bother about, say, just distribution of what
nobody much wants, or of what is so abundant that everyone's needs
are easily satisfied. And of course one could extend this recognition of
what Rawls calls 'the circumstances of justice' in such a way as to
bring in those other very general facts which cause other moral issues
actually to arise.

But second, and very differently, Rawls also lets in a very liberal
allowance of what he calls 'general facts about human society'. His
hypothetical formulators of principles of justice, though lurking behind 'the veil of ignorance', 'understand political affairs and the principles of economic theory; they know the basis of social organisation

[1] Rawls, *A Theory of Justice* (1972), sec. 24 etc.

and the laws of human psychology' – there are, indeed, to be
no 'limitations on general information, that is, on general laws and
theories'. It thus looks as if Rawls sees no reason to exclude, and
indeed is perfectly willing to bring in, not only the whole of what
Kant rules out as 'anthropology', but a large, indeed unlimited,
body of empirical (though general) information as well. So there
appears to be head-on conflict here: how real is that appearance?

Well, we can at least begin, I think, in a reconciliatory sort of way.
For it is clear enough that Rawls does not really mean to say that,
if principles of justice are to be formulated, we actually *need to have*
– if only because, after all, nobody could have – absolutely compre-
sensive knowledge of all general laws and theories, or even of general
laws and theories in politics, economics, and psychology; it is, rather,
most (though not quite all) of his point that we need not be supposed
not to have such knowledge – it need not be excluded. And his case
for that would be, of course, that knowledge of this wholly general
sort is *non-biasing*; it is all general, non-particular. The prime conceptual function of 'the veil of ignorance' is to deprive each party
to the transaction of such particular knowledge of *his own* case as
would incline or enable him, in formulating principles, to seek to
bias his formulation in his own favour. But if that is what the veil of
ignorance is for – if that is the guiding light by which we decide
what information to exclude – it may well appear that we have no
reason to exclude *any* knowledge of 'general facts' or 'general laws
and theories', and so might as well, for theoretical simplicity, let it
all in.

There are, however, two respects in which there is more to be said.
In the first place, although it is a large part of Rawls's contention
that his liberal allowance of general information need not (as non-
biasing) be excluded, that is not the whole story; he does suppose
that at least some of it is actually required. Why is that? Because, he
interestingly holds (or at least I think he does), in formulating principles of justice we need to know at least enough about human
psychology to know what principles stand a decent chance of being,
not merely formally adopted, but acted upon, really seriously
accepted and 'supported' in actual practice.

I think it is clear enough that Kant would not like this; and I am
somewhat inclined to believe that Kant would be right. I think one
might argue that Rawls's position here assimilates moral philosophy
too closely to legislation. His imaginative fiction of rational choosers
of principles is in fact plainly derived, at no great distance, *from* the
case of legislation (perhaps passing on the way Kant's 'legislating'
members of 'the kingdom of ends'); and I think it arguable that,

here, this provenance is misleading. Actual legislation is indeed, in large part and so far as it is intelligently undertaken, a pragmatic pursuit. Since it usually carries along with it a somewhat cumbersome and costly apparatus of surveillance, investigation, litigation, and enforcement – a rather extensive and expensive use of public resources – it is plain common sense to raise the question whether some proposed legislative provision stands a good chance, or any chance, of being decently complied with. However heinous one may take some form of behaviour to be, one may reasonably think there is a case against making it *illegal* if one judges such a law to be likely to be generally disregarded; one is concerned here in large part with social practicality, and there is simply no practical point in requiring persons by law to do what they will certainly not do, even if so required. Legislation, if ineffective, is inefficient at best, and should be condemned as such. But the proposition that principles of justice – or, more widely, moral principles – are in comparable case looks odd to my eye. Would it count against a moral principle of, say, charity that people were in fact not very much disposed to be charitable? Why should it? If I propose a quasi-legal rule for, say, the conduct of members of my college, it will be apposite to remark that it will certainly not be obeyed; for, if it will not be obeyed, its promulgation as a rule will certainly be useless, and may be positively damaging. But if I judge or pronounce some form of behaviour to be morally wrong, is it even relevant to observe that, given what people are like, they are not actually going to be inclined to abstain from such behaviour? I think it clear that Kant would say, and I am (I think) inclined to agree with him, that morality differs from legislation, and is not even quasi-legislation, in that it simply does not have to be practical, or practicable, or practised in *that* sort of way. Rawls says that a conception of justice should, as he puts it, 'generate its own support': but it is not clear to me how, as a conception of justice, it would necessarily be any the worse if it did not – though, of course, its not doing so would be very much to be regretted. The question what principles of conduct, given the facts about human beings and their general circumstances, are actually going to be effectively adopted and followed is no doubt important enough, and empirical enough; but I do not see that it is not, as Kant surely would have held that it was, strictly extraneous to moral philosophy.

The second respect in which there is more to be said is perhaps more controversial, or more a matter of opinion. It is conspicuous that all the general information which Rawls takes to be not excluded by the veil of ignorance is information about humans – human society, human psychology, terrestrial politics and economics. This he consciously acknowledges. 'I have assumed', he writes, 'all along that the parties know that they are subject to the conditions of human life ... The freedom of pure intelligences not subject to these constraints, and the freedom of God, is outside the scope of the theory.'[2] Now that may very well strike one as a sensible restriction; but it is disconcerting that Rawls explicitly makes the further claim that this limitation is not un-Kantian. 'It might appear', he writes, 'that Kant meant his doctrine to apply to all rational beings as such and therefore to God and the angels as well ... I do not believe that Kant held this view.' But it is surely not a matter of opinion that Kant *did* hold that view. In his own words, 'Everyone must admit that if a law is to have moral force, i.e. to be the basis of an obligation, it must carry with it absolute necessity; that, for example, the precept "Thou shalt not lie", is not valid for men alone, as if other rational beings had no need to observe it ... that, therefore, the basis of obligation must not be sought in the nature of man, or in the circumstances in the world in which he is placed.' I am not suggesting that Kant never said, elsewhere, anything that would in any way qualify this rather plain statement, but only that as it stands it is both plain and unqualified. I suspect that false antitheses are operating here. It is true that Kant did not believe that his theory applied to 'God and the angels', or perhaps even to 'pure intelligences', *just as* it did to persons; for God and the angels presumably, and perhaps pure intelligences also, would not present the specific problem of 'practical reason' in conflict with, or at any rate potentially in conflict with, 'inclinations' to act otherwise than the moral law prescribes. But what makes his theory applicable to persons is, in his opinion, not at all that they are specifically *human* persons, or occupants of this particular planet rather than some other one; it is, as he says, that they are rational beings; and he takes it not only as obvious, but as straight off universally agreed, that the obligations of morality would bear upon, or extend to, any rational beings *other* than humans, if (apart from God and the angels) any such existed. And on this point again I am inclined to think that Kant has reason on his side. It is difficult to avoid on this topic a perhaps rather laughable air of science-fiction fantasy; nevertheless, it does appear to me quite reasonable to hold that specimens from some other planet, or perhaps hitherto unencountered occupants of our own, would, if *ex hypothesi* rational beings, not properly be judged to fall outside all moral concern

[2] Op. cit., p. 257.

simply on the ground that they were not human. The moral disabilities of animals, so far as they exist, are surely to be ascribed to their non-rationality, not to non-humanness. Or one might put it like this: if, as Rawls insists, I am not to know my age, sex, nationality, abilities, date, and so forth, why should it be relevant that I *should* know my zoological species and galactic location? If so, then Kant, I believe, would rightly urge against Rawls that there is no *moral* relevance in all the general information that he so generously allows about specifically human psychology, human society, and so on. For there is no reason to think that morality has uniquely, or by definition, to do with the doings of specimens of that particular species.

So far, then, I have, I believe, found myself on Kant's side. I do not see that, to pursue enquiry into 'the basis of obligation', we need to gather information, interesting though it doubtless is as a further question, as to what sort of principles are likely in fact to 'generate their own support'; for I do not see what would be wrong, what would be evidence of philosophical error, in reaching the conclusion, dismal though it certainly would be, that certain defensible principles might not in fact be generally, operatively accepted at all. Nor do I see that we need, or even can relevantly bring in, a lot, or even a little, of general information about humans specifically as humans; for, as Kant said, not humanness, but reason, is what makes us both capable of and subject to moral appraisal. But – no empirical information *at all*? At this point my Kantian loyalties (such as they are) begin to give way.

For surely Kant does not really give us (or himself) enough to go on. He invites us to seek the basis of obligation '*a priori* simply in the conceptions of pure reason'. What does that mean? It means, in effect, that we are to consider what principles (presupposing *only* an 'inclination' sometimes to act otherwise than they prescribe) a number or aggregate of beings would all adopt, as being adoptable by and applicable to them all, given *only* that they are all rational beings. And that seems to me a question too totally unspecific to admit of anything much in the way of an answer. Why, one might for instance ask, would such beings adopt any principles at all? Because – the answer must be – they have occasion from time to time to *do* things, and thus have occasion from time to time to raise the question of what it would be right or wrong to *do*. For we are talking, of course, about practical principles; and that means at once that we should think of our rational beings not merely as rational (as 'pure intelligences') but as rational *agents*. But an agent, or at any rate a rational agent, has ends or purposes that he seeks to realise in action; and thus, though we are not yet anywhere near to insisting that our beings are human, we are taking them to be something more than merely rational. Next, why does it *matter* what a rational agent does? Why does the question of right and wrong even arise? It is at any rate a large part of the answer to say: because he may have ends that it would actually be damaging to him to realise, or in seeking which he would frustrate realisation of the ends of others, or damage them. And thus we are supposing our beings to be not merely rational, nor merely rational agents, but in some degree *vulnerable* to harm at their own hands or at those of others; and we are supposing that ends are not necessarily all harmoniously co-attainable. But all this, though very general information, and indeed not information necessarily about humans, is *empirical* information; it does not follow from the bare concept of rational beings that they have these further characteristics or are placed in these circumstances. Kant, it might be said, does clearly take very general facts of this sort for granted; but it can surely then be said that, in so far as he does so, he is making use for the purposes of his argument of knowledge of just the sort that Rawls sketches under his title of 'the circumstances of justice', and so, since these circumstances are clearly empirical circumstances, is not fully faithful to his own requirement that the argument should proceed *purely a priori*.

However, there may, after all, be an issue of mere nomenclature here. For perhaps, after all, it is a somewhat arbitrary matter where the line is drawn between foundations and superstructure, or between fundamental and more or less derivative principles. It might not be impossible for Kant to have held that, given *merely* the pure conception of rational beings, one could elicit some vastly abstract principle of a sort of *equality*. Perhaps, one might argue, any rational being as such would have to recognise that, if any practical principles were ever to be actually adopted, or anything ever to be done as to which any question of right or wrong could arise, then at any rate there would be no reason for any rational being to be regarded, or to regard himself, as relevantly *differently* situated from any other. It might possibly be held that that, though admittedly not much, is nevertheless the *whole* of 'the metaphysic' of morality, the whole of what is really fundamental in its principles. It is, one might conceivably hold, an empirical matter whether, among the members of any aggregate of rational beings, any issues calling for the exercise of practical judgement do ever arise; it is an empirical matter what sort of issues they might be, or in what sort of ways it might be of practical importance that this or that should be done or not done.

But all this, it might be maintained, is not part of the *foundation* of moral philosophy; it belongs to the superstructure that begins to emerge when we add to the foundation specific empirical information; the only really fundamental proposition is that, among rational beings, the situation of each, and the claims and rights of each if he should have occasion to make any claims or seek to exercise any rights, are not discriminable from those of any other. Rational beings are equal, and none is more equal than others.

Well, I suppose it not impossible to maintain that that *is* the metaphysic of morals; but I do not think it by any means clear that Kant claimed no more, or even that the claim by itself is particularly interesting. For my own part I believe that we must be just a bit empirical – at least to the extent that, in seeking the basis and *rationale* of moral principles, we should allow ourselves to ask why they are wanted, and what they are supposed to do for us. Kant had, of course, a special problem, for him a quite difficult one and one to which he gives special attention, as to what is – as he calls it – the 'interest' of morality; I think I would prefer the topic to be delimited in a way that, though perhaps not perfectly 'pure', would be rich enough to make it quite evident why the topic is interesting.

4

ON INEQUALITY AND VIOLENCE, AND THE DIFFERENCES WE MAKE BETWEEN THEM

Ted Honderich

JUST about all political philosophy of the recommending kind is factless and presumptuous. That it has an honest intellectual use, which it does, and which of course is different from its use as reassurance and the like, is only to be explained by the want of something better.

We can but agree that all of philosophy, in order to come within sight of its several ends, must have far less to do with empirical fact than those disciplines which have its discovery and explanation as their only end. However, in the political philosophy which implicitly or explicitly recommends action to us, or more likely inaction, premises of empirical fact necessarily have a larger importance than elsewhere in philosophy.

A reason for this larger importance is that recommendations of a quite specific nature are made. We are in fact urged to take a political side. Political philosophy of this kind is different even from moral philosophy of the traditional kind. There, one is urged only towards such indecisive parties as the Utilitarian and such indecisive commitments as to integrity. The Principle of Utility by itself, like a principle of integrity, does not decide particular questions in private morality for one. It is understood that to settle questions of conduct in marriage, say, one needs something in addition to general principles, which by themselves do not tell one what to do. The additional factual premises are not supplied, and so, very reasonably, recommendations of a specific nature are not made. One is not told what to do in marriage.

In political philosophy of the recommending kind, one is told what to do in politics. For such recommendations to rise to being *argued* recommendations, they clearly need to be preceded by premises about society, empirical premises of a pretty particular kind. Typically they are not. Nor does one have much confidence that what is said for our guidance was in fact derived, in private reflection off the page, from factual premises worth the name.

If political philosophy of the kind in question is in fact as little empirical as the rest of philosophy, and has such need to be more so that it may with justice be called factless, it is therefore presumptuous in its conclusions. However, there is also presumption in it for an entirely different reason.

The issue of political violence, to come down to that, is typically handled in a mere essay or a mere chapter, which does nonetheless finish with a conclusion on the principal question. We may be told that violence, leaving aside a few chosen revolutions now dignified or indeed holied by time, is savage iniquity. We may be given to understand, differently, perhaps in something that falls short of plain speech, that violence of the Left must reluctantly be welcomed. It may be allowed, as certainly it should be, that what has actually been set out in support of the chosen conclusion is no more than a *simulacrum* of the argument for it, or, certainly better, only *one part* of that argument. Still, we are offered the intimation that all of the real thing, the conclusive argument itself, exists somewhere else.

This political philosophy, then, begins without essential premises of fact, proceeds by way of intimation, and delivers conclusions to us nonetheless. Let us make a beginning at trying to put things right.

I. LIFETIMES

In the United States, on average, non-whites live for about seven years less than whites.[1] About 25 *million* individuals now alive will have an average of seven years less of life than, on average, other members of their society. If there are no very fundamental economic and social changes in America, it is likely that the next 'generation', the non-whites who are alive 20 years from now, will have an improved life-expectancy but still one that is very considerably smaller than that of their white contemporaries. The rate of improvement in the past gives one basis among several for this guess about the future.[2] One can guess, more precisely, that the non-

[1] *Statistical Abstract of the United States 1973* (Washington, 1974), Table 78, p. 57.

[2] In 1920 the gap between non-whites and whites was about 10 years,

whites alive 20 years from now, if fundamental economic and social changes do not come about, will have an average lifetime five years smaller than their white contemporaries.

The population of England and Wales has been divided into five of what are called social classes. They might also be called occupational groups, since they are in fact defined by the occupations of their members. They are labelled Professional, Intermediate, Skilled, Partly-skilled and Unskilled. On average, the life-expectancy of men in the fifth social class, *at age* 25, is 3.5 years less than the life-expectancy of their counterparts in the first social class.[3] The American figures for whites and non-whites, in contrast, have to do with life-expectancy at birth.

It is certain, although the figures are unavailable, that the average whole lifetime, the average life-expectancy at birth, of English and Welsh males who become unskilled workers, is considerably more than 3.5 years smaller than that of their counterparts who become members of the professions. There is evidence of several kinds for this.[4] Thus it is almost certain that the 1.2 *million* men now alive who are unskilled will have shorter lives than professional men by about five years. One can guess that in 20 years' time, if fundamental social and economic changes are not made in Britain, the unskilled workers then living will be in an improved position but still have a life-expectancy very considerably smaller than that of the professions.

Let us have before us, beside the truths and suppositions about individual lifetimes in contemporary America and Britain, certain uncontentious generalisations about all Western economically-developed societies. We can proceed towards these by remembering that non-whites in America and unskilled workers in Britain have greatly less material wealth and income than other groups in their societies.[5] There are, of course, some non-whites who are better off than some whites, and some unskilled workers who are better off than some members of some other occupational groups. On the whole, nonetheless, non-whites in America and unskilled workers

in 1930 about 13 years, in 1940 about 11 years, in 1950 about 8 years, in 1960 about 7 years, and in 1970 about 7 years. Op. cit., Table 78, p. 57.

[3] Calculated from standard mortality indices in *The Registrar General's Decennial Supplement, England and Wales, 1961: Occupational Mortality Tables* (London, 1971).

[4] The difference in life expectancies between the fifth and the first social class is insignificant at age 65, 2.1 years at 55, 3 years at 45, 3.3 years at 35, and 3.5 years at 25. (Calculated from standard mortality indices, op. cit.)

[5] See, for example, A. B. Atkinson, *Wealth, Income and Inequality* (Harmondsworth, 1973).

and their families in Britain each are large parts of a poorest group in each of the two societies. We have, then, a correlation between an economic fact and a fact about lifetimes. It is unsurprising. Indeed, the fact that the people in question come at the bottom of scales of wealth and income is the principal part of the complex cause of their shorter lives. This consideration, and many related truths about groups in the other economically-developed societies, give rise to two generalisations about all such societies.

The first one has to do with roughly the one-tenth of the present population of each society that has less wealth and income than any other tenth in that society. The generalisation is that the worst-off tenth now living in each of the developed societies will have considerably shorter lives than the individuals in the best-off tenth. It is as good as certain that they will live less long, on average, by five years or more. We must wait for precision until the time, if ever it comes, when more statistical work is done. The second generalisation, as may be anticipated, is that if there are not fundamental social and economic changes in the societies in question, the situation will be better in 20 years but not greatly better.

There are now, in all of the bottom tenths of the economically-developed societies, something like 65 *million* individuals.

To turn to a related subject-matter, the table below[6] gives a few

LIFE-EXPECTANCY AT BIRTH

	Gabon	Guinea	Nigeria	India	Colombia
Male	25	26	37	42	44
Female	45	28	37	41	46

	France	West Germany	America	England & Wales
Male	69	68	67	69
Female	76	74	74	75

specimen life-expectancies at birth for males and females, first for economically less-developed societies and then for developed societies. Males born in Gabon have an average lifetime of 25 years. Males born in Britain, taking all social classes together, have an average lifetime of 69, well over twice as long. On *average*, males in Gabon die well before what is regarded as middle age in Britain.

The average lifetime of males and females taken together in all

---

[6] Source: *United Nations Demographic Yearbook, 1972* (New York, 1973), Table 27, p. 600. Except for figures for America, which come from *United Nations Demographic Yearbook, 1969* (New York, 1970), Table 46, p. 640. The figures in my table, like the figures in the source-tables, have to do with different recent years.

the less-developed societies, by one common definition of the latter, is about 42 years. The average lifetime of males and females together in developed countries, again with the latter defined in one common way, is about 71.[7] About *half the world's population*, then, have average lifetimes about 29 years shorter than another quarter of the world's population. It is not too much to say that what we have before us are *different kinds* of human lifetime.

The average figures for the two groups of societies, as the specimen figures indicate, hide still greater inequalities, those holding between particular societies. There is also the greater difference in lifetimes between the top tenth of population in all the developed countries and the bottom tenth of population in the less-developed countries. There are no figures available, to my knowledge, for the latter tenth. Given evidence of various kinds, it is certain that that bottom tenth in less-developed societies have average lifetimes very much more than 29 years shorter than the average lifetimes of the top tenth in developed societies. Their lives, on average, are in the neighbourhood of 40 years shorter. It is not too much to say, then, that the wealthiest in the wealthy countries have two lives for each single life of the poor in the poorest countries.

There is a likelihood that these inequalities in life-expectancy between developed and less-developed societies, and groups within them, will be smaller in 20 years. In the recent past, medical advances have improved life-expectancies in the less-developed societies, and it is likely that further advances will be made. Nonetheless, unless there is a transformation in the relations between the wealthy and the poor parts of the world, there will remain an immense difference in lifetimes 20 years from now.

The numbers of people involved in these propositions about the less-developed societies are of course great. The population of the less-developed societies, as defined, about half of the world's population, includes about 1,700 million people. The bottom tenth then includes about 170 *million people*.

There arises the question of the possibility of any real change, either in the inequalities of lifetime within developed societies or in the inequalities of lifetime between developed and less-developed societies. Some will be inclined to suppose that whatever morality may say or not say, we do not have the relevant capability. There is error in talk of large changes in lifetimes that might follow on fundamental social and economic changes. It may be objected, in effect, that it is already inevitable that the next generation of the

[7] Simon Kuznets, 'The Gap: Concept, Measurement, Trends', p. 34, in *The Gap Between Rich and Poor Nations* (London, 1972), edited by Gustav Ranis.

groups in question will have a life-expectancy much like that of the present generation of the same groups.

This is mistaken, certainly or probably. Given the wealth and efficiency of the developed societies, proved in many different ways, it is clear enough that we could change very radically the life-expectancy of the groups in question. One needs to reflect, in part, on the magnitude of just such changes in the past. To consider the inequalities *within* developed societies, the following table gives the change in life-expectancy of American whites, at birth, over a period of 40 years.[8]

1920	54.9
1940	64.2
1960	70.6

One fact of relevance, then, is that in each of two 20-year periods in the past, the life-expectancy of American whites was improved to a considerably greater extent than would be required in to a considerably greater extent than would be required in the coming 20 years if blacks were to come up to the level of whites.

It is to be admitted, certainly, that the case is not clear with respect to the possibility of change in the lifetime inequalities between developed and less-developed societies. Nonetheless, it is beyond question that the inequalities could be dramatically reduced. The lifetime inequalities are consequences of economic inequalities. It is my own view that no amount of economic theory can put in doubt the truth that the present economic inequalities are open to change, change which would not be damaging to present economic totals and which would dramatically reduce lifetime inequalities.

It is worth remarking in this connection, to those who are struck by how very little *has* been achieved, that not much more than nothing has been attempted. In 1964 a number of the economically-developed countries pledged to 'contribute' a percentage of their future gross national products to the less-developed countries. This 'contribution' was to include loans and private investment. The figure agreed upon was 1 per cent. Since that time, a number of the countries in question have failed to reach this percentage. None has exceeded it by much. The pledged total of 1 per cent of the gross national products of the developed countries in question has not been met in any year.[9] This is not the *kind* of thing to be kept in mind in considering the question of capability. A better thing is the 'war efforts' of the past.

[8] Source: *Statistical Abstract of the United States, 1973*, Table 78, p. 57.

[9] Robert McNamara, *Address to the Board of Governors* of the International Bank for Reconstruction and Development (1970), p. 8. The situation, I think, remains unchanged.

All of these generalisations about lifetimes have *all* of their importance in the fact that they have to do with *individual human experience*. It is a banal truth that typically we escape this proposition, or give it the attention of a moment. It is necessary to come closer to the reality of experience. We may do so through one woman's recorded recollection of her daughter.

She was doing fine, real fine. I thought she was going to be fine, too. I did. There wasn't a thing wrong with her, and suddenly she was in real trouble, bad trouble, yes sir, she was. She started coughing, like her throat was hurting, and I thought she must be catching a cold or something. I thought I'd better go get some hot water, but it wasn't easy, because there were the other kids, and it's far away to go. So I sent my husband when he came home, and I tried to hold her, and I sang and sang, and it helped. But she got real hot, and she was sleepy all right, but I knew it wasn't good, no sir. I'd rather hear her cry, that's what I kept saying. My boy, he knew it too. He said, 'Ma, she's real quiet, isn't she?' Then I started praying, and I thought maybe it'll go the way it came, real fast, and by morning there won't be anything but Rachel feeling a little tired, that's all. We got the water to her, and I tried to get her to take something, a little cereal, like she was doing all along. I didn't have any more milk – maybe that's how it started. And I had a can of tomato juice, that we had in case of real trouble, and I opened it and tried to get it down her. But she'd throw it all back at me, and I gave up, to tell the truth. I figured it was best to let her rest, and then she could fight back with all the strength she had, and as I said, maybe by the morning she'd be the winner, and then I could go get a bottle of milk from my boss man and we could really care for her real good, until she'd be back to her self again. But it got worse, I guess, and by morning she was so bad there was nothing she'd take, and hot all over. And then she went, all of a sudden. There was no more breathing, and it must have been around noon by the light.[10]

To my mind, no apology whatever is owed to those who may say that they do not expect to find emotional matter within serious reflection. On the contrary, one must feel remiss for offering so small a reminder of human experience, or feel a despondency in the realisation that so little will be tolerated.

[10] Robert Coles, *Still Hungry in America* (Cleveland, 1969), pp. 27–8.

2. VIOLENCE

The facts of violence are not so much in need of being brought forward. It is a part of what I shall discuss in this essay that we have an immediate and a sharp awareness of them. Nonetheless, should anyone persist in regarding the effects of violence as no more than calculable expenses to be paid for the march of history, it will be as well to assert what should need no asserting, that here too we find facts of human experience. Bombs injure, maim, and kill. They end or devastate the lives of their first victims and they bring agony or ruin to the lives of their second victims, those who suffer through others' being injured, maimed, or killed. The effects of explosions are not only those which we find detailed in our newspapers as they happen. A man who is blinded or a girl who loses a hand lives on, and, for everyone who is killed, there are others affected.

If these are the things of importance about political violence, there is nonetheless need for a general definition, unlike the case of inequality. Political violence, roughly defined, is *a considerable or destroying use of force against persons or things, a use of force prohibited by law, directed to a change in the policies, personnel or system of government, and hence also directed to changes in the existence of individuals in the society and perhaps other societies.* There are other definitions of political violence, certainly, including definitions thought to be more enlightened or virtuous, but I shall not consider them.[11]

It will be as well to have in mind some extent or magnitude of political violence. What I shall have in mind in what follows is roughly the level of violence with which we have become familiar in Britain, America and elsewhere in the world during the past decade. To put the matter differently, if no more precisely, I shall not have in mind political violence at the level of civil war. Nor, of course, shall we be concerned with war between nations, which does not fall under the definition of political violence.

Finally, it may be worth pointing out that more will be in question than exactly the violence which has been most common during the past decade. There can be violence directed to other ends than those which are most familiar. We shall be concerned with political violence generally, both actual and possible.

---

[11] See Jerome A. Shaffer (ed.), *Violence* (New York, 1971), which contains several essays on the definition of violence.

3. FACTS AND REASONINGS

There are the facts of violence, then, and there are what we may
call, if we persist in the use of an anodyne label, the facts of inequality. The latter, of which we have considered only one particular set, claim our attention not only because they consist in
inequalities: situations such that one group of people has *less* of
something than another. It is not merely that some people have less,
but that they have *so little*, judged in an absolute rather than a
comparative way. They are in conditions of deprivation or distress or
worse. The circumstance is not an unreal one which can be imagined,
where inequality does not matter much because the worst-off are
nonetheless splendidly-off.

My intentions in this essay, which have to do with the facts of
inequality and the facts of violence, are two in number. One of
them, with whatever success, has already been realised. It is to make
a contribution, no more than a small one, and however 'unphilo-
sophical', to a realisation of the facts of inequality. The particular set
of facts noticed, those about inequality in quantity of life, have a
natural priority. *Time alive* is not all that matters, but it matters
very much indeed. Still, I do not mean to give this set of inequalities
a greater importance, or for that matter a lesser importance, than
others. The other facts of inequality may be separated into two
further sets. There are those many inequalities which have to do
with economic and social life. The list begins with inequalities in
food, shelter and health. The extent of such inequalities is only
barely indicated, by the known immense disparities in wealth and
income. The third set of inequalities are political in kind, and have
to do with certain freedoms and the lack of them. It is here that
one finds demands for equality in national self-determination, and
demands for equality between peoples in the possession of lands to
which there are historical rights.

It cannot be that rationality allows us to avoid informing ourselves of these things which are more or less directly relevant to
violence. No more is meant than said: that we are obliged in
rationality *to inform ourselves*. A part of this, and something to be
distinguished from responses of feeling to the facts of inequality, and
from judgements about them, is a decent approach to human experience in its detail. What is needed first is knowledge, knowledge
of particulars. No one should overlook, for example, that shorter
lifetimes are in clear ways within the anticipation of very many of
those who have them and also within the experience of others.
With respect to the latter point, there is the fact that if she had

lived longer, the death of the daughter would not ever have been within the experience of the mother.

If we were better informed of the facts of inequality, we could with propriety pass on to following things. What is customarily done, as I have remarked, is to press on improperly, to conclusions. What we shall do here, somewhat less improperly, is to consider some further matters. We shall not come to a conclusion about the rightness, the permissibility, the wrongfulness or the heinousness of political violence. The further matters we shall consider, like the facts of inequality and violence, have a natural place near the beginning of an orderly enquiry.

A welter of responses, assumptions, propositions, theories and doctrines comes in between factual premises about inequality and violence and final conclusions about the morality of violence. I mean, in saying they come in, that they must be considered. All of these things are reasons or reasonings, or else they can be improved into reasons or reasonings. All of them, obviously, must be made decently clear and explicit before their value is judged. In the end, of course, since they point in different directions, some of them must be rejected, or regarded as of lesser weight.

Here are some examples, all of one kind. We may believe that some governments, perhaps democratic ones, have a rightful authority over the members of the societies in question, and hence that the members have an obligation of obedience. We may believe that all members of a society, simply by living in it, acquire an obligation to keep some or all of its laws. We may have some idealised conception of the society of justice, and suppose that our actual society is within sight of realising this conception. Very differently we may have some ordered set of fundamental moral principles, or some belief as to the best or the only acceptable way of drawing moral conclusions, perhaps a way that is thought to guarantee fairness.[12] Differently, we may be committed to a number of propositions, perhaps got by historical enquiry, about the probability that violence will secure or give rise to social change. Differently again, we may suppose that some political violence has important affinities with the practice of democracy.

Whatever their final value, such reasons and reasonings are

---

[12] I have in mind such a procedure as the one made clear by R. M. Hare, *Freedom and Reason* (Oxford, 1963). For an economical and acute account of reasonings found in the history of political theory, see Leslie J. Macfarlane, *Political Disobedience* (London, 1971). Hannah Arendt, in 'On Violence', an essay in *Crises of the Republic* (Harmondsworth, 1973), discusses some of them enlighteningly.

certainly of relevance to any verdict on violence. Still, these are examples of reasons and reasonings of a kind which are correctly described as being at a certain distance from the facts, the facts of inequality and of violence. There are things which are closer to the facts and which may be considerably more persuasive for many people, whether or not they should be such. Some of these latter things, indeed, may determine the weight given to the more distant reasons and reasonings.

They often have the character of unreflective responses and assumptions, but, as I have said, they can be other than that. My second intention in this essay is to look at four of them, perhaps the four which are most important. They have to do with feelings about inequality and violence, the existence of moral prohibitions on certain kinds of action, the supposed irrationality of violence, and the possibility of having satisfactory principles of equality.

4. FEELINGS

If we were to assemble the facts of inequality before ourselves as best we could, as we have not done, what would be our untutored feelings about them? Among the facts would be those at which we have looked. (i) Within economically-developed societies a bottom tenth of individuals, about 65 million people, have lives at least five years shorter on average than other members of their societies. (ii) About half the world's population, that of the less-developed societies, have average lifetimes about 29 years shorter than another quarter of the world's population. (iii) One can say with reason that the worst-off in the less-developed countries, about 170 milion people, have *one* life for the *two* lives of the best-off in the developed countries. Among the facts of inequality before us, as well, would be those of socio-economic and political kinds. Also, for all these general facts, there would be particulars, particulars of human experience.

We are, we may suppose, people who are moved to some decent degree by the situations of others and have only an ordinary amount of prejudice. We are not possessed by ideology or doctrine. We may, as people do, incline to certain social and economic beliefs, but these are not so much a part of us that we have no independent attitude to the facts of inequality.

What would be our untutored feelings about them? The question could do with sharper expression, but let us take it as we have it. Our feelings in the imagined state of knowledge would be considerably different from our ordinary responses now in our actual state of ignorance. As I have already implied, we feel less than we might about the facts of inequality, much less, simply because we are ignorant of them. That, however, is not my present concern, which may be approached by noticing that our untutored feelings would have a certain *character*. Many of us, faced with the facts of inequality, would be appalled, dismayed, saddened, affected, sympathetic, wearied, bitter or resentful. The character of these feelings, in a word, is one of *quietness*.

Suppose that on another occasion we have assembled before us the facts of violence. Suppose we have before us killing, wounding, such destruction of property as touches closely on the lives of individuals, and also the consequences of these several things. The difference between what we are imagining and what is the case, between our having full knowledge and our having the knowledge we actually have, is far less here than with the inequalities.

Many or all of us would feel horror, repugnance, disgust, bitterness or rage. The terms 'atrocity' and 'savagery' would very likely have a place in the expression of these emotions. To come to the principal point, these emotions do not have about them the quietness of the emotions called up by the facts of inequality. They have a different character.

This difference is a fact about the feelings which we would have, given a fuller knowledge of inequality and violence, but obviously there is a related fact about the feelings we actually do have, with the knowledge we actually do have. It has seemed to me right to come to the matter by way of the insistence that we be more responsible about informing ourselves. Certainly it is the difference in *informed* feelings, as they might be called, which is most important. In what follows, nonetheless, we shall almost inevitably have in mind our feelings as they are, and this will not be disastrous. It will certainly not be to the advantage of my argument, but rather the reverse.

Feelings about inequality and violence are obviously of great effect on final moral views about violence. Furthermore, it is certainly possible to regard the responses as *reasons*, or to derive reasons from them. That is, it can be argued that we ought to be directed in our judgements by such differences in feeling, that such differences are right determinants of judgement.

The general ideas that we are guided by feeling in morality, and that we ought to be, are somehow true. That is, some understanding of these ideas makes them beyond denial. Obviously, both matters are complex ones. Let us look a bit at the second one, to the effect that we ought to be guided by differences in feeling.

It is clear enough that we must pay attention to what can be called the circumstance of feeling. We must look to the question of how it is that we come to feel as we do. Few people will say, except in heat, or with personal excuse, that we should not enquire into this. Very nearly all recent moral philosophy, in one way or another, gives explicit adherence to a general proposition of this kind about feeling, despite the fact that this philosophy has not got down to hard cases and hard details. What I should like to consider is whether our circumstance is such that we can give an unquestioned importance to our feelings about inequality and violence. There are a number of quite plain propositions which are of relevance.

One notable difference between any consideration of the two orders of fact is that the *agents* of violence are inevitably in the foreground and the agents of inequality are not immediately to be seen. The man who sets a bomb or shoots another man is precisely within our focus. Not so with agents of inequality. We may of course set out to find them. We may attempt some distinction of the kind that has informed whole traditions of reflection and politics, and issued in works with such titles as *Their Morals and Ours*.[13]

If we attempt this, we may have some tolerable success. We shall certainly find a class of people who may be said to accede to the system of inequalities, and who could contribute to change. It does not stand in the way of this enterprise that their motivations and personalities are not greatly different from those of the victims of inequality. They do not contribute to change and, unlike almost all of the victims of inequality, they could do so. Their simplest contribution would be part of their wealth.

At least three relevant things are true of this class of agents of inequality. One is that very nearly all of us are members of the class. A second is that the class is immense and hence, so to speak, anonymous. Its members are not some few identified individuals. The third is that the relation of these agents to the facts of inequality is quite unlike the relation of the agents of violence to the facts of that order. No one with his own hand sets a fuse which secures an immense loss of living time for American blacks or a part of the British population. Much of the latter difference, which I shall not pause to detail, remains if we narrow down our conception of the agents of inequality to individuals who actively obstruct change or, differently, individuals who by their own actions do more or less directly make for the distress of individual victims of inequality.

Our feeling about violence, then, has very much to do with its

[13] By Leon Trotsky.

agents, while our feeling about inequality has less or indeed little to do with its agents. The agents of inequality are pretty well out of sight or, if they are in sight, they are ourselves, they are many and impersonal, and they are distant from their work. The character of our feeling about violence, against the character of our feeling about inequality, is in significant part explained by the matter of agents.

However, to move towards the principal point, there is reason for saying that our feelings about inequality and violence are principally relevant in so far as they are feelings about victims rather than agents. That, although we shall in a way come back to the question, will be agreed by almost all who consider inequality and violence, no matter to what conclusion they are inclined. What matters is suffering, distress and deprivation, and not what may be taken to be an agent's callous deliberateness in intention, taken by itself. We thus have a consideration which must lead us in some degree to discount the vehemence, indeed the violence, of our feeling about violence. If that vehemence were more the product of an awareness of victims, and less the product of an awareness of agents, the circumstance would be importantly different.

There is a complication with which we shall be faced. There are those who will urge upon us a persistent Utilitarianism, or one or another doctrine akin to it. They will object that if it is agreed that our concern must principally be with victims, it must also be agreed as a consequence that we must concern ourselves with agents, conceived just as causers of distress, makers of victims. That is, we must look upon agents of both our classes as we look upon ordinary non-political lawbreakers if we subscribe to the deterrence theory of punishment. Like an ordinary offender, a man who sets a bomb is a man who is likely to act in the same way again and also a man who encourages others to do likewise.

It may thus be suggested, by way of a ramshackle argument, that we should in no way discount our feeling about violence on the ground that it is to some significant degree called up by agents. The argument, in essence, will be that any discounting of feeling leads to inhibition of it, that inhibition will have its effect with respect to what is done to agents, and that if less is done there will be more victims.

Of course, the same sort of premise may also be taken to lead in another direction, towards doubt about our quiet response to the facts of inequality. That is, the premise may be thought also to contribute to the conclusion that we should have stronger feelings about the agents of inequality, or compensate in our reflection for the weakness of our feelings. I shall not examine either this argument or the previous one about violence. All I wish to notice is that we are not in fact persistently Utilitarian, or anything like it. Our responses to the agents of violence perhaps *are* in part responses to causes of distress or, in the relevant sense, makers of victims. However, our responses are very much more than that. They are accusatory or vengeful. The machine that maims a worker and the man who maims another man are regarded by us in quite different ways. In the latter case, there is the fact of our beliefs and attitudes having to do with responsibility and culpability of persons. Hence, even should we be inclined to give some attention to the Utilitarian objection about feeling, it would remain the case that our feeling about the facts of violence has much to do with agents regarded as other than past and perhaps future causes of distress.

In sum, the different characters of our feelings about violence and inequality has in part to do with the awareness and the want of awareness of agents. To the extent that the resulting feelings are not related to the matter of prevention, they are not of the first importance. What is of the first importance is feeling about victims. We have, then, a reason for questioning the contrast in our feelings about violence and inequality.

A second plain proposition about our different responses to inequality and violence has to do with the *familiarity* of inequality, which is everywhere, and the *unfamiliarity* of violence. The magnitude of inequalities, and the absolute level of experience of those who are worst-off, are not things of which we have much grasp. Still, if we were to assemble the facts of inequality, we would not then have a grasp of something with which we had had no previous familiarity. As for violence not being within the experience of most of us, that is no doubt a generality pertaining only to most times and most places. As such, it stands high among useful generalisations in political philosophy.

It is to be remarked, then, that the quiet feelings evoked by inequality are in part to be explained by the relative familiarity of the subject-matter. The feelings evoked by violence are in part to be explained by the relative unfamiliarity of violence. There is support for this in the truism that there is a deadening or quieting of feeling in certain circumstances, usually in war, when violence becomes familiar.

The suggestion that must emerge here is that the moral relevance of feelings is the less if they owe something, perhaps a good deal, to the familiarity or unfamiliarity of their objects. It surely cannot be that the 'natural' death of a child or the murder of a man has a significantly different value in virtue of there being many or few such deaths, many or few murders. One may think of ways in which the proposition might be qualified, but the qualifications are of a secondary importance. Thus our circumstance in responding to inequality and violence is for a second reason one in which our first feelings are not to be accorded an unquestioned deference.

A third thing to be considered has to do with the common perception of inequality as *entrenched*. Violence is rightly seen differently. Setting a bomb is a human action which like other human actions might not have been performed. The man could have done otherwise. That, however the belief is to be analysed, is our belief. The action is something, too, which quickly raises in the mind the possibility of prevention by others. The inequalities, by contrast, and for good reason, do not have the perceived character of things that easily might not have been, or things that we can briskly set about altering.

The point again is that if our feelings about human experience are in part given their character by factors external to that experience, such a fact must be paid attention. If the quiet of our feelings about inequality is in part owed to a perception of inequality as settled and resistant, this is a fact to be paid attention. The terribleness of human experience, the terribleness of having a child whose lifetime is five years, remains just that, whatever may be true about persistence and change. If the inequalities were not merely entrenched, but in fact necessary and inevitable, which is different, the situation would be otherwise. To think that they are in fact necessary and inevitable is a simple error corrected by some reflection on history.

It is to be admitted, certainly, that it would be irrational to come to a verdict about political violence without paying careful attention to the probability of its actually achieving ends of social change. That is something of which I shall have more to say. However, it is one thing to take the matter into account, in full consciousness and in the right place, and another thing not to notice its effect on our feelings about the human experience of inequality.

Fourthly, it is at least arguable that our feelings about the inequalities and about violence are influenced by the correct perception of the inequalities as constituting a state of *order*, and violence as constituting a circumstance of *disorder*. Inequality is a product of law, of diverse settled institutions, of custom and indeed of assent. The vast majority of those who are worst-off do not resist, because they cannot. Violence is otherwise. A man shot by a political assassin is one of two figures in a circumstance of a wholly different character, a circumstance of anarchy. No restraint is put on one's feeling about his death by a recognition of it as ordained.

To repeat, if our concern is with responses of feeling to the experience of others, it is important to be sure that we take into account precisely such responses. The pain and distress of others should not come upon one, in the first instance, as items of order or of disorder. It may be that they should be so regarded, at some later point in reflection. They should not be regarded in this way in the first instance if a primary matter is not be confused. If, therefore, pain and distress *do* in fact have an effect upon us which is partly a consequence of something that is external to them, we must recognise this fact.

A fifth consideration has to do with the difference, not necessarily a reasonable difference, in our responses to being attacked or wounded on the one hand, and, on the other, being distressed or made to suffer for much longer periods but not as a consequence of an unnerving aggressive action. Before one argues too quickly from the primitive impulse to choose, say, lasting hunger rather than an injury, it is useful to consider what one would choose for another person, perhaps a person about whom one cares. It is safe to observe that first impulses are not certain to be last judgements. A sixth consideration has to do with the indiscriminateness or the undirectedness of much political violence. One thing to be remarked here is that the particular victims of inequality are not carefully chosen either. However, I shall leave undiscussed these considerations, the fifth and sixth, and finish here with something else.

Engels, in *Anti-Duhring*, characterises all of morality as class morality.[14] It is, in his view, an instrument of the ruling class or an instrument of an oppressed but rising class. A somewhat less *simpliste* view is advanced by Marx and Engels in the *German Ideology*.[15] Bentham and Mill also have views which touch on the general matter.[16] One proposition in this area, one which does not presuppose a ruling class's *devising* of morality, is that some moral feeling has some of its genesis in a self-identification which is general among the members of ascendant classes.

The relative quietness of our feelings about inequality, and the violence of our feelings about violence, are related to our own places in the world. You who are reading this essay, in all likelihood,

---

[14] *Herr Eugen Duhring's Revolution in Science (Anti-Duhring)*, trans. E. Burns (New York), p. 109.

[15] Marx–Engels, *The German Ideology*, ed. R. Pascal (London, 1939).

[16] Bentham, *The Handbook of Fallacies*, p. 207. Mill, *On Liberty*, p. 70 (Everyman edition).

are a beneficiary of the system of inequality and, perhaps more important, have no human connection with the victims of that system. By contrast, in many ordinary situations in life, you discount the feelings and doubt the judgements of individuals who are in positions of benefit and relationship analogous to your own.

It is remarkable that such suggestions of self-deception are dismissed by those who are familiar with a society some of whose fundamental institutions are constructed so as to defeat such things as self-deceiving responses to groups other than one's own. It will be remarkable, too, if such suggestions of self-deception continue to be dismissed by philosophers. No recent work of moral philosophy lacks a device against self-deceiving self-interest in its recommended system of reflection. In some cases, the device is most of the system.

Some may regard some or all of the foregoing seven reflections on inequality and on violence as tasteless or ill-judged. This may have to do with a failure to recognise that there are *two* orders of fact, each of them compelling, each of them terrible. Not to recognise this is to fail in feeling and judgement. Again, there is an inclination to suppose that the question of political violence, like any serious moral question, is one for ourselves as *moral judges*. That is, it is a question for the moral consciousness or the moral self, or perhaps the conscience. It is not one of which we can rightly treat by bringing in empirical psychology, propositions about the causes of feeling. This inclination, to my mind, is not one to be encouraged. The moral consciousness, somehow insulated from our attitudes and situations, is a fiction, and not a good one.

5. PROHIBITIONS

There are people who say, whether or not they would always do as they say, that there are certain kinds of act which are absolutely prohibited. These are acts about which there can never be a moral question, acts which must never be done whatever the circumstances. Those who express this view, which is connected with religious tradition, do not have in mind such 'truisms' as this, that an act is prohibited if *all* that is known of it is that it would cause suffering. They have in mind certain familiar acts, identified in quite different ways. One kind may be the killing of another person.

It is unlikely that many people would hesitate if they were faced with a straight choice between killing a man on the one hand, and, on the other hand, 'inaction' of which they *believed with certainty* that it would give rise to catastrophic consequences, perhaps many deaths. If, as is also far from being the case, they were faced with a choice between an act of killing and, on the other hand, 'inaction' taken to involve the *near-certainty* of catastrophic consequences, many would choose the killing and would defend their choice. Doctrines about absolute moral prohibitions have lost any force they may once have had.

Nonetheless, there is no doubt that there exists an inclination or perhaps something more than that, a conviction, against certain acts and those who perform them. It is not the claim that there is an *absolute* prohibition, but it is somewhere in the direction of that conclusion. What is in question here, as before, is the idea that an act of killing, say, is somehow wrong in itself, and not that it is wrong because in fact it will not be effective in securing social or economic change. There is thought to be a kind of moral constraint upon us which does not have anything to do with the consequences of action or inaction. It is a constraint which has to do with acts in themselves, and one which sometimes may rightly be effective in preventing individuals from doing what would have the best consequences.

This is the second of the responses to inequality and political violence which I wish to consider in this essay. It may be an unconsidered reaction to acts of violence and to those who perform them. Alternatively, it may be more reflective. In both forms, rightly or wrongly, it has been persuasive with many people.

The kind of inclination or conviction in question may of course arise in cases that do not have to do with political violence. Bernard Williams, in *Utilitarianism, For and Against*, considers the example of a chemist, without a job and hence with his family in difficulty, who is offered work in a laboratory whose research is into chemical and biological warfare.[17] He, unlike his wife, is particularly opposed to such warfare and to the research. However, he understands that if he refuses the job, the research will proceed anyway. More important, he knows that if he refuses the job, it will go to a particular man who is likely to push along the research with greater zeal than he himself would. The chemist nonetheless refuses the job. We have recommended to us that he has done the right thing. The attempt to support this recommendation has to do with two things, integrity and responsibility.

In refusing the job, we are to understand, the chemist's action flowed from deep attitudes which are fundamental to the person he is. He has not acted as a consequence of the attitudes or actions of another, in such a way as to alienate himself from his own actions, and hence

[17] J. J. C. Smart and Bernard Williams, *Utilitarianism: For and Against* (London, 1973), pp. 97–8.

in such a way as to diminish or destroy his own integrity, his integrity in the most literal sense. He would have diminished or destroyed his integrity if he had taken the job, as a consequence of the fact that the other chemist would be more diligent in the research. He would, in that case, have been acting as a consequence of the attitudes and actions of the other man.[18]

To pass on to responsibility, the chemist does take the view, understandably enough, that one of the two possible states of affairs would be *better* than the other. The better one, of course, is the one in which he himself does take the job and hence the research goes forward more slowly than it would in the hands of the other man. However, the chemist also takes it that it is not his business to engage in this state of affairs. It is not *his* business to prepare, however less efficiently than someone else might, for chemical and biological warfare. There is a great difference for him between this possible state of affairs and the worse one. Although he himself is involved in the coming about of the worse state of affairs, *the other chemist does the job* and hence 'a vital link in the production of the eventual outcome is provided by *someone else's* doing something'.[19]

It is allowed that in refusing to take the job the first chemist is responsible, in some sense of the word, for the fact that the research will go forward more quickly than it might. However, this will only come about through the other man's actions. The first chemist cannot be said to *make* this happen, and, it is suggested, he rightly does not accept a full responsibility for the outcome.

In all of this we may have an illumination of the common inclination against certain acts. Certainly there is a great deal of difference between the case of the chemist and the case of a man who contemplates an act of political violence. Nonetheless, any considerations which apply to the chemist also apply to the other man. We may have the inclination that he should be such a man as the chemist. He should be of a certain integrity, and he should maintain that integrity by not engaging in violence, even though he believes that the consequences of his engaging in violence will be or are likely to be better than the consequences of his not doing so.

The inclination needs examination, and for several reasons it will be best to proceed by way of the example of the chemist. There is one preliminary. The inclination is in conflict with several general attitudes to the effect that we ought always to act in such a way as to produce the best or the least bad state of affairs. One such general attitude is that we ought always to act in such a way as to produce

[18] Op. cit., pp. 116–17, pp. 103–4.   [19] Op. cit., p. 94.

the least total of distress. The case of the chemist is indeed offered against this proposition, which is the Principle of Utility in one formulation. However, the inclination also comes into play against the attitude, to speak very quickly indeed, that we should always act in such a way as to produce *that state of affairs which most avoids inequality and distress.*

This attitude, which has informed some of my earlier remarks, and of which I shall say more, is at least the fundamental part of the most common of reflective moralities. It, like Utilitarianism, is 'consequentialist'. It takes into account only what may be called the consequences of action, although more consequences than are considered in Utilitarianism. It conflicts with the inclination having to do with integrity which has been mentioned. In order to be consistent, and I think more relevant, let us have in mind this particular consequentialist attitude. Let us imagine what is certainly reasonable, that the chemist in refusing the job does something which makes *inequality and distress* more likely. His action conflicts with the particular consequentialist principle to the effect that we should pursue the states of affairs which include, or are likely to produce, the least inequality and distress.

The main difficulty about the case, it seems to me, is that of actually finding what consideration or principle it is which is supposed to lead us to agree that the chemist's act in refusing the job is right. That consideration or principle is not actually supplied to us. Let us see what, if anything, can be found.

We are told that the chemist preserves his integrity in refusing the job. This may amount to different things. The first of them is the matter of fact that the chemist, in refusing the job, is acting in accordance with deep attitudes of his own. His action is in no sense in conflict with these attitudes, whatever they are. Hence we can say, if obscurely, that there exists a unity or a whole. Integrity, in a literal sense, is maintained. However, we here have no consideration whatever that might lead us to agree that refusing the job is the right thing to do. It seems obvious enough that there is no connection whatever between the described integrity and right acts. An act of integrity in this sense, given certain deep attitudes on the part of an agent, will be an act of absolute immorality. Nothing follows about the rightness or wrongness of the act from the fact that it is in line with an agent's deep attitudes, which presumably may be of any kind.

To say the chemist preserves his integrity by refusing the job, however, may be to do something other than state a morally irrelevant and somewhat obscure matter of fact. It may be to approve of him, to commend him. It may be to approve of him or to commend him because, as we may say, he is true to himself. The chemist perseveres in certain deep attitudes. Here there is more obscurity, but it may be that the attitudes are to the effect that *he himself, with his own hands, should not carry forward research into chemical and biological war.* He persists in this attitude even when he sees that it issues in making chemical and biological war more likely. The chemist, then, is true to himself.

There are several related things to be said about this second speculation as to the matter of integrity. One is that there seems to be very little relevant connection between a man's being commendable in the given way and his act's being right. A man, obviously, can be commendable for the reason that he is true to himself no matter what act he performs, so long as he himself is committed to it. All that is required is that he sticks to his convictions, whatever they are. An appallingly wrong act, perhaps one of pointless torture, does not move a bit in the direction of being right when we learn that the torturer is being true to himself. What changes, perhaps, is our view of him.

There is the possibility of a confusion at this point. Surely, someone may object, we can support a man in his act, to which he is committed, for the reason that things work out better in the end if people are true to themselves. More importantly, we may sometimes even support a man if *we* think his act is somehow wrong. Several questions are raised by this objection, but it would be confusion to think that it is an effective one. The objector asserts the value of our being true to ourselves in order to object to consequentialism. However, the objection itself derives from consequentialism. In part it is that the effects, perhaps in terms of distress and inequality, will be better if people are true to themselves. However, what we are trying to find in the case of the chemist is a consideration or a reason of a non-consequentialist kind, a consideration or a reason for doing what is likely *not* to have the best effects.

The second thing to be said about commending the chemist is to be distinguished from the point that his act may be wrong even if he is true to some commitment. It is that if we are even to commend him, and, more important, if there is to be so much as a *question* of commending him, we must believe that he does have something that is distinguishable as a *moral* attitude or a *moral* commitment. We cannot commend a man for integrity on the ground that he is, so to speak, true to his selfishness. An absolutely unswerving record of acting in one's own interest does not establish integrity.

What then is the chemist's moral attitude or commitment? As we have noticed already, he does have *an* attitude: he is opposed to carrying forward research into chemical and biological warfare with his own hands, even though the only alternative is *more effective* research by someone else. Is that a moral commitment? It will occur to everyone that the chemist, in leaving the job to the man who will do more effective research, is simply engaged in keeping his own hands clean. Better that someone else should make a larger contribution to a terrible eventuality than that he should make a smaller one. Better that chemical and biological war should be slightly *more* likely than that he himself should have his hands in it. The chemist may be said to be engaged, if one puts the point in Williams's own way, which might be thought to endanger it by overstatement, in 'self-indulgent squeamishness'.[20]

Williams replies that the point is not independent of the assertion of a consequentialist morality. If the point were addressed to the chemist, it would necessarily be no more than an invitation to reconsider his decision, and in particular to reconsider it from a consequentialist point of view. The criticism would not consist in an independent argument, which is what is required, but simply a reiteration of the opposed morality.

This reply seems to me partly right and importantly wrong. The criticism is in a certain sense not an argument, but it need not be merely an invitation to reconsider either. It may amount to the suggestion that it is only self-indulgence which can be discovered to explain the chemist's decision, at least until more is said. It may amount, again, to a challenge to produce *a moral explanation* or *a moral reason*. We are indeed told that the unpleasant feelings which the chemist would have if he did the job would be 'emotional expressions of a thought that to accept would be wrong'.[21] However, we are not told the thought, or given to understand anything much about its nature.

What we seem to end with, then, if we look to what is said about 'integrity' in order to find a moral consideration or principle of relevance, is something different, the feeling that the imagined chemist would indeed only be engaged in a kind of self-indulgence.

We do not get further on towards finding a consideration or principle, it seems, if we direct our attention to what is said about responsibility. To recall, it is allowed that the chemist is in some sense responsible for the research going forward more quickly than it might, since that, as he knows, is the upshot of his refusing to do it himself. However, he is less responsible than he would be if he were

<hr />

[20] Op. cit., pp. 102–3.   [21] Op. cit., p. 103.

to do it himself. He is less responsible in that a vital link is the other man's activity.

There is the possibility of having the wrong thing in mind here. Certainly the chemist's responsibility for research done by himself, *and*, as we can say, *freely chosen*, would be greater than his responsibility for the other man's research. What one should have in mind, presumably, is something else: what the chemist's responsibility would be if he went ahead with the research for the strong or indeed coercive reason that otherwise the other man would do it more efficiently. If the chemist did that, would he have a lesser responsibility than he has when he refuses the job?

In any case it is far from evident that the rightness of actions has to do with responsibility in such a way that the argument about the chemist is at all persuasive. Let us assume it to be a fact that the chemist in refusing the job is less responsible for the research than if he were to do it himself because of the coercive reason. Let us add in, for what it is worth, that in not taking the job he does not *make* the other man's research happen. Do we now have a consideration or a principle which might lead us to agree that he does the right thing in refusing the job?

I cannot see that here, or elsewhere, we find such a thing. It is essential to the argument, of course, that the consideration be produced. It would not be enough to suppose that it can be perceived, but not reported, by those of especially refined moral vision.

Finally and differently, notice that any moral consideration having to do with integrity or responsibility, supposing it can be found and got clear, is of fairly small importance. In a second example,[22] which involves a man's straight choice between killing one person and acting in such a way that someone else will kill twenty, it is allowed that the man's integrity and responsibility cannot stand in the way of his taking one life in order to save twenty.

In the case of the chemist, too, we are likely to attribute more weight to some consideration of integrity than we should. That is, if we feel inclined to side with the chemist in his decision, we may too quickly attribute this inclination to a consideration of integrity. This comes about, I think, because the case as described is indeterminate. Different possibilities are left open. This in fact brings it into line with reality, but it also makes it indecisive as a proof or persuasion about integrity.

Very briefly, we have been assuming that what the chemist should do, if he is to choose the state of affairs most likely to avoid distress

[22] Op. cit., pp. 88–9.

and inequality, is to take the job, knowing he will do it less efficiently. But that is not entirely clear. One rightly takes it, in thinking of the situation, that there is only a probability that there will be a chemical and biological war to which the research will contribute. But *how small* a probability is in question? If we take it, unreflectively, to be *very* small, so that a war is in fact very improbable, then any inclination we have to side with the chemist may perhaps be explained by our consequential attitudes. That is, we may be moved by the consideration, as people generally are, that a possible circumstance very unlikely to obtain must count for less than one which is certain or probable. What *is* certain or probable, if the chemist takes the job, is that he will be distressed, that he will not have registered a protest, and so on.[23]

It remains to transfer these conclusions from the example of the chemist, where attention is not likely to be led away from the principal question by passion or aversion, back to the subject of political violence. What I wish to suggest is that one response to violence and its agents, a response having to do with something other than consequences of actions, is at least unclear, and certainly not something of large moral importance. Whatever is to be said against violence, there appears to be no large argument to be found in suppositions of the kind we have considered, about integrity, responsibility, and hence about certain moral prohibitions.

6. IRRATIONALITY

Political violence is said to be irrational, and said so often enough that the opinion has a persuasiveness for that fact alone. Let us consider the matter, which is in fact large and ramifying. That it *is* this, rather than something easily manageable, is much of what I wish to maintain.

Some lesser but bedevilling things need to be noticed before we come to what is of most consequence. First, it at least appears that a good deal of slipshod self-persuasion and perhaps persuasion of others goes forward in this area. Let us look at one example. Karl Popper, near the beginning of his essay on 'Utopia and Violence', which has to do with political violence as we have understood it and also with war, writes as follows:

It ... need not be a vain hope – that violence can be reduced, *and brought under the control of reason.*

[23] Williams considers this sort of suggestion – that consequentialist attitudes may be seen as supporting the chemist's decision. His remarks, I think, do not really undercut the suggestion.

This is perhaps why I, like many others, believe in reason; why I call myself a rationalist. I am a rationalist because I see in the attitude of reasonableness *the only alternative* to violence.[24]

Near the end of the essay, following on a reflection which brings together 'rationalism' with a belief in human equality, and violence with a belief in inequality, there is this observation:

Reason . . . is *the precise opposite* of an instrument of power and violence . . . [25]

We are offered an explanation elsewhere in the essay of 'reason' or 'rationality' or 'reasonableness'. It is explained as a certain set of ways of ending disputes, ways which are related at least by the fact that they are all non-violent. They include give-and-take discussion, argument, arbitration, willingness to be convinced, willingness to admit error, and so on.

The sentences quoted may be taken to express sentiments of the right kind. However, they may also be looked at more critically, as indeed they should be. As may be confirmed by reading the essay, they do not have in them propositions which are argued for elsewhere. Still, they are not mere bluff declarations that 'reasonableness' is right and violence is wrong. They are more than that, which is not to say that they have argument in them.

(i) In part they are an instance of the simple enterprise of persuasion-by-naming. That is, one set of ways of ending disputes is given a good name or rather three good names. Of course, there is some warrant in ordinary language for using the mentioned terms for the defined ways of ending disputes. There is most warrant for naming them the ways of 'reasonableness'. It is a small fact, and of no use in serious reflection. As we shall see in a moment, it is perfectly possible to describe some violence as 'reasonable', 'rational', or as proceeding from 'reason'.

(ii) In part, the quoted sentences declare that there exists a fundamental opposition between violence and 'reasonableness', which opposition invites one towards a general judgement on violence. However, if one is to take the sentences seriously, one needs to know what opposed features of violence and 'reasonableness' are in question, and why these may be thought to make 'reasonableness' invariably right. These questions are not adequately answered, and

[24] *Conjectures and Refutations: The Growth of Scientific Knowledge* (London, 1963), p. 355. My italics. For a related discussion of Popper, see Roy Edgley, 'Reason and Violence', in S. Körner, ed., *Practical Reason* (Oxford, 1974).
[25] Op. cit., p. 363. My italics.

so we are left without argument. In the place of adequate answers, there is the remarkably unsupported linking of 'reasonableness' with equality and violence with inequality, and perhaps one other relevant contribution. However, it can stand by itself for consideration.

(iii) That is, one may speculate that the quoted sentences also have in them this piece of persuasion. *'Reasonableness', which is give-and-take discussion and so on, is alone rational, the only choice for a rationalist. Hence it is always superior to violence, which is never rational.* What does the word 'rational' mean here? If we continue to take it to mean something about give-and-take discussion and so on, the proposition that reasonableness is rational is not a premise for the given conclusion or indeed anything much, since it is merely tautological. If no different and suitable meaning for 'rational' is given or suggested, we have only rhetoric.

Might the piece of persuasion be turned into something better? Elsewhere in the essay, Popper mentions in passing an entirely familiar and indeed a fundamental conception of rationality. 'An action is rational if it makes the best use of the available means in order to achieve a certain end.'[26] Irrationality thus consists in the adoption of means which do not in fact serve one's end, or serve it at too great a cost. By the use of these conceptions we can certainly escape tautology.

Is it obvious, however, as presumably it should be in the absence of argument, that 'reasonableness' as defined is always or generally rational, the best means to the end? It is not. Is violence the precise opposite, whatever that may be, of rationality in this sense? Is it never the best means to the end? That is obviously not obvious. As it happens, indeed, it is maintained by Popper in the essay that a good deal of violence is *not* irrational in the given sense, but rational.[27] That is, violence against those who are intolerant or threaten violence is defended as the best means. We thus come to a question about political violence rather than a generalisation to be used against it.

Before considering this major question, there are three other distractions we may put aside quickly. One, which is also brought to mind by 'Utopia and Violence', is the idea that violence is unreasonable because it is the result of speculation about a utopia, a transformed society. This speculation is poor stuff, and the activity which follows from it is therefore ill-founded. One thing to be said here is that it is plainly mistaken to suppose that all political violence

[26] Op. cit., p. 358.   [27] Op. cit., p. 357.

has to do with the large goal of a transformed society. Most political violence has had smaller ends. It is equally mistaken to run together all reflection which *does* have to do with transformations of society. It is not all of the same quality or kind. For example, not all of it has to do with speculative philosophy of history, as in Hegel and Marx.

The second distracting supposition is that the agents of violence are figures of irrationality in that they are self-deceived. That is, their actions are in fact not done from motives which have to do with the facts of inequality. Their thoughts, and their protestations, are mistaken. What needs to be said about this is that it would be a remarkable fact, one that would distinguish one kind of human endeavour from all others, if those who engage in violence were *never* subject to anything but what they themselves take to be their ends. Equally, it would be remarkable if campaigns of violence with supposed political ends were ever *the product*, or even in large part the product, of desires unrelated to those ends. It thus seems to me mistaken to suppose that senseless and unrecognised hostility, and like things, never have anything to do with campaigns of political violence, or that they come near to composing it.

The third supposition also has to do with the agents of violence. It is not to be assumed, as often it seems to be, that their own views and defences of their conduct are the only possible views and defences. We do not suppose, generally, that what can be said for or against a line of action is no more than can be said by those persons who are or might be engaged in it. No such requirement survives reflection. No one would deny, certainly, that lines of action and their outcomes are in different ways determined by the beliefs and passions of the agents. Their beliefs and passions, then, must enter into anyone's consideration of the value of their conduct. This granted, it remains mistaken to fix on the agents and to suppose that political violence is to be seen only or precisely as those who are engaged in it do see it.

To turn now to the major subject-matter, what may come to mind is something like this question: *Is political violence generally irrational in that it gives rise to distress itself and yet is uncertain to achieve its ends?* It is all right as a question, but only as a culminating, final question. Something like it nonetheless appears to be the *only* question about irrationality which is considered by many philosophers who offer pronouncements. At any rate, they answer only it or something like it. What is certain is that any effective answer to so general and presupposing a question must be supported by explicit answers to quite a number of antecedent questions.

Violence differs considerably and the same is true of its ends. One obvious essential, then, before answering the general question, appears to be a separation of kinds of violence and kinds of end. Is political violence which will almost certainly consist only in damage to property, rather than injury or death, a rational means of pursuing equality, or greater equality, in lifetimes and in the quality of life? What of violence which carries a risk of a relatively small number of injuries or deaths, although it seeks to avoid them, and has the same end? What of violence, still with the same end, which consists in intentional injury? What of violence, again with the same end, which consists in intentionally causing death?

What of the rationality of violence of each of these kinds but with the different end of political equality? What of violence of each of these kinds but with the end not of *achieving* any of the mentioned kinds of equality, but the end of increasing the probability that these ends will be secured in a given time?

There is point in remarking that we can count sixteen questions here, and that more can be added, each of them independent and of importance. Indeed, before considering such additions, each of the sixteen questions needs to be replaced by several which are different in that they contain numbers. Certainly such numerical questions will be regarded as offensive by many, but they are far from unknown elsewhere in human life and they are certainly unavoidable.

Let us in what follows have in mind but one of them: *Is violence which causes several thousand injuries or deaths, despite attempts to avoid most of them, a rational means of pursuing equalities in lifetime and in quality of life for a society's worst-off tenth, numbering more than five million people?* It will be obvious enough to anyone who hesitates for reflection that we are far from being able to *assume* an answer. This has to do with the fact that the question also raises others.

Putting aside problems having to do with uncertainty for a moment, let us suppose that the violence in question would in fact produce the equalities. Would it be worth it? If we are familiar with the existence of such choices, where different kinds of thing must be compared, we certainly are not familiar with a defensible way of answering them. Partly this is a matter of fundamental principles, of which I shall have more to say in the last part of this essay. Partly it is a matter of judging the nature of kinds of human experience. There is no agreed method. We do not have a way of assessing injuries and deaths on the one hand and, on the other hand, the various inequalities and deprivations. We must somehow judge of such matters if we are to arrive at reasoned conclusions about the rationality of violence. Anyone who argues that some violence is rational must obviously deal with comparative questions of this kind. Anyone arguing that political violence is irrational must also do so, although not for so obvious a reason.

To take up what was put aside, the matter of uncertainty, I have already assumed in these remarks that it may be that some violence is rational even if it is not certain to succeed. Although sometimes those who condemn violence seem to suppose that it must always be certain of success in order to be rational, this is a proposition for which argument is obviously needed. There obviously are circumstances in human life where something that is not certain to succeed, or even something that is unlikely to succeed, is rationally attempted. These, of course, are situations of greater or lesser extremity. Very roughly, then, there is the question of how probable it must be that the given violence will be successful if it is to be rational. The answer, which I shall certainly not try to give, will depend in good part on comparisons of the facts of violence and the facts of inequality.

The question will bring to mind yet another, which is as essential. Any view of the rationality of a kind of violence will depend on a factual judgement, more likely many such judgements, of the actual probability of success, as distinct from the probability necessary for rationality. What is to be said here will have much but not everything to do with the evidence of history. The same applies to the other relevant factual question of probability: How probable is it that given ends of political violence will or would be achieved by non-violent means?

These latter questions, about uncertainty, are like the others in having presuppositions which must themselves be fixed. What period of time is to be assumed in the last question about achieving ends by non-violent means? That question, if made explicit, must mention a period in which the ends will or would be achieved. The fact of mortality, and hence the length of human lifetimes, suggest a period. I shall not pursue the matter, except to say that it is easier to argue against violence, from a premise about things being better for future generations as a result of non-violent progress, if one's place in a present generation is satisfactory.

Enough has been said to establish that the ready response to political violence which consists in abusing it as irrational is open to question, indeed open to many questions. What has been said, equally, establishes that any unreflective response which consists in the opposite thing, accepting violence as rational, is as jejune. One's conclusion, which there is point in asserting, must be that the question is an open one.

Such a conclusion is likely to give rise to several different although related responses, which I shall not attempt to discuss adequately. One is that violence must be mistaken in that it causes harm or tragedy and *its rationality has not been shown.* If a general comment is of use here, it is that the choice is not necessarily one between violence, whose rationality is not established, and something else, whose rationality *is* established. There are the same kinds of diffi-culty to be faced in considering the alternative to violence: non-violent activity which appears to have a lesser chance of securing an acceptable change in the facts of inequality. Perhaps it does not need saying again that a different view, to the effect that this other political activity is already established as rational, is likely to derive in good part from an insufficient appreciation of the facts of in-equality. A relevant generalisation, obviously, is that situations of extremity enforce consideration of the rationality of terrible means.

One other thing that may come to mind as a consequence of my conclusion about an open question is that accredited members of societies, as they might be called, are more able to guess what should be done about the facts of inequality. Accredited members include governments and their personnel, leaders of traditional political parties, and so on. Whatever one may think in general of the right of governments to take decisions, it may be supposed that they are in a superior position of knowledge, or of ignorance, when compared to those who contemplate or engage in political violence.

When this is a piece of unexamined piety, as often it is, perhaps there is room for that familiar jibe that the wars and catastrophes owed to the accredited members of society do not recommend their judgement. If we depart from piety, and from the jibe, we are bound to find difficulty rather than simplicity. Part of it has to do with the connections between power and judgement, or want of judgement.[28]

My general conclusion here, then, is that common responses to political violence, having to do with its supposed irrationality, are themselves unreasonable. In the end, when the work of enquiry and reflection has been done, it may be that the strongest arguments against political violence will indeed be those having to do with the probabilities of success. No doubt we can conclude, now, that such arguments will sometimes be as conclusive as arguments in this area

[28] Stuart Hampshire discusses and defends Bertrand Russell's relevant condemnation of governments in 'Russell, Radicalism, and Reason', in *Philosophy and Political Action* (London, 1972), edited by Virginia Held, Kai Nielsen and Charles Parsons.

ever can be. No doubt there are situations in which political violence cannot be justified.

It may also become evident in the end, less comfortingly, that violence would be justified in these situations if it worked. That is, it may become evident that in these situations, as in others, violence which *did* secure change in inequalities would be preferable to no violence and no change. What may be thought to follow from such a proposition is not our concern now.

7. PRINCIPLES OF EQUALITY

Classical Utilitarianism as a basic morality appears to have had its day, and to have remaining to it only a twilight in economic theory. At the same time, as implied above, it is impossible to leave out of morality a proposition to the effect that the distress of individuals is to be decreased, and, as a second priority, their satisfaction increased. The extent of each person's distress, and also the number of persons distressed, *must* be facts relevant to moral decisions about actions, policies, practices and whatever. What needs to be added to a proposition about distress, obviously, is something about equality. It is made necessary by the fact that the proposition about distress allows for inequality. That Classical Utilitarianism allows for inequality, and indeed calls for it in certain circumstances, is its familiar and fundamental weakness.

What emerges, although far from clearly, is that what we must have as the foundation of an acceptable morality is a principle or a set of principles which gives importance to the avoidance of both distress and inequality. This would also emerge, incidentally, from an attempt to rely solely on a principle of equality. What we must also have, in addition to the fundamental principle or principles, although this is not our present concern, is a set of subordinate conceptions, rules and so on. One of these, to give a single example, would have to do with forms of government. These latter things would be consequences of the fundamental principles.

To announce these needs, however, is to say something less than wonderfully useful. While the conviction that we should have such fundamental principles is not uncommon, we have not got them. I do not mean that they have not yet been put in decent order, although that appears to me to be true.[29] Rather, the point is that we do not have them in place within our own thinking. As a consequence we

---

[29] An extended attempt has been made by John Rawls in *A Theory of Justice* (Oxford 1972).

find ourselves in *some* confusion about what I have called the facts of inequality. So it is, or should be, with the facts of violence and with any conclusion about its justification.

To provide the basic principles would be to provide the most important one of the reasonings, as they were called above, which stand between premises of fact and substantial conclusions about violence. The full and final devising of the principles cannot be our present business. Let us finish, rather, by reflecting a bit on the difficulty of the enterprise and hence the difficulty of emerging from the mentioned confusion about the facts of inequality and of violence. Are we, as some suppose, in so much or such deep difficulty about principles that a kind of despair is in place, an acceptance of early defeat and of what follows from it?

There are problems, certainly, with any proposition about the avoidance of distress. These are usually discussed in connection with Utilitarianism. There are also thought to be difficulties in the other part of the enterprise, pertaining to equality. It is these at which I should like to look. They arise in the course of attempting to settle one's mind about equality itself, and hence *before* the stage at which equality and the avoidance of distress are brought together, and a kind of compromise is struck.

If one picks up a piece of philosophical writing on equality, there is a decent chance that it will describe equalitarian thinking as weak, or as incoherent, or as lacking a defensible and substantial principle, or as coming to very little in the end.[30] These dismissals are independent of the point already noticed, that considerations of equality must finally be brought into conjunction with something else. A pastiche derived from these writings on equality, a decently representative one, goes as follows.

[30] The following recent writings, while of different kinds, qualities and sympathies, share at least the feature of overlooking what I call The Principle of Equality: S. I. Benn and R. S. Peters, *Social Principles and the Democratic State* (London, 1959), Chapter Five; W. T. Blackstone, 'On the Meaning and Justification of the Equality Principle', *Ethics*, 1967; Norman E. Bowie, 'Equality and Distributive Justice', *Philosophy*, 1970; John Charvet, 'The Idea of Equality as a Substantive Principle of Society', *Political Studies*, 1969; J. R. Lucas, *The Principles of Politics* (Oxford, 1966), Section 56, and 'Against Equality', *Philosophy*, 1965; Felix E. Oppenheim, 'Egalitarianism as a Descriptive Concept', *American Philosophy Quarterly*, 1970; D. D. Raphael, *Problems of Political Philosophy* (London, 1970), pp. 183–94; John Rees, *Equality* (London, 1971), Chapters Seven and Eight; Nicholas Rescher, *Distributive Justice* (Indianapolis, 1966), Chapter Four; Bernard Williams, 'The Idea of Equality', in Peter Laslett and W. G. Runciman, editors, *Philosophy, Politics and Society*, Second Series (Oxford, 1962).

Consider the *Principle of Absolute Equality*, which is that everyone is to be treated absolutely equally in every respect. This is absurd. It is absurd because, for example, not everyone can possibly live by the seaside. Also, we cannot think of treating the sick as we treat the healthy. If more needed to be said of the principle, there is the fact that there is no earthly chance of its being realised, and that if it were realised, the resulting dull uniformity would be appalling.

Let us, then, be guided by the idea just mentioned, that the sick are not to be treated equally with the well. Indeed the only sensible thinking about equality begins from the observable facts that men are different or unequal in some respects and perhaps the same or equal in other respects. The sensible general idea of equality, in fact, is that those who are in fact equal in a certain respect ought to be treated equally, and those who are in fact unequal ought to be treated unequally. This is the *Principle of Formal Equality*.

If it derives from Aristotle, however, it does not carry us at all far. It gives no direction at all until one has found what actual equalities do exist among men. Clearly they are not equal in intelligence, industry and a great deal else. Indeed, it seems that they *are* equal *only* in having certain primitive needs and desires, and, if one can ever get the matter clear, in being *individuals*. That is, they are such that they should be treated as ends rather than means.

Given the overwhelming natural differences or inequalities between men, and these few equalities, it is merely confusion to suppose that men ought in *many* respects to be treated equally. Nothing of this kind follows from the Principle of Formal Equality. The most that one can reasonably say is that they ought to be treated equally in such basic ways as these: none should have his primitive needs and desires frustrated and none should be deprived of what is called human respect.

We may take this consequence of the second principle and regard it as a principle by itself, that of *Minimal Equality*. It does not requiring anything like a large redistribution of wealth, or greater participation in social decisions, or an end of social distinctions. It does not require much. What it comes to is something far less than equalitarians have imagined. There is in fact no large and defensible principle of equality.

Equalitarians have also offered many other principles. There is the *Principle of Equal Opportunity* and there is the *Principle of Equality of Wealth*. They have claimed too, if not often, that those who are of *equal merit* should be treated equally, and that those of *equal need* should be treated equally. The latter principle, sometimes expressed as 'to each according to his need', implies the existence of unequal needs, and so is not the Principle of Minimal Equality.

These principles taken together are inconsistent. Equal opportunity issues in inequality of wealth. When these inconsistencies are seen, something must in any case be given up, but how is the Equalitarian to choose? Moreover, it is quite unclear how these latter principles are related to the previous two, those of Formal Equality and Minimal Equality.

If the foregoing sketch were truly a sketch of the best that can be done with notions of equality, we would have some reason for being intellectually dismayed by the prospect of trying to get some moral grip on the state of our societies, on the facts of inequality. However, the situation is otherwise. What follows is only a part of what might be said.

Is there really no general and substantial principle of equality, no unqualified ideal which is fundamental to equalitarian feeling, and which would enter into the construction of a basic morality? The first principle mentioned in the sketch, that everyone is to be treated equally in every respect, is certainly unqualified. This, the Principle of Absolute Equality, *is* nonsense. It is also nonsense, though, to suggest that it is all that is possible by way of an unqualified ideal.

Notice that it is a principle about *treatment*: that is, roughly, what is to be *done for* and *done to* people. To fix on the idea of treatment is to miss what is at the very bottom of ordinary thought about equality. There is something else to fix upon, and it is, roughly, the *experience* of individuals, or the quality of experience. It consists, still to speak generally, in distress and satisfaction. There is then what has the right to be called, simply, *The Principle of Equality*. In one form it is that there is a presumption that everyone should be equal in satisfaction and distress.

This principle does not carry the consequence that we must treat everyone alike, the sick with the well. Nor, to return to the frivolous example of the seaside, does it have the other overwhelming disability of the Principle of Absolute Equality. That is, it does not run up against the truth that certain large physical impossibilities stand in the way of equal treatment. The Principle of Equality does not have these consequences, because of differences between individuals. Since everyone's going to the seaside is not a condition of equal satisfaction, we should not have to have everyone at the seaside to realise the principle. Again, since individuals are different, they can obviously be equal in satisfaction without living the same and producing a flat uniformity.

It may be objected to The Principle of Equality that there is no earthly possibility of its realisation. It is, in that respect, like other principles and ideals. It does not follow that it should not direct our efforts. As we know, incidentally, it cannot be supposed that it is *all* that should direct our efforts. To mention the pertinent argument, equality of distress in a society is not preferable to an inequality of satisfaction.

Another objection may be expected from many philosophers. They are those who have assumed, with Aristotle, that all principles of equality necessarily rest on natural or factual equalities and inequalities. They have assumed that one must find an equality of fact, perhaps intelligence, in order to *justify* an equality of treatment.

There is no such general requirement and certainly there is no such requirement on The Principle of Equality. Indeed, to think one is in place appears to require some confusion with an obscure aesthetic principle, having to do with symmetry, or perhaps some speculation that we must act in accordance with the instructions of a god, instructions which he has made implicit in his creation. The Principle of Equality, if anything does, stands as self-recommending in moral thought. It does presuppose certain similar potentialities in all men, which is an entirely different matter from finding a justification in these similarities. It directs our attention not to factual *equalities* but rather to factual *inequalities*. We are not to mimic factual equalities but rather to compensate for factual inequalities.

To return briefly to the sketch, and to the Principle of Formal Equality, it should now be clear that we have no need to search out sufficient similarity between men so as to secure the small conclusion that primitive needs and desires should be satisfied and that persons should be accorded a certain respect. That is, we need not struggle towards and end with the Principle of Minimal Equality. We already have a principle which secures the things in question and also a great deal more.

This is not to say that there is no place for the Principle of Formal Equality. Indeed in its most important use or application, it follows as a consequence from The Principle of Equality. Given that one wants to secure or maintain equal satisfaction, it follows that if two persons are *equally satisfied* then *equal treatment* is in order. If they are *unequally satisfied* then *unequal treatment* is in order.

In working out the equalitarian part of a basic morality, or, better, in working towards a basic morality by way of equalitarian attitudes, one will certainly have to deal with conflicts between secondary principles of equality. Obviously, the principle of equal opportunity does conflict with other things. However, it is only if one has a remarkably simple view of human existence, and is forgetful of an immense amount of moral and religious reflection, that it will come as a surprise that principles do conflict, and some must be discarded. It is no cause for despair. What one needs to do is something which is possible, some decision-making guided by The Principle of Equality.

There would be no point in going only a little way further here with these reflections. What I wish to suggest here is that in considering the facts of inequality, or, as they might as rightly be called, the facts of distress, we are not at sea. In particular, while it would be footling to suggest that there are no problems, we are not so confused about basic principles as to be unable to make a decent response. It is not that the facts of inequality, or of violence, must defeat moral theory and commit us to a passivity.

5

AGREEMENT, OBJECTIVITY AND THE SENTIMENT OF HUMANITY IN MORALS

Christopher Cherry

I

FAIRLY recently, I came upon the following passage in a review of a book by Colin M. Turnbull, called *The Mountain People*:

A child dumped on the ground is seized and eaten by a leopard. The mother is delighted; for not only does she no longer have to carry the child about and feed it, but it follows that there is likely to be a gorged leopard near by, a sleepy animal which can easily be killed and eaten. An old woman who has been abandoned falls down the mountainside because she is blind, so a crowd gathers to laugh at the spectacle of her distress. A man about to die of gunshot wounds makes a last request for tea. As he feebly raises it to his lips, it is snatched from him by his sister, who runs away delighted. A child develops intestinal obstruction; so his father calls in the neighbours to enjoy the joke of his distended belly.

It is difficult to imagine a society in which the family means nothing; in which altruism is mere stupidity; in which love is regarded as dangerous or idiotic; in which there are no values higher than the individual's need for food. But such a society exists.[1]

It is indeed difficult – if not more difficult than difficult – to imagine such a society (I suspect, indeed, that the difficulties involved in imagining such *a people* will not vanish if we are invited,

[1] The reviewer was Anthony Storr, writing in the *Observer*.

instead, to imagine such *people*; and accordingly that certain familiar juggling motions with the concept of *society* must prove facile and of limited value. But I let that pass for the moment. I shall do a very little juggling myself, but only in order to separate off a different sort of difficulty suggested to me by the passage.) Why is it at the very least difficult? The answer which comes most immediately to mind is that a society of the sort described either could not have got off the ground to enable us to study the peculiar nastiness of its members, or else could not possibly survive long enough to give that study any permanent or general value. We can, however, expand this answer in a slightly less trite, but certainly not profound, way. While maintaining that no society could have grown and maintained itself from such inauspicious *beginnings*, we might nevertheless allow that a society should *end* thus: that we are effectively witnessing its death-throes. (We are all too acquainted with such a phenomenon – and not simply as witnesses.) If we settle for this, we shall of course have to seek an explanation for the tragedy. But, more to my point, we shall have to take care to characterise our study not simply as one of a particular society of people, but as one of something – perhaps several sorts of thing – which can *befall* a people severally when, for one reason or another, their society is collapsing about their ears.

So it seems to be less difficult to suppose that people should be severally *reduced* to the state described if we bear in mind that what makes them a viable people is precisely what has been, or is in the process of being, destroyed. To put things more – perhaps far more – cagily: the supposition is no less preposterous than, and is formally rather similar to, the supposition that, for example, a formerly flourishing species of creature might be unfortune enough to undergo mutations of such a sort as to sever, in the case of that mutant species, 'essential' connections between pain and pain behaviour (evasion, retaliation upon the inflicter of pain, and so forth).

So far, then, I have suggested that if we are to imagine such a people as Turnbull (and Storr) depict, we shall do well to – and arguably must – posit some background of catastrophic degeneration. That is to say, the description occasioning the difficulties is incomplete and stands in need of supplementation. We are offered no more than a frozen *tranche* which requires extending in at least a backwards direction – an extension which cannot simply consist of more, and more detailed, descriptions of the *same* sort. Perhaps this is a somewhat baroque way of approaching a pervasive and vexatious feature of the topic of essences: we are called upon to decide whether or not a given property is essential to something's being a society, or to some creature's being human. We play at isolating and abstracting that feature from whatever it may be, and then puzzle as to what we shall make of the resulting fiction. The trouble with this game is that, for the purpose of the exercise, we treat the remaining features as constant, and only contingently connected with the problematic feature we have abstracted. We fail to appreciate that, and how, the problematic feature structures, gives form to, the features from which it has been abstracted.

Whilst I believe one would soon cease to be banal if one pursued in this way what I just now called 'the topic of essences,' I do not propose to do so, although I shall come upon it again, from a rather different direction, at the end of this lecture. For the moment, I want to draw attention to a different sort of difficulty, for I think it *is* different, to imagining a people described as Storr describes them. It is not, as the other was, a difficulty engendered by reflection upon the conditions of social viability, but one engendered by reflection upon the nature of moral consciousness – if I may be permitted such a general expression. To put the matter in a correspondingly general way: my reluctance to swallow, my puzzled resistance to accepting, the description as it stands, has as a further source the suggestion in the passage I quoted – which I am sure did not strike the writer – *that consciousness and moral consciousness are very distinct animals.* I shall not try to explain and develop what I mean by further reference to the Ik, for having almost outrun their usefulness they can be left to their own unpleasant devices. However, before I have done with them entirely I shall indicate what I do not *merely* mean. I do not *merely* mean to imply that we ought to find perplexing the suggestion that a people might find a continued employment for terms like, for instance, 'son' and 'mother' when the attitudes they display towards, and the treatment they mete out to, their biological kin disclose a capricious callousness, a total lack of humanity (I do not, though perhaps one might, say 'viciousness', given that the people in question are described as taking *positive pleasure* in acting in unspeakable ways towards those whom they acknowledge as sons, or mothers). There certainly *are* perplexities here which have been aired in one form or another;[2] but I shan't give them further airing here. What I mean is at once more basic and more comprehensive. I mean that we ought to remark, and find perplexing, any suggestion that moral consciousness and consciousness are so organised, are so distinguishable, that it is possible to suppose an absence of the first to affect in only the most

[2] See, for instance, Melden's *Rights and Right Conduct*; and the discussion by Phillips and Mounce in their book *Moral Practices*.

minimal respects the extent and range of the second.[3] So now two things must be done. The first, and by far the easier, is to kill off the Ik; the second is to explain, and in due course develop in connection with what I have to say about the sentiment of humanity, one sort of inadequacy in a certain view of moral consciousness – the view, as I have cryptically described it, that moral consciousness is at root quite distinct from consciousness *tout court*.

First, then, the Ik. I located, and discussed briefly, *one* sort of difficulty to imagining people like the Ik: the difficulty of imagining *a* people like the Ik. The difficulty which I have distinguished, and which will now occupy me, is no more one of societal viability than the difficulty in the suggestion that one might have a concept of self-identity without a concept of other-identity has to do with getting by in the world (though no doubt the problems would be real enough). Again, the account of moral consciousness I shall examine is not one having to do with any particular group, although it is one which appears to me to be encapsulated in the description of the moral constitution of a particular group. It is a quite general account of how we ought to view the relationship between being aware and being morally aware; and it is to this account that I shall now turn my attention.

II

The question: What is it for there to be beings (namely, human beings) which possess moral consciousness? has appeared to many, whether or not they have recognised the fact, to be a question distinct from the question: What is it for there to be beings (namely, human beings) which possess consciousness? It has appeared distinct in the respect that it has seemed to call for an answer additional to, and different in kind from, any called for by the second question. (Sometimes rather similar preoccupations yield rather similar, but confused and hybrid, questions like: *How* has it come to pass that there are beings which possess not merely consciousness but moral consciousness? Thus, certain writers tell us that the trouble with evolutionary theory is that it cannot account for *moral* consciousness – by which they understand disinterested moral awareness or

[3] There are parallels between this suggestion and the view, to which some sceptics have almost eagerly committed themselves, that knowledge of others and knowledge of self are so related – or unrelated – that it makes sense to suppose that the absence – in this case, an irremediable absence – of the first should in no way affect the extent and range of the second. One parallel that cannot however be drawn is this, that while Kant has shown the senselessness of the second view he has done nothing to rebut the first suggestion.

something of the sort – as if what they are happy to regard as sauce for the goose cannot be sauce for the gander. Many instructive confusions converge here, such as the confused notion that while the language of neurophysiology can stop us worrying about the origins of most forms of awareness and experience, it cannot help us with *moral* awareness and *moral* experience. But of course neurophysiology is disinterested. This sort of confusion shows itself in some current pronouncements about machines: they can think, we may concede, but they cannot think *morally*.)

As I have formulated it, the separation thesis is alarmingly ambiguous, and it is high time to make amends. So let me say what I do not deny in denying separatism. I do not deny the possibility that a *person*, or even a group of persons, should conceptualise and yet possess no moral concepts, or analogues to moral concepts (but it is significant that I see such a possibility as standing in need of both argument and explanation). I do not even deny such a possibility in the case of some *species* of brute, or of non-human creature, although, as I remark later, I think the contrary *can* be argued. (I am not impressed, incidentally, by the claim that we have good experimental evidence for the existence of such brutes. Apart from anything else, I take it to be a truth of logic that if a thing can speak it *will* speak; and I remain unpersuaded when told that whilst there are no apparent physiological obstacles to speech in, for example, chimpanzees they nonetheless prefer to communicate their thoughts by conventional means of another sort.) *A fortiori*, we don't have to find it especially puzzling – though perhaps depressing – that people who are highly sophisticated intellectually should think, speak and act in morally outrageous ways without recognising the outrage, without the slightest inkling of what all the fuss is about.[4] (I do not, of course, mean to deny that there are moral theorists who would be hard put to accommodate even this: Aquinas, perhaps, and Aristotle.) But I do, and we surely should, find puzzling the separatist suggestion that – questions of intellectual sophistication and *naïveté* quite apart – the connection between the capacity to conceptualise in anything like the way we do and the capacity to discern and make moral distinctions, while not fortuitous like that between, say, common sense and height, and while not strictly contingent, like that between, say, height and bodyweight, is at any rate a connection which, so to speak, holds in *one* direction only. (Separatism does not, of course, embrace the asinine proposition

---

[4] It is again significant, however, that even on this plane we are inclined to say of such people that they could recognise moral outrage *if only they could be bothered*.

that beings are conceivable who possess the capacity to make, and act upon, moral distinctions, while lacking the capacity to conceptualise.)

Let me illustrate what I mean. Whatever its merits and demerits, separatism reveals itself in many philosophies which in almost all other respects are very different from one another. Intuitionists are conspicuously separatists. It is solely by a *further* grace of God that reflecting, self-conscious beings are equipped to discern moral goodness and evil, for the territory of the ethical is discontinuous with that of the non-ethical somewhat in the way that two spaces, and hence their respective populations, may be imagined as distinct. It might have been the case (though, as it happens, it is not) not only that our acquaintance was exclusively with the non-ethical territory, but furthermore that the exclusive aquaintance we enjoyed was more or less identical with – or, for that matter, profounder than – the non-exclusive acquaintance which we happen to enjoy. Although acquaintance with the ethical presupposes acquaintance with the non-ethical, want of the first could not be such as to make impossible, or in any sizeable or obvious way interfere with or affect, the topographical features of the second.

Now, there is a further feature of intuitionism which is relevant to what I shall have to say in a moment about the sentiment of humanity. In an essay entitled *Freedom and Resentment*, Professor Strawson castigates the Intuitionist for sometimes appealing to intuitions of 'fittingness'. The appeal, he says, is to a 'pitiful intellectualist trinket' which a philosopher wears 'as a charm against the recognition of his own humanity'.[5] I think Strawson is right. But the notion of *humanity* to which he appeals is obscure; for the term 'humanity' has both specific and non-specific uses. The non-specific are more dangerous but at the same time more rewarding philosophically. I shall return later to this matter.

Not only Intuitionists but, what is both more curious and perhaps more reprehensible, many Naturalists seem to be separatists. Mr Warnock's brand of Naturalism[6] furnishes a good example of one sort of separatist thesis. On one interpretation at least, Warnock implies that a person can offer a comprehensive description of anything whatsoever, of 'the world', without thereby committing

[5] British Academy Henriette Hertz lecture, 1962. See p. 209.

[6] At any rate, that brand to be found in Chapter VI (especially on pp. 66–8) of his book *Contemporary Moral Philosophy*. I have written elsewhere about a number of problems connected with the sort of account given by, e.g., Warnock of the relationship between facts and values and so I shall be brief.

himself in any way to morally evaluating. Certainly the descriptions he offers cannot fail to contain enormously many references to features which, according to Warnock, are necessarily criteria of moral evaluation. However, it does not follow, Warnock claims, that one who offers such descriptions thereby engages in moral evaluation. The inclination and capacity to refer to, and *a fortiori* to conceptualise, such features are quite *separate* from the capacity and inclination, which it so happens we possess, to put them to moral employment – and these features, note, are supposed to be 'necessary criteria of moral value'!

> That there are ... necessary criteria of moral value does not imply that anyone, let alone everyone, necessarily evaluates things with reference to those criteria; it is only that we *must* do so *if* we are prepared, as we may not be, to consider the question 'from the moral point of view'.[7]

But what, then, *is it* to consider a question – to raise a matter, to view a state of affairs – 'from the moral point of view'? What further operation is demanded; and what further operation *is* there? To put it in a different way: if a person always may, and presumably often will, speak of the world in terms making reference to features which are necessarily involved in 'the moral point of view' without embracing that point of view, what possible effect could his failure ever to embrace that point of view have upon his conceptualisation of the world? The answer must be: no obvious effect. And an analogous answer must surely be given to the – for my purposes, crucial – question: What difference would it make to our conceptualisings if we (not only never embraced that point of view but) had not the remotest notion of such a point of view? What would we not be able to say, and think, which we do say and think?

I would argue that this variety of separatist account is *at best* appropriate only to one area of the fact-value domain; that there exists a wide range of *facts* and *features* which are conceptualised, and conceptualisable, only by virtue of the moral interest; and hence that a wide range of thoughts and statements, namely statements of those facts and making reference to those features, would not be possible if that interest did not exist, for they can have no life outside, and independent of, that interest. But I do not want to get bogged down here.

I think we may state the position represented by Warnock in the following way: the moral point of view, as he calls it, is conceptually dispensable although it is, as it happens, available. It is not conceptually peremptory in that it makes no *direct* contribution to the activity of conceptualising 'the world'; and for this reason it might never have, though as a matter of fact it has, suggested itself. Had it not, there would have been no conceptual havoc. If I am right, something further emerges, though perhaps not so much a new point as an opportunity to reformulate the same point with an importantly different emphasis: adoption of the moral point of view comes to be seen as an indulgence, however desirable – as an activity supplementary to, and characterisable apart from, the hard-headed business of making ourselves aware of, and of charting that awareness of, the world.

III

I do not intend to pursue separatism further in the context either of intuitionism or of (one variety of) naturalism. For there appears to be a very important – and to some, perhaps, very obvious – sort of answer, which I have so far chosen to neglect, to the question: What is it for beings to possess moral, as contrasted with other forms of, awareness? I have in mind what may be called *the sentimental answer*; but for the moment please treat the implicit reference to Hume as unrewarding though not dangerous.[8] Suppose we view the

[8] Despite my plea about Hume, I should of course acknowledge immediately one or two of the several ways in which Hume formulates what I take to be the crucial question and answer in any discussion of the 'achievement of moral consciousness'.

Question:
'*What is that to me?* There are few occasions when this question is not pertinent ...' (*Enquiry concerning the Principles of Morals*, Section V, Part I; *Liberal Arts*, p. 45.)
Answer (which I glean):
'... *reason* instructs us in the several tendencies of actions, and *humanity* makes a distinction in favour of those which are useful and beneficial.' (Op. cit., Appendix I, p. 105.)
'... there is some benevolence, however small, infused into our bosom; some spark of friendship for humankind; some particle of the dove kneaded into our frame, along with the elements of the wolf and serpent ... these generous sentiments must still direct the determinations of our mind and, where everything else is equal, produce a cool preference of what is useful and serviceable to mankind above what is pernicious and dangerous.' (Op. cit., Section IX, Part I, p. 92.)
'The notion of morals implies some sentiment common to all mankind ... It also implies some sentiment so universal and comprehensive as to extend to all mankind, and render the actions and conduct, even of the persons the most remote, an object of applause or censure ... These two requisite circumstances belong alone to the sentiment of humanity ....' (Op. cit., Section IX, Part I, p. 93.)

achievement of moral consciousness as a supplementary, and in certain senses expendable, achievement, one which is secondary to and, in a way which I have already indicated, distinct from the achievement of consciousness *tout court*. It will be secondary and distinct in that it will equip us to ask and answer in respect of certain *independently* conceptualised items – namely, the fruits of a distinct and earlier achievement – a type of question we would not be able to ask and answer simply on the basis of that earlier achievement: How is it that this or that item matters in a certain sort of way to me and others? Now, the sentimental solution I have in mind to this problem runs as follows: we possess a (or, the) sentiment of humanity and it is this that bestows upon certain items of our experience a *supplementary* moral 'meaning' which, logically, they might have lacked without thereby ceasing to be items – the *same* items – of our experience. The sentiment of humanity adds a colour and tone which would otherwise have been lacking, but not a structure.

Now on a fairly superficial level, the sentiment of humanity may be intended either as a generic expression designating a cluster of specific (moral) sentiments or affections, or as the name of some allegedly special *sui generis* moral emotion. But no matter which possibility is intended, its introduction is supposed necessary to account for the possibility both of raising and of providing an answer to the question: How can there be (or, what is it for there to be) moral consciousness? – or, if we prefer Hume's formulation: What is that to me?

At this point it may be objected that the notion does not, and really cannot be expected to, provide an explanation, even in part, of moral consciousness in any sense other than a recharacterisation. For it merely reiterates, in different and perhaps somewhat vapid words, that there *is* such a phenomenon (we shouldn't, for example, hope to *explain* what it is for there to be honourable and decent treatment of others by hypostatising a sense of honour, or a sense of decency). However, this objection is too glib in at least two respects. In the first place, it ignores the – by no means contemptible – pressures upon us to treat the notion as a springboard for (or even as a summary characterisation of) the deployment of techniques thought necessary to the achievement of a distinct point of view, namely, the moral point of view. So here is a species of separatist view: a point of view must be adopted *from* some point and be a view *of* something; and on the present account the view is *from* a point made available by one aspect of ourselves – our humanity – and it is a view *of* some given state-of-affairs anteriorly conceptualised by another, *different* aspect of ourselves. The conceptual availability of that state-of-affairs has to do only *accidentally* with our humanity. I shall return to this almost immediately.

The objection is too glib, also, in its total disregard for what sentimentalism achieves simply *by contextual exclusion.* However unsatisfactory its own implications, sentimentalism alerts us of, puts us on our guard against, the lunacy of certain rival -*isms.* What is here called for is, of course, an excursus, which I obviously cannot undertake, into eighteenth-century debates about reason and sense. Instead I shall simply re-echo Strawson's words, and take up my first point again.

I shall concentrate upon, without striving to keep distinct, two connected aspects of this first point: first, and more generally, upon the role in which a separatist thesis casts the sentiment of humanity; and secondly, upon the idea that, as I have described it, certain distinct and supplementary techniques appear necessary to an achievement of the moral point of view.

What is that to me? (Why does that matter to me?) is, I'd imagine, the most venerable question in moral philosophy. It seems to split very naturally into two sub-questions the links between which are crucial and yet highly problematic. *Why does that matter* to me? asks (in the context of the present discussion) after the possibility of such a thing as a moral point of view, after the possibility of the fact that human beings are, among other things, moral beings. Why does that matter *to me*? asks why, given that there is a moral point of view available, I should in the least concern myself with it. It is, at first sight, spendidly economical to appeal for help to a sentiment of humanity. For it advises us that we happen to be constitutionally ready and able – in differing degrees, of course – *to concern ourselves with things which don't, on the face of it, concern us.* And so we seem able to kill two birds with one stone: to adopt the moral point of view is, precisely, to concern myself with matters which don't concern me. As Hume tells us at one point: 'The notion of morals implies some sentiment . . . so universal and comprehensive as to extend to all mankind, and render the actions and conduct, even of the persons the most remote, an object of applause or censure. . . .'[9]

At second sight, however, the appeal is too economical. To begin with, we don't have to suppose, with Hume, that the sentiment of humanity is the isolable *intermediary* between 'actions and conduct' and 'applause or censure', conveying to the latter the information that in the former it will find an appropriate object. Rather than serving as messenger-boy between cognition and reaction may it not be what determines the form of the cognition?

[9] Op. cit., Section IX, Part I, p. 93.

Secondly, it cannot, even for Hume, simply *happen that* certain of the 'actions and conduct ... of persons most remote' become 'an object of applause or censure'. For he himself writes, almost immediately following the passage I have just quoted, that a man 'must ... depart from his private and particular situation and must choose a point of view common to him with others: he must move some universal principle of the human frame and touch a string to which all mankind have an accord and symphony'.[10] And the 'must ... depart' at least suggests to me that a man must master, and apply certain techniques.

Let us see how these two points bear upon the question: Why does that matter to me? The first intimates that there would be no '*that*' or – what perhaps comes to the same thing – not the same 'that', *unless it did matter*. The 'that' in question presupposes a certain sort of human concern, and would be impossible without it. (This might be construed as a moralised form of Kant's formula that 'I' entails an 'it'.) Now although it has appeared far from obvious, I think the moralised formula is absolutely correct for some values of 'that'. That is to say, we do not take an independent conceptual interest in certain kinds of action and conduct and, *what's more*, because there happens in addition to be 'a notion of morals', a sentiment of humanity, end by finding such actions and conduct objects of applause or censure. On the contrary: it is because there is a notion of morals, a sentiment of humanity, that we have a conceptual concern with such matters. To put the matter properly and non-causally: there are not two interests, a 'moral' on the one hand and an anterior, more basic interest on the other. There is one interest, which we may, if we are inclined, call 'the sentimental'.

Professor Bernard Williams has said something very similar, but in a different context and so in rather different terms.[11] He writes that concepts of virtue and vice (such as cowardice, sentimentality and treachery), and institutional notions (like face or one's job or property or stealing or a debt) are such that

> if it were not for the evaluative interest, if it were not for the kind of human interest that those concepts respond to, it's not that you'd have a different evaluative flag ... you wouldn't have the concept at all. ... the point about concepts like face or one's job or property or stealing or a debt is that the deployment of these concepts is intimately bound up with an entire set of institutions, and the proposal to get rid of its [*sic*] evaluative force is not a

[10] Loc. cit.

[11] *The Listener*, 4 February 1971, pp. 136–40, repr. in B. Magee, *Modern British Philosophy* (Secker & Warburg, 1975), ch. 9.

proposal for a kind of logical reform about what words we use to describe the world, nor, merely, how we commend what is there: this would be a proposal to change our entire view of our social relations. Similarly with assessments of human character: the things which given societies find it fit to pick out as characteristics of human beings, to praise, condemn, remark and so on, are tied up with the kind of expectations they have of human beings.

I do not pretend, and nor I think would Williams, that there are not obscurities and difficulties in this line of argument. The most formidable (for me, at least) lie not in the presentation of the argument but in its scope – in its bearing upon separatism. Even if it is acceptable in outline, the gains are pretty modest. It would establish not that conceptualising beings must be beings with moral or 'sentimental' interests (consciousness as involving moral consciousness), but that beings without such interests would display conceptual deficiencies of proportions undreamed of by, and inexplicable in terms of the assumptions of, the separatist. Viewed from the vantage-point of our system, the other would reveal immense lacunae. Now, what is remarkable is neither the fact nor the extent *but the nature* of the lacunae. For what would be missing, if the sentiment of humanity were missing, would be not just attitudes, emotions and reactions but characterisations of those things which typically elicit in us such attitudes, emotions and reactions. To lack the sentiment of humanity would be to lack object as much as emotion.

Is the stronger thesis – the thesis that conceptualising creatures must be creatures with moral interests – entirely preposterous? Not *entirely*, I think: but to attempt to sustain it, in some less confused and less confusing formulation, would take a time – and a heroism – which I do not possess. Instead, I shall merely indicate the direction in which any argument would have to travel. If the thesis is that an interest in *applauding and censuring* is a precondition of the formation not of certain but of *all* concepts, then it *is* preposterous. If, differently, it is that one who appeals to the sentiment of humanity is *really* appealing, or ought *really* to be appealing, to some such precondition, then it is not. He would have to show that such an appeal is necessary to account for our ability to discriminate if not between self and others, at least between self and others *as human beings*, and, via such discriminations, to ascribe to oneself and other selves things like pain and pleasure, suffering and happiness. We may see him as countering with his appeal what he takes to be profoundly false analogical accounts of these matters – false because analogical procedures are bound to lead to the idea that we hold *unsupported* beliefs about selves. Further, he might look for support to Wittgenstein's discussions (of other minds, etc.), in the *Philosophical Investigations* and elsewhere, summed up in his observation that 'My attitude towards him is an attitude towards a soul. I am not of the opinion that he has a soul.' We must remember, however, that the *explanatory* (as opposed to the rhetorical) force of the appeal will show up, if at all, only against a Cartesian background.

It is tempting, though no doubt unscholarly, to construe in this rock-bottom epistemic way observations like 'The humanity of one man is the humanity of everyone.' And yet the whole enterprise bristles with difficulties (I don't mean exegetical ones). In the first place, the subject has changed: the sentiment of humanity no longer has to do with moral as contrasted with other interests, but with all indifferently. Now unless we conclude, as some have concluded, that it is sheer superstition to suppose we can isolate a *peculiar* kind of interest (or point of view) called 'moral', we shall, in trying to account for the peculiarly moral, very likely reintroduce under some other name a peculiar sentiment or collection of sentiments. In the second place, it may be said that the sentiment of humanity as a rock-bottom epistemic notion ceases not only to be a sentiment but also to account for anything: it merely vetoes anything which *does* look like an explanation.

Well, perhaps we *should* be sceptical about the idea of a peculiarly 'moral' interest; and perhaps, therefore, the unmoralising of the sentiment of humanity renders unnecessary attempts at such 'explanations'. If so, the unmoralised notion could not be expected to subsume or furnish techniques for achieving a 'moral', as contrasted with other forms of, awareness – techniques commonly imagined essential if one is to achieve a distinctively 'moral' point of view by departing from this 'private and particular situation'. If this is right, not only is the sentiment of humanity not what makes possible our reactive life towards anteriorly conceptualised states of affairs: it is not even something which creates a public, moral world out of a private, idiocentric one. I conclude by saying something about the sentiment of humanity unmoralised: human-ness.

IV

There is a basic – and highly formal, though not empty – sense of 'humanity' in which it means 'human-ness'. It is certainly not, in this sense, the name of some specific and determinate (moral) emotion or (moral) disposition like compassion, decency, or readiness to relieve the sufferings of others; and it is not, on the other hand, a quick way of characterising either what is, or what makes possible, moral awareness as contrasted with some more basic species of aware-ness: it is not a sentiment.[12] Humanity in the sense of human-ness has to do with those 'connections', established by nature, which constitute human beings – with the procedures, and in particular language-using procedures, deemed distinctive of human beings.

When we speak of 'humanity' in any one of these senses we shall as likely as not find ourselves speaking before long of 'agreement' or of 'accord'. Nowadays the notions seem to be locked together. Thus, when we wish to draw attention to features common to, and perhaps peculiar to, human beings we are pretty irresistibly led to speak of 'basic agreements' or of 'distinctive accords' between human beings. Now, I want to suggest that the notions of *agreement* and *accord* are, despite the manner in which they obtrude, highly misleading when used in connection with the sense of 'humanity' with which I am now, and in conclusion, concerned. This sense at least of 'humanity' is, as it were, *too basic to be done justice to* by such notions.

There is a tangle of considerations in why this is so. While making no attempt to disentangle them, I shall lead off with a familiar con-sideration which perhaps does not go very deep but which is useful instrumentally. Agreement is, characteristically, something which is arrived at, reached, achieved, and so, characteristically, something which one may always fail to achieve. Of course, even on the level of this first consideration, we need not, and indeed it would be absurd to, imagine that agreement must be hard-won, or that it must be reached, if it is reached, as the end-product of rational and systematic debate. We may simply happen to find ourselves in agree-ment with others about this matter or that. Nonetheless, we must suppose agreement to be an *active* achievement in this weak sense of 'active', that it may in any particular instance fail (not to obtain, but) to be attained. With respect to agreement we are, unlike colour schemes and food and wine, agents and not patients: to agree is something we do rather than something which befalls us.

And yet one scarcely needs reminding of the strong philosophical pressures upon us to appeal to the concept of agreement in contexts where the notion of an active and contingent achievement has, and calculatedly has, no place; where we are invited to see ourselves as patients who suffer 'agreement' as their lot rather than agents who

[12] I think, incidentally, that the principal task facing the reader of Hume's second Enquiry is that of deciding which of these several senses Hume intends at particular points – when, that is, he does not complicate matters even further by inventing some additional and *sui generis* moral sentiment which he calls 'humanity'.

achieve it.[13] The contexts are those where we are concerned to point to connections which nature, and not man, has established in man. On such occasions, we may be appealing either, more superficially, to *humanity* as 'agreement' in (certain sorts of) 'feelings' as opposed to agreement about the facts of the matter or, more deeply, to *humanity* as 'human-ness', as that set of quite basic connections exemplified by human beings. The interesting and troubling thing about Hume is that we are never sure when he is being superficial and when profound:

> Ut ridentibus arrident, ita flentibus adflent
> Humani vultus.
> (As the human face smiles at those who smile, so does it weep at those who weep. Horace, *The Art of Poetry*, 101–2.)[14]

Does Hume, and shall we, treat these words as moral law or descriptive law?

But irrespective of whether the intention is the more superficial or the deeper, we are alike seduced into speaking of an 'agreement' which I shall henceforth call 'passive agreement'. Now, the misgivings I have expressed about passive agreement are not simply that it is passive. If this were so, they would bear alike, which I do not think they do, upon both the superficial and the deep sense of 'humanity'. However, I find it very hard to explain satisfactorily why I do not think they do so; and I have a fear that, in trying to explain myself, I shall be solemnly engaged in making a distinction without a difference. Suppose we are struck by the fact that people feel alike, react in very much the same ways to the same sort of things – that they as it were aim their 'feelings' at pretty much identical targets. We notice, for instance, that moral practices are far less diverse than some would have us believe – that the moral precepts communicated to, say, the Murray Island youth are almost identical with those communicated to the youth of Tunbridge Wells. In such a case we are struck by, and will probably have recourse to speak of, the phenomenon of 'passive agreement' in what I have called the superficial sense. But imagine, now, someone saying that this way of putting things fails to capture, or only partially captures, what he is *really* struck by. He is not, he tells us, struck by the (doubtless, non-contingent) fact that the range of *objects* of feelings is much the

---

[13] We should recognise that a number of philosophical lines converge here: those followed by Natural Law theorists, Wittgenstein and (more erratically) Hume.

[14] See footnote 2 to Part II, Section V of *An Enquiry concerning the Principles of Morals*.

same for all men; but by the (doubtless, non-contingent) fact that all men *have* feelings – and not only feelings). That is to say, he is struck not so much by the fact that people feel contempt or reverence or pride for much the same things as by the fact that, wherever one looks, people *are capable of* feeling contempt or reverence or pride.

You may immediately suspect that we have on our hands only one fact, and not two. I will be reminded that contempt, etc., must have objects and that there are logical limits to the possible range of such objects. Now, even if such reminders showed, and I do not believe that they do, that there is at bottom only one fact, they certainly do not, and could not, show that there is only one *focus of interest*. For whereas in the first instance what one is struck by is the fact that the same sorts of thing excite in all, or most, men contempt or reverence or pride, in the second what one is really struck by is the fact that *there should exist such phenomena* as contempt and reverence and pride. The interest which declares itself in Hume's observation that 'the humanity of one man is the humanity of everyone' may be either one of these two. If it is of the first kind, it focuses upon the fact that men's feelings have much the same catchment area. If it is of the second, ontological, kind, it focuses upon the fact that there should exist such a phenomenon as humanness: that there should be entities, namely, human beings, which are the carriers, the instruments, of an elaborate network of feelings, responses, capacities and the like. (The second interest has obvious connections with, but is not merely a particular case of, the metaphysical form of the principle of Sufficient Reason, and connects with some things Wittgenstein says in his *Lecture on Ethics*.)

If my distinction in terms of foci of interest is accepted, we should be less than happy to talk of 'agreement in humanity', at least where the second interest is at stake. Both interests have to do with something we *do not have a hand in*, and if that were all, it might not be too objectionable to mark the fact by retaining the concept of *passive agreement* – or, for that matter, of *coincidence*. But the second sort of interest, unlike the first, has in addition to do with something *we* do not have a hand in. For the second interest in humanity is an interest in the *definition* of human beings: in, to use an old-fashioned expression, the essence of man. Now, talk of 'essence' is inimical to talk of 'agreement'. In as far as we opt to think in terms of 'humanness', of 'human essence', to that extent we opt to rule out the possibility of treating what we are thinking of not so much as something which might not have happened, but more importantly as something which might not have happened *to us*.

6

PSYCHO-ANALYSIS, HUMAN NATURE AND HUMAN CONDUCT

Ian Gregory

THERE is, I gloomily suspect, little which is *significantly* new that remain to be said about psycho-analysis by philosophers. The almost profligate theorising that goes on within the psycho-analytic journals will, no doubt, continue unabated. It simply strikes me as unlikely that such theorising will generate further issues of the kind that excite the philosophical mind. Though in making such an observation, I recognise that I lay claim upon the future in a manner that many might believe to be unwise. The place of psycho-analysis upon the intellectual map, the implications that psycho-analytic theory and practice have for the various kinds of judgements that we make about human behaviour, have been exhaustively discussed in recent times. Rather more specifically, whether psycho-analysis should be accorded the dignity of being labelled a 'science', what the significance is of psycho-analysis for those complex problems bounded by the notions of Reason, Freedom, Motivation, have occasioned much fruitful philosophical debate. It is not any wish of mine to add to the literature on these problems in the forlorn hope that even slightly different answers might be forthcoming.

Psycho-analysis is typified by its profusion of schools. The history of psycho-analysis is a story of schism and countervailing attempts to enforce orthodoxy. There may be such a profusion of schools but the figure of Freud dominates them all. To say that all psycho-analytic theorising is a footnote to Freud would be a pardonable exaggeration. Most psycho-analytic thought represents an elaboration of or a reaction against (or both) Freud's leading ideas. The ideas of Freud, like all ideas of worth, far from imposing a straitjacket upon us have that kind of fertility that inspires in others more of the same. The story of psycho-analysis is the story of such inspiration.

This due to Freud apart, the one element that all schools of analysis have in common is the belief that what is crucial to the therapy of those who come to, or are brought to, the analyst for help is the achievement of insight into their plight. There is a primary emphasis upon the need to communicate with the patient. This is in stark contrast to those schools of therapy that place a primary emphasis upon the manipulation of the physical states of their patients via drugs, electrical treatment and the like. Indeed those who object to the labelling of patients as 'mentally ill' often suggest that many schools of analysis belie their therapeutic method with an inappropriate mode of theorising which talk of people being 'mentally ill', with its physical connotations, reflects. Still the warrantedness or otherwise of extending the concept of illness from the physical to the mental sphere is not our concern.

This paper will fall (roughly) into three parts. I will sketch in a highly informal manner three psycho-analytic portraits of man: Freudian, Kleinian, Neo-Freudian. The implications of such portraits of man will be traced with a view to discerning what is embodied within such pictures about man the moral agent. A natural development of this concern will lead us to consideration of some problems raised by our intuitive and unreflective conceptions of man as an-other relating animal and the relationship they might have to the alternative portraits we are offered of man. I am not interested in any problems that might be thought to arise out of the therapeutic concern of psycho-analysis. Hopefully these very attenuated remarks will take on more substance as I proceed. I doubt if I will say anything new. I will simply make very explicit what has been said before.

Let me start with the problem of *Weltanschauung*. The word seems to be ambiguous between two rather different possibilities. One very common meaning is that embodied in the phrase 'a philosophy of life'. As such it relates to a way of viewing the world that bears upon the values and hence the attitudes and actions of the particular people concerned who have adopted that philosophy of life. It is essentially a scheme of values regulative of people's lives. Classical analysis has always been sternly insistent that psychoanalysis cannot be seen as supportive of such *Weltanschauung*. Freud rejected the idea of an analytic *Weltanschauung* and one sees this stricture continually re-emphasised in the writings of those most strongly to be identified with the orthodox tradition of Freud. Hartmann, for instance, in his Freud Lecture warns us against those who, under the guise of being analysts, through their theory and practice rationalise their particular *Weltanschauung*. The scientific status of psycho-analysis is incompatible with the peddling of such wares. One cannot derive evaluative conclusions from descriptive premisses. He notes that psycho-analytic findings can be used in the service of enormously varied *Weltanschauung* – and have been. He reinforces the warning he utters about the buttressing of *Weltanschauung* by analytic theory and practice by condemning those patients who take from the practice of therapy into their lives those attitudes that inform the therapist's practice. In their lives they now 'embody deep interpretation, the broad range of communication, unlimited self-revelation, widest permissiveness, the discarding of every consideration which stands in the way of full psychological understanding as practised in analysis . . . the avoidance of what we consider moral value judgements, characteristic of the analyst's attitude toward the patient'. These attitudes of mind, these tactics of the analyst become regarded as the only correct ways to deal with interpersonal relationships outside of analysis. Because this is the way of the analyst within the analytic session, this lends no weight to such ways of proceeding as regulative of the way in which lives should be led outside of such a peculiar context.

Weltanschauung in this sense is not, I think, of crucial importance for the problems of this paper. It is a second sense that it can enjoy that interests us more. In this sense *Weltanschauung* is to be identified with enormously pervasive presuppositions that inform our conception of the kind of creature man is. These presuppositions may be held more or less reflectively, may or may not herald some fresh vision of man. And no doubt finds reflection, on occasion, in *Weltanschauung* in the first sense. Psycho-analysis is an attempt to lay bare the nature of man, his mental development and functioning. Given this, we have to be alert to the possibility that *Weltanschauung* in the latter noted sense could play a crucial role in the construction of such theory. It is to be expected that different *Weltanschauung* would find reflection in different theoretical constructions. If *Weltanschauung* were not capable of empirical testing, were perhaps only subject to philosophical criticism, this might occasion gloom as to the possibility of finally determining which analytic theory did most justice to man and his nature. I must now give substance to these very general remarks.

Classical analysis, after the manner of Freud, has as its goal the understanding of human behaviour in all of its manifestations, both normal and abnormal, such understanding to be achieved via an instinct theory that reveals the ultimate determinants of human behaviour. The instincts are the ultimate determinants of human behaviour in that, no matter how transmuted, modified or disguised, all explanation of human behaviour must, in the last measure, embody some reference to such instincts. All that men do is expressive of certain primary instincts. The higher as well as the lower of human activities have a common genesis. Thus the whole of culture is seen as a manifestation of drive activity. The all-pervasive influence of the instincts is not easily detectable and shrewd analytic work is required to reveal the presence of the primary instincts in the enormously varied range of human action and activities. It is the function of the defence mechanisms to deflect the primary instincts from expression in ways that calm the anxieties of the ego, often into forms of behaviour that are socially acceptable, socially valued.

Putting all this into the language of Freud's metapsychology we can say that the id rules the roost. It is often complained, I think with good reason, that the original Freudian schemes left little, indeed no room, for reason to play an independent role. The therapeutic practice might well have redressed the balance but in principle the ego was a derivative of the id. While the functions of the ego are not to be identified with purely rational functions, rationality is part of the sphere of the ego. And the conception of the ego as always engaged in a more or less losing battle with the forces of the id, its emerging out of the undifferentiated id, its energies being id derived, occasions little comfort for those who see the exercise of reason as having an independent role to play in the domain of human activity. These articulations of the relationship of the ego to the id are just another way of saying that the real determinants of human behaviour are to be located within the unconscious.

The instincts being the kinds of things that they are, they have as their aim instinctual satisfaction. The satisfaction attained may be more or less direct. But if they are the ultimate determinants of human behaviour the implication is clear. Man can only be a creature geared to instinctual satisfaction, is wholly subject to the dictates of the pleasure principle. Man may achieve a certain guile in pursuing his satisfaction, i.e. he becomes subject to the reality principle, but his end is always the same, his own gratification. He is, in short, wholly self-absorbed, utterly selfish, not capable of forswearing instinctual satisfaction.

Analytic theories are frequently categorised as either instinct or object theories. Classical Freudianism of the kind outlined is clearly an instinct theory. When talking of object theories, we must bear in mind that the term 'object' does not mean, as it rather suggests, some perfectly impersonal entity towards which action or desire is directed. It connotes a person, part of a person, something symbolic of a person. Perhaps only in psycho-analysis could such an inappropriate term be used to designate the essentially human. As characterised by Rycroft, in his 'Critical Dictionary of Psychoanalysis', the precise difference between instinct and object psychologies lies in the possibility or not, of man having the capacity to forgo instinctual satisfaction. Within object psychology, the central need and desire of the individual is to relate to objects, other persons. This importantly implies that in order to attain to an object relationship, instinctual satisfaction may be fore-sworn. For instance, the object for the young child is the mother. No doubt the orientation of the child towards its mother is rooted, in part, in its desire for instinctual satisfaction. The presupposition of object psychology is that, from the very start, the individual has the capacity for seeking out an object for its own sake. Men's attitudes toward each other are not just a function of the pleasure they might afford each other. The object may be a vehicle of pleasure. The striving however is to establish a relationship with each other.

Now Kleinian psycho-analysis is an object psychology. There is much in Klein that is reminiscent of Freud; a theory of instinct in which aggression is singled out for especial attention, a general acceptance of Freud's metapsychology and his theory of defence mechanisms. Gorer notes that Kleinian psychology is known as the 'British School' because it seems to be so in attune with the British tendency to conceive of human nature as basically evil. And it is true that the Kleinian account of the world of the young child with its emphasis upon the phenomenon of aggression, internally and externally directed, a world comprised of 'the most monstrous and murderous and cannibalistic fantasies and wishes' does convey the most horrendous picture of the world of the young child.

A picture of man that is founded on the presupposition that man can forgo instinctual satisfaction carries with it certain expectations that should be mirrored in the theory rooted in such a presupposition. One's expectations in this matter are realised within Kleinian psychology. It is clear that a measure of altruism is part of man's natural equipment. No doubt allied to selfishness but present all the same. Where there are intimations of altruism, the possibility of love as a natural phenomenon is catered for. Klein indeed does talk of an *inherent* capacity for love, which capacity is of crucial importance for her theory of the depressive position. And the closely related notion of reparative guilt.

The concept of love, whatever its precise significance, carries within itself the reality of embracing an object for its own sake, without regard for the pleasure that it might afford. In addition, alarm at the possibility of the loss of the loved object, dismay if it is felt that through one's own actions, harm should be inflicted upon that object and, finally, the high regard in terms of which the object is viewed. All these elements within love find expression within Klein's theory of the depressive position and underlie that guilt, which in sharp contrast to the Freudian conception of guilt as persecutory, is reparative. Money Kyrle in his elaboration of the Kleinian theory of the super ego points out that such a story allows for the possibility of an ethic of love contrary to the ethic that is embodied within the harsh persecutory super ego of classical Freudianism. Klein herself, in a rather utopian vein, conceives of a world in which love might pervade human relationships rather more than at present. This attainment arising out of the mechanism of making child analysis as much part of everyone's upbringing as school education is now. The child analysis will fulfil the function of modifying and lessening the aggressive instincts of the child, thereby making more effective in all lives, the child's 'ever growing, deeply rooted desire to be loved and to love and to be at peace with the world around it'. If this realisation of the inherent capacity to love can be achieved in childhood through successful analysis, then adult life will reflect this achievement.

Kleinian and Freudian analytic theory have one crucial factor in common, apart from so much in the detail of theory. They are both individualistic psychologies. That is to say, the primary determinants of human behaviour are to be located within the individual. There is no denying that social situations in which men find themselves by accident of birth and the like, bear importantly upon the forms of behaviour characteristic of individual men or whole groups of men. But there are elements in man's make-up that must find expression and which are invariant between cultures. The environment shapes the mode of expression. Not that expression occurs. There are intractable elements in man that no environment can gainsay.

The primary determinants of men's behaviour are not social. They are elements in human nature. And human nature imposes distinct limits upon man's modifiability.

Now Neo-Freudianism can be characterised in all kinds of way *vis-à-vis* Freudianism; a rejection of its libidinal theory, (in the main) a rejection of his metapsychology with a consequent lack of concern for the psychological development of the individual. Much more positively, a greater interest in the life circumstances of those who are suffering in a manner demanding of therapeutic help. This is a reflection of the Neo-Freudian commitment to the basic premiss that the source of the problems in living that people have is to be found in cultural conditions. Social factors are the primary determinants in the shaping of men's lives. The emphasis upon cultural factors is not univocal in its significance. Precisely what are the crucial social determinants tends to vary from theorist to theorist. For some, it is cultural factors in a straightforward anthropological sense. This in contrast to the Marxist interpretation of what constitutes such factors, in for instance the writings of Fromm. But for our purposes such attention to detail is not that important.

The neurotic condition is the peculiar obsession of the Neo-Freudian. 'There is perhaps no phenomenon which shows more clearly the result of man's failure in productive and integrated living than neurosis. Every neurosis is the result of a conflict between man's inherent powers and those forces which block their development.' Forces that block the development of man's inherent powers are predominantly social and cultural. This very naturally goes along with the doctrine that the creation of different social environments will, if they are of the right kind, lead to an amelioration of men's unhappiness. This optimism is the all-pervading characteristic of those whom one thinks of immediately as Neo-Freudian – Adler, Horney, Fromm. The elements in our social life that create those tensions that find expression in neurotic behaviour are remediable. And must be if man is to achieve self-realisation or to enjoy those interpersonal relationships through which he will find self-fulfilment. When some approximation to the ideal state is attained, then lives will be characterised by love; mutuality will pervade personal relationships. The outcome of the curing of neurosis is the ability to have significant relationships with others. Man comes to trust, respect, care for others, and perceive others as ends rather than as means.

I have a huge sense of having parodied the schools of analytic thought to which I have drawn your attention. But I hope that, in essence, I have captured some important aspect of such schemes of thought. Given the particular interests I have, I can only plead not ignorance but convenience. And press on.

I believe that one can discern in these different kinds of analytic schemes of thought, different images of man the moral agent. The rest of this paper will be devoted to an examination of some of the problems arising out of these images of man *qua* moral agent. All this against the background of these analytic portraits of man.

There are a number of dichotomies that importantly characterise attitudes typically adopted towards morality and man's capacity for the same. I am going to specify four such dichotomies. No doubt there are others that are as important. The four I have in mind are:

A. Morality is of the most compelling importance. Or it is not.
B. Morality is importantly concerned with the attitudes and states of mind of the moral agent. Or it is not.
C. Man is naturally moral. Or he is not.
D. Man has the capacity for significant moral improvement. Or he has not.

These dichotomies are quite separate from each other. Clusters of typically associated attitudes however are usually found if we lay bare the deeply pervasive elements that structure a man's conception of morality, his sense of what is morally possible on the part of man. This seems to be vindicated as an observation if we look to the implications of the analytic images of man that have been briefly alluded to.

It is a commonplace to observe that Freud must be counted a moral pessimist. The account we are offered of man's instinctual core chimes in so well, at some level anyway, with all those manifestations with which we are only too familiar of man's sheer brutality and depravity. It is not uncommon for analysts within the Freudian tradition to claim that recent historical events underline the psycho-analytic assertion that the aggressive and destructive forces are part and parcel of human nature and belong to the basic equipment of mind. Freud's rejection of the thesis that the abolition of private property would somehow eliminate so much in human behaviour that is unpleasant is not consonant with a sense of optimism regarding men's moral possibilities.

Now an optimist is defined as a person who has the disposition to take a bright and hopeful view of things. That is, one who has a general tendency to be confident that, has the expectation that, some good will be attained. Colloquially, a person who looks on the bright side of things. In the particular context of optimism regarding men's moral possibilities, a moral optimist may be characterised as one who believes that the real possibility exists of the enlargement of man's other regarding capacity, his altruistic propensities. More specifically, that the future will show human relationships more pervaded than they have been, or indeed are, by the virtues of love, decency, compassion, gentleness, respect for persons, concern and the like. Even more specifically, that there will be much less in the future of those ways of behaving that so affront our moral consciousness. Much less of those actions which embody manifest inhumanity between men. Much less of that behaviour that creates in us a sense of outrage, a sense that certain kinds of behaviour if indulged in almost put persons so indulging beyond the human ken.

An extreme version of such an optimism would be found in the idea that man is naturally good. Where this goes beyond the doctrine that man is by nature moral, that is always sees the relevance of moral considerations, to the belief that other things being equal he would always carry into actions those considerations of a moral kind he recognises to be relevant to how he behaves. Moral considerations bind us in a way that no other kind of consideration can and recognising this, it is only circumstances that so distort man's perception of things that he fails to do that which he recognises as binding. The natural corollary of the doctrine that man is naturally good is to locate the blatant failure of man to exercise this natural tendency as rooted in his environment. The fundamental distortion that occurs of this natural tendency towards the good must reside elsewhere than in man. Where else apart from in society? In one way or another, all the morally dubious elements in man are caused by circumstance. They are not of his nature. Be that as it may, it is not clear that one needs to be committed to the doctrine of the natural goodness of man, if one is to believe that the real possibility exists of moral improvement on the part of the whole of mankind.

If such an amelioration were to occur of man's moral state, this would have as a necessary consequence that there would exist a much greater measure of human happiness. The reduction of selfishness in human affairs, necessarily entails more people realising their own desires and coming to enjoy them. Very considerable selfishness necessarily brings it about that large numbers of people never do what they want to do, realise themselves in the ways they wish to do. Their interests, needs, wants, are always being sacrificed at the altar of those who through force, social position and the like can coerce others in their whims. All such unhappiness in principle is largely removable from the human scene.

All the foregoing in stark contrast to the moral pessimist. A pessimist tritely enough is one who looks on the dark side of things, takes a depressing view of the human situation, here now and forever. In our terms he is a person who asserts that selfishness will always predominate in human affairs. Misery is endemic to the human condition. This misery reflecting to a very large degree, the sheer amount of self-concern that permeates human relationships. The fitful flashes of altruistic concern that enliven human affairs have to be seen for what they are – the temporary triumph of other regarding tendencies over natural and normally assertive selfishness. Man's nature limits irredeemably man's moral potential. Even if men have the capacity for moral action, i.e. recognise moral considerations to be to the point, the actual exercise of that capacity is rare. This has always been true. It will always be true.

Optimism can normally be conceived of as ill- or well-founded. Whether the general attitude of moral optimism we are addressing ourselves can be so judged seems to be unclear. One might have expectations of a person on a particular occasion and be disappointed. One may well see that in the light of how that person has behaved in the past in such circumstances that one was perhaps unduly optimistic. Or one's optimism may be shown to be vindicated. But that such particular manifestations of optimism are capable of being so judged might be thought to lend no weight to the tenability or otherwise of this general commitment to moral optimism. Exactly what kind of commitment we have in those cases in which we label people moral optimists or pessimists is most murky.

After all, both the optimist and the pessimist have access to exactly the same evidence. Man's behaviour seems to exhibit both a significant amount of good and evil. Each side seizes upon that kind of behaviour appropriate to, supportive of the general tenor of their commitment. It is undeniably true, so it is thought, that there is a great deal of other-regarding behaviour, i.e. behaviour that puts another's interests before one's own. There is undeniably a great deal of behaviour that seems to be a straightforward manifestation of self-concern. There seems to be an extrapolation from the available evidence to draw conclusions that are equally in accord with the evidence. And there furthermore seems to be no half-way house between moral optimism and pessimism. We either accept the possibility of a significant extension of altruistic concern or we do not. All of us at the bottom of our being must have an opinion that we characterise as optimistic or pessimistic regarding men's moral possibilties.

Moral optimism is perfectly compatible with the expectations that we might have here and now of individual men's behaviour. It is the claim upon the future that highlights the nature of the distinction we are alluding to. One feels tempted to speculate about the ways in which the phenomenology of the different moral worlds which must be inhabited by moral optimists and pessimists vary. That there must be such variations seems inevitable. It is to be expected that it might be reflected in the quality of the interpersonal relationships that each enjoys. It is not our concern but interesting work surely remains to be done in this area. The elements of spontaneity, calculatedness, trust must be measurably different in so far as they enter into human relationships.

Inevitably along with these different perspectives upon man the moral agent one tends to get rather different conceptions of the role that morality plays within people's lives. A moral pessimist will see in morality a regulative device that acts as a check upon those elements within man that would otherwise tend to destroy the very possibility of social life. Morality acts as a bulwark against all man's strongest natural inclinations. Morality has as its proper business the amelioration of the human predicament, the enlargement of human sympathy. Things have a natural tendency to go badly and morality is a device to try and countervail that tendency. This characterisation of morality is Warnockian and captures nicely the view of morality as an attempt at overcoming the *status naturae*. But the reason for pessimism resides in the fact that the very strongest tendencies in man are rooted in self-interest, self-concern. Morality is not to be seen as expressive of those elements within man that represent how he most truly is. Of course, if asked to characterise all those elements that can countervail man's natural selfishness one has recourse to notions like love, compassion, concern, respect for others and so on. But by nature our commitment to such virtues is fitful and therein lies the source of one's pessimism.

If one sees morality as a regulative device, the possibility must be allowed for that, given the end that such a device is designed to fulfil, alternative devices might be found that serve those ends that much better. The contingent nature of our commitment to morality is now revealed. It is not true that moral considerations are of their very nature more binding upon us than any other kind of consideration. Their compelling nature turns upon their oiling the wheels of social intercourse. A moral optimist in contrast will see in moral concern, the exercise of those elements in man that are most truly revelatory of his nature. Man's selfishness, addiction to pleasure, represents some kind of distortion of his true nature. In acting morally, man most realises his own inner nature. For this reason, amongst others, moral considerations are of the most compelling importance.

Perhaps at this stage I could just draw attention to the fit that might exist between the rather cursory points I have just made and the analytic portraits of man to which in equal cursory manner I have drawn attention.

Whatever is meant by asserting that man is naturally moral, what it does not mean is that man is naturally selfish to the exclusion of anything else. The Freudian picture of man carries within itself the implication that man is not naturally moral. I take it that the assertion that man is naturally moral is not in any degree equivalent to the observation that it makes perfectly good sense to talk of egoism being a possible morality. That precluded, it seems to be entailed that talk about man being naturally moral demands recognition of an altruistic element within man's make-up. And, as noted, both the Kleinian and Neo-Freudian accounts of man embody some such recognition. To differing degrees, they are optimistic regarding the possible quality of human relationships – certainly much more optimistic than the vision of man contained within the id psychology of Freud. Indeed the optimism of Neo-Freudianism is viewed by some with profound distaste. The attraction of Neo-Freudianism to an educated public resides in its articulation of a possible mode of human existence far removed from that which we contemporaneously enjoy. The emphasis upon social factors as the most important element in the aetiology of neurotic conditions is highly consonant with the blander pictures of man that now tend to enjoy currency. Man is not to blame; rather it is circumstances that conspire against him. Many have suspected that within the Neo-Freudian tradition, one is being offered rationalisations of a moral vision. The Neo-Freudians would be prime candidates for the observation that we are being offered *Weltanschauung* under the guise of science.

It is certainly true that the identification of the fulfilled life, self-realisation and the like, with those forms of human existence that exemplify to the highest degree a measure of altruism, looks very like exhortation to the moral life. And Fromm, for instance, is most insistent that man is committed irreducibly to the moral sphere. If an individual violates his moral and intellectual integrity he weakens or even totally paralyses his personality. He is unhappy and he suffers. If his way of living is approved by his culture, the suffering may not be conscious, it may be felt to be related to things entirely separate from his real problem. The problem of mental health cannot be separated from the basic human problem; achieving the aims of mental life-independence, integrity and the ability to love. Man in short cries out for moral satisfaction. Only then can he fulfil himself. No considerations can be more important than moral considerations. But what is explicit in Fromm is implicit in other Neo-Freudians. They are critics of society, optimistic about man's moral possibilities. Indeed only to the extent that man measures up to what might be, will he achieve maturity and mental health.

The acceptability or otherwise of analytic theories often looks more like a matter of the embodied perspectives of man being acceptable to an intuitive sense of the kind of creature man is. Rieff in his *The Triumph of the Therapeutic* talks of some analytic theories being 'surrogate political theories'. This remark captures very accurately what one sometimes feels about much analytic dispute.

That is, it represents ideological conflict rather than any other kind of conflict. I suppose that what is meant by the equation of analytic theory and 'surrogate political theory' is that, dressed up in the garb of empirical or quasi empirical modes of speech, we have rationalisation of a sense of man's moral possibilities, of preferred forms of social existence. It is clear that Rieff has particularly in mind Neo-Freudian theorists. He has a strong sense that they portray much too an optimistic picture of the human condition. He condemns their 'cheery platitudes', rejects their belief that the amelioration of the plight of humanity lies at hand. His own vision of man is darker, more blighted, more in accord with the image of man that finds such powerful expression in the id psychology of Freud.

Now it is characteristic of most pessimistic images of man that while asserting that selfishness must predominate in human affairs, while recognising the element of destructive aggression that necessarily enters into interpersonal relationships, to rather regret these facts. There is no tendency to deny the reality of those weak fitful altruistic elements over which pure self-concern triumphs. The altruism of man, no matter how weak, is expressive of an authentic element in man's nature. The Freudian picture of man, however at rock bottom, seems to be peculiarly gloomy.

A measure of altruism might be thought to enter into any conception of morality in two ways, (a) as a precondition of the very possibility of morality, (b) as an important element in the substance of morality, perhaps its very core. To elaborate: even if morality is viewed primarily as a regulative device which has as its end the amelioration of the human predicament, it might well be thought necessary that, in order to be the kind of regulative device that it is, there be in the make-up of a man a measure of non-malevolence, beneficence, sense of common humanity. Unless there existed some such sentiment on the part of man, there would never be any motivation to be moral. I do not want to deny that there are qualities of mind, personal characteristics that are highly valued morally that have nothing to do with others. But it is surely undeniable that for most people, the most important moral values are just those that involve a concern for other people. If one's motives in acting sincerely bear testimony to a desire to help other people then one is morally commended. If one's actions exhibit respect for persons, involve treating them as ends rather than means, manifest concern for others, one thereby demonstrates a proper appreciation of the nature of moral concern.

Why I say that the Freudian image of man is peculiarly gloomy is that, if it is true that man is bent purely upon instinctual satisfaction, can see others purely as vehicles of pleasure, it makes it unclear how such a picture of man can do justice to the elements of altruism just mentioned that seem so important to any account of the nature of morality. Because it seems to carry the implication that all apparent cases of altruism are not as they appear, indeed *could* not be what they appear.

Men exhibit their altruistic propensities in an enormously varied number of ways, the particular ways always being a product of the kind of situations with which they, along with others, find themselves confronted. The kinds of demands that are made of us, the claims that we recognise others as making upon us, all arise out of the circumstances of people's lives. There are many ways of exhibiting the same manner of altruistic response. That is to say, being compassionate can take different forms according to the plight of those towards whom we behave compassionately. And so on. Disregarding the differences between the different manners of altruistic response, we normally think that they all have one crucial thing in common. Our concern, compassion, love, gentleness, trust and the like, are all thought to arise out of, and involve some immediate response on our part to, the plight, personal qualities, life style of others. Their responses to us in like manner. We imagine the very fabric of our interpersonal relationships to involve some such fundamental element. The very stuff of social life is rooted in our belief that there is such immediacy of response to the situations of others and that this response is expressive of a genuine part of the make-up of man.

What the Freudian image of man intimates, so it seems to me, is that this altruistic mode of response, which pervades the entirety of our interpersonal relationships and more particularly our conception of morality, is ultimately a sham. It is true that there is no change suggested to the descriptive content of the world of human relationships. At one level things are as they always are. Men still behave compassionately, exhibit concern for others, deal gently with others and the like. But, if man is wholly selfish, then man's altruism must be a sham. A sham which is practised by the entirety of humanity and which is recreated in the life of each newly born individual. The defence mechanisms have as their role to disguise from us the true mainsprings of our actions. Via aim inhibition, sublimation *et al.*, the ego manages to hide from us, our obsession with the furtherance of our own ends, our hostility towards others. It is not that on occasion we are deceived and deceive others through our actions as to the attitudes we have towards them. That is clearly so. Though our success in deceiving others is normally thought to be parasitic upon paradigm cases of not so deceiving others. It is that we always are deceiving both ourselves and others about our attitudes towards each other.

The situation seems not to be unlike the situation in which we meet a man who seems to be most concerned, attentive to the interests of others. We admire enormously his altruistic concern. We then learn that he takes a drug which has just such an effect. We further learn that prior to taking this drug he was a man who in his life style manifested profound contempt for the interest of others. We further observe that, if he ceases taking this drug, the old tendencies re-affirm themselves. Surely in this case, we feel that his other-regarding capacity, so clearly exhibited in his life style while under the drug, is deeply fraudulent. The manipulation that has occurred to modify his natural response while at one level clearly desirable, precludes his response being *his*. And as such is a deceit. Is the account offered within the Freudian picture much different in essence from the imaginary case outlined? It is true it involves not just one man but the whole of mankind in sham and deceit. In principle it remains the same. Given that mankind practises this deceit, it occasions little surprise that on occasion this proves too great a strain upon his true nature and that there enters into the relationships he enjoys with others, elements more reminiscent of his deep-down authentic nature. Pessimism regarding the human predicament is inevitable and wholly appropriate.

It might be thought to be a version of a crude reductionism to argue in this manner. Why should we doubt the significance and value of our moral commitments and more generally altruistic impulses because they have such a dubious aetiology? After all what is true of the altruistic impulse is true of all the higher human activities. Science, art, philosophy still possess value despite their doubtful genesis. Perhaps the impulse towards intellectual activity is really a disguised form of coprophilia but it is still valued, and rightly so. To imagine otherwise is to commit the genetic fallacy.

It might be suggested that, if morality is valued purely as a regulative device, exactly the same situation obtains as in the case of science. It serves its purpose, retains its value, no matter what the source of moral concern. I am unclear that we do ever view morality as purely a regulative device. Morality is especially valued because it is the kind of regulative device that it is, embodies as responses the values that it does. Again, if we do view morality as a regula-tive device and value it, why do we value it as a regulative device? Would not any such answer to this question reintroduce back into the discussion some mention of something looking suspiciously like altruistic concern? And if I am right it is the authenticity of such concern that the Freudian image of man deeply threatens. Morality is intimately bound up with questions of motive, the states of mind embodied in action. Judgements of moral worth often reflect this aspect of morality. The suggestion that all those attitudes of mind we most admire and value within the moral domain are a sham carries the clear implication that morality itself is a fraud. Our insistence that it may be of the most compelling importance is just another way (perhaps) of deceiving ourselves further. Because morality is (to some important degree) bound up with matters of motive, we cannot not concern ourselves with issues of a genetic nature.

What are we to say about all this? The contrast between the respective analytic images I have outlined is indeed stark. The intimations of the Freudian image of man are that, at the deepest level, our unreflective beliefs about the nature of a large part of our interpersonal relationships are mistaken. There exists a pervasive belief that there genuinely exists within human beings a capacity for altruism. This belief is mistaken. All those ways of behaving that give substance to what we mean by altruism are really manifestations of obsessive self-concern. This thesis that man is irredeemably selfish carries certain other implications for the possibilities of man *qua* moral agent. Man has no natural capacity for morality. Lacking that capacity, any talk of moral optimism is out of place. In addition, entailed by the notion of the deep inauthenticity of altruistic response, there goes along with this the idea that morality itself is a fraud. What else could it be seeing that it trades upon so many elements that are to be located within those ways of talking that form the domain of altruism? In contrast both the Kleinian and Neo-Freudian accounts of the nature of man start from the very pre-supposition that man has, at least, the capacity for altruistic response. Other people are not simply vehicles of pleasure. We can relate to them for their own sake. In order to achieve an object relationship we may be prepared to forgo instinctual satisfaction. This presupposition seems to suggest very strongly, perhaps even entail, that man is naturally moral, that talk of moral optimism is intelligible. There is even the suggestion within both schemes of thought that moral optimism may *in fact* be in place. Kleinian psychology is less optimistic overall than Neo-Freudianism with its characteristic belief that manipulation of social orders and institution will make it easier for people to relate in accord with the need that they naturally have. But in both Kleinian and Neo-Freudian psychologies, there is clearly discernible a sense that lives based upon mutuality of relationships represent an ideal mode of human existence. Interpersonal relationships, that mirror what so much in morality represents as of most worth, are indeed possible and to be aimed at. The embracing of moralities that give substance to concern for others are the forms of living that most guarantee the quality of interpersonal relationships that are the measure of man's mental well-being. In short, is more in keeping with so much that normally informs our perspectives upon man the moral agent, upon man the enjoyer of human relationships.

A question that is of utmost importance and which deserves much more time than I will give to it is: to what extent can scientific findings coerce our natural and unreflective views of man? Or is talk of coercion in this context out of place? Perhaps more to the point is that in that area of human activity, namely the domain of human relationships, it might be the case that, unless scientific findings so-called, capture our intuitive sense of how things are, they will likely find themselves rejected. Any would-be scientific endeavour that carries within itself the implication that we are fundamentally mistaken in those ways of conceiving the human world that are so natural to us, is doomed not to receive intellectual credence. Putting it more into the context of our particular problems: Is it conceivable that we could ever become convinced that so much in the interpersonal relationships we enjoy, is not as it appears? Is it an intelligible supposition that all those species of non self-interested behaviour which we hold in peculiarly high regard could be demonstrated not to be what they appear? And for the reason that they are all variations around the desire that all men have for self-gratification.

There are two problems here. The first relates to what it could be to live in a world where our deepest beliefs about the nature of human existence are demonstrably fraudulent. The second about the nature of the divide between those who see man as utterly self-seeking and those who deny that he is. Though these two problems are intimately bound up with each other. Perhaps I could start with the latter problem first.

We are asked to choose between a view of human action as, on occasion, exhibiting a lack of self-concern and of human action as always reflecting some self-interest such that self-interest is what provides the motivation for action. It is fairly clear, so it seems to me, that this is not the kind of issue capable of empirical resolution. No test could be devised that would settle the issue as to who is right. It is no doubt true that in general terms to live in a world which always manifests a desire to achieve one's own ends is different phenomenologically from one in which there is catered for the possibility of non self-interested action. With respect to particular actions and the expectations we might have of people, it is not true that predictions regarding likely behaviour in specifiable circumstances will be different. There is no dispute about the facts; just what they signify. A man might have the tendency to act in those ways we label as compassionate in given conditions. And, predictably enough in those circumstances being realised, act in that manner we call compassionate. The predictability of such a person's behaviour would be the same whether it was viewed as either authentically altruistic or as really selfish. The facts of people's behaviour do not compel any particular interpretation of that behaviour upon us. Else this particular debate would have foundered already.

It furthermore seems unlikely that evidence relating to neurophysiological states could help resolve such a dispute. Freud himself always envisaged the possibility that a final account of human behaviour would be biological in kind. It was a confession of ignorance that most explanation of human behaviour was cast in the highly informal modes of common speech. Such explanatory schemes only afford us partial explanation of human behaviour. Whatever the identity thesis maintains it seems highly implausible to identify acting altruistically or, conversely, acting selfishly with brain states. The characterisation of human behaviour as either self-concerned or as altruistic must go beyond mere consideration of brain states. In addition, the infinitely large number of ways in which behaviour as an instance of selfishness might be manifested precludes the possibility of identifying, in all instances of such human behaviour, some brain state with which the state of being exclusively self-concerned could be identified.

It might be suggested that the implausibility of labelling all human action as essentially selfish is shown when we come across instances of human behaviour which lend themselves so much more easily to the altruistic mode of speech. Stock examples of this would be a woman who gives up an enormously promising career in order to nurse an ailing parent or a man who sacrifices his life in order to save another. Our linguistic sensibilities are affronted by the attempt to interpret such behaviour as selfish in kind. Our sense of the reality of the quality of those actions is likewise affronted. The altruistic modes of speech enable us so much more naturally to describe such ways of behaving. It might be retorted to these trite observations that this is simply a reflection of our strong adherence to the beliefs encompassed in our unreflective ways of characterising such action. But it is just these beliefs that are under scrutiny.

This line of argument leads naturally into the first question that was raised in connection with the suggestion that we are mistaken as to the reality of our other regarding capacities. It is rather being suggested that our commitment to those beliefs we have about man being by nature a creature capable of forswearing self-interest is purely contingent. Being contingent we can be persuaded by a more objective and detached study of the reality of some imagined elements in human relationships to see the world of interpersonal relationships in some other way. We could, in principle, jettison what we take to be entailed by all those ways of talking that suggest a measure of altruism on man's part. We perhaps might go on talking in the same way but attach different significance to what is being said. This is a profoundly difficult problem the nature of which I am unclear about. It seems to involve questions bearing upon the most fundamental presuppositions of those ways of talking that take as their subject-matter, the very nature of human relationships. It is not, to reiterate, that it is being suggested that in *some* beliefs we might have about some phenomenon, involving other people and their interests, needs, wants and desires, we are mistaken, but that in *every* respect involving others and their lot, we are mistaken if we believe that we can order our relationships with those people in the light of some altruistic concern. Given that we believe that altruism does not just involve acting in certain ways but crucially involves, in addition, concern for another, which concern is *the ground* of our so acting, if the Freudian image of man were demonstrated to be true, it would thereby be shown that we are deluded in our natural tendency to look on a better side of man.

I do not want to suggest that our ways of talking, of seeing the world are sacrosanct. Conceptual changes can and must occur to mirror the advance of knowledge. But I feel tempted to say that, so intrinsic to our ways of thinking and talking about human relationships is our belief that man can forgo his own ends, that any attempt to infect with uncertainty this universal and normal perspective upon the quality of human relationships must be rejected. Our sense of certainty regarding the reality of men's other-regarding capacities must always outweigh any speculation that such is not the reality of things. In so far as interpersonal relationships become an occasion of study, any such study has to mirror what intuitively we know to be the case. It is only particular aspects of interpersonal relationships that can become a subject for study. That, in the fullest sense, interpersonal relationships exist cannot become a matter of doubt. They form the very fabric of human existence. What we mean when we talk of human beings demands a recognition of some measure of a capacity for other relating, on the part of those who are human beings. Human beings may choose to pursue their own ends but they recognise the claims that others may lay at their feet. The conception of man as bent upon instinctual satisfaction seems to preclude any such recognition. If it is insisted that man is wholly self-seeking, then, if this is equivalent to the assertion that all altruistic manifestation is a sham, one can only be doubtful of any theory which, embodying this commitment, seeks to lay bare the nature of much human phenomena.

Where does all this leave us? What are the implications of this for psycho-analytic theory? The analytic portraits of man that have been our subject for discussion embody enormously different images of man. It appears that the nature of these commitments is not empirical in nature. They represent ultimate stances on the nature of man: man as wholly selfish, man as not wholly selfish, man as naturally moral, man as a creature capable of much moral achievement and the like. It seems inevitable that these different perspectives must shape the development of theory. The most fundamental of these divides being that represented by instinct and object psychologies. It would be interesting to carry out in detail an examination of the way in which theory is so shaped. A lot of psycho-analytic theory will be neutral between the competing *Weltanschauung* that find expression in analytic theory – e.g. theory of defence mechanisms, various clinical theories. But wherever the differences in analytic theory are expressive of some ultimate view of man not amenable to empirical testing, it looks rather like a matter of making one's choice. Though it is clear that, from what I have said, I rather believe that where we are confronted with choosing between instinct theory as represented by Freud and any kind of object psychology, we are left with no real choice at all, object psychologies being so much more in accord with our perfectly natural view of human relationships. In recognising selfishness as an endemic feature of the human scene as present constituted, there is no tendency to deny the reality of so much that goes under the heading of altruism.

The reluctance to accept that the human situation is irremediably blighted is both the source and the attraction of Neo-Freudian thought. And the amelioration of the plight of humanity is inevitably seen in social terms. The manipulation of social circumstances on a large scale is thought to hold the key to the creation of that environment which releases those capacities in man, that the present social structure effectively precludes from exercise. The primary determinants of human behaviour, attitudes and the like are social in kind. All this in contrast to the strongly individualistic theories of Freud and Klein. So much in these disputes puts one in mind of the disputes of political theory. Once the terms of reference of a species of theory have been drawn out, then the construction of the detail of that theory can commence. If the desire is to be taken seriously as scientific then due precision and the like in the formulation of theory must be observed. And between the competing theories of the Neo-Freudians there can be some kind of adjudication. But it is unclear what kind of test settles the issue of whether man is primarily determined by his nature or by environment. Whatever the apparent facts they are interpretable in terms of the respectively incompatible beliefs. There clearly is some intimate connection between a sense of man's possibilities and where one locates the source of his failing. It is not being suggested that there exist logical entailments in this murky area, just strong tendencies.

Where we take as our concern Man, it cannot be otherwise than our preconceptions of what is most peculiarly human influence the shaping of our theory. This implies that all debate about the nature of man, his manifestations of the typically human is rooted in *Weltanschauung*. Some of these elements of *Weltanschauung* are unmitigatedly metaphysical in nature. Not capable of empirical testing, capable of philosophical scrutiny, not capable of final resolution. These *Weltanschauung* can be shared by otherwise different kinds of theories, different in the sense that they may be divided by yet other sharply incompatible *Weltanschauung*, cf. Kleinian and Neo-Freudian analytic theory. There is no reason to suppose, however, that this renders futile all the empirical work that goes on under the name of psycho-analytic activity. To suppose so is to fall victim to the idea of a final science of man that encompass all there is to know about man. The inspiration of these *Weltanschauung* is realised in our much greater awareness of elements in men's lives that affect them. That there is no final adjudication between the primary importance of these elements in men's lives is neither here nor there.

A few final comments: all psycho-analytic theory embodies *Weltanschauung* in the sense that has primarily concerned us. That is to say, all analytic theory gives expression to deeply pervasive presuppositions about the nature of man. Detailed investigation is needed to pursue the precise way in which *Weltanschauung* enter into the theoretical structures of competing analytic theories. I suspect that some elements of *Weltanschauung* arise out of more fundamental elements of *Weltanschauung* as those more fundamental elements are given theoretical expression. Freudian psychoanalytic theory of the kind I have outlined must embody some such *Weltanschauung*. That it is true that it seems not to give support to *Weltanschauung* in the sense of a scheme of values regulative of people's lives, in the manner of Neo-Freudianism, and some guises, Kleinianism, stems from the fact that it scarcely starts to do justice to all those elements in man's make-up that form the core of the most important part of morality. Where one is in a realm that is barely recognisable for what it is, the expectation must be that justice will not be done to so much that is crucially related to what is parodied. That Kleinianism and Neo-Freudianism do justice to what most people regard as the most distinctive element in man, i.e. his capacity for human relationships, means that necessarily much more to the forefront of such minds will be a sense of man's moral possibilities. To recommend the extension of all those capacities that so illuminate the human condition, the capacity for love, concern for others, exercise of gentleness and the like seems the merest moral good-sense. The difficult problems of morality are the problems involved in determining which actions give substance to such formal notions. One would be rightly suspect of analytic theory that started to sketch in for us the detail of lives characterised by love under the guise of psycho-analytic theory. It may be true that we all have to make up our own minds about the substance of our moral lives. What surely must be true is that, if we are concerned to give expression to our sympathy with others, then we are much more likely to stumble upon those actions that do ameliorate the lot of others. And ourselves in so far as good is its own reward.

There are, no doubt, relatively few people who now embrace the perhaps crude id psychology of Freud as I have outlined it. And no doubt their reasons are various. Some, I am sure, are rooted in empirical considerations. All I have suggested by way of example is that an element of extreme importance in determining our acceptance of a kind of analytic theory lies in commitments of a nature that are certainly not empirical, not capable of empirical refutation. They are beliefs of a kind that, in a sense, we may demand be recognised within analytic theory. This demand is perfectly compatible with there being large areas of agreement between theories as to the facts of man's mental structures. The beliefs that we demand be so recognised characterise our conception of the nature of man and his various possibilities. Given the endless debate about just what his nature is, whether he has any particular nature, what the prospects are for man, why should we ever expect a final resolution of these problems within one kind of analytic theory?

7

THE NATURAL SUPREMACY OF CONSCIENCE

Justin Gosling

I WANT to start this paper by drawing a distinction between two uses of the word 'conscience' in order to get clear just what it is I shall talk about. The distinction I want to make can perhaps best be brought out by reference to a type of situation which could equally well be described in one or other of two ways, each way illustrating one use of the word 'conscience'. Suppose then that we have a man who has been brought up to think that it is a good thing to help the poor. This lesson he has been taught, at least in part, by being told stories about beggars asking for money. The good person gives money to the beggars and the wicked person callously refuses it. One year he decides to book himself a holiday in Spain. Before he goes, however, he has a conversation with a social scientist friend. This friend points out to him that the one thing he should not do when in Spain is give money to beggars. Beggary, he argues, is a social evil and one which will only be removed if people take a stand and refuse to go on giving money when asked. The appropriate action to take is to inform the beggar of the whereabouts of the local employment exchange, or take him along to an employer, or do one or other of various rather embarrassing things. If the worst comes to the worst, it is better simply to walk away than to give money. Our man goes to Spain convinced by this argument and realising the unsophisticated and over-simple nature of his earlier moral approach. Before long, a beggar comes up to him and asks for money. Let's suppose that he refuses to give it, because of his newly acquired conviction. Now it seems to me that when he returns he could describe this situation in one or other of two ways without there being any difference as regards the facts that he is asserting. First he might say, 'I could not in conscience give him the money, after my conversation with you, but I felt awful about it for weeks afterwards.' Or alternatively he might say, 'Well, I couldn't give him the money, after my talk with you – it wouldn't have been right – but my conscience gave me hell for weeks afterwards.' Now, I think that whichever way he describes it, it really doesn't matter. The interest of this example is that the word 'conscience' in the one case gets attached to what upon reflection the person thinks it right to do, and in the other gets attached to his moral feelings, his moral reaction to the situation. In what follows I shall not be concerned with this second use of the word 'conscience'. No doubt characteristically with most of us the two tend to go together except in situations, like that described, of conversion from old and long-held views. What I shall be concerned with, however, is that use of the notion of 'conscience', where it catches what a person on reflection considers is the right thing to do.

Now I take it that there are certain views which are fairly familiar among people in what can roughly be called 'the Western world', and these views can be summed up as follows. First of all, it is felt that a person should follow his conscience. This means two things: one, that he should do those things which are in fact in accordance with his moral views, and the other, that he should do those things *because* they are in accordance with his moral views. Secondly, the view is not typically that a person should, on those rare occasions when his conscience stirs itself from its habitual lethargy, do what it says, but that a person should have a conscience, that is to say that in matters of moral concern he should actually have moral views and act on the views that he has. To the extent that he exercises and obeys his conscience a person is to be praised. To the extent that he ignores his conscience, or in circumstances appropriate to its exercise follows other motives, he is to be censured.

I hope that the view sketched is recognisable. I now want first to elaborate one or two points in it, and then add some nuances for the sake of verisimilitude. The points I wish to elaborate concern following one's conscience. To begin with, the relevant behaviour does not have to be the result on each occasion of conscientious deliberation. I may consider that I ought in conscience to entertain my pupils more. This entertainment will, no doubt, be a matter of conscience. I shall not, for all that, start the planning of each party by reference to fundamental principles, nor govern the production of each witty quip by reference to what I think right. Secondly, whether the behaviour attributed to conscience is in this way loosely related to deliberation from first principles, or whether it is the direct result, it is not sufficient that the deliberation simply start and finish with considerations of what is right or wrong. A given man may have fallen in love with an upright woman. In order to win her respect he realises that he must allow moral principles to guide his decisions. A good many of these will now be a function of what he thinks right. But although his deliberation is thus in conscientious form, he is not acting as he does because he thinks it right in the sense required by advocates of conscience, but because he hopes to win her respect. In order to count as being honest and so on because he thinks it right, his adoption of those principles would have not to be dependent on their supposed utility in serving another end – unless, of course, the end was that which definitionally gives point to morality. In other words, a person who follows his conscience has to adopt the courses he does because of his interest in morality, and this is not itself to be derivative from some other interest.

Now for some nuances. I have already tried to soften the picture of constant intervention of considerations about what is right as entailed by concern for conscience. It is also quite possible for someone who insists on the importance of exercising and following one's conscience to hold that there are areas where its exercise shows something amiss. Thus parents may be expected to be fond of their children. If we found in a given case that each kiss or present or entertainment was subjected to the test of right and wrong, some of us might think that all was not well, that it would be morally better if conscience were not so energetic. In old-fashioned terminology, it is possible to distinguish between charity and justice and confine conscience to the latter. So it is compatible with the emphasis on the importance of conscience that I have sketched, though not entailed by it, to limit the areas where the exercise of conscience is desirable.

Further, however extensive one may feel the range of conscience to be, one may consider it important without thinking that it is the sole determinant of praise and blame. It may always be something in a person's favour that he exercises and follows his conscience, but there may be other considerations. We may feel that the campaign for the preservation of law and order is retrograde, or that protests against the courts and police are anarchic. Or we may think that a given parent's reference of everything to principle shows insensitivity. The fact that in each case those involved are following their consciences may be a point in their favour, but it does not thereby still all criticism.

In making these points my intention has been to bring out the possible variety of emphasis on the importance of conscience. Of course, a given person may hold that on every question we should always start from deliberation as to what is right and wrong, and that praise or blame of the agent is determined solely by whether or not he did what he did because he thought it right. My point is that one does not have to aspire to such austere heights in order to give the emphasis to conscience that I wish to discuss, and I think few people go to this extreme. Finally, it should be acknowledged that not everyone does stress the importance of conscience in the ways indicated. It is, however, I think, true that many do in varying degrees, and it is the implications, not the propriety or extent, of such emphasis that I wish to discuss.

Anyone who does give this emphasis is to some extent claiming that conscience has, at least in some areas, some natural supremacy, that the individual should acknowledge its authority and others encourage its development. In appropriate matters conscience ought to hold sway. The emphasis is in fact a moral view to the effect that people ought to ask certain sorts of questions and abide by their answers. What I want to bring out in what follows is that this kind of view about conscience is something which fits ill with quite a number of moral positions. If we take 'moral' fairly broadly, so that it is sufficient for being a moral position that the position embody views as to what the best way is for men to behave and what constitutes a good man, then I think there are a good many moral views on which it becomes a puzzle why anyone should have any enthusiasm at all about the development or exercise of conscience. I hope to bring this fact out through examples, from which it will emerge that any moral view that does embody these encouragements must have some special feature or features to explain it. I shall then produce some examples where it is only to be expected that one would find such enthusiasm. There is no claim that the examples exhaust the possibilities – far from it – and I apologise in advance for the fact that for expository purposes the views are more like theoretical possibilities than real life entities.

It may help, before embarking on examples, to recall what the view on conscience is that I am discussing. The important points are as follows:

1. A person should have views on what is right and wrong.
2. Where appropriate he should apply those views in deliberating.
3. He should act as deliberation according to those views determines.
4. It should be moral and not any other concern that is responsible for the fact that the deliberation takes the form it does and that he acts accordingly. This amounts to encouraging the

development of a desire for what is right giving rise to operative deliberation.

The first example I want to take is one of morality in the Platonic mould. Now Plato, I take it, thought that you could discover what the nature of man was, that he was primarily a soul, a psychic being, and that the characteristic function of the soul was to think, govern, deliberate, rule and generally care for those things over which it had governance. A fully developed soul, therefore, i.e. a good soul and therefore a good man, would be someone who had these capacities developed to the full. Now, and I think this emerges very clearly in Plato himself, there is no obvious reason why we should encourage people, in general at least, to ask themselves what the right thing is to do, or should think that it tells in a person's favour that at least he did what he did because he thought that it was the best thing to do or because he thought that it was right. In Plato's sort of view, where the ideal involves the development of a certain expertise, there is no great kudos to be gained, morally, simply from doing what you think best. The ideal person is, indeed, a person who does think, he does exercise his thought, he will do what he thinks best. He will do what he thinks best because he knows what's best, and Plato holds him up for admiration. But he has no inclination to admire anyone short of that simply because he does what he *thinks* is best. Indeed, the exercise of thought outside the context of a given political and educational set-up is something which is obviously, in Plato's eyes, highly dangerous. It is far better, if one hasn't been through the Platonic course of studies, to do what is in fact best because, say, you have some trustworthy instructor, some philosopher guiding you, who does know how you should act, even though you yourself don't know and perhaps don't have any views on whether or not it is right. So long as you are in the right context and are in fact doing what you are told, the reasons *why* you do what you are told are not particularly important. It would be better if you could think, but not therefore better if you did think. In short, one would not expect to find, nor does one find in Plato, any enthusiasm for conscience. It is more important to do what is right than what one thinks is right.

It is perhaps worth noting that for these purposes it does not matter whether or not Plato is right in supposing that the truth of statements about worth can be known. The important feature of his position is that he holds up for admiration a condition of expertise. A view which held that the ideal was to pursue physical or intellectual development would for these purposes be in the Platonic mould, just so long as it was possible to learn how to achieve these goals. That is enough to produce the emphasis on experts as against eager tryers.

The second example I wish to take is one of a consequentialist style of view, a view whereby whether or not certain acts are the right acts, whether or not someone should be commended for doing them, is a matter of what the consequences are of behaving in the way that the person in question is behaving. On such a view, what we are all after in morality is a given end-state, and we are interested in actions only in so far as they are liable to produce this state. Now suppose that we take it that each act is to be assessed as the right act in so far as it is, overall, more conducive to the end-state than any rivals, or at least not less conducive than any rivals. Among the other bits of behaviour that would need to be assessed by reference to these consequences would be the practice of praising people for doing as they thought best, and that of discouraging people from encouraging others to ignore what their consciences told them. This set of practices would clearly stand in need of justification. It would have to be shown that on the whole they did lead to desired consequences. As it is assumed that the encouragements are likely to be successful, it would have to be shown that the result of their being successful would be the achievement of the desired end.

The first thing to be said, therefore, is that it would be an empirical thesis that certain ways of going about making decisions are most likely to produce the consequences aimed at, and the ways in question consist in working out how best to achieve the consequences and acting accordingly. To begin with, this is certainly not self-evident. There are examples, such as the law, etiquette, schools and such like, which have aims very like those usually attributed to morality by consequentialists, and of similar complexity, where one does not find anything analogous to the cited concessions to conscience. Few legal systems encourage citizens to ask on each occasion what the purposes of the law or state are and then act as they think most likely to serve those purposes. Still less do they generally condone misdemeanours done from such motives. The emphasis is heavily on conformity, and there is little worry about the motive for conformity. Thus a man might be a trustee for a trust set up for a doll hospital. He thinks the money would be better used supporting research into industrial unrest – better in that the general aims of society would thereby be more effectively served. So he diverts the funds illegally to support this research. The motive will not, however, necessarily help him – though of course in any given legal system it could. Generally, however, it is just this sort of individualism that the law is out to discourage, and for the obvious reason that individual judgement is likely to be so variable that we should not know where we stood. In such circumstances it is liable to seem important to make it clear that individual judgement is to be discouraged, and one obvious way is to be indifferent to the motive and to stress obedience. No one is blamed for keeping the law for fear of punishment or because it never occurs to him to break it. No particular type of motive is required for praise or leads by its absence to censure. The important thing is that the law be kept. Yet this is sufficiently like the proposed case with morality for one to expect similar obviousness with each.

In fact, of course, it is as implausible with morality as with the law. In so far as you encourage members of a large group to pursue a complicated aim such as group harmony by developing freelance deliberation, you introduce grit into the social works. This is partly because the complexity of the deliberations makes success unlikely; partly because our stupidity makes it unlikely; but also, of course, it helps to have some confidence in how others are going to act in given circumstances, and this leads to pressure for some reliable conformity in specifiable areas. Within the context of conformity individual judgement may – or may not – be desirable, but there will be areas where it should be discouraged.

So if we are aiming at a determinate form of good society, or general happiness, or anything of this sort, it looks as though the likelihood is that we will not have a very good chance of achieving it if we are encouraging all men to ask themselves, when they make their decisions, 'How can I on this occasion best achieve this end?' Certainly it is not on any such view axiomatic that it's a good thing for people so to make up their minds. The only way in which it could seem to become this latter would be if one argued, say, that people are much happier, or, something which doesn't lend itself so much apparently to any empirical testing, they are so much better, if they do simply use their own judgement on all occasions in this way.

Now the first, the 'happiness' style of thesis, seems highly improbable, if you consider the kind of question a person is being asked to raise, one which involves intricate reference to future consequences and developments of his actions. If you try to get everyone to exercise this kind of judgement, you are putting a great load of responsibility on them and a great strain on their thinking faculties. A great many people simply shrink from any such addition to their lives. Not having to think is at least as plausible a candidate for a source of happiness as having to think. If, on the other hand, one says, 'Well, it is just better, one can simply see the intrinsic worth of thinking', then one has for present purposes ceased to hold a consequentialist position, because one is not now assessing the worth of actions by reference to their consequences only, but partly at least by reference to the motives from which the actions are performed.

Now these considerations have, traditionally, led people to abandon the view that when it comes to making up their minds people should ask themselves this question about the overall consequences of what they are likely to do. When we are on the question of how people should make up their minds, then we should encourage them to use certain rules, at least in general, and when the good concerned is some kind of communal good, then there is quite an argument in favour of having certain rules which are generally accepted so that we all know more or less where we stand. Now the rules, no doubt, will be devised as ones such that if everybody does tend to keep to them, then the chances of producing our desired end are far higher than if people go freelance in the matter. But the question of individual decision is now transferred to the rules and the question as to whether or not the action that has been done was the right action is also transferred to the rules. So now the position that a person should do what he thinks is right, and so on, is no longer the position that a person should do what on reflection he considers will lead to the greatest happiness, and should do it because it does that. It becomes a thesis that he should do what he thinks is in accordance with the rules, and do it because it *is* in accordance with the rules. It still, of course, comes out as advocating the development and operation of a particular kind of motive but the position looks more defensible than the previous one. For it is slightly more plausible at first blush to suppose that there would be more chance of getting more obedience to the rules if people did do what the rules said because the rules said it. This motive should secure the occurrence of right acts. But while the first part of this seems near to being truistic, the second part is not at all so obvious. That is to say, of course there would be more obedience to the rules if more people did what the rules said, but it isn't clear that that particular way of looking at the rules is the best way of getting people to conform to them. Yet it would have to be established that it was if we were to justify the sort of encouragement of the exercise of conscience that I sketched at the beginning of this talk. It could, after all, well be that it would be more effective as a means of getting people to obey such moral rules as hold in our society, to encourage the development of a general admiration for the good John Bull Englishman, and then fit into our portrayal of the John Bull Englishman the obedience to just those rules that we want. And now, it won't be because this is what the rules say that anybody will be obeying the rules, but because this is how a John Bull Englishman would behave. Or alternatively, a hope of heaven and fear of hell could well be stronger motives in a given society than the ones proposed. This is not to say that of course in some other society it may not well be true. The temperament of the people in the society may be such that you achieve your ends better if you can develop this particular form of devotion to the rules. But it isn't at all self-evident and indeed, at first sight, it doesn't seem to me very plausible, even if more plausible than the previous effort. Once again, if we compare with the law, we find no insistence there on any special motive, but contentment with a variety so long as they are variously successful. Similarly one would expect, in this kind of morality, no talk of the treason of doing the right thing for the wrong reason. If it is good to give to charity, we simply want to ensure that the giving is done, and whether from pride, rivalry, fear or by inadvertence does not matter. Nor, again, is it going to be a very likely thesis that people who do things because the rules say that they should do these things, are a happier lot than people who keep to them for other reasons. There does seem to be a recognisable type of person for whom an adequate reason for doing anything is that some accepted set of social rules says that these things should be done. But this class of persons is not noted for its particularly cheerful countenance. Again, we might say that a society where people keep rules because they are the rules is thereby better than one where the rules are kept for any other reason. But once again this would simply be importing another element into one's view and one which few consequentialists would relish. There is, however, a further point about this version of rule consequentialism. Part reason for moving in this direction was that the ends of morality were supposedly some common goals of the various members of society. It just seemed highly implausible to say that a free-for-all, letting each person decide for himself, was likely to achieve these goals, and plausibility in face of this was achieved by talking about rules, which are instituted as the generally recognised rules in the group concerned. If these are good rules, then the social ends might well be achieved by general conformity to them. But now this seems to produce a position which makes at least one line in common views about conscience even more awkward. For one thing that does seem to be typical of common views about conscience is that even if two people differ as to what the best rules are, if they differ on fairly basic matters, nevertheless it is in somebody's favour that he does actually follow the principles that he has. But this allows, of course, straight away for a plurality of rules, indeed, for the very kind of situation which was thought on 'act' consequentialism to be likely to lead to chaos in the achievement of goals. It seems even, indeed, to allow for some variety in the ideas as to what goals are supposed to be achieved. It may be all very well to enter into debate with the other members of your community in order to produce some changing of the rules, but the whole idea about the original move was that you would better achieve your ends by a degree of conformity. This will not incline one to encourage a person to think his moral views out for himself and act on *his* views of what's best to do, for that amounts to encouraging him to devise and act on his own rules. Yet commonly it is thought to be in a person's favour that he does this.

In all this I have been talking as though there were a clear dividing line between act and rule consequentialism, despite the fact that this has been disputed. I have no wish to get entangled in this dispute, so I shall merely state dogmatically that it seems to me that a threefold distinction is needed in considering act/rule disputes. First, there is a contrast between saying that an act is right if, and only if, no other act would have/have had better consequences, and saying that an act is right if and only if it accords with a rule that belongs to a set of rules such that there is no other set whose observance produces better results. Secondly, there is a dispute over whether, by using reference to the justifying end, one would be able to produce a satisfactory justification of actions which would not be justifiable by reference to any justifiable set of rules. Thirdly, there is a contrast between advocating that when people have to make up their minds what they should do, they always refer to the justifying end; or that they only refer to rules; or that they always refer to rules except when they consider the circumstances peculiar and then they refer to the end. When we treat the views about conscience sketched at the beginning we are clearly concerned with the third contrast, for we are concerned with what approaches to decision we want to encourage. We might agree that whatever can be justified by reference to an ideal set of rules could be justified by reference to the justifying goal for each case, but still believe that the chances of the average citizen coming up with that justification were slim, so that we opt for a rule-biased version of decision-making. Even if we opted for a half-way house of general rule-observance with occasional reference to goals in a crisis, it would not affect my point. It would still be true that if we also insisted that people followed their consciences we should be holding that one should encourage first a desire for the common good and to keep the rules geared to it; and secondly a tendency to argue from the rules except where circumstances seemed unusual. The justification for encouraging these things would have to be that the good in view was more likely to be achieved if this motive and deliberative practice were widespread. Further, the suspicion of doing the right things for other reasons would be justified only by showing that other motives interfered with the securing of the ends. This justification would still have to be supplied; the position is still unobvious, and indeed implausible. In the same way as the version I considered, it would be hard to justify much tolerance of action on different rules just so long as they were thought by the agent to serve the end well.

The position might, perhaps, be more clearly stated as follows: a consequentialist view is one that holds that an act is a right act if, and only if, no other act has better consequences. Strictly, encouraging conscience would be encouraging individuals to act on their deliberations about consequences. For plausibility one suggests encouraging them to use rules instead and introduces a second sense of 'what one thinks right', making all or most deliberative thinking about what is right a matter of considering the rules.

So far, what I am trying to bring out is that whether or not one is going to be inclined to give any important role to conscience, whether one is going to encourage its development, exercise of and obedience to it, will depend very much on the kind of moral view that is being put forward, and the degree of encouragement that is likely to be given to it will depend on the view in question. On a Platonic style of view one would only encourage people who actually knew what was best to do what they thought was best. On a consequentialist view, one would only encourage people on each occasion to act in accordance with their consciences on the hypothesis of a highly rational society of almost computer-style intelligence, if then. On the more 'rulish' kind of view, one would only encourage it if one had a population which was temperamentally of a sort which was very attracted to rule-keeping. Even then, nothing could be made of tolerance of diverging consciences. But the second point, which I think is an important one, and has by now emerged, is that what the encouragements to exercise development of conscience amount to varies very much according to the moral view that you have got. It isn't that there is something called conscience that is in each case being encouraged. It's rather that we have a pair of formulae – 'doing what you think is right because you think it's right' and 'learning to develop views on what's right'. For a Platonic person this means encouraging people to do what they think is best because they think it's best. But then, we all have views on what's best, in Plato's view most of them highly erroneous, and so it becomes very implausible to suppose that Plato is going to encourage people in that way. What we are encouraging them to get views on is, in the last analysis, how our actions, or people's actions, fit into the general operation of the universe at large. When we move to our act, consequentialist, then encouraging the person to exercise his conscience cashes out as encouraging him to raise a question about the consequences of each action and how best to achieve them, and encouraging him always to act in accordance with his conclusions with regard to that question. When he goes rulish, he is being encouraged to ask himself what the rules say and to do what the rules say because the rules say it. In any case he is also being encouraged to develop a desire for the good, the common good, rule-keeping or whatever, according to the view in question. So the apparently uniform thesis that we should always do what we think is right, comes out as in fact taking quite a different form according to the context which is being considered.

I want to develop this point a little further now, by considering two examples where, in contrast to the examples that I have considered so far, the emphasis on conscience seems very natural. There is, I think, a broad range of moral views which set up as the ideal for the behaviour of men some model of friendship or family relationships. They consider that the good man is the man who considers his fellow men in a certain light and acts towards them in a certain way, and we are encouraged either to consider other men as though they were our friends, or as though they were members of the same family. Now I am not concerned with whether or not this is a realistic ideal, but it is, it seems to me, one that's been about. Christianity and many other religions, I suppose, are examples of this, and those Marxists who take it that Christianity is all right except for all the religious mythology that clutters it up, also hold that some such ideal should operate. A good man is one who manifests this ideal. People who emphasise the notion of the brotherhood of man, or the family of man, and so forth, are liable to have some such ideal in mind. Now such views may vary at many points. They will no doubt have rather different versions of the family, or of friendship, to operate as the model, and that I am not going to be worried about, nor am I going to go into the detailed differences. What I do want to remark is that, of course, if you hold some such view, then straight away you are showing an interest not simply in the consequences of acts. You are showing interest in the wills of the agents. You are wanting the situation where men have goodwill towards each other and this, of course, is shown in their actions. You are liable, therefore, to make allowance for acts which actually have a rather unfortunate effect if they are, despite some ignorance or some quirky view on the part of the agent, nevertheless done with the right sort of intention, with the right sort of motive. You have already got built into your moral ideal a concern that a certain sort of motive should be developed, a sort of attitude on the part of men towards their fellow men. You may not indeed want to say that, granted that a person has acted in accordance with what he thinks is right, then it doesn't matter what he has done. You may sometimes think that the effects of what a person has done are so deleterious to the general situation of the society, to the development of the kind of mutual attitudes in which you are interested, that indeed his attention should be drawn to it, and perhaps it shows a quite unwarranted insensitivity on his part. Nevertheless, in so far as we can establish that he quite sincerely did act as he did from the motive that we are trying to encourage, that has to be in his favour, because one of the things we are trying to encourage is just that motive. So one would expect it to be thought important that a person should have a conscience and that it should be exercised. Further, even within a given morality, notions like 'brotherhood' are liable to allow indeterminacy both of interpretation and as to what precepts they support. It would not, therefore, be surprising to find some preparedness to recognise the existence of the important motive despite difference of view on the ideal form of friendship, love, brotherhood or whatever. Such differences may show in divergence of precepts, but still be manifestations of the desired attitude. No doubt there will be limits to the permitted variety ('Always frustrate the wishes of your fellow men' might be a difficult candidate), but there is no requirement of conformity to recognised social rules of the sort we found on the rule-consequentialist view.

On this kind of view, again, doing what the person thinks is right just doesn't come out as the same as what it does on any of the views considered hitherto. Doing what the person thinks is right now comes out as doing what he thinks is the friendly sort of thing to do, because he thinks it's the friendly sort of thing, or whatever it may be. That is what is being encouraged in encouraging a person to do what he thinks is right because he thinks it's right. In being encouraged to exercise his conscience he is being encouraged to develop this way of thinking about his fellow men. Yet while the formula now, in this context, yields something different, still in this kind of context it is to be expected that this set of encouragements using this kind of formula will occur. Now it may be that they don't, or it may be that they are overlaid in any particular case with other interests, because moralities are complex matters. Still, one would expect in a morality embodying this kind of ideal to find some concern for conscience of the sort sketched at the beginning. If we look back at the points made at the beginning this will become clearer. To start with the fourth point, since the ideal is a spread in the development and influence of goodwill, one would obviously expect some hostility to other motives ousting this one. There may be matters where this one has no bearing, but in areas where one is wanting it to operate it is to be expected that one would want other motives not to usurp its position. Someone who gives to charity in order to win a reputation for himself is giving more importance to his progress than to the benefit of others, and this shows him to be falling short of the attitude idealised. On the other three points the matter is slightly more complicated. On such ideals it is to be expected that deliberation in some areas might be deplored, and it is not altogether clear what doing what one thinks is right because one thinks it right amounts to. It might be felt that everything should be spontaneous and beautiful. But while no doubt on such ideals warmth and spontaneity are valuable, one has to be very romantic not to recognise that not everything that gushes from a full heart shows consideration and goodwill. Quite apart from the fact that most hearts are not full of goodwill to start with, so that thought might be a restraint on their outpourings, it is also true that goodwill can be expressed by thoughtfulness and often needs reflection to ensure its best expression – or at least, the spontaneous candidate is not the only plausible one. As a person's reflections will give his considered view of the behaviour friendship demands, it is to be expected that such ideals will require him to act on such reflections, and so long as the view of friendship or family relations involved is not too gushing, it is likely that some reflection about the sort of behaviour required will be encouraged. This opens up the possibility of sincere difference of opinion about standards, but that would generally be felt better than unthinking or coerced uniformity, either of which in different ways shows a lack of the spirit hoped for in such moralities. But as on the other views considered hitherto, not every kind of deliberation will count as a deliberation of conscience.

Just as on the act–consequentialist view, only those deliberations count as conscientious deliberations which are directed to that end which is the end morality is about, and on the rulish view only those deliberations count as conscientious deliberations which concern what the moral rules allow, so now only those deliberations which are about how one can act in a friendly way, and those which come from a desire to act in that way, count as deliberations of conscience.

To come to the last example, there is another general style of view, which is not, I hope, unfamiliar, and which can often seem very like the one I have just discussed. It is not altogether uncommon for people to hold that one hasn't started behaving morally or thinking morally so long as one is simply taking one's views on how to run one's life and how to organise one's life from other people. Suppose you have a woman who simply won't take a stand on any question of any importance about her life, whether it be whether or not to take a job, how to bring up children, or on whether or not abortion is wrong. She always tends to take the matter home to see what her husband thinks, and take her views from him. One is inclined to think that she hasn't grown up yet, she hasn't got any moral views. Whereas if she did have, it wouldn't much matter what the views were. So long as she had thought for herself about these important matters of life and how to conduct herself and had decided for herself, she would thereby have moral views, and they would be her morality.

Now commonly, this sort of view is held in a way which makes it rather obvious that the holder of the view considers that it is admirable to have moral views. There is something immature about the woman who is always taking her views from her husband. There is something desirable about becoming adult. To have moral views now is to have views on how to conduct your life, which you accept because you have wondered for yourself how to conduct your life and you are prepared to take responsibility for the decisions you have taken, and face life full on and in your own right. People who hold this kind of view are, very naturally, very keen that people should and should be encouraged to do what they think is right because they think it right, and to have views on what is right. But now, there is no particular form of consideration which makes it the conscientious consideration or consideration of what is right. Encouraging people to do what they think is right is encouraging them to have some views on how to live and then to have the courage to act in accordance with the views they have decided upon. You can't now say, 'Oh, but they aren't concerned with friendly behaviour', or 'They aren't concerned with the social rules', or 'They aren't concerned with whatever the social goals are that our consequentialist had in mind' – and 'therefore it isn't a view on what's right'. No style of rule is entailed by the fact that anybody takes, on this view of 'moral', a moral view. It may be that some styles are ruled out, but if so it's a very rare and select breed. There is a vast range of possibilities that can be included, ideals quite hostile to each other. Enthusiasm for conscience, therefore, comes out as enthusiasm for a society of self-determining adults. Usually, no doubt, it is for a *society* of self-determining adults, so that some forms of self-determination might win less than whole-hearted enthusiasm – but still an individual is at least to be praised to the extent that he has formed his own views and acts up to them. Also, while there is no particular style of reason that marks it as moral, moral reasons have a special status in the agent's personality. If he acts for other reasons, where these special ones are appropriate, then he is being untrue to himself. Thus he may give way to public opinion against his accepted view, but if so he has succumbed and failed to behave as an adult moral agent. Or it may be that he has done what his views would require, but this is sheer luck. He has been wondering what would please public opinion. He is still guilty of moral pusillanimity. In short, one would expect some frowning on doing what is right for other reasons than because it is right, which here comes out as frowning on doing what accords with one's principles for other reasons than that they do just that.

Now this variety in what the encouragements to the exercise and the development of conscience amount to, is, I think, of some importance because quite often in discussions of conscience we are under the illusion that we have some common phenomenon to discuss. I am leaving aside that sense of the word 'conscience' which tends to get referred to immediate moral reactions, but when we are discussing conscience, when people are insisting that it is very important that people should do what they think is right, they still, often, tend to think that we do have a topic to discuss, that this is very clear and that only if we are utterly disingenuous can we claim otherwise. And this seems to me, quite simply, false. The situation seems rather to be, as I have said, that we have a formula, and now we have a choice. When we start raising questions like whether, and if so why, we should allow authority to conscience, either we are wondering whether, on whatever view it is that we are considering, we should give importance to whatever we would be giving importance to if we allowed this formula to cash out as something on this view: or, alternatively, we are taking some particular view and we are wondering of other views whether they can allow for the exercise of what would be conscience on this view. Thus, if we take, say, an act consequentialist view, we can either be asking whether an act consequentialist can allow importance to raising questions about how to achieve in each act those consequences, and if so how he would justify it; or we might be asking our question from a Christian standpoint and now we should be asking whether an act consequentialist could justify raising questions about how to be friendly, or how to love one's brother, or whatever may be the way in which we put it. Now each of these questions is no doubt an interesting question. The point is that they are very different questions and it's of some interest, I think, to start getting them clear. At least we might then have some hope of stating precisely the question we wish to answer. It's also of some interest that when we are treating the matter as I have, simply in terms of a formula cashing out, it's only certain styles of moral view in which one would at all expect that there would be any concern for what on that view the formula produces as conscience: that on certain sorts of rulish views, consequentialist views, Platonic style ideals, it becomes really quite a problem why anybody should worry about conscience at all. Now of course if we make this notion of conscience definitional of morality, then exhibiting that these views get into difficulties is exhibiting that in that sense of 'morality' they aren't really moralities. Alternatively, if you take a broader view of 'morality', we can discover that one or other of certain things has to hold of moral views if they are to accommodate the encouragements that I listed earlier on.

In all this I have been discussing the natural primacy of conscience in a rather weird way. I have not taken a particular phenomenon and asked whether it does or should have authority. Nor have I asked how men are constituted so that they concede authority to this phenomenon. I hope it is now clear why I have not done this. There seems to be rather a wide range of possibilities that might be covered by the term 'conscience', and consequently there is a likelihood that different people are interested in different ones. At any rate there is no one phenomenon that is clearly in question. Of course, if one admits this, it remains possible to put these questions about nature. For any given interpretation of 'conscience' one will have a morality, or a psychological investigation or what have you, that determines that interpretation. Let's suppose that we have a utilitarian style morality. One could now ask not only, as I have done, whether one should encourage conscience, but also whether human beings do have the relevant desire or tendency to treat certain considerations seriously. Here several problems arise. For instance, is the question whether human beings are capable of a concern for the greatest happiness of the greatest number? or is it whether only when this desire is aroused do humans find (real) happiness? or whether the pursuit of other objectives involves the frustration of a strong inherent *nisus* in human beings, so leading to constant felt dissatisfaction? or is it, more radically, that all human desire is and is only for the general happiness? Even at this sketchy level these are rather obviously different questions. Pursuing them reveals the difficulty of being precise about just what the facts would have to be to support an answer one way or the other. Also, however, the fact that there are various questions raises the question of just what one is wanting to claim for one's morality. Clearly, in some sense people usually want to claim that the morality they advocate answers to human nature. At the very least they will be claiming that people are capable of responding to the considerations put forward as important. The crunch comes when we want to know what more is claimed. And here the thesis is usually hidden in a plethora of underlined '*really*'s. Men really want happiness, or to love and be loved, or to develop and express their own personalities. But these 'really's are just signs that we want time to fumble a little longer. They do not of themselves give us a clear thesis. This is not to say, however, that theses could not be worked out, simply that they need to be. Once they are, and we have an interpretation of 'conscience', then we can ask whether or not conscience does, on that interpretation, play the role required for the thesis.

So far I have concentrated on questions raised by moral views. The word 'conscience' is, of course, used also in psychological and educational contexts, sometimes, but sometimes not, as part of a moral thesis. The fact remains that one cannot assume connections between 'conscience' as that has to be interpreted for one discussion and 'conscience' as required for another; but for any precise enough interpretation one can ask one or another of various questions about its role.

I must apologise for labouring this point, but I find myself largely in the dark in discussions of conscience. If what I have said is right then one might hope, for any given discussion, to characterise, say, the relevant moral position, give the relevant interpretation of 'conscience', give the sense in which one wants to consider whether it answers to human nature. Then we might even be able to decide whether or not something is true.

8

REASON AND HAPPINESS[1]

Roger Scruton

ARE moral judgements objective? This is a question of great complexity, and in what follows I shall try to cast some light on what it means, and on how it might be answered.

First of all we must know what we mean in referring to 'moral judgements'. If we are talking of a form of words, then how is that form to be isolated? If we are not talking of a form of words, then of what *are* we talking? Here is an opening for the sceptic, but let us not be too disheartened. It is clear that we possess an intuitive conception of morality, and that our moral opinions, so called, often find expression in moral judgements. We seem also to be able to recognise these judgements. For example, we may often know when people are being praised or condemned from a moral point of view, rather than from the point of view of prudence, politics or art.

How, then, are moral judgements recognised? Clearly there need be no such thing as a specifically moral vocabulary; the terms 'good', 'right' and 'ought' have many uses besides moral ones, and moral judgements can be recognisably expressed in the use of terms other than these. Kant suggested that we should distinguish the moral use of 'ought' by its categorical nature: it does not need to be, and indeed, according to Kant, it cannot be, completed by an 'if . . .', by a reference to what is needed or desired. A moral obligation is a categorical injunction that is indifferent to the individual interest. Others argue that moral judgements are distinguished not by their form (or 'force', to borrow from a more recent theory) but by their

---

[1] Previous versions of this paper were read by Dr Hans Kamp, Mr Mark Platts, and Mr Ian McFetridge, and I am grateful for their comments. I am particularly indebted to Dr John Casey, whose unpublished lectures on Virtue inspired much of the discussion in the second part.

subject-matter. The moral point of view is not, as Kant would suppose, the point of view of the impartial legislator, but rather the point of view of the man with certain interests, specifically, interests in human happiness and welfare. For reasons that will be apparent shortly, I shall follow Kant's suggestion, and concentrate on the categorical use of 'ought'. If there is such a use, then I shall call it a 'moral' use, but, as we shall see, absolutely nothing hangs on this use of the word 'moral'.[2]

'It matters in no way what you want; you ought to be kind.' Here, then, in the second proposition, is a judgement of the kind I shall call 'moral'. Many people have maintained that judgements of that form – statements of categorical obligation – are subjective, in the following sense: that there is nothing to which we can appeal that will settle, for all rational men, no matter what their individual peculiarities, the question what is right. Reason cannot *constrain* a man to accept any moral judgement.[3]

How do we set about proving that moral judgements are not subjective in this sense? There are, I think, two paths that can be recognised. One – which I shall call the path of truth – peters out in a sterile desert of logical analysis, while the other – which I shall call the path of reason – holds, I think, some promise of a successful outcome.

Let us begin with the path of truth. It might be said that a judgement is objective if it makes sense to say that it is true or false. Subjectivists in ethics have sometimes maintained that it is a consequence of their position that there is no true or false in moral judgement,

[2] It should be pointed out, all the same, that enormous difficulties stand in the way of any purely *syntactical* definition of the moral 'ought'. For we may use the term 'ought' whenever we wish to refer to a norm, and there are norms whose existence does not derive from human interest, and yet which are not moral. If I say 'The eclipse ought to occur at 3.20', then, grammatically speaking, I have uttered a categorical 'ought'. But I have not made a moral judgement. Any view that attempts to overcome this objection by ruling that 'ought' is simply *ambiguous* should be regarded with suspicion: are we so sure that we can tell when a term has more than one sense? (On these questions see Roger Wertheimer's interesting, if somewhat negative, discussion in *The Significance of Sense*, Cornell, 1972.) In the course of this paper I suggest tests for the moral use of 'ought' that are not merely syntactic; but these tests emerge as a consequence of our moral philosophy, and cannot be included in its premises.

[3] Philosophers of a Quinean cast of mind will of course insist that the same is true of *any* judgement. But it is not necessary to decide this issue, since, even for the Quinean, there will be 'constraints' imposed by one's scheme of concepts, and the question then becomes whether these constraints apply in the case of moral judgements, or whether they are unique to the empirical (or 'scientific') realm.

since no 'scientific' or 'descriptive' world-view, however complete, can determine the moral judgements of a rational man. Now it is clear that moral judgements can be said to be true or false, and moreover that they stand to each other in relations (of implication, presupposition, contradiction etc.) that are themselves subordinate to the concept of truth. But there is more than one explanation of this fact. Consider the example of 'nice': an adjective of commendation, which can be used in combination with a noun and a predicative 'is' to form a declarative sentence, a sentence which can be described as true or false. It is by no means clear that there is such a thing as a standard of niceness that must be accepted by all rational men; for the term 'nice' is introduced into our language without reference to such a standard. One can imagine, indeed, indefinitely many adjectives that are given meaning through entirely 'subjective' conditions, adjectives which it is deemed correct (from the point of view of linguistic usage) to apply to the object of some attitude or preference, whether or not this application has a *basis* in the object that would be acceptable in principle to all rational men. But the judgement that results from this application – being of subject/predicate form – will also admit of the concept of truth.

The suggestion must therefore be amended. It will be said that, in talking of when it makes *sense* to apply the concept of truth, we have been relying merely on certain grammatical intuitions. But these intuitions stand in need of some validating theory, a theory that will order them in a systematic way. It might be said that we have treated moral discourse as a system of deontic logic, but that we have offered no interpretation of that system. The concept of truth requires a description of truth *conditions*.

The suggestion might be, then, that we prove the objectivity of a moral judgement by establishing a condition for its truth: an interpretation of the judgement that makes clear to us precisely what judgement it *is*, an interpretation that enables us to treat the judgement as other than a mere counter in a game of uninterpreted signs. Such an interpretation will be designed to tell us, in a systematic way, just when a deontic judgement is true, and moreover, it will be designed to show us which of the judgements involving 'ought' are logically valid or invalid, and which are contingent, which inferences between moral judgements are truth-preserving and which are not.

Now suppose we produce such a theory: do we now have a proof of the objectivity of moral judgement? It might be said that we do not. For it could be argued that a semantic theory is only an arbitrary interpretation: without supplementation it will give us no rule or standard that is objective in the requisite sense. It can do this only if it also indicates some procedure of verification (to put it vaguely) for the sentences of our deontic logic, and it was no part of the conditions for the theory that it should do that.

In a sense this objection is entirely justified. For it would certainly establish the objectivity of moral judgements if it could be shown how we might move by logic from an 'is' to an 'ought'. Present-tense empirical judgements are objective in that their truth conditions are typically also verification conditions, or are logically connected with verification conditions. Hence their truth can be established objectively by observation of the world. Someone who observes the existence of a state of affairs and yet who professes to dissent from the judgement that describes it is someone who does not understand that judgement, for he does not understand the conditions for its truth, the conditions which *give its meaning* under the standard interpretation. A semantic theory that had the merit of showing how 'ought' judgements are built up from empirical judgements would indeed establish their objectivity: truth conditions and verification conditions would at last coincide and Hume's problem would be no more. But of course it is no part of the function of a semantic theory that it should do this, and indeed it is difficult to see how it could do this and still provide a useful account of the validity of deontic arguments.

But that is not quite the end of the story. For it is not only empirical judgements that possess objectivity in the sense that interests us. In particular, objectivity may be attributed to certain judgements of a modal form, judgements describing the necessity, possibility, or impossibility of a state of affairs. But consider the proposition 'Necessarily $(x)(x=x)$'. Can this be deduced from any statement of empirical fact? If we think that this proposition is itself necessary then indeed it does follow from an empirical statement; but from *any* empirical statement. That will scarcely encourage us in the enterprise of distinguishing modal propositions through their empirical truth conditions: the idea of an empirical truth condition (a truth condition which states merely *how things are*), will now be out of place. On the other hand, if we do not consider the proposition as necessary, then we find ourselves as perplexed in our search for an empirical basis for it, as we do when searching for an empirical basis for morality.

But few of those who accept that there is a coherent notion of necessity would deny that propositions of the form 'Necessarily p' are objective in the sense under consideration. It is an objective truth that necessarily everything is identical with itself in the sense that all rational men must agree to the proposition $(x)(x=x)$, on pain of not understanding the concept of identity involved in its formulation. But how do we verify the judgement that necessarily $(x)(x=x)$? In giving a positive answer to this question we may find ourselves tempted towards the view that the proposition is after all not a genuine statement of necessity, but rather something more like an extremely general contingent truth.

Let us return a moment to the assumption (common among philosophers interested in these matters), that the categorical 'ought' functions like a modality. On this view we treat 'ought' as a one-place propositional operator, roughly translatable as 'It ought to be the case that . . .'; obligation and permission are then treated syntactically in the manner of necessity and possibility. A semantic theory for deontic statements will naturally take as its starting point the intuitions that govern the interpretation of modal logic. Just as we interpret necessity as truth under every interpretation – or truth in all possible worlds – so we might construe obligatoriness as something like truth in any *ideal* world. That is to say, 'It ought to be the case that p' is true in a given world if p is true in any world that is ideal relative to the given one – any world in which all existing obligations are fulfilled.[4]

The details of such an interpretation need not concern us. However, it is worth lingering over certain philosophical questions that are raised by it. While no semantic theory aims at telling us which individual sentences are contingently true (as opposed to logically true) it nonetheless must make certain important assumptions about the truth of its individual sentences, and these may not be compatible with every intuition that we have. In interpretating deontic logic we assume a world that is ideal relative to ours – a world that is perfect from the point of view of the categorical imperatives laid down in our world. In this sense – as Hintikka points out[5] – we attempt to construct a Kantian 'Kingdom of Ends': the hypothetical state of affairs that is conceived through moral judgement and which functions as the standard against which our actions may be judged. Now it is a well-known fact that moral principles may conflict in a particular case. For example, it is wrong to lie about one's feelings,

---

[4] For developments of this idea see: Stig Kanger, 'New Foundations for Ethical Theory', and Jaakko Hintikka, 'Some main Problems of Deontic Logic', both in *Deontic Logic: Introductory and Systematic Readings*, ed. Risto Hilpinen (Dordrecht, 1971). Perhaps the most elegant statement of the formal analogy between the concept of obligation and the alethic modalities occurs in Richard Montague, 'Logical Necessity, Physical Necessity, Ethics, and Quantifiers', *Inquiry*, 1960.

[5] Hintikka, op. cit., pp. 73–5.

and it is also wrong knowingly to wound someone who may suffer greatly as a consequence. And yet many men encounter situations in their lives in which these two principles openly conflict: an action which, under one description, is enjoined by one principle is also under some other description, forbidden by another. Moreover, it is not true that such a situation can be counted merely as *refuting* one or other of the principles.[6] Merely to reject a principle because of such a conflict is to fail in sincerity: it is to take a light-hearted view of what is perhaps the most serious of all moral predicaments. Our moral opinions are not mere hypotheses that stand before the evidence in order to be refuted or confirmed. Furthermore, it is possible to imagine a conflict created by a *single* principle: a principle which condemns equally two courses of action in a particular case, when those are the only two courses of action that are open.[7]

Now we can conclude at once that this permanent possibility of dilemmas in our world must be reconciled with the absence of dilemmas from the ideal world, the world in which all obligations are fulfilled. But can we always imagine a perfect world where our dilemmas are resolved? Suppose that an action admits of two descriptions, under one of which it is enjoined, and under the other of which it is forbidden. (For example, my action, which is a case of saving your feelings, is also a case of telling a lie.) In our world there is no contradiction in supposing both that 'It ought to be the case that a is done', and 'It is not true that it ought to be the case that b is done', where $a = b$; for 'ought' contexts are referentially opaque. But what would it be like to imagine this dilemma resolved? Must we imagine a world in which it is not the case that $a = b$? And can we do that? Surely what ought to be done in our world is *this* action, namely a, while what is forbidden is also *this* action, namely b. Suppose, then, that someone looks back on the action a, that he has done, thinking that he ought not to have done it. Must he imagine a 'possible world' in which a is other than it is? It is perhaps in the attempt to avoid this kind of difficulty that Kant regarded his Kingdom of Ends as a realm of 'purely intelligible beings', free from all 'empirical determinations', such as those active in the creation of dilemmas.[8] But that is highly unsatisfactory. Our moral

[6] On this point, see B. A. O. Williams, 'Ethical Consistency', *P.A.S.S.*, 1965.

[7] Examples are suggested by the discussion in John Casey, 'Actions and Consequences', in *Morality and Moral Reasoning*, ed. John Casey (London, 1971).

[8] Cf. *Foundations of the Metaphysic of Morals*, pp. 454 ff. (Original pagination.)

obligation is to do *this, here, now*; an action that is empirically determined. One may indeed wonder what use morality is to the 'purely intelligible being' when he is free from all empirical predicaments.

That is by no means all that needs to be said. There are doubtless ways of reconstructing deontic logic so as to avoid the problem of dilemmas.[9] On the other hand, the problem seems to be a natural (if perhaps not inevitable) consequence of the assumption that deontic operators are modalities, whose effect on the propositions that follow them is to be described in terms of the concept of truth. And it might be precisely at this point that we should resist the attempt to explore the meaning of moral judgements through the notion of a truth condition, by arguing that the concept of truth has, after all, a deviant role to play in the assessment of moral utterances, that, like imperatives, these utterances admit of no application of the concept of truth that will provide the clue to our general problem: the problem of which judgement is the right one, or which it would be rational to accept. Even if we find some means of accommodating dilemmas within the standard semantic framework, then we still find that the path of truth has led us nowhere. For if we ask ourselves what the truth of any merely contingent moral judgement consists in – one whose truth value cannot be decided by logical theory – then the answer we are given is this: truth is nothing but correspondence with an ideal state of affairs. If that is so, then we are back where we started. For how are we to gather the objective support for our moral opinions that we are seeking? Experience of *this* imperfect world is surely less than adequate. The whole idea of empirical support must therefore be abandoned. But how else are moral opinions to be supported? Notice that the parallel with modal judgements here ceases to be illuminating. For the truth of modal judgements can be established objectively, even in the case of judgements that are not logical truths from the standpoint of semantic theory. For we can establish the truth of 'p is necessary' in at least some cases, by referring to such considerations as agreed usage, what is to count as 'understanding' p and so on. There is, then, some epistemological basis for our decisions as to which modal propositions are true and which are not. But we have no similar considerations to which we might appeal in the case of moral judgements: we do not establish the truth of moral judgements by appeal

---

[9] It is important to see, however, that the logical possibility of irresoluble dilemmas is admitted, as soon as we accept that there are or could be imperatives that are categorical. Therefore, if deontic logic is to be what it claims to be, it must accommodate dilemmas, and not dismiss them.

to the meanings of words, or by reference to what it is to 'understand' a moral judgement. The skeleton of semantic theory remains, therefore, a mere skeleton. We might reasonably doubt that we have been dealing with a genuine application of the concept of truth.

We have pursued the path of truth to the point where it seems to peter out in a bewildering series of questions. But the advocate of truth will doubtless not be discouraged – not yet at least. For he will argue that we have treated of one class of moral judgements only, and that there are many other classes, such as the recognisably moral judgements employing the notion of goodness or value, that do not create the same kinds of problem. Indeed it is often argued that the notion of a good or virtuous man plays a part in moral thought at least as important as the part played by the notion of moral obligation. Moreover, it is quite easy to envisage informal explanations of the idea of goodness that indicate immediately a method of objective verification. It has been suggested, for example, that a specimen *x* is a good *x* to the extent that it possesses those properties that contribute to the continued existence and flourishing of its kind. This informal explanation of the truth conditions of '*A* is a good *x*' serves at once to indicate how judgements of value might be verified.

That is only one suggestion – albeit characteristic of a certain kind of ethical 'naturalism' – and there is no space to consider it in detail. I shall merely indicate why I think that the defence of moral objectivity depends on an account of the justification of categorical imperatives. Here we have but to refer to a well-known argument of Hare's (an argument that has its origins in Hume). Either moral judgements are action-guiding, or else they are not. To say that they are action-guiding is to say that accepting a moral judgement is like accepting a command: it commits one logically to action, or at least, to some attitude in favour of acting in a certain way. (That is what we *mean* by 'acceptance' of a moral judgement.[10]) If moral judgements are action-guiding then the question 'What should I do?' is solved for me – other things being equal – once I have accepted a moral judgement that bears on the present situation. If they are not action-guiding then of course the question 'What should I do?' may still arise. But it seems that, if moral judgements have the kind of relation to the world characteristic of judgements of empirical fact – if they have truth conditions, in the sense of states of affairs whose presence can be objectively verified – then it is very doubtful that they can also have an action-guiding force. For

[10] Cf. R. M. Hare, *The Language of Morals* (Oxford, 1952) Pt. II.

suppose that I agree (sincerely) to a given description of the state of affairs in which I act. Surely the question 'What should I do?' may still arise for me. Or if it does not arise, then it needs to be shown why it does not arise: what is it about this description that compels me to favour a particular course of action? If there are moral judgements that are 'descriptive' then of course they are objective. But we see that this does not show that they provide objective answers to the questions that they are designed to solve. On the other hand, if we accept the argument that I have attributed to Hare, then it does seem to be the case that categorical imperatives provide objective answers. Sincerely to accept the judgement 'You ought to do X' involves a decision to act. Hence the question 'What should I do?' no longer arises. I have already, in accepting the imperative, made up my mind.

However, there are two important reservations to be made. First we must acknowledge the possibility of akrasia, or weakness of will. It is possible to accept that I ought to do something, and yet decide not to do it, for example, by giving way to a weakness. Our analysis must therefore be qualified; we must say that *in the normal case* to accept a categorical imperative is to decide to act. Secondly, we must recognise that we have not been speaking of the moral use of 'ought' but rather of the 'deliberative' use.[11] I may make up my mind to one course of action while accepting a moral judgement in favour of another. To accept a deliberative 'ought', on the other hand, is to make up one's mind; the acceptance of a deliberative judgement involves an intention. In the case of a moral judgement we have to deal not with intention but rather with attitude, an attitude being a general commitment that may or may not express itself in particular intentions. Once again, the 'ought' judgement will provide an answer to a practical question, for its acceptance involves a motive to act. But in the particular case this motive might be over-ridden, so that a decision is taken in conflict with the principle. On the other hand, it is not the case that some further factor must be introduced to explain how it is that, having accepted a moral principle, a man then acts in accordance with it. Other things being equal, his moral values will tell us what he does. We must say then that in the normal case, and *other things being equal*, to accept a categorical imperative is to decide to act.

The categorical 'ought' is distinguished by two features: first, by its special relation to the concept of truth, exemplified in the problem of dilemmas; secondly, by its connection with practical reason. I

11 Williams, op. cit., pp. 123–4.

have suggested in effect that we envisage these features in the following way. We have certain attitudes, attitudes in favour of particular forms of conduct, particular motives, and particular ways of life. Attitudes, unlike beliefs, and unlike intentions, may openly and consciously conflict; when they do so we are faced with a dilemma. There is a problem, then, as to how we justify these attitudes. In particular, we wish to know how we might arrive at an objective justification. This is a problem of practical reason, and cannot be solved through the study of truth (which is the province of pure or theoretical reason).

Now moral judgements can be seen in either of two ways – either as expressions of our moral attitudes, or as descriptions of the facts on which these attitudes are based. In the second case the question of an objective justification is solved at once. But this proves to have no bearing on the practical problem of objectivity: the question whether there are objective reasons for our attitudes (and hence for acting as we do) still remains. For it still needs to be shown that our 'descriptive' judgements of value indicate objective reason for acting. Simply to concentrate on the problem of truth is to ignore the question of objectivity. It does not matter, therefore, if we succeed in finding judgements – such as our purely 'descriptive' judgements of value – for which the search for truth conditions also leads to an objective procedure of verification.

If we neglect the categorical imperative, then, we are apt to find that the problem of objectivity eludes our grasp. The distinguishing features of the categorical imperative are precisely those features that lead us to construe it as an expression of attitude rather than as an expression of belief. It is the attitude that seeks expression in a categorical imperative that we may describe as moral. Moral 'opinions' are attitudes, and not beliefs. But we can also see that it is unimportant from our point of view that categorical imperatives should or should not exist. We are concerned to justify a certain kind of 'conclusion' to a practical argument, the 'conclusion' manifest in a moral attitude. If we also assume that there is a form of judgement which precisely captures this attitude, then it follows that the conditions laid down on the moral attitude must govern the logic of that judgement. It is precisely these conditions that lead to the problem of dilemmas. But suppose that we allow that there is such a judgement – the categorical 'ought' of Kant and Hare. We then see the deontic operator 'ought', whose logic we studied earlier, as an essential feature in a language-game whose object is not the pursuit of truth so much as the pursuit of rational agreement in activity and attitude. The declarative form of the categorical 'ought', and its consequent susceptibility to semantic analysis, is a subterfuge, a way of constraining moral judgements through the syntax of truth, thereby promoting rational argument. Our attitudes stand to each other in certain logical or quasi-logical relations. One attitude may presuppose or involve another; attitudes may be inconsistent or complementary; and so on. It is in virtue of these facts that the concept of truth gains a foothold in moral argument. Nonetheless, the real reasons to be given in support of a moral judgement are not truth conditions but rather practical reasons, reasons which show the rightness of an attitude, and not the existence of a fact. The argument from dilemmas serves merely to reinforce this supposition.

Naturalism in ethics is therefore logically sterile – it brings us no nearer to the refutation of scepticism. Equally sterile is the form of prescriptivism that confines itself to a study of the deductive relations of categorical 'oughts'. Such a theory, emphasising as it does this special form of judgement, fails to see beyond the judgement to the real phenomena of moral thought, to the attitudes that conclude our moral reasoning, and which impose on the moral judgement its categorical form.

Let us turn, then, to the path of reason, reason being here construed in its practical application. Now the first question that arises is what is meant by 'reason'. We can see at once that there are at least two ways in which reasons may enter into a practical situation: first internally, as the reasons which the agent may have for acting as he does; secondly externally, as it were, as the reasons which an observer might give in support of the agent's action. The problem of objectivity is a problem about the reasoning that *issues* in action. It is a problem that only presents itself from the point of view of the first person: 'Why should *I* accept *this* as a reason for acting?' Such a problem is not solved by describing the 'this' in question from an external point of view, from the point of view, for example, of one who considers the advantage of society as a whole.[12] Here we might point to the parallel with epistemology, where the question is 'How can *I* have the knowledge that I have, given my capacities and experience?' The problems of practical reason require, it seems to me, the same emphasis on the first person case that is accorded to the problems of epistemology. In what follows I shall be developing the practical parallel to what Bennett (following Carnap) has called 'methodological solipsism'.[13] I shall be interested in the problems

[12] We may conclude at once, therefore, that Utilitarianism provides no direct answer to our problem.
[13] J. F. Bennett: 'The Simplicity of the Soul', *J. Phil.* 1967, see esp. p. 654.

that confront the individual, and the rational solutions that he himself can offer to them.

It follows that the notion of crucial importance for us is the notion of accepting, and acting from, a reason. Now I can acknowledge that there is in fact a reason for giving up smoking – namely, that it is damaging to the health. But that may not be my reason for giving up smoking, either because I decide not to give it up, or because I give it up, but for another reason (say, because it disturbs my wife). To accept a reason for doing x is to be inclined to do x *because* of one's belief that a certain proposition is true. In this sense to accept a reason for doing x is, in the normal case, to do x, in so far as one acts rationally, and in so far as one has no reason to the contrary. Accepting a reason is a practical matter; we judge a man's rationality by his ability to *act according to reason*, and this is our primary criterion for the acceptance of a practical reason.

Now clearly there are first person reasons for action that are objective in the sense we are considering: reasons relative to desires. For example, suppose that a man wants to travel to Paris as quickly as possible, and that the quickest way is by aeroplane, then, other things being equal, it is clearly true that he ought to catch the aeroplane. Putting it in this way leaves the distinction between pure and practical reason obscure. For it seems to suggest that we have a special case of theoretical reasoning: X desires Y, Z is the means to Y, therefore X ought to do Z. But of course the conclusion is an 'ought', and here stands proxy for the action or decision to act.[14] To accept this reason is, other things being equal, to intend to act. A better way of displaying the reasoning involved is this: X desires Y, Z is the means to Y and X knows this, therefore X intends to do Z. Here we have expressed the process from an observer's point of view. It remains only to translate it into terms appropriate to the first person case: Would that Y! (Expression of desire): Z is the means to Y (Expression of belief): Therefore Z (The decision itself).

This process of reasoning is objective in the sense required: a man whose beliefs and desires do not generally combine in this way, so as to lead to appropriate action, is our paradigm of an irrational man. It would indeed be difficult to describe such a man as making choices, acting intentionally, forming policies, with the result that

---

[14] Some philosophers (including Aristotle) have spoken of the conclusion of practical reasoning as an action. However, an action may fall under more than one description, but will not be justified by the practical syllogism under each of these descriptions. This suggests that we should speak of the intention, rather than the act, as the true conclusion.

for such a man, the whole question 'What shall I do?' is without significance.

This argument seems to show that reasoning about *means* is objective. Such is the kind of reasoning described in Kant's hypothetical imperative. Now Kant considered the validity of the hypothetical imperative to be 'analytic',[15] and in this he has been followed by more recent philosophers, notably by Hare.[16] According to this view, there is a contradiction involved in supposing that someone accepts the premises of a 'practical syllogism' and fails to derive the practical conclusion. However, it seems to me that we can perfectly well attach sense, in the individual case, to the supposition that a man should sincerely assent to the premise 'I want Υ, Z is the means to Υ, and Z is in my power', make no mistake of reasoning, and yet not draw the practical conclusion, even when there is no reason to the contrary. In other words, the objectivity of this form of argument should not be described simply in terms of the law of non-contradiction. It depends, rather, on what must *generally* be true if a man is to count as a rational agent, as an agent who can accept and act on practical reasons. This point is important, for it seems to show that there is at least one form of argument that is recognisably 'valid', even though its validity cannot be reduced to the usual logic of propositions, and therefore cannot be subsumed under the concept of truth. The point is to some extent obscured by the current emphasis on decision, as though that were the only area in which practical reasoning is expressed. Now it is perhaps a logical truth that if someone intends X and believes that the means to X is Υ, then he also intends Υ; to intend otherwise would involve a *change of mind*. But here practical reasoning is 'analytically valid' because of a logical truth about the concept of intention. [17]

From the point of view of ethics we cannot rest content with this. For we need to establish the objectivity of reasoning about ends, and modern moral philosophy has tended not to raise the question how ends might be justified. There is a prevailing prejudice that practical reason is about means only, and that the choice of ends is, in the last

---

[15] Kant, op. cit., pp. 417–18. Thomas E. Hill Jr., in 'The Hypothetical Imperative', *Phil. Rev.* 1973, gives reasons for doubting that this was Kant's view.

[16] Hare, op. cit., p. 37.

[17] Thus modern philosophers have often argued that the form of reasoning 'X wants Υ, X believes that Z is the means to Υ, therefore X decides on Z' is logically conclusive, by surreptitiously interpreting 'X wants Υ' as 'X decides on Υ'. Examples are: Donald Davidson, 'How is Weakness of the Will Possible' in *Moral Concepts*, ed. Joel Feinberg (London, 1969); and G. H. Von Wright, *The Varieties of Goodness* (London, 1963) pp. 168–71.

analysis, idiosyncratic, and not constrained by any standard of
validity. In other words, it is generally assumed that ends in themselves *cannot* be justified. One explanation of this prejudice is the
persistent failure to distinguish ends from needs. Animals pursue the
satisfaction of their needs, and show a capacity to choose the appropriate means to this. But they do not in any other sense have *ends*
of action. That is to say, they are unable to form long-term policies,
policies which may involve the partial frustration of their immediate
desires.[18] To pursue an end entails having some *conception* of that
end, and this involves making judgements about the future. Moreover, it is necessary to be able to conceive of this future state of
affairs as desirable, and that involves the capacity to form a rational
picture of the state of affairs, through which it may be compared
with alternatives and thereby assessed. A lion moved by hunger
pursues food, but not through any conception of what it *is* to satisfy
hunger. That is why we think of the lion as *driven* by his instincts.
Don Giovanni pursues Zerlina, but not so as to fulfil a need (for
why bother, in that case, with *this* particular woman?). He acts on
the basis of a conception of the desirability of possessing Zerlina,
with her particular charms, and her particular innocence, in the face
of all the obstacles presented by her approaching marriage to
Masetto. Human beings are also, indeed, susceptible to desires unqualified by the 'rational picture' of an end. The traditional miser,
who desires money not as a means but merely in order to have it
beside him, is perhaps in this condition. But it is significant that here
we feel tempted to describe the desire differently; we speak of
obsession, compulsion, and so on. The impulse of the miser can
rarely be considered as the rational pursuit of an end:

> 'Tis strange the Miser should his cares employ,
> To gain those Riches he can ne'er enjoy.

The picture we have is that of a man driven willy-nilly by a force
that is greater than himself. Sometimes, too, our desires are mixed,
having a 'compulsive' element: the desires of Molière's and Da
Ponte's cunning Don Juan are so portrayed in Mozart's brilliant
music.

It is, I think, too simple to describe the difference between men
and animals by saying that human beings have both desires and
intentions, whereas animals have only desires. But clearly the difference has to do with the capacity of rational agents to deliberate: to
act for a reason, and to choose on the basis of reason. Anna Karenina

[18] Cf. Kenny's discussion of long-term and short-term desires: Anthony
Kenny: *Action, Emotion and Will* (London, 1963) p. 124.

might, in a sense, be said to have *given way* to her passion for Vronsky, but she certainly did so only after deliberation, and after forming a proper conception of what was desirable. She made for herself a picture of the happiness that she (and others) would enjoy, a picture that, if true, might very well have provided sufficient reason for her action. Unfortunately the picture was false.

In forming a picture of an end of action we engage in something like reasoning. Can we establish any principle of validity for this reasoning? Kant thought that we could not justify our ends of action as moral agents except *a priori*. For to justify them in any other way is to refer them to some further end, and so degrade them into means. It is therefore to stand convicted of the 'heteronomy of the will'. We know the validity of individual categorical imperatives by testing them against certain *a priori* principles, and the question how this *a priori* knowledge is possible was one to which Kant was disposed to give a metaphysical answer.

In a similar manner, modern philosophers have tended to assume that in giving reasons for an end of action we are necessarily assuming the existence of some further end to which the first is now conceived as instrumental. In which case, of course, the question simply arises all over again: the pursuit of reasons is endless, and endlessly inconclusive. If this is so, then of course we shall never succeed in providing an objective justification for an end of action. We will have to presuppose some at least of our ends as mere facts, about which dispute is possible but pointless.

To avoid this difficulty, we must establish that there are objective reasons for action that are reasons independently of our particular desires. This seems to be what Kant meant in referring to the *objective necessity* of the categorical imperative. If all reasons are relative to desires then clearly I can give to the evil man (the man with evil desires) no reason that he *must* accept which is also a reason for being good. It seems to me that Kant has here located the heart of our problem. Morals will be objective only if we can show that, if a man accepts practical reasons at all, then he can in principle be brought to acknowledge that he has reasons for being good. These reasons will be, in a sense, *a priori*, since they will be derived from the abstract idea of a practical reason; they will not be relative to particular desires.

But how *can* there be reasons that are not relative to desires, and yet which are also practical? I wish to examine the traditional view that such reasons might be found through the study of happiness.

Kant regarded the appeal to happiness as a violation of autonomy:

if what justifies one in doing good is that such is the way to happiness, then the maxim governing one's conduct is not the categorical imperative – 'You ought to do good' – but rather the hypothetical imperative – 'You ought to do good if you want to be happy.' I believe this line of reasoning to be fundamentally mistaken. It seems to me that the reference to happiness is compatible with treating what is justified by this reference (the present action) as an end. The reference to happiness might provide, then, genuine reason for an end of action. Practical reason has as its object not only actions, but also attitudes, emotions and motives. Take the case of friendship. It is because his action gives pleasure that the true friend does what he does: giving pleasure is his ultimate end of action, and his reason for doing what he does. But motives may arise from dispositions, and there is such a thing as justifying, or reasoning in favour of, a disposition. In this way we might try to show that every man, whatever his desires, has a reason to aim at friendship. But in showing this, we do not describe any further end at which the friend aims in every act of friendship. We justify a certain end, in the particular case, without describing that end as a means to something further. To say that an action was done out of friendship is already to describe an end. Indeed, there is a sense in which there cannot be a further end which is still compatible with this motive. To say that I was friendly towards X because I hoped to gain something – say wealth or esteem – through this friendship is to give a reason for saying that I was not moved by *friendship* towards X. But this does not mean that one cannot give a justification for the general disposition to friendship, independently of its deployment in the particular case. For example one can show that a certain disposition is part of happiness without describing happiness as one's aim in the exercise of that disposition. If this is so, then there is no contradiction between saying that one values doing what one ought to do categorically – for its own sake, as an end – and that there is a further reason for valuing it, namely, that such is the way to happiness.[19]

In talking of practical reason I have so far spoken only of reasons for acting. But the question of the objectivity of morals rests on another kind of practical reason – reason used in favour of an attitude. The above digression into the notion of a virtuous motive was simply one way of showing what should by now be obvious, that reasons in favour of an end of action are not reasons given for the particular action directed towards that end, but rather reasons given for the motive of that action, that is, for the state of mind which

[19] The strategy of this argument is, of course, based on Aristotle's *Nichomachean Ethics*.

involves *choosing* that end. In the case of the categorical imperative we might say that the reasons in question are reasons given in favour of an attitude, the attitude of valuing the particular end of action. It is this attitude that provides the motive of action – the Kantian 'Good Will' that is expressed in moral conduct. It follows then, that Kant was wrong in thinking that to attempt to give further reasons for categorical imperatives is to fall into the error of the 'heteronomy of the will'. This would be true only if we were concerned to justify the action enjoined by the imperative, done from whatever motive, rather than the attitude expressed in that action (the Good Will itself).

How then do we prove the objectivity of morals? It seems to me that it would be sufficient if we could show two things. First, that every man has reason to acquire moral attitudes. Secondly, that the objects of moral attitudes are restricted, so that every man has reason to approve of some things and disapprove of others. Now of course one can imagine situations in which even the most established maxims of practical wisdom fail to apply. A man may be starving, dying, incapacitated; for such a man morality might be inoperative or profoundly futile. But to prove the objectivity of morals it is sufficient to show that the normal situation of the normal man is such that he has better reason to aim at being moral than otherwise. And it is important to recognise that this 'normal' situation is what we must always assume, in advance of the happy and unhappy accidents of which we can now have no foreknowledge. We are concerned to discover what dispositions, and what desires, it behoves us to cultivate. Our actual desires are therefore irrelevant.

There can be no doubt that there are moral attitudes, and that they play an important part in our lives. Men have a sense of justice; they feel bound to each other by relations of allegiance and trust; they feel guilt, remorse, shame and compunction for their deeds; they feel anger, and distaste, admiration and respect, towards actions that have no direct bearing on their own state or welfare. In short, men take up a critical attitude, not only towards the actions of others, but also towards actions of their own, and a principle of indifference or impartiality seems implied in this comparison. Those qualities that we admire or reproach in others we also find in ourselves; if they arouse admiration or antipathy when we see them in others, then they must also arouse self-complaisance and remorse when we find them in ourselves. Without pursuing the matter further, we might say that we acquire attitudes to certain human qualities (specifically, dispositions and intentions), that are *normative*.

These attitudes involve the desire that men in general should pursue certain of these qualities and recoil from others. If one were to continue this piece of natural history, he would soon realise that the qualities that are the proper objects of these attitudes are those qualities of another (and therefore of himself) that find expression in intentional action. It is those qualities that we regard as part of a man's moral character, for it is on the basis of those qualities that we form or remove our trust. Now to act intentionally is to act with an end in view, for a reason. A normative attitude must therefore aim at rational agreement about ends, and this will involve agreement in reasons for acting.

Once we have fully described such normative attitudes we shall be able to formulate more clearly the distinction between the man who merely wants something, and the man who also *values* something that he wants. The second man's desire contains an element of self-consciousness that transforms not only his efforts to obtain what he desires, but also the kind of satisfaction that he experiences on obtaining it.

It is clear that there can be practical reasons for being courageous (in general), or for being disposed to friendship, not because one already has a desire for these things but because the satisfactions that they make possible are intrinsically desirable. Similarly there can be practical reasons for having normative attitudes, even though the having of these attitudes is not strictly speaking something that we do. An attitude can be acquired through repeated imitation, in the manner of a virtue. For example, I can repeatedly aim at a certain thing, train myself to exhibit anger and resentment against those who despise it, and so on, rather in the manner of the timid man of whom Aristotle speaks, who trains himself to react with anger where previously he would have reacted with fear.[20] Part of this process of changing one's attitude consists in the deliberate formation of a picture. Such a picture will involve the voluntary contemplation of some features of a thing at the expense of others, where this is not a matter of choosing to believe something (whatever that might mean) but rather of choosing to give it emphasis. Our attitudes may therefore remain within our power, even when the beliefs they depend on are inexorable. It is within one's power to have values, even if one is at present without them. So now let us return to our two principal questions. Are there objective reasons for acquiring moral attitudes? And if so, are there objective reasons for valuing some things rather than others?

[20] See Aristotle, op. cit., 1126a.

With regard to the first of these questions it might be thought that it would be sufficient to develop our natural history of the moral attitudes to the point where it seems inevitable – a part of 'human nature' – that a man should have such attitudes. But to appeal to human nature at this point is, I think, to abandon the enterprise of objectivity. The 'unnatural' man need only ask why he should be other than he is. Until we can show that, if he accepts reasons at all, then he must see that he has a reason to aim at being 'natural', then nothing of interest will have been proved.

How then can we show that there is such a reason – a reason independent of particular desires, and hence a reason that can be offered also to the evil man? I think that the answer must lie in the kind of satisfaction that is consequent on valuing something (rather than merely wanting it) and it is here I think that some reference to happiness is essential. Both Aristotle and Kant[21] held that all men aim at happiness. Perhaps, at least, all men have *reason* to aim at happiness (whatever their immediate desires). If this is so, and if it is also a necessary truth that happiness is only possible for a creature with values, then an essential part of our point will be established.

Now the term 'happiness' admits of many uses, not all of them relevant to this 'proof'. But, leaving common usage aside, we can without absurdity develop a notion of happiness that corresponds well enough to what both Kant and Aristotle had in mind, and which is also the peculiar property of rational beings. Happiness, in this sense, is a state, capable of considerable duration – even a lifetime – and indeed, doubtfully said to endure for a moment, or a day, or even a month, unless cut short by accident. In this it is to be distinguished from pleasure. Moreover, unlike pleasure, it does not have an object. There is nonetheless a sense in which happiness is directed, in that one's life and circumstances provide the reason and not just the cause for one's state. Again, happiness is unlike pleasure in that it involves the judgement that one's circumstances are intrinsically worthwhile; the happy man thinks of himself as possessing something valuable. Indeed, perfect happiness, as commonly conceived, involves the capacity to assign a positive value to all that one possesses, in particular to one's own personality and one's own state of mind. In happiness what one is is what one thinks it a good thing to be. Happiness in the sense I am considering is therefore sharply to be distinguished from those soporific states of mind – as described, for example, in Huxley's *Brave New World* – where the faculty of judgement is entirely suspended. Nor can happiness be reduced to

[21] Aristotle, op. cit., 1097b; Kant, op. cit., pp. 415–16.

the mere satisfaction of existing desires.[22] No animal can be happy on this definition, nor, as Aristotle remarked, can a child. This may sound absurd, until we reflect that by 'happiness' we wish to indicate a state at which all rational beings might aim. It clearly involves the grossest of self-deceptions for any adult to aim at that state normally described as the 'happiness' of a child, for this is a state which it makes sense to regret or yearn for, but which cannot be rationally pursued.

On this account we must I think acknowledge that there is already involved in happiness the particular kind of attitude that is expressed in moral judgement. One is seeing one's own state from outside as well as from within, and one's contentment is rendered secure by the fact that it accompanies this external vision of how things are. The totally amoral man is therefore not capable of happiness. This may seem paradoxical, but in fact it is not. For by 'totally amoral' I mean 'making no demands of a normative kind on the conduct of others' and therefore 'not seeing his own conduct in relation to any ideal or norm'. This means having no conception of what a man should be or do, only of what he is or does. (A policy of complete tolerance might perhaps lead to this paradoxical position; but of course it could then no longer be a policy.) Clearly, even Don Juan was not totally amoral in this sense. It is possible that Camus's '*étranger*' is struggling towards total amorality, but one can see him, in the novel, moving inexorably towards a kind of moping unhappiness as well.

Now we must demonstrate that every rational man has a reason to aim at this state. As a matter of fact, we could easily show that there is *a* reason to aim at this state: for it is a state in which one does not suffer through one's consciousness but on the contrary takes pleasure in consciousness. And to relate an end in this way to pleasure and suffering is to give a reason for pursuing it. This is surely a paradigm case of an objective reason, in that someone who did not recognise this fact as a reason would to that extent show that he did not understand the idea of a reason for acting. For there is a conceptual connection between pleasure and desire. To desire what is unpleasant is (other things being equal) to desire to have what one will not desire to keep: not a contradiction exactly, but a paradigm case of practical irrationality. This, indeed, is the nearest equivalent in practical reason to the notion of 'inconsistency', which modern philosophers (notably Hare) have attempted to exalt into a universal criterion for irrationality of whatever kind.

[22] A point worth emphasising against the crasser kinds of Utilitarianism, particularly those that lean on the Theory of Preference.

But it is not enough to show that there is *a* reason for pursuing happiness. For there is a similar reason for pursuing the empty satisfactions of *Brave New World*, or the pleasures of animal appetite. Clearly, then, we must show that a man has a reason not only for pursuing happiness, but also for preferring it to all its unreal or ephemeral substitutes. My instinct is to believe that we can in principle show that this is so, although I am very unsure how the argument should proceed. It seems to me, first, that we should distinguish two different ways in which we might argue for the conclusion that all men have a reason to aim at happiness rather than, say, merely physical pleasure. First, empirically, and secondly, by some form of *a priori* reasoning. I take it that only the second of these is of interest to us. In other words, while we could attempt to persuade the evil man that circumstances are such that it would be better for him should he pursue happiness rather than pleasure, we would be weakening the argument: the idea of a fully objective reason would cease to gain support from it.

Can we argue *a priori* to our conclusion? Here is a suggestion. Suppose that we pursue some pleasure or satisfaction to which we attach no value, something that we merely desire. Having obtained this thing, what satisfaction will remain to us? We cannot reflect on what we have done and be satisfied with it, without engaging in the kind of reasoning characteristic of the happy man. Therefore, either we must enter a state of quiescence, in which neither pleasure nor pain predominates, or else we must embark again on the pursuit of another object: some further pleasure of the same or a different kind. If it is of a different kind, then our state is like that of the animal, drawn now to this thing, now to that. I cannot *now* form the decision to aim at that state, since, involving as it does no particular object of desire, it gives me nothing coherent at which to aim. Hence, if my policy is, now, to adopt this kind of satisfaction as my aim, I must have an idea of the kind of thing I shall bring myself to desire – a drug, say, sleep, food, or sensual pleasure. Since this is my aim I must desire it 'infinitely': my desire will never be absolutely satisfied; it can only cease.[23] How, then, can I picture to myself this state as desirable? In what does my satisfaction with such a state consist? Such a state seems no more desirable than the state of the neurotic, who not only desires always to wash his hands but also has the means to fulfil his desire constantly available.

There has scarcely been a moralist who has not in some such manner argued that happiness is the aim of all rational beings. It

---

[23] Aquinas: *Summa Theologica*, Ia 2ae 30, 4.

is no part of my purpose here to elaborate on the argument, even if I could. I only wish to remark that, if we can get this far, and show that every rational agent has a reason for aiming at happiness rather than the other ends that might conflict with it, then we ought to be able to go one step further and show that it is no longer an open question what a man may value. For if a man must have values, then he will value some things rather than others. The description I gave of a normative attitude is already sufficiently rich to lay severe restrictions on its object. Just as there are only some things that a man can rationally fear, so then are there only some things that a man can rationally value. All men will therefore have reason to value precisely those things.

It is important to recognise that the theory of moral reason that I have sketched may be defended against a certain popular objection. The Kantian will say that morality, as I have described it, is something 'impure', a self-congratulatory activity engaged in for selfish reasons. This objection is confused on at least three accounts. First, the action done *from* a moral attitude is not done for the reasons (whatever they may be) that are given *for* that moral attitude. The parallel with the case of friendship is exact. We have reasons for aiming at a certain state of mind involving the choice of an end, but these reasons cannot be reinterpreted as reasons *for* that end when it is chosen. Secondly, happiness is not related to the exercise of morality as end to means. Happiness is a form of satisfaction *in* the exercise of morality, and cannot be described independently. Morality is therefore a part of happiness, and not a means to it. Thirdly, it follows from this that the kind of reasons given for an end will not be reasons which can be assimilated to the means/ends paradigm. Rather, they will be addressed directly to the rational imagination. They will begin from the question: 'Imagine yourself in this situation; how would you, and how must you, then feel about your life and circumstances?' Without imagination no man can answer such a question: perhaps it follows that, without imagination, no man will see that he has reason to be good.

But this is the point at which I wish to leave the argument. I have tried to show what is meant by objectivity in morals, and also to indicate the logical space in which the answer to moral scepticism must be found. The rest is the task of philosophical psychology: in particular, of the theory of attitude and choice. Here I have only wished to suggest that the notion of happiness will have an important part to play in any answer that we may arrive at.

Finally, I should like to mention two points that might encourage the conviction that it is not after all impossible to prove the objectivity of morals. First, it is not necessary that we should prove objectivity in the strong sense of giving a *procedure* for deciding of any action whether or not it should be done. This is a question that only poses itself for the man with a moral sense, the man with values, as we say. It is sufficient if we can show, for example, that it is rational to admire certain traits of character and rational to despise certain others. For if we can show this, then there is no longer properly speaking any 'free choice' of values, and the decision what to do will never be arbitrary or unfounded. Secondly, it must be remembered that no practical reason can be conclusive: all practical reasons are *prima facie* reasons. The most we can ever say is that you have a reason to pursue *x* rather than *y*, other things being equal; 'other things' being precisely those factors that have not yet been brought into question. For it does not make sense to speak of a conclusive practical reason. Conclusiveness is a property of proof: a proof is conclusive if its premises entail its conclusion, and entailment is a semantic relation, subordinate to the concept of truth. Conclusiveness belongs, therefore, to theoretical and not to practical reason. But this should not be regarded as a weakness in practical reason. On the contrary, it is its strength. For if one reason does not convince the evil man, then we know that there will always be others, and the search for them need never be abandoned as hopeless.

9

NEEDS, DESIRES AND MORAL TURPITUDE

Richard Wollheim

1. Need and Desire have obvious affinities. In this lecture I shall consider how they are to be distinguished, and how they may be confused: distinguished, that is, within philosophy, and confused in life itself. I shall then consider, very briefly, how this possibility of confusion bears upon morality and moral assessment.

2. To understand Need let us begin by looking at the phenomenon in a very simple form.

We say of a plant that it needs water or a heavier soil. We say this – we must do so in the second case, though we don't have to in the first – of a particular plant and because of its present condition. We are talking, in other words, of an occurrent need. In addition to occurrent needs there are also standing or dispositional needs. The two kinds of need are closely related, but in this lecture I shall confine myself to occurrent needs.

When we assign an (occurrent) need to a plant we presuppose two cycles. One runs from the plant's lacking something or other – say x – to its having x. The other runs from the plant's ailing in a certain respect – say r – to its recovering in r. The two cycles are related thus: The event in which the first cycle originates (the plant's lacking x) initiates the second cycle, so it ails in r, and the event on which the first cycle terminates (the plant's having x) closes the second cycle, so it recovers in r. In assigning the need for x to the plant we are situating it somewhere in the first cycle,[1] and should it reach the end of that cycle we shall say that its need is satisfied.

[1] The first, though not necessarily the second. For, if there is a time-lag between the plant's lacking x and this taking effect, it will for this period need x but not ail.

On these, the conditions for the plant's needing x, some observations: The first, which will prove the most significant as far as need generally is concerned, is that need presupposes a norm. This is so because the second cycle presupposes a norm in that to ail and to recover is to fall away from, then to return to, a standard of well-being. And note – this is my next observation – it is essential to need as I understand it that recovery – recovery, that is, in the relevant respect – should be possible. If it isn't, then we cannot assign to the plant a need: unless, of course, there is some further respect in which it ails and in which it can recover, for this might give rise to a need. However, in talking of the possibility of recovery, I do not require that the plant should actually recover when it has what it needs. For recovery in this respect may depend on recovery in some other respect, and, if this for some reason or other is not forthcoming, the plant will continue to ail in the original respect. Thirdly, the terms 'lack' and 'have' are used in a very skeletal sense; in that they take on substance according to the kind of thing that is needed. In having water and in having a heavier soil a plant will stand very differently to what it has. And it can lack something that it never had.[2] One advantage of using 'lack' and 'have' skeletally is that the conditions of need can be stated with great generality. Another advantage is that it reflects what is surely an epistemological fact: that in ascribing a need to a plant we do not necessarily know how the plant must be brought into contact with that which it lacks if its need for this is to be satisfied.

My final observation is intended to meet a possible objection. I have characterised the object of the plant's need as indifferently that which the plant initially lacks, so that it ails, and that which (with good fortune) it ultimately has, with the consequence that it recovers. But this, an objection might run, assumes an identity between the two which in point of fact does not always hold: nor do we in ascribing a need have to presuppose that it does. The object of need is properly characterised just as that whose possession brings about the plant's recovery: and any reference to that whose lack brought about its ailing drops out of the analysis of need. Although, of course, where that whose lack caused the plant to ail happens to

[2] This might be thought to produce a difficulty for conceiving of the relations between the two cycles along the lines I have suggested. For where the plant never had x, it did not have x even before its ailing in r was initiated. How then can its lack of x be said to have initiated its ailing in r? But in changing circumstances a lack not previously operative can become operative. A man may lose his job because of lack of education though he was just as uneducated when he held it.

be the same as that whose possession causes it to recover, then this is indeed the object of need *but not under that description*.[3]

We can readily see the kind of case that this objection has in mind: A plant has been placed in too light a soil. Lacking a heavier soil it ails. Ailing it undergoes certain internal changes which mean that, if it were not transplanted, it would die. However, a treatment has recently been devised, not involving a change of soil, which, if adopted, would produce recovery in the plant. In this kind of case, should we not say that what the plant needs is this treatment, and is not reference to a heavier soil quite out of place? Well, to this the initial response is obvious: that is, that, for all that has been said, there may be an underlying description, in chemical or physical terms, under which both the heavier soil and the treatment can be brought so that the object of need can then be identified through it, through this description. There may be. But there may be cases – some – where no such thing holds. What are we to say in such cases?

Now I maintain that, in those cases where the identity of that whose lack brings about the plant's ailing in a certain respect and that whose possession brings about its recovery in that respect does not hold, we should still insist on some significant relation holding between them before we are entitled to say that the latter is the object of the plant's need. We should, as a minimum, think of the treatment as a substitute for the heavier soil before we say that what the plant needs is the treatment. And to say that one thing is a substitute for another requires independent empirical support over and above the fact that the two have a common causal efficacy. My reason for insisting on some such relation holding between the two is this: If we do not, and if, without further reservation, we allow that, if the treatment brings about the plant's recovery in the relevant respect, it is what the plant needs, then we have lost an important distinction. We have lost the distinction between, on the one hand, the satisfaction of a need and, on the other hand, the removal or alleviation of it. Once a plant ails in a certain respect and hence needs something, there are ways in which it might recover – recover, I mean, in that respect – and yet its need go unsatisfied. If its need is to be satisfied, this, I maintain, can be only if it recovers through having either that whose lack brought about its ailing or some substitute for this.

If this is so, then it follows that even in those cases where the object of the plant's need is not that whose lack brought about its ailing

---

[3] I have been led to take this objection seriously by Mr Mendel Kramer.

but is rather that whose possession brings about its recovery, it is not the object of need solely in virtue of this fact: nor can all reference to that whose lack brought about the plant's ailing be allowed to drop out of the picture: and for the same reason. And that is because not every recovery is due to the satisfaction of a need, and to discriminate we need to refer to the cause of the ailment.

3. And now I should like to look at the phenomenon of Need in a somewhat more complex form.

We say of an animal that it needs water or sexual activity. To what extent do the conditions that I have proposed for a plant's needing something or other apply here? Are the animal's needs to be understood in terms of two cycles one of which is dependent from the other?

Some philosophers have answered No. They have argued that something must be put into the account of the animal's needs which is not required to account for the plant's needs, and, when this something is put in, there is no longer any use for what made up the original account. This something is behaviour. In assigning some (occurrent) need to an animal we presuppose a behaviour-cycle which has two characteristics both of which are 'behavioural' or in a crude sense observable. The first characteristic it shares with all behaviour-cycles expressive of need, and consists in what might generally be called 'activity under stress'. The second characteristic it shares with those behaviour-cycles expressive of the same need. and consists in its terminating on a certain result, i.e. the animal's having something or other – say x. In assigning the need for x to the animal we are situating it somewhere in such a cycle. This account of the animal's need I shall call the behaviourist account.[4]

Now the obvious difficulty that such an account faces is that a need can go unsatisfied or its pursuit be interrupted. A dog in need of sexual activity falls asleep, or in following a bitch across the road it is frightened by a passing car and for a while its ardour flags. In both cases the last event in the behaviour-cycle as we have it – sleep in the one case, terror in the other – is evidently unreliable as to what the animal needs. But this, it might be thought, is because we haven't distinguished some event which happens to terminate the

---

[4] The account I shall consider has some resemblance to, though it is in no way modelled upon, the analysis of desire given in Bertrand Russell, *The Analysis of Mind* (London, 1921) chap. III. Russell's analysis has been criticised in Anthony Kenny, *Action, Emotion, and Will* (London, 1963) and David Pears, 'Russell's Theory of Desire' to be published in *Russell in Review* (Toronto, 1974).

behaviour-cycle from that event on which the behaviour-cycle terminates; and an obvious suggestion for making this distinction is by reference to some such supposition as 'when the behaviour-cycle would stop/would have stopped, if...': where 'stop' is a deliberately neutral term between 'terminate' and 'be terminated', and the conditional makes reference to the absence of interference, interruption, inhibition, etc. But such a supposition, which in effect is about the natural course of the behaviour-cycle, only requires explicitly what is anyhow an implicit requirement of the behaviourist account: that there should be a criterion of identity for a behaviour-cycle. For without such a criterion how could we ever think of a fresh piece of behaviour as being, either actually or hypothetically, the continuation or resumption of a given behaviour-cycle – as opposed, that is, to the start of a new one? Yet, if the behaviourist account is to hold up, this is what at times we must be able to think.

However, the kind of supposition to which I have referred not only requires that there should be a criterion of identity for a behaviour-cycle, it also places a constraint upon the form that this criterion must take. The criterion must be backward-looking rather than forward-looking. For, if it were forward-looking how could it do what we ask of it – that is, distinguish between the true and the false end of the behaviour-cycle? Now, it might be argued that, even before this point, the behaviourist account of an animal's need has had to abandon its distinctive claim: the claim, that is, to give a total account of need in terms of behaviour or, more specifically, of behavioural characteristics. For in supposing that a behaviour-cycle would continue in such-and-such a way – that it would, for instance, adapt to certain obstacles – are we not, the argument would run, presupposing some internal factor which would explain its constancy?[5] But whether this is so or not, by the time we have introduced into the behaviourist account a backward-looking criterion for the identity of a behaviour-cycle its original claim has lapsed. For a backward-looking criterion will necessarily look to the initiating event of the behaviour-cycle, and, since that cannot be equated, for obvious reasons, with a piece of behaviour nor, for less obvious but well-rehearsed reasons, with an external stimulus,[6] it must be an internal event. So to account for the animal's need we

[5] Cf. David Armstrong, *A Materialist Theory of the Mind* (London, 1968) chaps 5 and 6.

[6] See e.g. Noam Chomsky, 'A Review of B. F. Skinner's *Verbal Behaviour*' reprinted in *The Structure of Language*, ed. Jerry A. Fodor and Jerrold J. Katz (Englefield Cliffs, N.J., 1963), and Charles Taylor, *The Explanation of Behaviour* (London, 1964) *passim*.

must go outside the behaviour-cycle or, more precisely, outside its purely behavioural characteristics.

What we have now to ask is what kind of internal event it is that characteristically initiates a behaviour-cycle that is expressive of need. And to this the most plausible answer would appear to be: The animal's lacking something where this leads to its ailing. I shan't argue for this, if only because of the absence of anything obvious to argue against: though later we shall have the opportunity of considering an alternative answer. If, however, I am right in my suggestion, and if an account of an animal's need that aims at completeness should include within itself what is in effect the first half of the account I proposed for the plant's need, should we stop there? Or ought we now to go on and introduce the rest of that account?

I shall argue that we ought to.

To find the criterion of identity for a behaviour-cycle in its initiating event means that for any given behaviour-cycle it is those and only those pieces of behaviour which are causally dependent, directly or indirectly, on the initiating event that belong to it. If, however, this criterion is to do what we expect of it – that is, to allow us to distinguish between the true and the false end of a behaviour-cycle, or, as I have put it, to plot the natural course of the behaviour-cycle – then we must be able to determine when the causal efficacy of the initiating event has been spent. How are we to do this?

One way which suggests itself would be to think that the causal efficacy of the initiating event has been spent when and only when the animal recovers in that respect in which as a consequence of the initiating event it ailed. Now, this would certainly have the effect of allowing us to set aside as false ends certain events on which the behaviour-cycle might stop: for instance, when the dog falls asleep or is momentarily terrified. But there are other events, which are also false ends but which we have no reason for setting aside so long as we attend exclusively to whether the animal recovers in a certain respect or not: for instance, the animal's being effectively distracted or sedated. The problem is, in other words, that which we encountered in the case of the plant's need once we felt it necessary to distinguish between cases where the plant's need is removed or alleviated and those where it is satisfied. Nor is the congruence between the two problems fortuitous. For it is surely reasonable to think that the causal efficacy of the initiating event of the animal's behaviour-cycle is spent when the animal's need is satisfied but remains unspent so long as the need is merely alleviated or removed.

Or to put it slightly differently: If we are to determine when the causal efficacy of the initiating event is spent, where this in turn is equated with the true end of the behaviour-cycle or the event on which it terminates, we should pay attention not just to how the animal ailed and whether it has recovered but also to how it has recovered. And here my suggestion would be that it is only if the animal recovers through having either that whose lack constituted the initiating event or some substitute for it, that we should think that the behaviour-cycle has terminated, that the efficacy of the initiating event is spent, and that the animal's need is satisfied. And this, of course, amounts to introducing into the account of the animal's need the whole of the account that I proposed for the plant's need.

At this stage, when the behaviourist account is in shreds, it is worth asking whether any of these shreds are worth preserving. Distinctively the behaviourist account tried to explain the animal's need exclusively in terms of behaviour, and it took a forward-looking view of that behaviour. There are, therefore, two questions that might be raised. The first question is, Granted that the animal's need does not consist in its behaviour, is the behaviour an essential part of its need or is it merely contingently associated with it? The second question is, Granted that the forward-looking view of behaviour does not by itself give us insight into the nature of the animal's need, how is it that it nevertheless seems to give us some vision of it?

On the second question the happy dispensation by which, other things being equal, the forward-looking view of behaviour will allow us to see what it is that the animal needs rests on the fact, just considered, that the event on which the behaviour-cycle terminates matches the event that initiates it. We may discover that a dog was in need of water by observing its drinking water because its drinking water matches the initial dehydration. But since the behaviour-cycle may be terminated short of the event on which it terminates, other things are not always equal, and then the forward-looking view shows us nothing. And when the forward-looking view does coincide with the backward-looking view, the backward-looking takes priority: for it is only when we have looked back that we know what to look forward to, it is only when we have identified the initiating event of the behaviour-cycle that we can recognize as such the event on which it terminates.

As to the first question, whether the behaviour is even part of the need, there is the preliminary difficulty, remarked on by philosophers of very different persuasions, of how to effect, with any conviction, the analytic-synthetic distinction within the domain of mental phenomena. That aside, I think that the problem becomes more accessible if we again increase the complexity of the form in which we consider the phenomenon of need.

4. In order to look at the phenomenon of Need in a yet more complex form, I shall make a further move up the evolutionary scale.

A man goes to his doctor for a check-up. His doctor observes to him that his condition is not good, and that this is so because of the poor quality of his diet. He lacks vitamins, and that is why he ails. The man is in the habit of believing his doctor, who is generally right, and is so on this occasion too. When he leaves the doctor, the man goes to the chemist, buys some vitamin tablets, takes them regularly, and after a few weeks he is much better. The doctor is satisfied with his recovery, and the man is pleased about his doctor's satisfaction.

Now here we have a fairly elaborate and sustained piece of behaviour. It is evidently connected with the man's need. It plays a very significant part in the satisfaction of the need. Yet there is, it seems to me, no temptation to think of the behaviour as part of, or essential to, the need.

Compare this case with another: A man lacks water and ails. He sets himself to get some water. He goes downstairs, goes to the tap, draws some water and drinks it. He recovers. He goes back upstairs and resumes whatever he was doing. The man needed water, and there seems to me to be very good reason for thinking that the man's behaviour, up to the point at which he drinks the water and recovers, is part of, or is essential to, his needing the water. For instance, I think that our understanding of what it is for a man to need water would be very different if we did not, in thinking of it, think of such behaviour. No such consideration holds in the case of the man's need for vitamins.

If we want to bring the two cases into line, so that the relevant differences will show up, we must insert into the description of the second case something which obviously belongs there and which I have omitted just because of its obviousness: a belief. The man goes downstairs in search of water because he believes that he needs water, and this belief remains with him until he drinks the water he has drawn. If we now set the two cases side by side, what leads us to think that in the second case the behaviour is, but in the first case it isn't, part of the need comes into focus. It is the significant difference in the relationship between the belief in which the behaviour originates and what is needed. The man who believes that he needs vitamins does not (or so it would appear) believe this because he needs vitamins, whereas the man who believes that he needs water does believe this because he needs water.[7]

Whether in these two cases the difference in relationship between the belief about the need and the need is actually such as to justify our thinking that in one case the behaviour is, in the other case it isn't, part of the need is a question with whose detail I shan't engage. But if I am right on the principle of the matter, something reasonably significant has emerged. What has emerged is that whether the behaviour is or isn't part of the need depends on whether something larger than the behaviour, and of which the behaviour is part, is itself part of the need. This something larger contains a belief, and whether it, the something larger, is part of the need, depends on the belief, or more precisely some feature of that belief. In other words, the question whether the behaviour-cycle is part of the need has become the question whether a further cycle of which it is only a segment is part of the need: and this further cycle I shall call, on account of the key role that the belief plays both in it and in its relationship to the need, 'the psychological cycle'.

I have another reason for doing so: in order to bring out an important transformation in the argument. We are now considering whether a very modified behaviourist account of need has anything to be said for it. In its original form the behaviourist account was a total account in that it tried to explain need exclusively in terms of behaviour – indeed exclusively in terms of the behavioural characteristics of behaviour. Such an account notoriously challenged the status of need as a psychological phenomenon. In its present modified form the behaviourist account is a fragmentary account, in that all that it claims is that behaviour has some role to play in the explanation or analysis of need. If, however, we look more closely at what this role is, it appears that, if the account is true, so far from depriving need of psychological status, it ensures it just such a status. Indeed, unless some such account is true, it is hard to see how need could be regarded as a psychological phenomenon. For what the modified behaviourist account guarantees is that the beliefs that we have about our needs need not be externally acquired: we have, in other words, the possibility of direct knowledge of them. It is to

[7] The man who needs water might not believe that he needs it. He might simply desire it, or to have it, and be aware of this. I am not here concerned with such a case. Hidé Ishiguro has pointed out to me the need for making this distinction, though she has argued – and here I would not agree with her – that the man who believes that he needs water is in much the same situation as the man who believes that he needs vitamins.

bring out this new turn to the argument that I have used the phrase 'psychological cycle' to describe that cycle to which the behaviour-cycle belongs if it, the behaviour-cycle, belongs to the need.

If, however, it is true that sometimes there is and sometimes there isn't a psychological cycle as part of the need, so that in some cases need is, and in other cases need isn't, a psychological phenomenon, is this not – philosophically at any rate – quite unsatisfactory? What is the rationale to such a 'mixed' phenomenon? If the situation is to be accounted for, perhaps a solution is to be sought along the following lines: that needs that are psychological, or to which the psychological cycle is essential, are themselves essential to the phenomenon of need as a whole. I want to suggest that something of this sort is so, but to do so I must bring into the foreground a feature of need about which I have so far said nothing except that it is important: namely, that need presupposes a norm.

Now the norm of well-being, as I have called it, is a very complex affair: complex both in its content and in its origins, in what it collects and in how it collects it. The norm will in part rest on physical or neuro-physiological considerations: in part it will rest on social or what are called cultural considerations. What we think we need will depend on our body, on our ideology, on the technology of our society, on the prevailing expectations of life and death. Estimates will diverge about the relative influence that these considerations have in the formation and constitution of the norm. However, no account or explanation of the norm exclusively in terms of these factors, or other such, would be adequate for what we must also attend to is the peculiar effect exercised upon us by those beliefs which we have about our needs and which we have because of our needs. These beliefs, I want to suggest, exercise a threefold effect upon the norm.

In the first place, they permit us some knowledge of the norm: or – to put it in less objectivist language – they contribute to the formation of the norm. Initially this might seem surprising: for if our beliefs about our needs presuppose a norm, how can they establish, or help to establish, the norm? To which the answer is, By the fact that they presuppose it. So: A man believes that he needs *x*. If his belief is true, he lacks *x* and he ails because he lacks *x*. If he ails because he lacks *x*, then there must be some norm that he falls away from in virtue of lacking *x*, but, until he lacked *x* and in consequence ailed, he might have had no sense that this is how the norm was: that it made him vulnerable in this respect. Consider, for instance, a man who had led a hard life and taken risks throughout it: when his children desert him, he feels the need for their affection, or for affection itself: and so he comes to realise how emotional security is part of well-being. How solitude, or excitement, or achievement are, for us, parts of well-being are things often learnt in this way.

Now, in principle any beliefs we have about our needs could be in this way informative: we could learn from them something about the norm of well-being. But there is good reason to think that those beliefs which we have about our needs and which we have because of our needs – rather than, say, because of what we have been told or of what we have read in books – are more likely to be a source of information about the norm. For in the case of those beliefs which come from outside, it would seem to be unlikely that we would ever subscribe to them unless we already conceived the norm in the way in which they presuppose. To this there are, of course, exceptions, so I talk only of likelihood.

Secondly, beliefs which we have about our needs and which we have because of our needs bear upon the norm that they presuppose in this way: that it is very largely because of them that the norm of well-being has the significance in our lives that it has. It is possible to overlook this. It is possible, for instance, to think that the physical or neuro-physiological considerations by themselves would be adequate to establish the significance that the norm of well-being has in our lives. We care about our needs, because they are the needs of our body. But reflection upon the fact of death and our pervasive acceptance of death should suffice to dispel this thought. Indeed, to appreciate the point that I am making, ultimately on behalf of psychological needs and what they do for need, we have only to consider a world in which our beliefs about our needs, all of them, would come from outside. In such a world we would come to learn of our needs, as we now come to learn of the distant past, as though from libraries rather than experience.

Thirdly – and this is related – those beliefs which we have about our needs and which we have because of our needs have a great part to play in determining the significance we attach not (this time) to the norm as such, but to this as opposed to that aspect of it: or, to put it more simply, they have a great part to play in our relative assessment of our needs.

Now, if I am right about this threefold effect that psychological needs exercise upon the norm of well-being – that they give us some knowledge of it, that they give us a sense of its significance, and that they allow us to make comparative judgements about its different aspects – then, I think, the claim would be established that psychological needs are essential to the phenomenon of need itself. For I think that our concept of need would be very different if we did not have what I shall summarily call an internal access to need. And, if in the course of following my argument, or of working out its implications for particular cases, you have come to think that the line between, on the one hand, those beliefs which we have about our needs and which we have because of our needs and, on the other hand, those beliefs which we have about our needs and which arise otherwise, or (the same thing) between psychological and non-psychological needs, is not all that sharp, that conclusion is perfectly consonant with my own views and coheres, I hope, with everything that I have been saying.

5. There is a phenomenon that I must make mention of at this stage, if only to excuse myself from discussing it at adequate length. The phenomenon is bodily sensation.

The first way in which bodily sensation enters the present discussion is that I have talked so far as though the only way in which behaviour can rightly be considered part of need is through the belief in which it originates, or some feature of that belief. But is there not some kind of behaviour which we also rightly consider to be part of need which originates not in belief but in bodily sensation? Indeed would not a more realistic account of the behaviour that I have had under consideration exhibit it as partly originating in bodily sensation? And the second way in which bodily sensation enters the discussion is that it would seem to follow from what I have said so far that animals do not have psychological needs. For unless we assume animals to have not just beliefs but beliefs about their needs, there is no way, it seems, in which their behaviour can become incorporated into a psychological cycle. Or, once again, can behaviour that originates in bodily sensation be rightly considered part of a need?

I am fairly convinced that the psychological cycle can originate in bodily sensation. The view of bodily sensation to which I am anyhow inclined – that is, of bodily sensation as a form of perception – facilitates this conviction, and this seems to me a consideration in favour of that view. With what other views of bodily sensation this conviction is compatible I do not know. So let me limit myself to two observations: First, that behaviour that originates in bodily sensation should not be considered all that differently from behaviour that originates in belief; and, secondly, that any view of bodily sensation that leads us to do so is correspondingly objectionable.[8]

[8] Throughout this discussion of need I have not discussed what might loosely be called 'hypothetical' needs, e.g. the burglar's need for a jemmy, the dictator's need for a brutal police force.

6. If a man needs x, then he must lack x. If, however, he desires x, it is not necessary that he should lack x: all that is necessary is that he should believe that he lacks x. This is the first difference between Need and Desire.

If a man needs x, then he must ail. If, however, he desires x, it is not necessary that he should ail. And if he desires x, and lacks x, it is still not necessary that he should ail. This is the second difference between Need and Desire.

If a man needs x, then, when his need is satisfied, he must (other things being equal) recover. If, however, he desires x, it is not necessary that, when his desire is satisfied, he should (even if other things are equal) recover. And if a man desires x, and lacks x, and ails, it it still not necessary that, when his desire is satisfied, he should (even if other things are equal) recover. This is the third difference between Need and Desire.

So, for instance, a man might desire his daughter's love: though (like Lear) he has it but believes he hasn't it. Or he might desire his daughter's love, not having it, and still lead a contented life: it might indeed be just his happiness without her that makes it difficult for his daughter to love him. Or he might desire his daughter's love and not have it and pine for it, yet if she were to love him, it would make no difference to him: he could not accept it, or perhaps he doesn't like her. Or another man might desire fame: and he might have it and not recognise it: or he might not have it and be none the worse off for it, though he thinks of it as an agreeable addition to life: or he might be unhappy in consequence of his neglect by the world and yet, when fame reaches him, it is truly a trial. If you think that these examples in any way draw upon the pathological, they can be varied: and anyhow the fact that desire can in this way conjoin with the pathological is itself highly significant.

These differences between Need and Desire rest upon two very general features of the situation. The first is that Need involves a departure from a norm: and the second is that the object of need constitutes a remedy. Neither of these two features is paralleled within Desire. And from this an important consequence follows. If a man needs x, his need constitutes an intrinsic claim to x. To deny this claim, we would have to deny the norm, or deny that deviation from it had occurred, or deny that x would restore him to it: and if we denied any one of these things, we would be denying that the man needed x. However, if a man desires x, his desire does not constitute an intrinsic claim to x.

At this stage it might be objected that I have misrepresented the situation of the man who desires x: and that I have done so in two interrelated ways. In the first place, if a man desires x, it is necessary that he should ail. And this is so because an unsatisfied desire is a condition that falls short of the norm of well-being. Secondly, and by extension, if a man desires x, it is necessary that, when the desire is satisfied, he should, other things being equal, recover: for the condition of unsatisfied desire will then come to an end, and he should return to the norm. This, I think, is quite wrong.

At the outset it must be pointed out that, even if there is something painful or (to use the most generalised term) negative about unsatisfied desire, it does not follow from this that the man who desires x ails. For there can be painful or negative conditions that are inseparable from, or part of, well-being. So independent reasons must be found for thinking that to desire x is to ail. Are they forthcoming?

First, it is worth noting that the objection before us does not really bring need and desire into uniformity. For the man who needs x ails because he lacks x: it is his lacking x that causes him to ail. It is only in a trivial or pleonastic sense that he ails because he needs x. However, if the man who desires x ails, he ails because he desires x: it must be his desire for x that causes him to ail. So if we hold that he does indeed ail, we must hold that to desire x is in itself to depart from the norm of well-being. We must hold, for instance, that the man who desires x would be better off if he didn't desire x. And this does not seem to be obviously true: neither in the way in which it is true that the man who needs x would be better off if he didn't need x, nor in the way in which it is true that the man who needs x would be better off if he didn't lack x. If at this stage it is asserted that, of course, the man who desires x would be better off if he didn't desire x, since he would be better off if his desire for x were satisfied, it seems to me that – apart from the doubtful character of the premiss, to which I shall turn – the argument is in error. For, *pace* the Cynic, it doesn't follow from the fact that it is better to have a desire satisfied than a desire unsatisfied, that it would be better not to have desired at all. Desire may be not merely a road, but the road, to happiness.

Secondly, if we really do hold that the man who desires x in desiring x departs from the norm of well-being, we are in effect holding that just to desire – that is, to desire *no matter what* – is to depart from the norm of well-being. No further restriction upon the object of desire is stipulated. Now, it is perfectly true that in the case of need I have argued for a similar proposition: that is, that just to need, or to need no matter what, is to ail. I haven't stipulated any restriction upon the object of need before need is said to be a mode of ailing: so why should I imply that some restriction is requisite in the case of desire? And the answer is that in the case of need the requisite constraint has already operated: for in ascribing a need to someone, we have already taken account precisely of whether he ails. But in ascribing a desire to someone, there is nothing we have taken account of except that mental state itself.

Thirdly, the view that the man who desires x must ail might seem to gain support from considering what happens when he has what he desires. For then his desire is satisfied: and this, it might be thought, implies that he is satisfied – which is then taken as tantamount to a return to the norm of well-being. So previously he must have fallen short of the norm. But to say that a man's desire is satisfied and to say that he is satisfied are two very different things. The point is evident when we realise that to say the first is to say that the man has, say, x, which he once desired, whereas to say the second is to say something about the effect on him of his having x. Indeed, this last point seems to me to be a corrective not just to the view that to have an unsatisfied desire is to ail but also to the somewhat broader view that an unsatisfied desire is a painful or negative condition. For that view too gains in the minds of some a degree of support from the illicit contrast of unsatisfied desire with, not satisfied desire, but the satisfaction that satisfied desire can (but, the truth is, need not) bring in train.

If the preceding argument about desire is correct, and I have not misrepresented the situation of the man who desires x, I can return to the assertion from which the argument took off, that, whereas, if a man needs x, his need constitutes an intrinsic claim to x, if a man desires x, his desire does not constitute an intrinsic claim to x. And on this assertion two observations to clarify what I have in mind. First of all, in talking of a claim I am talking of something that a man's nature makes, or fails to make, indifferently upon himself, or his attention, and others, or their attention. For it seems to me that in facing the claims of individual human nature, in endorsing or rejecting them, in the choice between approbation and disapproval, even in the matter of tolerance itself, the issues are not radically different when raised in connection with ourselves and our needs and desires from what they are when raised in connection with others and their needs and their desires. That we seldom resolve the two types of issue consistently – that we are generally markedly more, or markedly less, indulgent to ourselves than to others – is another and deeper matter. And, secondly, in saying that a desire does not constitute the same kind of claim as a need, I am certainly not saying that it does not constitute a claim. It certainly does. It is only that the nature of the claim – that is, its content and extent – do not admit of ready-made determination. We may need to know more about the desire. For instance, we might think that we should first understand the desire, and that the real claim is made by the underlying situation. Or we might think that to do this would be precisely to go against the desire, in that the real claim it is making is that it should not be understood. Or we might think that issues of well-being or happiness must be brought in, and that we cannot respond to the desire until we know how its satisfaction would bear upon them. And there are many other possibilities.

7. I have, I hope, said enough about Needs and Desires to show that anyone who confused them – who took a desire for a need or vice versa – would be in serious error. For not only are the phenomena very different, but they have very different consequences. And in saying this I am thinking particularly of the fact that a need implies a claim of a kind that a desire does not. The question therefore arises whether there is a tendency to confuse needs and desires: and if there is, it must then be asked how this comes about.

That needs and desires are confused is surely beyond doubt. There is a whole field of political discussion, which under certain forms of cultivation has proved reasonably fruitful, where what is centrally in dispute is whether this or that satisfaction that a citizen demands or might demand from society is the satisfaction of a need or the satisfaction of a desire.[9] Since opinions are often divided, it must be assumed that at least one of the disputants is in error, and so confusion is possible. And the same kind of dispute, with the same division of opinion, can arise, we know, in private life, between, say, two persons, one of whom asks for freedom – and, according to the other, at his or her expense – for some satisfaction. Is what he wants satisfied a need, or is it a desire? Once again, one must be wrong, and so need and desire can be confused.

If this is so, how does it come about? One obvious answer, which must surely cover a number of cases, is that the disputants genuinely disagree over the facts. They disagree whether a norm is involved, or whether what is wanted relates to the individual's well-being.

[9] These issues are discussed, though in varying terminology, in, e.g., S. I. Benn and R. S. Peters, *Social Principles and the Democratic State* (London, 1959); Brian Barry, *Political Argument* (London, 1965); Herbert Marcuse, *Five Lectures* (Boston, 1970); W. G. Runciman, *Relative Deprivation and Social Justice* (London, 1972); John Rawls, *A Theory of Justice* (London, 1972); Ivan Illich, *Tools for Conviviality* (London, 1973); Joel Feinberg, *Social Philosophy* (Englefield Cliffs, N.J., 1973).

There are, however, a number of cases where that kind of explanation seems inappropriate. It may indeed be the case that the disputants, when the matter is put to them, will express different opinions on the facts, but this disagreement seems more the effect than the cause of the dispute. And there will be cases where such disagreement even at some late stage is not forthcoming: no facts are challenged.

Another answer to the question how needs and desires can be confused is that there can be confusion about the concepts themselves. By extension individuals may dispute whether a certain satisfaction is that of a need or of a desire because they have a different understanding, one from another, of these concepts. I would not want to deny that such cases can occur, but I would find it hard to believe that they are very widespread. This, however, is because of a thesis to which I subscribe but which I would not wish to assume without further argument, which time does not permit. That thesis is that concepts like need and desire are so deeply entrenched in that primitive psychological theory which we use to make ourselves comprehensible to ourselves, and others to us, that it is reasonable to suppose that, at least within a given culture, there is general agreement upon them. Nevertheless I think that even without this assumption it would be implausible to hold that all the remaining cases of confusion between need and desire can be put down to conceptual confusion.

And now I want to suggest another explanation and that is that the confusion is motivated, and the motive I have in mind is just that which might arise from consideration of, or reflection upon, the very different consequences (as I have called them) that the two phenomena have. In other words, we have a good motive for confusing needs and desires in the fact that we can thereby assert, alternatively deny, the kind of claim that a need implies and a desire doesn't. The most obvious way in which this motive would manifest itself would be, in regard to others, to misrepresent their needs as desires, and, in regard to ourselves, to misrepresent our desires as needs. Though this is clearly not the only, nor the only significant, way in which it may make itself felt.

However, this suggestion may seem to offer an explanation of how needs and desires can come to be confused only on the most superficial understanding of that phenomenon, unless something which is quite integral to the suggestion is kept in mind. I have already said that the claims made by a man's nature – made, that is, by his needs and desires – are claims that are just as much upon his attention as upon that of others. And in suggesting that a man might be motivated to confuse needs and desires so as to alter the existing balance of claims, I had thought of *him* as being amongst the first to accept the new claims. Or to put it another way: The misrepresentations of need and desire to which he is impelled are, amongst other things, ways in which he misrepresents certain needs and certain desires *to himself*. When we consider this in the specific context of his own needs and desires we have a phenomenon of an interesting but neglected kind. The phenomenon is that whereby a man represents his desires to himself as needs with the aim of getting them thought of – perhaps above all by himself – as having claims to satisfaction to which they are not in fact entitled. The phenomenon is subtly recorded in the many ways in which we talk of our most pressing desires in language appropriated from need. We feel naked and exposed without the love that we demand: we have to discharge the energy which otherwise remains pent up inside us: we thirst for excitement. For this confusion of need and desire I have coined the term 'moral turpitude', and it was not because I hoped to examine the phenomenon but because I wanted to draw attention to the kind of phenomenon to which it belongs that I incorporated the phrase in the title of this lecture. If I had to characterise the kind of phenomenon summarily I would say that, in the first place, it consists in the internal employment of a strategy, and, secondly, in the employment of this strategy there is a characteristic exercise of a virtue or a vice.

To the idea of such a phenomenon a number of objections might be raised. For instance, it might seem to some inappropriate to think of strategy in connection with our inner relations: the argument being that to think of strategy implies a measure of freedom or will that we are wrong to presuppose in this domain. My feeling would be that, if we are ever right to presuppose will, it is just in this domain that we may. Doubts that we may legitimately hold about the operation of will in our relations with others come in large part, I would think, from reflection upon the dubious and tangled outcome of these inner relations.[10] And again – and the two points are related – to the objection that, even if we accept such internal strategy, we should not consider it as subject to moral appraisal, I would feel that here, if anywhere, the virtues and vices have an undisputed application. Certainly the moral life rests on these transactions and, if they cannot be reclaimed for moral scrutiny, that life remains unexamined at its core. As it does in so much contemporary moral philosophy.

[10] If by any chance it is not already clear, I have not thought of the confusions and misrepresentations I have been talking about, nor (more generally) of internal strategy, as restricted to *conscious* mental activity.

10

MY ROLE AND ITS DUTIES[1]

Martin Hollis

RECIPES for the Good Society used to run, in caricature, something like this:

1. Take about 2000 *hom. sap.*, analyse each into essence and accidents and discard the accidents.
2. Place essences in a large casserole, add socialising syrup and stew until conflict disappears.
3. Serve with a pinch of salt.

Such recipes have produced many classic dishes in political theory, the exact ingredients varying with the chef. In particular the magic formula for the socialising syrup varies with the analysis of human nature. For instance, if men are essentially greedy egoists in pursuit of riches, fame and honour, then the syrup will be a blend of fear and reward for co-operation. If men are by nature rational and sympathetic, they need only to be stewed in Enlightened education. If men are crucially sinful children of God, then the syrup will be distilled, at any rate by a conservative chef, from notions like authority, law, tradition and property, and tinged with a dash of anti-intellectualism. Ingredients vary but the recipe always presumes an essential human nature. The idea that political cookery is wholly an empirical, rule-of-thumb business is a fairly recent one and traditional chefs would certainly retort that Michael Oakeshott, for example, cannot cook. I hope this paper may lend some power to their elbows.

In denying that there is any essential human nature, the modern

[1] My warm thanks are due to Alan Dawe, Bryan Heading and Quentin Skinner for many helpful comments on an earlier draft and discussions of the issues involved.

social theorist often has two main objections in mind. One is that societies are not molecular compounds of pre-social, individual atoms; the other that facts about human behaviour imply nothing about the Good Society. I shall try to show that neither objection has the intended force, since a belief in essential human natures does not imply a pre-social atomism; since any social theory rests on assumptions about human nature; and since those assumptions cannot be ethically neutral – hence the gesture in my title to Bradley's famous white elephant, now almost a century old and still an embarrassment.[2]

The paper will not proceed, however, by full frontal assault in support of Bradley and demands no rush to borrow his *Ethical Studies*. 'My Station' has yielded to 'My Role' and ethics are not the prime concern. This is a paper about the self and the explanation of social action in terms of Role, with only a final salute to Virtue. It will be in four parts. In the first I shall rehearse a broad but familiar distinction between passive and active conceptions of human nature and undertake to show that they do not form a continuum. In the second the notion of Role will be translated from the stage into each conception, with different results. In the third 'normative' explanation (or the explanation of social action in terms of the requirements of roles) will be argued to stand to active conceptions of man as causal explanation stands to passive conceptions. Finally a hesitant thesis will be proposed that the free man is the man who chooses a set of consistent roles and plays them rationally, the Good Society being one where the social self can be free. The scope of the essay is thus absurdly ambitious but, in echo of Montaigne, 'all I say is by way of discourse and nothing by way of advice. I should not speak so boldly, if it were my duty to be believed.' I shall be content if I can make the notion of Role do some work for once.

I

Passive and active conceptions of man are both to be found in the amorphous thought of the Enlightenment, which has so shaped modern social theory. The root idea is that the laws of human nature can be harnessed to produce a society which satisfies human nature. It is instructively ambivalent. It presumes first that there are indeed, in Hume's phrase, 'constant and universal principles of human nature' (*Enquiries* VIII), second that social engineers have a power of initiative, apparently transcending these constant and

[2] F. H. Bradley, 'My Station and Its Duties' in his *Ethical Studies* (Oxford, 1876; O.U.P. paperback, 1962) chap. v.

universal principles, and thirdly that human nature is constant
enough to yield a criterion of progress yet mutable enough to satisfy
it. In other words human nature is sometimes taken as passive and
sometimes as active and these perspectives, I shall claim, are not
complementary but conflicting.[3]

Talk of 'constant and universal principles of human nature'
suggests that we are natural creatures in a rational world of cause
and effect. This has become a dominant theme in social science, with
the implication that we are at most more complex than other natural
objects. 'Man is not fashioned out of a more precious clay; Nature
has used only one and the same dough in which she has merely varied
the leaven', as La Mettrie put it in *L'Homme Machine*. Human
beings are essentially programmed creatures and their output is a
function of their input, with or without the intervention of whatever lies between, itself presumably in any case the product of earlier
inputs and its own feedback. Programmed creatures can be manipulated by selecting the input or adjusting the programme – hence
the talk of social engineering. Since the conception is far too
familiar to need any introduction, it will be enough simply to dub
the organism it portrays Plastic Man.

Plastic Man has many variants and I impute no simple-minded-
ness to his proponents. He has been proposed in very different terms
by sociologists, psychologists, biochemists and others and I am
making no claim about the likeliest starting point. In general Plastic
Man is the work of social structure and inner programming and the
spectrum of variants from social to individual concerns their relative
standing. If the programming results from the socialisation of very
raw material, then sociology is queen of the social sciences; if social
institutions are formed in response to the group behaviour of men
with individual and identifiable drives and dispositions, then psychology or biology is a likelier candidate; if structure and programming

---

[3] That there are two perspectives is a commonplace of sociology. In a
large literature I have found Alan Dawe, 'The Two Sociologies' (*British
Journal of Sociology*, 1970; reprinted in *Sociological Perspectives*, Penguin
in association with the Open University Press, 1971), especially lucid and
suggestive. The perspectives are the passive and the active, not to be confused with another celebrated dispute between *homo sociologicus* and *homo
psychologicus*, which usually occurs within the passive conception and is,
in any case, a separate question. Debate between passive and active is also
familiar in philosophy, where it usually takes more oblique forms – what
the mind itself contributes to the interpretation of experience, for instance,
or whether action needs its own canons of explanation. In tracing both
conceptions to the Enlightenment, my aim is schematic rather than historical and I am not doubting the influence of later conservative thinkers on
the passive conception nor of romantics on the active.

are both explanatory, then we await the higher synthesis which will mark out the scope of each science. At present the full spectrum is open and I make no rash attempt to close it.

There is point nonetheless in using the single label of Plastic Man. Passive conceptions of man are deterministic and naturalistic. They are deterministic in that the only scientific explanation of human behaviour countenanced is in terms of causal laws. (This is less committal than it sounds, since it leaves the analysis of 'causal law' open. Laws may be construed, with hard determinism, as logically or mechanically necessary or it may be thought enough, with soft determinism, that they be regular in some Humean sense. Equally there is room for teleological explanation, provided that other goal-directed systems like mice and machines are also similarly explicable and provided there is always a causal explanation of any teleological system taken as a whole.) They are naturalistic in that, in principle, explanation continues for ever and in the same mode. There is no reason in nature to halt a chain of explanation at any point – the scientist's interests may be selective, his life short and his understanding finite but nature is a total system without internal boundaries or *ceteris paribus* clauses. Natural and social sciences attack the same one world. They do not differ in method of validation. Human agency is a natural and determined phenomenon and does not provide, in Leibniz's phrase, 'a necessary being with which we can stop'.

Consequently the gamut of variants of Plastic Man includes only a thin kind of individualism. The 'individual' is unique merely in so far as he is the only instance of the intersection of a complex of laws. (As with any other natural phenomenon, there may be a random element too; but what is random is to that extent inexplicable and there is no source of individuality here.) His identity is thrust upon him by contact with a central value system, induction into socio-economic relationships, his drives and dispositions, the mechanics of his unconscious or genetic programming. Psychology too is a generalising subject and the instincts of *homo psychologicus* are no more nuggets of selfhood than are the marginal differentiations of *homo sociologicus*. The difference between numerical and qualitative identity (except perhaps as it applies to physical bodies) is one of degree and the point at stake between psychologism and sociologism is not whether Plastic Man is an individual.

The strength of a passive conception lies in its single canon of explanation and well-worked-out range of causal models; its weakness in the absence of a self to apply them to. The reverse holds for active conceptions. The antiphonal theme in Enlightenment thought is that we are rational creatures in a natural world of cause and effect. With the aid of reason we can master nature, manipulate society, change culture and indeed shape our own selves. As a political premiss shared by many liberals, socialists, revolutionaries and anarchists, the idea is too familiar to need rehearsal. But its epistemology is obscure and the self so cavalierly posited requires a fresh account of the explanation of human action.

Whereas Plastic Man, being formed by adaptive response to the interplay of nature and nurture, is only spuriously individual, his rival needs a degree of autonomy. There must be a self whose activity is sufficient explanation of some social behaviour. In calling him Autonomous Man, we are demanding a subject self, the I of 'The I and the Me', perhaps given more independence than G. H. Mead intended.[4] Autonomous Man is the self of popular common sense and everyday morals, who picks his own way through the world as he interprets it and even the toughest sociologists and philosophers find him a stout ghost to exorcise.

Autonomous Man has mixed origins and qualities. The bare idea is that he is the explanation of his own actions but the idea derives from more sources than the Enlightenment and can be fleshed out in conflicting ways. It owes something to the theology of the soul and something to the metaphysics of substances. It raises questions of privacy, self-consciousness, identity and rationality, to mention but a few. There is no space here to attempt a review of the differing claims made for an irreducible self and I shall follow a single thread. Let us focus on the notion of autonomy.

A language of action is often distinguished from a language of behaviour. Crudely, agents interpret, reflect, plan, decide, act intentionally, hope, regret and are responsible for at least what they tried to do and should have foreseen; patients are programmed, provoked and conditioned. Two such languages can be worked out with great detail and subtlety, so that each contains an analogue of everything in the other. (There is no evident reason why, for instance, the former should have a monopoly of ethics or the latter of psychoanalysis.) I take it that this much is uncontentious – the hot questions concern their relation and reference. Do both have application? If so, do both refer to the same thing? If so, is one primary and the other parasitic on it? If both apply but to a different sort of referent, how do the referents relate? This battleground is as old as philosophy.

[4] For a highly individualistic (and doubtless contentious) interpretation of Mead, see Herbert Blumer, 'Sociological Implications of the Thought of G. H. Mead', *American Journal of Sociology* (1966).

The neatest way to assert the existence of Autonomous Man is to claim that human action falls under the concepts of the language of action and then to deny that it can be wholly explained in terms of causal laws. In other words, an active conception of man is most neatly presented as a thesis about explanation.[5] This does not absolve one from giving an account of human nature, since, I venture to assert, the merit of any theory of explanation depends finally on the true nature of what it explains. But it makes the initial problem more tractable, by creating a clear duty to supply an alternative to causal explanation. The duty falls most evidently on those who reject all causal explanation of human action. But it is no less incumbent on those who compromise with determinism. The notion of autonomy applies in the gap between partial determinism and total explanation. Thus the determinism of Hume and his descendants, in replacing concepts of logical or mechanical necessity with those of regularity or probability, makes no concession to autonomy – Hume has a no less passive conception of man than Hobbes. I declared earlier that the strength of active conceptions is their positing of a self and their weakness a lack of models of explanation. It will be seen that this is misleading, since, without the explanatory model, the self is a mere we-know-not-what.

At any rate, enough has been said to recall the two broad conceptions of human nature in Enlightenment thought. One gives us Plastic Man subject to a determinism whose only limit is randomness or Uncertainty. The other replaces even stochastic with partial determinism, to allow Autonomous Man an individual self, and owes us a suitable mode of explanation. It has yet to be shown that there is more than an apparent conflict between passive and active and that they do not form a continuum. With this and the need for another mode of explanation in mind, we shall next set our heroes on the social stage.

II

There might be no problem in relating human nature to social institutions. It might be that individuals are simply the raw material which the social factor moulds and transforms. Or it might be, conversely, that institutions result solely from deliberate contracts among

[5] Alan Dawe (loc. cit), approaching sociologically, throws the conceptions into instructive relief by contrasting two kinds of question. A passive conception is typified by the 'Problem of Order' (how society integrates the behaviour of its members) and an active conception by the 'Problem of Control' (how men manipulate their social context). There is much to interest philosophers in these paradigmatic problems.

pre-social individuals. But few thinkers have risked the divine
simplicity of either extreme. In the main passive conceptions attach
some sense to the notion of an individual self and active conceptions
recognise some external social facts. This is perhaps why the conceptions seem to form a continuum – both need a way of fusing the
separate individuals who interact with the stock of characters which
society provides and neither can therefore resist the concept of Role.
The relative emphasis given to individual or character seems a
matter of degree. In this section I shall introduce the concept of
Role, intending to use it finally to fill out the notion of autonomy.
But I shall try to show that Role behaves differently in passive and
active conceptions and that the social self is no easy compromise
between 'private' self and social 'self'.

'Role' is usually defined in terms of normative expectations
attached to a social position – what Bradley calls in better English
the duties of a station. This reference to norms or duties is crucial.
Indeed it is presumably implicit even in the seemingly weaker definition of Role as the active dimension of a social position, since only
activity sanctioned by norms is relevant. For instance, army quartermasters are wont to keep more items in their store than they ever
record in their ledgers. This is quartermasterly activity; but it does
not in itself show that their role includes holding reserves for the
benefit of careless friends. It is in the role, however, if quartermasters
who play strictly by the book are liable to the censure (as opposed
to the mere disgruntlement) of their friends. A role involves 'rights'
and 'duties', the quotation marks being there this time to signal
that no ethical questions are being begged – there is no simple
inference from a quartermaster's 'duties' to his duties. Nor need
the 'duties' be legal or explicit, as the example shows (in anticipation
of points to be made later). With these caveats, then, a role is a set
of normative expectations attached to a social position.

This definition has a passive flavour to it, as it makes roles external
to individuals. So it will aid discussion if we turn to the theatre to see
how a character in a play is related to the actor who plays him.
The relation looks simple at first. According to what we might call
the Townswomen's Guild view, the actor dresses up for the occasion
and pretends to be the character, the character is supplied complete
by the playwright, and the producer, as hidden master of ceremonies,
sees that the pretence is faithful. But even this no-nonsense view of
theatre lets us read the dramaturgical analogy in two conflicting
ways. On the one hand the actor who dons and doffs the mask is
wholly distinct from the *dramatis persona* and owes no part of his
private identity to the stage. Analogously, we might look to an

extreme individualism which treats social life as a contract and a construct to be explained in terms of individual desires. On the other hand the script is complete, at least in traditional drama, and the character exists only in the play. Analogously, the actor is presumably in turn a character in the larger play of his own life. His identity is socially created and his behaviour is to be explained in terms of a programme he did not write. One analogy points to Autonomous Man, the other to Plastic Man.

Yet, even if the Townswomen's Guild view were a true one, neither analogy would be so unambiguous. That the actor is distinct from the character may indicate only that within a passive conception, *homo psychologicus* is at least as important as *homo sociologicus*. That the script is written in advance may be a red herring, given that, in its own terms, it is a story about individuals and not about characters, who exist only in the context of an audience. (Nor is the existence of a script any more sinister for an active conception than theologians have found the idea of an omniscient Creator, who knows already what I shall choose to do tomorrow.) Even with a stage set for amateur theatricals, there is no such thing as *the* dramaturgical analogy nor even the two dramaturgical analogies.

The plot thickens further as soon as theatre ceases to be seen as pretence. The mark of great acting is that the character lives in the actor and becomes part of his self-definition. The actor does not so much impersonate the character as personify him.[6] But now the fusion of 'private' self with social 'self' is no easier to grasp in the theatre than in everyday life. The phenomenon is opaque and, although some plays and performances put a clear interpretation on it, the interpretation can be disputed. Accordingly there are conflicting theories of the nature of acting and once again there is no such thing as *the* dramaturgical analogy.

The basic ambiguity is brought out by asking whether the role creates the agent or the agent creates the role. For Plastic Man it is crucial that all aspects of role-behaviour be determinate. Social facts and individual programmes (in whatever proportions) account for everything in the everyday drama. What roles there are, who is inducted into them and how, the machinery for keeping them going and adapting them are matters directly involved in the explanation. Even if allowance is made for the 'subjective meanings' which men attach to their experiences, this apparent concession is quickly nullified by adding that what notions like 'socialisation' and

---

[6] I owe this point to Malcolm Bradbury. See M. Bradbury, B. Heading and M. Hollis, 'The Man and the Mask: A Discussion of Role Theory' in *Role*, ed. J. A. Jackson (Cambridge, 1971).

'internalisation' cannot explain, other sciences like socio-linguistics can. In effect, therefore, the playing of roles is always *explanandum* and never *explanans*. However handy it is for picking out features of social life worth explanation, the notion of Role is theoretically otiose, which is perhaps why it can often be deleted throughout works on Role Theory without loss of content. For Plastic Man it is only a metaphor that the world is a stage.

For Autonomous Man the notion of Role offers an *explanans*. The Individual is sometimes said to be an invention of liberal political theory and moral philosophy, an abstract and absurd angel in a historical vacuum. This has led even moralists to reject autonomy. Bradley, for instance, working with a social-cum-organic theory of individual identity, pronounces that 'there is nothing better than my station and its duties nor anything higher or more truly beautiful. It holds and will hold its own against the worship of the "individual", whatever form that may take'. 'My station', he adds in thunderous illustration, laughs at individualism's 'adoration of star-gazing virgins with souls above their spheres.' And indeed Autonomous Man has all too often been Bunthorne without even a hard, gem-like flame. But the notion of Role offers a more robust line. By taking the requirements of roles as partly fixed and granting that a man's identity becomes partly that of the roles he chooses, we may be able to retain an Individual, who is self-creative and self-explantory but no angel. Moreover we may also be able to restate a sort of social contract theory by treating social institutions as the (often unforeseen) result of agreement about roles and their 'duties'. For Autonomous Man it is a categorial fact that the world is a stage.

'Role' is *explanandum* in a passive conception of man, *explanans* in an active one. This is why there is no continuum. How roles and their 'duties' can explain social action autonomously, is the topic of the next section. Star-gazing virgins read on.

III

With an abrupt change of example, although not of theme, I turn next to a discussion by Quentin Skinner of an episode in eighteenth-century British politics.[7] Mr Skinner's subject is Bolingbroke's per-

[7] Q. Skinner, 'The Principles and Practice of Opposition: the Case of Bolingbroke versus Walpole' in *Historical Perspectives: Studies in English Thought and Society 1500–1900*, ed. N. McKendrick (London, 1974). Skinner's interpretation of Bolingbroke is self-confessedly contentious but I borrow it without apology to other historians who might wish to object, since it illustrates the philosophical point, whether it is correct or not. I also

sistent attack on the ministry of Sir Robert Walpole in the 1730s. By invoking a role perspective, I shall try to show how reference to a structure of 'duties' can explain the conduct of an autonomous agent.

Mr Skinner discerns two main lines in Bolingbroke's attack, one being that Walpole's ministry had no business to retain a sizeable land force when Britain was no longer involved in any major European war, and the other being that the ministry was too free with places and pensions for its supporters. He asks why these lines were the ones Bolingbroke pursued. This question has not usually been raised by historians, he claims, since they have been distracted by another one, why Bolingbroke attacked Walpole at all. Their answer to this latter question has been either that Bolingbroke was an adventurer or that he was a patriot. Those who see him as an adventurer have had no interest in the choice of the form of attack, since an adventurer uses whatever lies to hand. Those who see him as a patriot have tended to suppose, in explanation of the lines chosen, that he was especially incensed by the practices mentioned. Skinner argues that both answers rest on a shared assumption that a man's professed principles (or ideology) enter into the explanation of his actions, only if he professes them sincerely. Thus if Bolingbroke was an adventurer, his professed principles provide no explanation; and, if he was a patriot, they explain at face value. Skinner rejects the assumption, however, on the ground that Bolingbroke's choice of lines of attack would have been the same, whether he was sincere or not. In the context of the time any opposition to the King's ministry was likely to seem *ipso facto* treasonable. So Bolingbroke had to appear as a patriot, one bent on defending the true liberties of England. Conveniently his Whig opponents' own ideology of constitutional liberty condemned especially the keeping of mercenaries and the centralisation of powers. So Bolingbroke could patriotically denounce a peacetime army as mercenaries and the award of places and pensions to supporters as failure to observe the separation of powers. Thus existing ideology and his professed patriotic principles explain his specific actions completely. He had found the only strategy likely to oust Walpole without provoking a charge of treason. Yet the explanation is wholly silent about Bolingbroke's motives, thus showing that professed principles can be explanatory, whether sincerely held or not.

---

have much in mind his admirable essay ' " Social Meaning" and the Explanation of Social Action' in *Philosophy, Politics and Society*, ed. P. Laslett, W. G. Runciman and Q. Skinner, Fourth Series (Blackwell, 1972).

Recast in the language of Role, Skinner's analysis is, in effect, that there was at the time a role of patriot, whose duties could be construed to require opposition to the King's ministry. This yields the following general explanatory schema:

(1) Role R required action A.
(2) The agent held a position involving Role R.
(3) The agent knew that R required A.
(4) The agent's reason for doing A was that R required A.

The first three conditions give the agent a reason for doing A, namely that it was his 'duty', and the fourth adds that this reason was his reason. It may be objected that the schema cannot explain action because it makes no mention of motive. Should we not add at least:

(5) The agent's motive for doing A was that R required A?

On the contrary, it is a positive merit that no mention is made of motives. The strength of Skinner's analysis of Bolingbroke is precisely that it leaves his motives enigmatic, a subject for a further and different enquiry. The most which might be made usefully explicit is that the agent acted willingly in doing A; but this too is not a remark about motive (except perhaps to imply that he had some motive or other) and is already implicit in the four conditions. In saying that the agent acted as he did because it was his 'duty', we leave it open whether he wanted to do his 'duty' because he had the role or whether he chose the role because it involved the 'duty'. In other words in 'He did A because it was his "duty" ' 'because' is ambiguous between reason and motive. It will emerge presently that passive and active conceptions of man regard the ambiguity differently.

Skinner's case, if right, is also rare. A single role rarely requires a unique course of action and, even where it does, there may still be more than one way of discharging the 'duty'. The usual case is that a role, while requiring some actions and forbidding others, leaves a range of permitted options. A role which permits A or B but forbids C in a situation can be invoked to explain why the agent did A rather than C but not why he did A rather than B. Admittedly this is something – an enquirer unaware that there was a role of patriot might wonder why Bolingbroke did not attack Walpole for stupidity or incompetence. But little of what we do is uniquely required by a single role.

The schema can be extended however:

(1) R_1 required $(A \ or \ B)$ and R_2 required $(A \ or \ C)$.
(2) The agent held positions involving R_1 and R_2.
(3) The agent knew what R_1 and R_2 required.
(4) The agent's reason for doing A was that $\{R_1 \ and \ R_2\}$ required A.

A consistent set of roles gives a clear-headed agent reason to do fewer actions than each role singly permits.[8] Where an agent willingly does the only action permitted by his role-set, then the requirements of the set explain his action, provided he knows what they are. Where even the whole set permits more than one action, the limits of social explanation have, I suggest, been reached. Despite the threat of final indeterminacy, however, the type of explanation seems to me interesting enough to merit a name. Let us call it 'normative explanation', noting again that, even as just elaborated, it makes no mention of motive.

Objections spring up at once, some to the very idea of definite roles and 'duties', some to the thesis that 'normative explanation' is explanatory. Under the former heading, first, is there ever a clear list of roles in any society? (For instance was there really an eighteenth-century role of patriot? Is there a contemporary role of cyclist, dope-pedlar, television personality or Englishman and how do we know?) Secondly are the 'duties' of a given role ever clear enough? (For instance is a Chancellor of the Exchequer whose budget leaks 'bound' to resign? Is a priest 'required' to believe in God? Is a professor 'forbidden' to seduce his own students?) Such questions are all too familiar to sociologists and there is no denying their bite. A general social theory is needed before positions, occupants, roles and 'duties' can be identified and, since each competing theory justifies a different social map, sociology still has far to go. But the philosopher's role does not include providing a social map and I shall ignore this sort of objection without a blush.

Objections to the proposed explanatory schema strike nearer home. The conditions are now:

(1) Roles $\{R_1 \ldots R_j\}$ required A.
(2) The agent held positions involving $\{R_1 \ldots R_j\}$.
(3) The agent knew that $\{R_1 \ldots R_j\}$ required A.
(4) The agent's reason for doing A was that $\{R_1 \ldots R_j\}$ required A.

[8] Equally Skinner could appeal to Bolingbroke's role-set to explain why, although all his contemporaries, including Walpole himself, saw themselves as patriots, not all applauded the attack on the ministry. Bolingbroke and his supporters could perhaps be shown to form a group with 'duties' and reasons for action of their own.

Several questions arise. First, do agents usually know what their roles require and, in any case, why the emphasis on knowledge rather than belief? Secondly, does the final condition distinguish reasons from motives clearly enough and, in any case, can motives be treated in the cavalier manner proposed? Thirdly, is it not fanciful to suppose that agents are often blessed with consistent role-sets? Fourthly what does the schema tell us about the self, unless to deny its existence?

In reply, first, I agree that normative explanation applies only to agents who are either highly socialised or highly rational; but this will turn out in a moment to be a merit. The schema specifies 'knowledge' for the sake of the view of rationality to be taken later. Besides, although an agent may sometimes act on the basis of false beliefs, including a false reckoning of his roles and 'duties', the falsity cannot in principle be universal, since that would make all explanation of social action finally psychological. Similarly a short-sighted bridge player may lead a card because he mistook it for the Knave of Hearts; but it cannot be universally true that the explanation of all leads by all players is independent of the cards actually held. Mention of 'knowledge' is intended to ensure that social facts enter essentially into the form of explanation of social action.

Secondly, the social game must be played by social rules and these rules supply the player with reasons. These reasons are indeed the player's reasons in so far as he takes part willingly. It does not matter why he ultimately plays the game, provided that he cannot get whatever it is he wants without playing. Similarly there are many motives for playing chess but, provided the player can satisfy them only by gaining the fruits of playing chess well, they are independent of his reasons for the moves he makes. Why an agent has the roles he does and why he acts within his roles as he does are very different sorts of question.

Thirdly, there is indeed no blinking the fact of role-conflict. Schematically an agent will often find that R_1 requires A, whereas R_2 forbids it (or requires B which excludes A). The doing of A cannot then be explained by reference to the agent's role-set, since a set which requires A and also requires *not-A* does not explain the doing of either. Role-conflict being endemic, we must be ready either to appeal outside the role-set altogether (for instance to a sexual appetite which prompts Bloggs to do what might cost Professor Bloggs his job) or to restore consistency. Too frequent appeal outside the role-set would destroy the pretensions of normative explanation. But consistency is not too hard to restore, if we include sorting

devices like hierarchy, immediacy or degree of sanction in the construction of the role-set. (Roughly, since Bloggs and Professor Bloggs
are doubtless in conflict in any case, abstention would show the
scope of normative explanation and indulgence its limits.) The
general degree of consistency assumed reflects an underlying conception of human nature, as will be argued presently.

Fourthly, what does emerge about the self? We said just now that
normative explanation applied only to agents who were either highly
socialised or highly rational. The two cases differ in that one points
to a passive and the other to an active conception of human nature.
A highly socialised agent certainly knows and does what his roles
require – *de tautologis non disputandum.* But, by the same token,
normative explanations within a passive conception of man do not
take us far, being only a preliminary to asking how roles are allotted,
normative expectations formed and men socialised into accepting
them. Analogously, the behaviour of bees can be explained in the
first instance by pointing to divisions of function between queens,
drones and workers and showing how the functions intermesh to
keep the hive going. But these are causal mechanisms to be explained
in turn in terms of inputs loosely labelled nature, nurture and environment. There is no break in the chain of explanation at the
boundary of the social world; nor, for those who deem psychology
more powerful than sociology, is there any break between social
states of mind and the psychological factors which cause them. As
argued earlier, a passive conception of human nature goes with a
claim that all explanations are causal and, although there is no harm
in using the notion of role, there is no great merit either, since the
key questions remain those of the relation of individual programming to social structure. From the passive side normative explanation does inded implicitly deny that there is a self.

Within an active conception of man normative explanations are
also incomplete but for a different reason. In so far as positions are
chosen by their occupants, explaining action in terms of the requirements of a consistent role-set is only part of the story. Given an
individualistic enough social theory, the scope for choice can be
made very wide. The agent not only has an existing stock of roles
to choose from but also can propose new interpretations of old roles
or new roles altogether. No doubt such proposals need the consent
of others; but what a single agent cannot do, a large enough group
can. No doubt some social institutions are unforeseen results of
choices, but other choices can be made later, if those results are unacceptable. No doubt it is historically inaccurate to speak of institutions arising from choice, but this objection has never been enough

to kill the theory of the Social Contract. Normative explanation can be squared with extreme individualism and so leaves as much room for the self as you please.

Like Bradley, however, I recoil at the prospect of hordes of star-gazing virgins with souls above their spheres. Rampant individualism also destroys the self and normative explanation must finally do more than explain the game in terms of its rules. Some social actions need to be seen as commitments to a role and so as acts of self-definition. In principle normative explanation can explain not only what a man does but also what he has become. But we are running ahead of the argument and shall be content to say here that normative explanation explains the voluntary social activity of the social self, while reserving for the private self whatever its proper sphere may be.

The difference between passive and active shows itself most clearly so far in the relation between reasons and motives. We said that in 'He did *A* because his role-set required *A*' 'because' was ambiguous between reason and motive and that the two conceptions of man regarded the ambiguity differently. In the active idiom, 'He did *A* because his role-set required *A*' asserts solely that this was his reason, leaving it as a further, although legitimate enough, question what moved him to take his 'duty' so seriously. Following Skinner, we know why Bolingbroke denounced the keeping of a large land force and, with more details supplied, we would know his reason for opposing Walpole at all; but we do not yet know his motive for the attack nor why he had the role-set from which his reasons derived. In the passive idiom reasons are explanatory only when they are causes and they are causes only when they are motives. The enquiry into Bolingbroke starts by asking whether he was a patriot or an adventurer and continues by seeing what beliefs and interests he had and how they caused him to act as he did. Admittedly the contrast is less clear than it sounds, as we have carefully avoided discussing Causation. But, by the same token, it is intended only as provisional.[9]

Provisionally, then, questions about Plastic Man are causal and cross the social and psychological boundaries into the rest of the natural world without a break, whereas questions about Autonomous Man are self-contained with limits. Normative explanation can be

[9] The relation between reasons and motives needs more care than I can give it here. So I am grateful to R. S. Peters for the general strategy of *The Concept of Motivation* (London, 1958) and for pointing out to me the help to be had from his other writings in following up the case I am presenting here. (See R. S. Peters, *Psychology and Ethical Development* (London, 1974) chaps 4 and 18.

applied in either idiom to the highly socialised in one case and to the highly rational in the other but, when applied to the social behaviour of Plastic Man, it is a species of causal and is only a first step to the more powerful causal explanation for which it is itself an *explanandum*. When applied to the social actions of Autonomous Man it is substantive.

IV

Inasmuch as a man acts autonomously, when he does his 'duty' for the reason that it is his 'duty', we see how to put the private self on the social stage. But we have yet to introduce a social self. So far the individual remains pre-social and even the set of his roles remains external to him. He is still an abstract and absurd angel. I want to suggest finally and fleetingly that the free social individual is the man who creates his own social identity by acting rationally within a consistent role-set of his own choosing and becomes what he has chosen by accepting his 'duties' as his duties. Few men take this course and few societies offer it.

That 'there is nothing better than my station and its duties nor anything higher or more truly beautiful' is often taken to be Bradley's final word. His famous essay gives that impression. I am born into my station, he seems to say, and inherit its duties. My identity derives from my station, the self being social and the individual a fiction. My 'duties' are indeed my duties and, in learning to understand and accept my station, I am learning to be moral. I am wholly a social creature, my station has resulted from organic evolution and is best for me, my path to virtue is obedience. In the very next essay, entitled 'Ideal Morality', however, Bradley recants. He points out that societies may be corrupt, implying presumably that my 'duty' is not always my duty, and adds that my station does not exhaust my duties in any case, since there is also a 'non-social ideal', for instance 'the realisation for myself of truth and beauty'. My ultimate moral goal is self-realisation, he holds, and, although individualism is never absolved of absurdity, this self is not in the end completely social.

I am not impressed by an organic view of society which holds that social stations are as easily identified and almost as immovable as those in a railway system. But I find Bradley's dilemma suggestive. He is convinced that social facts and theory are relevant both to the philosophical problem of personal identity and to ethics; yet personal identity is not social identity and social systems are not always ideal. In effect he rejects a passive conception of man but finds enough truth in it to be uncertain what to make of an active conception. This is also a problem for our present discussion.

In the active mode, normative explanation applies only to well-informed, reflective and consistent agents blessed with consistent role-sets. Yet, in speaking of an active conception of human nature, we have presented Autonomous Man as if he were any and everyone. To escape a charge of fatuous myopia, I propose to take Autonomous Man as not a description but, so to speak, a prescription. Inasmuch as all social theories presuppose a view of human nature, an active conception holds that all men are potentially Autonomous. Yet not everyone succeeds in acting autonomously all the time – not all social actions can be explained normatively. If we grant, moreover, that, in making a choice of roles, we choose not only what to do but also what to become (roles being not always hobbies but sometimes self-definitions), we can propose a definition of freedom in society. A free social agent is man who chooses his roles rationally and plays them rationally.

By rational action I mean action whose explanation is that the best reasons for it were also the agent's own reasons. (There is some prevarication here as to whether the 'best reasons' must rest only on true beliefs but, since I judge it possible to budget for false beliefs without making a paranoiac as rational as anyone else, I shall not pursue this difficult topic now.) Rationality so defined, however, is relative to goals – that cyanide is lethal is a good reason for a suicide to drink it. The rationality of goals, once we have run out of further goals to which the previous goal is in turn a rational means, is an old but inescapable problem in ethics and politics. That is why the paper began and will end with recipes for the Good Society. To link reason and freedom we must presuppose a suitable view of human nature. To link both to virtue we need a thesis about final goals. Even those who agree to see autonomy in terms of commitment to rationally chosen roles may doubt whether there is virtue in autonomy.

To show that questions about goals are inescapable let us raise this doubt in sharper form. We have so far insisted that normative explanation applies only to the agent whose role-set is consistent. Consistency, I have implied, is a condition of freedom. This can certainly be doubted. A contrary thesis (which gives a plausible reading of Erving Goffman and can perhaps be traced as far back as Thrasymachos) is that self-realisation is best achieved by control of one's social setting secured by clever manipulation of an inconsistent role-set. Machiavelli observes that 'A prince, therefore, being compelled knowingly to adopt the beast, ought to choose the fox has succeeded best. But it is necessary to know well how to snares and the fox cannot defend himself against wolves. Therefore, it is necessary to be a fox to discover the snares and a lion to terrify the wolves. Those who rely simply on the lion do not understand what they are about . . . he who has known best how to employ the fox has succeeded best. But it is neccessary to know well how to disguise this characteristic and to be a great pretender and dissembler . . .' (*The Prince*, chap. 18). It appears that freedom to pursue one's own good in one's own way is to have mastered the art of the fox. Autonomous Man, it seems, is rational but inconsistent.

Such examples raise a crucial query about the relation of private to social self. But, before taking this up, it is worth noting that they do not establish what they seem to. Machiavelli says that the Prince's role requires him to be liberal and to keep faith; yet, if he does so, he becomes bankrupt and despised and so unable to perform the role of Prince; hence he must seem to be liberal and to keep faith, while secretly ensuring that his liberality costs him nothing and that he breaks faith whenever necessary. This suggests that the role of Prince is inconsistent, but it implies only that the role is not what it seems. It involves an element of role-distance, that is of distance from the public 'duties' of the role. But a Prince, who 'knows what he is about', can still play the real role consistently, by playing the apparent role inconsistently in such a way as to seem consistent to his audience, while his victims gnash their teeth at his inconsistency. This dizzying advice is perhaps Machiavelli's recipe for virtue in a corrupt society. Equally Goffman's notes on how to work the system appear to show that perpetual role-distance pays but leave it possible that some roles involve distance, if they are to be played successfully. The same possibility would make it hard to isolate Bolingbroke's motives, since he may have been both a patriot and a fox.

Nonetheless such examples do suggest an individualist account of autonomy, in which the private self has its identity independent of all the roles it plays. If men are indeed pre-social individuals who enter the social arena for gain, amusement or even their own idea of virtue, then it may suit them to have inconsistent role-sets. On the other hand, if they become persons only by acquiring social relations to others, then the normative explanation of their actions must sometimes reveal their motives. In either case it may sometimes be a virtue to appear consistent, yet a vice to be consistent. But Machiavelli's advice is directed on the former interpretation to a pre-social individual and on the latter interpretation to a Prince. Goffman may be right to advocate role-distance on the grounds that the man who internalises all the roles society allots him is too passive to be free; but we must also ask whether Goffman himself is a pre-social individual with wants to satisfy or a transitional social self seeking an identity he can accept.

I have space only to confess my own view. I confess to believing that there can be no self where all roles are played with distance (an idea I find useful in reflecting on alienation and anomie). In this sense man is a social animal. But, given existing social forms, to play without distance is to be passive. The free man therefore distances himself from the outward aspects of his roles, while choosing and committing himself to real roles whose duties are among his motives. With the skill of the fox he ensures that his apparent roles appear consistent and his real roles are consistent, so that his actions have both apparent and final normative explanations. That is, finally, the sense in which he is autonomous.

This credo leaves much unanswered, in particular whether Autonomous Man is Plastic Man grown active through exercise or whether he had and retains some undefined private self. It leaves the degree of individualism in the explanation of the structure of roles and institutions teasingly unclear. It shirks hard questions about personal identity and sincerity. So, by way of excuse, I shall hastily sum up what the paper has tried to maintain. We began with the usual objection to traditional political theories, that they rest on a metaphysical and ethically charged view of human nature. It turns out, however, that presumptions about human nature are still crucial to social theory and the explanation of behaviour. In the broadest terms, passive and active conceptions vie with one another, each requiring a different model of explanation and each model of explanation presupposing a view of human nature. The playing of roles furnishes a case study. Social action can often be explained by reference to the requirements of an agent's role-set. Such normative explanations are silent about motives and answer no causal questions about the existing structure of roles. So they are treated within a passive conception as a first step to a fuller but no less causal explanation. Within an active conception, however, they promise to fill the gap between partial determinism and complete explanation with an account which allows autonomy. This seems to throw active conceptions back on a pre-social atomism which sees men as private selves or abstract and absurd angels. But it need not, if the autonomous social self exists only when rationally chosen duties are among the motives of the agent. There is some truth, but not, I hope, too much, in Bradley's *obiter dictum*, 'we have found ourselves, when we have found our station and its duties, our function as an organ in the social organism'.

As a final gesture of intent, let us revert to recipes for the Good Society. For Plastic Man the Good Society is one which minimises the gap between desire and reward. In so far as science can manipulate him, the recipe is so to socialise him that he wants what society gives. In so far as he is not yet fully malleable, the recipe is to give him an interest in keeping the peace. For Autonomous Man the Good Society allows and aids his creation of a social identity but the recipe remains hidden. As to what either account requires in the way of roles and means to play them, given the claims not only of freedom but also of equality, justice, comfort, self-respect and other ideals which men propose, I prudently say nothing.

11

THREE VIEWS CONCERNING HUMAN FREEDOM

John Watkins

*In memory of Imre Lakatos, who exemplified to the
end the ideal of personal autonomy presented here*

Contents

1. INTRODUCTION

ULTIMATELY, the only good reason for restricting the freedom of
responsible adults is to protect other people's freedom, to increase the
overall enjoyment of freedom.

That, I take it, is the central principle of classical liberalism. And
I salute it. But what is human freedom? Or, to put it in a less
essentialist way, what view of human freedom should we adopt if we
hold that freedom should be maximised?

I will begin by considering two older views: the *empiricist* view of,
for example, Hobbes and Hume; and the *apriorist* view of Spinoza

and Kant.[1] I shall argue that both these views are inadequate. I shall also argue that, although they are inadequate in very different ways, there is a common explanation for their inadequacy, namely, that both views were developed within a determinist framework. I will then outline a third view of human freedom within an indeterminist framework.

My title contains an allusion to a famous paper by Karl Popper.[2] There are close ties between, respectively, the three views of human knowledge which he examined there, and the three views of human freedom that I shall examine here. My eventual aim in this paper is to outline a post-Kantian conception of personal autonomy which reflects the shift from Kantian determinism and apriorism to Popperian indeterminism and conjecturalism.

2. THE EMPIRICIST VIEW: DOING WHAT ONE WANTS TO DO

The empiricist view that I will now consider is admirably straightforward and uncomplicated: a man is free when he is able to do what he wants to do (or, as Hobbes put it, when he 'is not hindered to do what he has a will to do').[3]

Hobbes and Hume were determinists and they needed a concept of freedom that could be reconciled with determinism, as this view can: it says that a man who can do what he has a will to do is free, no matter how his will may have been causally determined.

On this view, the amount of freedom in a political community is something that might perhaps, in principle, be maximised by skilful legislation.[4] Taking the wants of its citizens as its data, the

[1] What I call the 'empiricist view' roughly corresponds to Berlin's 'negative concept' of freedom; and what I call the 'apriorist view' has some resemblance to his 'positive concept', at least as he initially presents it (Isaiah Berlin, *Two Concepts of Liberty: an Inaugural Lecture* (Oxford: Clarendon Press, 1958) pp. 16 f.). However, he soon proceeds to what I regard as collectivised, romantic and illiberal perversions of this individualist and rationalist idea, which seems, in his treatment, almost to get swallowed up by its monstrous progeny.

[2] 'Three Views Concerning Human Knowledge', first published in *Contemporary British Philosophy*: Third Series, ed. H. D. Lewis (London: Allen & Unwin, 1956); reprinted in K. R. Popper, *Conjectures and Refutations* (London: Routledge & Kegan Paul, 1963) chap. 3.

[3] Actually, this view (at least as it was worked out by Hobbes) is not quite as straightforward and uncomplicated as it at first seems; see my *Hobbes's System of Ideas*, second edition (London: Hutchinson, 1973) chap. 7, especially pp. 95–6 and 128 f.

[4] I have worded this cautiously in view of the notorious difficulties (culminating in Arrow's Impossibility Theorem) which attend the idea of the optimum collective satisfaction of individuals' preferences. I have reviewed

government should try to estimate the extent to which the unrestricted pursuit of any one of these wants would generate hindrances to
the satisfaction of other wants; and it should then try to devise a legal
system that minimises the net total both of legal hindrances, and of
hindrances generated by individuals' behaviour, to people doing
what they want to do.

I will now indicate why I find this view of human freedom
inadequate.

Consider, first, cases of what may be called *pleasurable servitude*.
A courtier, say, or a protégé of an underworld boss, enjoys a volup-
tuous life; his enjoyment of it depends on a thorough-going subservience to another man; but he has become inured to this.

This man scores a high mark for personal freedom by the empiricist yardstick: he spends most of the day (and probably a
good deal of the night) doing what he wants to do. But for an old-
style liberal there is surely something shameful about his state of
subservience, even though he is happily adjusted to it. (Mill did not
even mention such cases in the chapter 'Of Individuality' in *On
Liberty*. He was sufficiently disturbed by cases of subservience to
external traditions and customs.)

Consider, next, a more extreme kind of case. A writer, say, lives
in a country recently taken over by a totalitarian regime. He finds
the regime morally and politically repugnant. His books are banned,
his phone is tapped, and he ekes out a living by poorly paid translation work. On the empiricist view, he enjoys a low degree of human
freedom. Next the regime decides to try to win him over: if he will
express approval of the regime and undertake some revisions of his
books, they will be republished and he will lead a comfortable life;
if he refuses, he will be sent to a labour-camp. He does refuse, and he
is sent to a labour-camp. On the empiricist view, he now enjoys an
even lower degree of freedom.

I have, of course, no quarrel so far with these empiricist appraisals.
But now let us alter the scenario. The regime takes him into solitary
confinement and tries to brain-wash him into submission; and they
succeed. Assume that they operate upon his mind with an almost
surgical precision, so that he emerges with his moral and political
ideas transformed, but with his faculties otherwise unimpaired. He
now gladly sets about eliminating the 'errors' in his past writing and
undertakes a big novel, full of optimism and hope, about life under

---

these difficulties in my 'Social Knowledge and the Public Interest', *Man
and the Social Sciences*, ed. W. A. Robson (London: Allen & Unwin, 1972)
pp. 185 f.

the new regime. He is rewarded with a luxury apartment, a chauffeur-driven car, and various literary awards.[5]

What, on the empiricist view, must we say about his freedom now? The answer seems clear: he now enjoys a high degree of freedom since he is hindered very little from doing those things that he now wants to do. But I, at least, am inclined to say that this man is now more thoroughly a captive of the regime than he would have been if he had defied their methods of persuasion and gone to a labour-camp.

3. HETERONOMY AND DETERMINISM

Except that the effects are more lasting, the imaginary case we have just considered is analogous to the well-known and much discussed case of post-hypnotic suggestion, in which a waking person carries out a suggestion made to him earlier, while in a hypnotised state; he feels himself to be behaving voluntarily, and offers more or less plausible reasons for what he is doing. But we want to protest that what he is now 'doing' is not really something that *he* is doing,[6] and that his 'reasons' for doing it are rationalisations subconsciously invented afterwards. His condition, as he acts out the hypnotist's suggestion, is a glaring example of what Kant called heteronomy: his behaviour, although he does not realise it, is governed by antecedent and external causes.

Now it seems to me that what is exceptional in this case, according to determinism, is only that the heteronomy of the subject is *obvious* to informed spectators. According to determinism, *all* human behaviour has been causally predetermined, down to the last detail, by causes external to the agent; however, these causes are mostly concealed, not only from the agent himself (who thereby *feels* free, just as our hypnotic subject does), but from spectators as well. In short,

[5] I presented this seeming counter-example to Hobbes's concept of liberty in 1965 (*Hobbes's System of Ideas*, first edition, §33 (2)).

R. S. Peters has drawn my attention to an article by S. I. Benn and W. L. Weinstein, 'Being Free to Act, and Being a Free Man', *Mind*, LXXX, 318 (April, 1971) with whose conclusions I am in full agreement. Thus they write: 'There are cases, indeed, in which one clearly does not have it [the freedom of an autonomous chooser], cases of manipulated choice. The hypnotised subject and the brain-washed are "not their own masters", not because the objective conditions of choice have been interfered with, but because the subjective conditions have. Though the subject may believe that he is choosing, the actions of other people may still sufficiently account for what he does; he may be as externally programmed as a computer' (p. 210).

[6] This phrase, which recurs rather frequently in my text, is adapted from A. I. Melden, *Free Action* (London: Routledge & Kegan Paul, 1961) p. 8.

it seems to me that determinism implies that all human agents are
always in a state of heteronomy.

But I do not expect that many of you will agree with me here.
I have not made a count, but I have the impression that only a
small minority of contemporary philosophers hold that full-fledged
determinism has destructive implications for human freedom.
Campbell has long held this view,[7] and so has Popper;[8] Melden[9]
and Munn[10] also share it. But I suspect that a much greater number
prefer to accept some version of what has come to be known as the
'reconcilability-thesis'.

The thesis that freedom and determinism are reconcilable has been
ably defended by various twentieth-century thinkers,[11] though without, I think, advancing far beyond Hume's very skilful defence of
it.[12] No doubt, the skill with which the reconcilability-thesis has been
defended has been important in securing its widespread acceptance.
But I think that a deeper factor has also been at work. The mar-
vellous progress of classical, deterministic physics from the seventeenth down to the end of the nineteenth century made determinism
increasingly seem, during that long period, an absolutely *inescapable*
doctrine.[13] Thus if the idea of human freedom was not to be scrapped

[7] In 1938 he wrote: 'Libertarianism is certainly inconsistent with a
rigidly determinist theory of the physical world. It is idle to pretend that
there can be open possibilities for psychical decision, while at the same time
holding that the physical events in which such decisions manifest themselves are determined in accordance with irrevocable law.' C. A. Campbell,
In Defence of Free Will (London: Allen & Unwin, 1967) p. 45.

[8] 'Physical determinism, we might say in retrospect, was a daydream of
omniscience which seemed to become more real with every advance in
physics until it became an apparently inescapable nightmare.' Karl R.
Popper, *Objective Knowledge: An Evolutionary Approach* (Oxford: Clarendon Press, 1972) p. 222.

[9] See the reference in note 6 above.

[10] Allan M. Munn, *Free-Will and Determinism* (London: MacGibbon &
Kee, 1960) pp. 205 f.

[11] See, for example, Bertrand Russell, 'The Elements of Ethics' (especially
section IV) in *Philosophical Essays* (1910) and Moritz Schlick, *Problems of
Ethics*, trans. David Rysim (1939) chap. VII. For a recent defence of the
reconcilability-thesis, see Adolf Grünbaum, 'Free Will and Laws of Human
Behavior', *American Philosophical Quarterly*, vol. 8, no. 4 (October 1971).

[12] I think that D. M. MacKay has introduced a novel consideration in his
ingenious attempt to reconcile free choice with mechanistic determinism
and scentific predictability; but I do not think that his attempt succeeds:
see my 'Freedom and Predictability: an Amendment to MacKay', *Brit. Jour.
Phil. Science*, vol. 22 (August, 1971). (MacKay's reply in the same issue of the
BJPS contains a bibliography.)

[13] 'The ordinary common-sense man has always had a belief in his
personal free-will ... Up to the seventeenth century [the validity of his

altogether, which would have been intolerable, philosophers supposed that it just *had* to be reconciled, somehow or other, with determinism. The reconcilability-thesis has behind it three centuries of single-minded philosophical endeavour. So it is little wonder that acceptance of that thesis became something like a fixed habit of thought among most philosophers. It became so fixed that when the main reason for the thesis began to disappear with the breakdown of determinism in contemporary physics, philosophers of this cast of mind scoffed at the idea that these new developments might have some bearing on the question of human freedom.[14] To put it rudely: they had come to feel so much at home in their deterministic prison that they were not enthusiastic when cracks started appearing in its walls.

My own view is that, now that we no longer *have* to reconcile ourselves as best we can with physical determinism, we can take a fresh look at the reconcilability-thesis, cheerfully free, unlike determinism-ridden philosophers in the past, to decide the matter either way according to how the argument goes.

I will confine myself to Hume's case for it. As you know, his thesis was two-pronged: freedom *is* reconcilable with determinism (=causal necessity); moreover, freedom is *not* reconcilable with indeterminism (=chance).

He began by laying down what might be called a law of excluded middle for causal determination and sheer chance: ' 'tis impossible to admit of any medium betwixt chance and an absolute necessity':[15]

---

belief] was not really denied. Though Christian theology might talk about an omniscient and omnipotent supreme being, it was a highly abstract theory. At the practical level the churches acted as if man did possess free-will ... The situation changed with the development during the seventeenth, eighteenth, and nineteenth centuries of physical science. Here for the first time in the history of man's thought appeared a rigorously deterministic theory, extending its range of application in all directions without encountering any apparently insurmountable obstacle; and by the middle of the nineteenth century there was every good reason to believe it would be eventually extended to a detailed description of man himself. What to do with man's belief in free-will when considered against the background of a universal deterministic physics? The continuing success of physics resulted in the abandonment of any direct attacks upon its determinism ...' Allan M. Munn, ibid., p. 213.

[14] See pp. 311–14 of the paper by Grünbaum referred to in note 11 for a recent statement of this dismissive view.

[15] *Treatise*, Bk. I, Part III, Sect. XIV (ed. Selby-Brigge, p. 171). This claim of Hume's has been criticised by Popper, *Objective Knowledge*, pp. 227 f. Hume's view was reiterated by Schlick: 'the alternative "either determination or chance" is a logical one, there is no escape from it, no third possibility' (in Feigl and Sellars, *Reading in Analysis* (New York, 1949) p. 532).

an event must either be caused or, alternatively, not caused; if caused, it comes about with necessity; if not caused, by chance. There is no middle possibility.

I shall argue later, with acknowledgements to Popper, that there is a whole range of middle possibilities. But when Hume's fork is accepted, as it usually is, resistance to determinism tends to crumble. For now, to reject the thesis that all human acts are causally pre-determined is to embrace the thesis that some human acts happen by chance. We would be out of the frying-pan into the fire. Or rather: we would be out of a perfectly tolerable condition and into an intolerable one. Hume supposed that his analysis of cause had drawn the string from determinism and rendered it innocuous. According to his analysis, to say that B was caused by A is not to say that B was compelled or necessitated by A to occur; it is only to say that A-like events are regularly succeeded by B-like events. And suppose that B is a human act while A is the agent's antecedent motives and beliefs. Then surely we want A to be causally succeeded by B. Surely it would be a nightmare world if such a succession were a matter of chance. According to this argument, it is *determinism* that allows us to regard a man's acts as *his* acts, as causally determined by his psychological make-up.

I claim that this argument is plausible only if we halt the causal regress at the motives and beliefs immediately behind an action. But why stop there? According to determinism, these motives and beliefs have antecedent causes which have antecedent causes . . .; if lifeless matter antedated living matter, these causal sequences go back eventually to causes that were purely physical.[16]

This very obvious implication of determinism is usually over-looked by reconciliationists; yet it seems to me to undermine their claim that it is *determinism* that allows us to regard a man's acts as *his* acts. And it creates an awkward problem concerning the *appropriateness* of a person's 'voluntary' movements to the thoughts and intentions behind them. Consider the movements of my hand and fingers as I write these words. According to determinism, the physical state of the universe at some distant time when there was only lifeless matter was such that, given the laws of nature, it was already causally predetermined that my hand would move as it is now moving.

[16] Although Russell was for the reconcilability-thesis in 1910 (see note 11 above), he had stressed the 'alien and inhuman' aspect of the physical determinism of contemporary science in 'A Free Man's Worship' (1903): 'Man is the product of causes which had no prevision of the end they were achieving; . . . his origin, his growth, his hopes and fears, his loves and his beliefs, are but the outcome of accidental collocations of atoms' (*Mysticism and Logic*, p. 47).

It was also causally predetermined that I would be thinking as I am now thinking. Again, it was causally predetermined that the birds in my garden would be chattering as they are now chattering.

Now there is no co-ordination between the birds' chattering and the movements of my hand. (The birds do not fall silent when I put down my pen.) Nor is there between the birds' chattering and my thinking. (The birds do not burst into song when I get a new thought.) And a determinist should not expect any such co-ordination: the three processes I have singled out are the contemporaneous end-products of three indefinitely long, hugely complicated, unplanned causal processes. It would be a miracle if they had somehow been keeping in step with each other.

Then why are the movements of my pen-holding hand so nicely appropriate to my thinking? Why is it that, no sooner have I decided to cross a word out, than my hand moves appropriately and the word gets crossed out? Determinism implies that my hand movements should not be regarded as *controlled* by my thinking: they were causally predetermined long before my thinking began.

This difficulty becomes obvious when physical determinism is allied (as it often is, and perhaps always should be) with *epiphenomenalism*, according to which thoughts and decisions are the mental shadows of physical changes in the brain and exercise no causal influence or feedback. But the difficulty is also present, if less obviously, in those versions of determinism that allow mental events to figure among the causal antecedents of bodily behaviour. My wife calls to me that tea is ready, and I reply that I will come in a moment. Let A be my wife's call, and let B be my thought and C be the movement of my lips, larynx, etc., as I reply; and let S be the physical state of the universe a long time ago. Determinism says that S, in conjunction with the laws of nature, predetermined A and B and C. But why did the mindless S predetermine C in such a way that C would be *appropriate* to B? And why did S predetermine the ensemble $B + C$ so that it would constitute an *appropriate* response to A? It looks as though the determinist will have to call in God to pre-establish this remarkable harmony.[17]

But a determinist might deal with this seeming implication of his position by *accepting* it ('Yes indeed; God did prearrange it all').[18]

[17] This is an adaptation of Alfred Landé's argument to the effect that determinism leads to a theological conspiracy-theory of *random sequences*. (See, for example, his 'Determinism versus Continuity in Modern Science', *Mind*, vol. 67 (April, 1958) and his *New Foundations of Quantum Mechanics* (Cambridge, University Press, 1965) chap. II.)

[18] Joseph Priestley, for instance, would have endorsed this implication unhesitatingly. He was a determinist and also a Christian; and for him a

So I now turn to Hume's claim that his analysis of causal determination as mere regular succession renders causal determinism innocuous
by depriving it of its air of compulsoriness and iron necessity.

A billiard-player who had metaphysical leanings but who was
unversed in Hume's philosophy might exclaim: 'I'm glad I'm not a
billiard-ball. A billiard-ball has no control over its movements. So
long as nothing hits it, it remains at rest; and when something hits it,
it moves in a predetermined way. I am different. I control my movements. Before making a stroke I survey the billiard-table to find the
most promising combination. Then I sight along my cue, mentally
estimating the required angle and momentum. I take a little time
positioning my body just right. Finally, I make a carefully controlled
arm-movement.'

If he said this in the presence of a Humean determinist he might
get the following two-point reply: '(1) Your arm-movement was just
as causally predetermined as the billiard-ball's movement. (2) But
neither the billiard-ball nor your arm was *compelled* or necessitated
to move as it did.' My guess is that any comforting effect of (2)
would be more than off-set by the discomforting effect of (1). Our
billiard-player snobbishly tries to keep a certain distance between
his controlled movements and the blind movements of the billiard-
balls that he pots and cannons so effortlessly. Now he is told (1) that
his movements are on the same causal level as theirs, but (2) that this
level is higher than he had supposed.[19] It is as if T. H. Huxley had
tried to soothe Bishop Wilberforce by assuring him that monkeys are
really very human.

4. THE APRIORIST VIEW: REASON AND AUTONOMY

I now turn to the great classical alternative to the empiricist view,
namely the apriorist view of human freedom, of which Spinoza and
Kant are the chief spokesmen in modern times.

---

decisive *objection* to libertarianism was that it would deprive God of His
ability to foresee what would happen in His own creation. (*The Doctrine of
Philosophical Necessity Illustrated*, 1777, sect. III, 'Of the Argument for
Necessity from the Divine Prescience'; reprinted in *Priestley's Writings on
Philosophy, Science and Politics*, ed. John A. Passmore (London: Collier-
Macmillan, 1965) p. 63.)

[19] As Hume put it: 'Let no one, therefore, put an invidious construction
on my words, by saying simply, that I assert the necessity of human actions,
and place them on the same footing with the operations of senseless matter.
I do not ascribe to the will that unintelligible necessity, which is suppos'd to
lie in matter. But I ascribe to matter, that intelligible quality, call it necessity
or not, which the most rigorous orthodoxy does or must allow to belong to the
will.' (*Treatise*, Bk. II, Part III, Sect. II, ed. Selby-Bigge, p. 410.)

Spinoza's view, put very briefly, was this. The human mind is mostly engaged in merely empirical thinking ('knowledge of the first kind'). This includes sensory experiences, memories and imaginings, and also inductive beliefs induced by repetitive experience. With respect to this kind of thinking the human mind is other-determined: physical stimuli impinge upon the sense-organs and disturbances are transmitted to the brain which gets modified in various small ways; new channels are formed in it; the nervous fluids flowing along these channels are paralleled by perceptions, dreams, imaginings, memories and associations of ideas. In all this the human mind is *passive*.

However, the human mind is capable of something else: rational or *a priori* reasoning (for simplicity's sake I am amalgamating Spinoza's 'second' and 'third' kinds of knowledge). Here, the mind is not impelled by anything external to it. This kind of intellectual activity is self-determining. It proceeds with a kind of necessity, but an internal necessity. There is no indeterminacy, no freedom of choice, as reason proceeds unerringly from one adequate idea to another, unfolding the inevitable consequences of self-evident axioms grasped by intellectual intuition. Nor is there any external pressure. When and only when a person is reasoning in this necessary way is he doing something unconstrained by anything external to himself, something purely active. Unhappiness and pain result from passivity. Activity is joyful: 'From this [third] kind of knowledge arises the highest possible peace of mind, that is to say, the highest joy.'[20]

On this view, neither our brain-washed convert nor a subject acting out a post-hypnotic suggestion is free. But Spinoza's view also implies that *all* of us are unfree as we go about our daily lives in the empirical world:[21] if we believe ourselves to be free in our practical decision-making it is because we are 'dreaming with our eyes open', unaware of the causal prehistory of our decisions.

Spinoza's idea of a-causal self-determination was taken over into Kant's moral philosophy. But instead of an intellect cognising eternal truth, Kant had practical reason imposing a universal and rationally necessary moral law upon itself; and in place of Spinoza's intellectual love of God, Kant put reverence for the moral law.

For my part, I regard the idea of freedom as a kind of emancipation, by the use of reason, from dependence on external factors as much more serious and interesting than the first view we considered.

[20] *Ethics*, Bk. V, prop. xxxii.
[21] 'It is evident from what I have said, that we are in many ways driven about by external causes, and that like waves of the sea driven by contrary winds we toss to and fro unwitting of the issue and of our fate.' (*Ethics*, Bk. III, prop. lix, note.)

But this second view, as set forth by Spinoza and by Kant, was crippled by the fact that both these great thinkers were thorough-going determinists whose determinism applied to human conduct equally with inanimate natural processes. This had the consequence that a man's rational thinking *cannot actually alter his bodily behaviour.* Kant tried to combine freedom and determinism in the following way: viewed as part of the empirical world, man is wholly heteronomous; viewed as a rational being, he is wholly autonomous. Kant boldly declared that 'no genuine contradiction is to be found between the freedom and the natural necessity ascribed to the very same human actions'.[22]

Like many other people, I cannot accept this 'two-world' solution of Kant's freedom-causality antinomy.[23] Of what use is a person's understanding of, and reverence for, the moral law if it does nothing to check or redirect or control his causally predetermined empirical behaviour? Kant came rather near tacitly conceding this point when he said that 'even the most hardened scoundrel' possesses, as a rational member of the intelligible world, a good will, even though, as a member of the sensible world, he possesses a bad will.[24] So Al Capone and Hitler were essentially men of good will, really; it was just that their empirical selves got causally implicated in the killing of other men.

5. BETWIXT CHANCE AND NECESSITY: DEGREES OF CONTROL

Yet there is much in this second view that should be rescued. As I see it, its rescue calls for three main steps. The *first* step is the overthrow of physical determinism. As we saw, the Spinoza-Kant view was paralysed by its deterministic framework: if a person's physical behaviour is causally predetermined down to the last detail, no *spielraum* is left for practical thinking to exercise any influence or control. But this is *only* a preliminary step and by no means sufficient *by itself* to reinstate the possibility that practical thinking may influence bodily behaviour. I agree with Popper that 'indeterminism is not enough': we also need a certain 'causal openness' of the physical towards the mental.[25] If there are physical indeterminacies,

[22] *Groundwork of the Metaphysic of Morals*, second edition, p. 115 (pp. 123–4 in H. J. Paton's translation, *The Moral Law*, London: Hutchinson).
[23] A new version of it has recently been advocated by Stephan Körner: see his *Abstraction in Science and Morals*, Eddington Memorial Lecture (Cambridge: University Press, 1971).   [24] Ibid., pp. 112–13 (pp. 122–3).
[25] Karl R. Popper, 'Indeterminism is Not Enough', *Encounter* (April, 1973) p. 20.

then there is a certain *spielraum* or gappiness in some physical processes, but whether this can be exploited by consciousness is a further
question. After taking this first step we would still be confronted by
Hume's 'law of excluded middle' and its implication that with the
introduction of indeterminism we should merely be out of the frying-
pan into the fire.

So the *second* step must be to show that there are middle possibilities between chance and necessity.

The need for this second step is revealed very clearly in an
important passage by Austin Farrer.[26] Farrer belonged to the
minority that takes physical determinism seriously: 'Over the whole
debate about the voluntary freedom of man there hangs the shadow
of physical determinism . . .' Does the indeterminacy of microphysics
offer any escape? He concluded that it does not on the following
grounds: (a) 'What would interest us would be an indeterminacy on
which conscious thought could (as it were) exercise a persuasive influence' (p. 4). (b) Now the system on which thought would have to
exercise such an influence is the nervous system; but the nervous
system is a *macro*-system. (c) And micro-indeterminacies yield, at the
macro-level, regularities which, though statistical, are as stable and
hard as those of a fully deterministic system.

But (c) above is, in effect, a special application of Hume's 'law':
it says that there may be chance-events at the micro-level as well as
causal determinacy at the macro-level; but there is no middle possibility. This conviction seems to have crippled Farrer's attempts to
solve the important problems that he posed so sharply.[27]

Our second step is still within the physical domain. We want to
show that, if there are micro-indeterminacies, then there can be a
macro-system B whose behaviour is by no means precisely determined, but which can be more or less strongly influenced or controlled by some physical adjuster A.

The *third* step in our rescue-operation would be, ideally, the

[26] Austin Farrer, *The Freedom of the Will* (London: Black, 1958) pp. 2–4.
[27] He seems to have been a would-be interactionist inhibited by the old
belief that something non-physical cannot interact with something physical.
He rejected psychophysical parallelism and epiphenomenalism, insisting
'that consciousness should do some real work, and not exhaust her efficacy
in the mere business of being conscious' (ibid., p. 99). But confronted by
the full-fledged interactionist, dualist, neo-Cartesian position presented by
Sir John Eccles in *The Neurophysiological Basis of Mind* he exclaimed:
'We will have nothing to do with the fantastic suggestion, that what the
supersensitive "reactors" in the cortex react to, is the initiative of a virtually
disembodied soul' (p. 87). He took refuge in a kind of identity-theory: 'We
say that the reactions of the reactors are, in cases of free will, themselves
the work of the soul . . . incarnate in . . . these very reactors' (p. 92).

development of a model for the more or less strong influence or control by A over B where B is again a macro-system (such as the nervous system) but A is mental.

So much for the programme; what about its implementation?

On the present occasion I am going to assume, without argument, that the *first* step (the overthrow of physical determinism) has already been taken by science. My authority is, of course, quantum mechanics, whose indeterminacies cannot, according to von Neumann's theorem, be imputed to hidden parameters, but have to be accepted as irreducible. (I have presented elsewhere arguments, mainly due to Landé and to Popper, for indeterminism that are independent of QM.)[28]

As to the *second* step: this is rather easy to take once the first has been taken. One way to take it is with the help of the propensity interpretation of probability which Popper developed in connection with his objectivist interpretation of quantum mechanics.[29]

The propensity interpretation was intended to absorb and supersede the frequency interpretation of probability. In von Mises's version of the latter, a central place is occupied by the idea of a 'given collective' of outcomes of a repeated experiment.[30] What *generates* the collective (or population, or sequence), what it is given *by*, does not receive much attention. Popper's propensity interpretation, on the other hand, gives a central place to the set-up that generates the collectives or random sequences. The set-up is conceived as a physical propensity-system which gives to each of the possible outcomes of an 'experiment' a certain weight or probability-value. From our point of view, it is important that the set-up may be

[28] In my contribution, 'The Unity of Popper's Thought', submitted back in 1968 to the forthcoming volume, *The Philosophy of Karl Popper* (The Library of Living Philosophers, ed. P. A. Schilpp).

I wanted to avoid duplication of that paper in this one. But the delayed publication of the former (though it has appeared in a German translation, by Gretl Albert, in *Grundprobleme der Grossen Philosophen*, ed. Josef Speck (Göttingen: Vandenhoeck & Ruprecht, 1972) and my desire to make the present paper reasonably self-contained have resulted in some overlapping. [Added in proof: *The Philosophy of Karl Popper* was published in 1974.]

[29] Karl R. Popper, 'Quantum Mechanics without "The Observer"', chap. 1 in *Quantum Mechanics and Reality*, ed. Mario Bunge, volume II of *Studies in the Foundations, Methodology, and Philosophy of Science* (Berlin and New York: Springer Verlag, 1967), and 'The Propensity Interpretation of Probability', *Brit. Jour. Phil. Science*, vol. 10 (May, 1959).

Popper himself does not seem to have exploited his propensity theory in his criticism (see note 15 above) of Hume's necessity/chance dichotomy.

[30] Richard von Mises, *Probability, Statistics and Truth*, Second English edition by Hilda Geiringer (London: Allen & Unwin) pp. 11–12.

adjustable and hence that the probability-values may be *controllable*. Consider the following set-up. There is a source that allows us to fire electrons, one at a time, at a diffraction apparatus with adjustable slits; beyond the slits there is a photographic plate, which is divided into regions. Assume that on one adjustment, A_1, of the slits, the set-up gives a probability-value of 0.01 to the outcome that an electron lands within a certain region, while on adjustment A_2 the probability-value is 0.02.

On the propensity-interpretation, such probability-values *exist*, in a dispositional sense, whether or not the set-up is activated. Suppose that the set-up is now activated, neither just a few times nor billions of times, but quite a large number of times, say 10,000 times on adjustment A_1 and 10,000 times on adjustment A_2. Then we should expect the actual statistical results to conform quite well, but by no means precisely, with the probability-values. Suppose that in the event we get, on A_1, an actual statistical result B_1 of 89 hits, and on A_2 a result B_2 of 217 hits.

Now the relation of B_1 to A_1 (and of B_2 to A_2) falls into neither of Hume's two allegedly exhaustive categories. Hume's 'law' might be expressed thus: for an event (or set of events) x, either (1) there exist antecedent conditions y such that y precisely predetermined x, or (2) for all antecedent conditions y, x is causally independent of y. If 'independent' is given a probabilistic interpretation, (2) becomes (2'): for any antecedent condition y, the probability of x given y equals the absolute probability of x. But neither of these alternatives holds if we put B_1 in place of x. Alternative (1) fails on the assumption (here taken for granted) that the individual electrons behave with a certain indeterminacy, so that the statistical result was not precisely determined. And alternative (2') is false since the adjustment of the set-up assuredly *influenced* the statistical result.

The source of Hume's mistake seems to have been this: he did not notice that a full-fledged doctrine of determinism involves *two* universal quantifiers. It says, not just that all events are determined, but that *all* events are determined in *every* detail (or are *completely* determined). Thus he took its contradictory to be, 'Some events are [completely] undetermined' when he should have taken it to be, 'Some events are not completely determined.' Our imagined set-up is a straightforward example of a physical situation that is only partially determined.

But perhaps I am labouring the obvious. Once it is conceded that, in addition to areas of causal determinacy, there are at the opposite extreme areas of indeterminacy, then surely there will be areas of partial determinacy in between. Once we are allowed out of the drill-hall into the casino, we must surely be allowed into places in-between – a dance-hall, for instance – where what happens is neither strictly regimented nor merely random. The *first* step being taken, the *second* step follows naturally.

What about the *third* step? Do we have a model which could account for the exercise of a degree of influence or control by *A* over *B*, where *A* is a man's mind and *B* is his body?

Here, my claim is only that there is no longer any good reason to suppose that such a model *cannot* be provided.[31] However, this modest claim is strong enough for the present purpose. I will make the point with the help of an analogy. Imagine that during the seventeenth century a certain doctrine came to be regarded by philosophers as absolutely indisputable, and that this doctrine implied that it is *impossible* that *white* sunlight should cause *reddening* of the skin: so philosophers were driven to search for ingenious hypotheses that would account for sunburn in some esoteric and round-about way.

What would be required for a philosophical rehabilitation of the stubborn conviction of common sense that the sun does cause sunburn? Well, it would certainly be rehabilitated if the proscribing doctrine were superseded by a theory that provided an actual model of the sunburn process. But it would be sufficient if the proscribing doctrine were just shown to be baseless. Then there would be nothing to inhibit our belief that the sun somehow causes sunburn, though the exact process may remain obscure to us.

The proscribing doctrines that drove so many philosophers after Descartes to hold that it is *impossible* for a man's mind to exercise a degree of control over his body boil down, so far as I can see, to these two: (1) A man's body is part of the physical world; if it were open to quasi-causal interference of an extra-physical kind, then there would be bits of the physical world that are physicalistically indeterminate. (2) Something immaterial cannot act on something material.

With the breakdown of physical determinism, (1) ceases to be an objection. As to (2): at least since 1600, when William Gilbert likened magnetic forces to the animating effects of the human soul,[32] there has existed within science the idea that *forces* act on things. Now the idea of a field of force *may* have been reconcilable with (2) so long as it was accompanied by the idea of a subtle material substratum or medium through which the forces are propagated. But with the

---

[31] My debts to Popper here are indicated in §4.1 of the paper referred to in note 28.

[32] William Gilbert, *De Magnete*, Book V, chap. xii.

abandonment of the ether, electromagnetic field theory called for a major revision of traditional ontological categories: a 'qualitatively new kind of entity' had been introduced,[33] an immaterial substance that acts on material things.

Thus the two great philosophical objections to interactionism have both been overtaken by scientific developments.

6. A THIRD VIEW

We can get a third view of human freedom by subjecting the second view to two major revisions: first, replacing the deterministic framework within which it was developed by a framework of the kind indicated above, a framework which allows a partial indeterminacy even at the macro-level and which allows that ideas may initiate actions; second, disengaging the idea of self-determination or autonomy from the apriorist theory of knowledge on which it was based. It is to this second revision that I now turn.

Spinoza's theory involved a dichotomy analogous to Hume's cause/chance dichotomy, but with two big differences: chance is replaced by *self-determination*; and this latter category is *not* a mere empty logical possibility. Yet Spinoza was no less certain than Hume that everything is *other*-determined down to the last detail. Then how is self-determination possible?

Spinoza's answer involved a kind of intellectualist escapism: although we are always situation-bound, it *is* possible to escape into a condition of pure, unconstrained activity. How? Well, there is one individual who is not situation-bound: there is nothing external to God to constrain *His* activity. Considered in one way, His activity consists of timelessly thinking the infinite system of necessary truth. Thus if a human individual succeeds in thinking through some part of that system he becomes, to that extent, one with God, participating in God's self-determining activity.

But it seems obvious that no one ever thinks in the manner here required. Consider the case of Spinoza himself when he was writing the *Ethics*. Obviously, he did not proceed by first cognising a few self-evident axioms, and then go on to derive, one after another, the

---

[33] David Bohm, *Causality and Chance in Modern Physics* (London: Routledge, 1957) p. 45. Or as Einstein put it: 'For this theory [the electrodynamics of Faraday and Maxwell] and its confirmation by Hertz's experiments showed that there are electromagnetic phenomena which by their very nature are detached from every ponderable matter — namely the waves in empty space which consist of electromagnetic "fields".' ('Autobiographical Notes', in *Albert Einstein: Philosopher-Scientist*, ed. P. A. Schilpp, The Library of Living Philosophers, vol. I, p. 25.)

numbered propositions that appear in the *Ethics*.[34] That book was hammered out in a sustained attempt to solve a sequence of interconnected problems (one of which was: how is self-determination possible in a deterministic world?). And although it required Spinoza's peculiar genius and temperament to discern the problems as he did, they were largely created for him by the work of other thinkers. (His problem-situation would have been very different if, for instance, Descartes had died at birth.)

No one, I take it, is fooled by the 'Euclidean' trappings of Spinoza's *Ethics*. But just suppose, first, that the *Ethics* had matched Euclid's *Elements* with respect to both the status of its axioms and the rigour of its demonstrations; and second, that Kant had been right about the synthetic *a priori* status of mathematical propositions. That still would not mean that the *Ethics* was the outcome of a special kind of unerring, *a priori* cognising. For we know that, whatever the status of its finished products may be, mathematical thinking, like other kinds of scientific thinking, is a problem-oriented, trial-and-error process.[35]

I conclude that it is not possible for anyone to escape from the exigencies of his empirical situation into a state of freedom by switching to a kind of pure, self-determining, error-free and inexorable *a priori* thinking; for there is no such thinking.

Yet I share Spinoza's view that freedom essentially involves the exercise of reason, just as I share Kant's view of the emancipating role of knowledge. Let us see how the idea of freedom, or autonomy, fares when we detach it from apriorism and relate it to what I take to be a more realistic view of the way reason is used in advancing knowledge, namely Popper's 'third view'.[36]

Only the bare essentials of this view are needed here. I will confine myself to four main features. First: all rational thinking is *problem*-oriented. Second: problems exist objectively, 'out there' so to speak; thus they may be underestimated or misappraised.[37] The third

---

[34] See the section on 'The Construction, Possession and Utilisation of Theories' in Gilbert Ryle, *The Concept of Mind* (London: Hutchinson, 1949) pp. 286 f.

In Spinoza's case, we know from the *Short Treatise on God, Man, and His Well-Being*, trans. and ed. A. Wolf (1910) reprinted (New York: Russell & Russell, 1963); and from the correspondence with Oldenburg in *The Correspondence of Spinoza*, trans. and ed. A. Wolf (London: Allen & Unwin, 1928) that there had been earlier versions of his system which differed significantly from the version in the *Ethics*.

[35] See I. Lakatos, 'Proofs and Refutations', *Brit. Jour. Phil. Science*, vol. 14 (1963–4). [36] See note 2 above.

[37] On the 'world 3' status of problems, see Karl R. Popper, *Objective Knowledge*, chap. 4. Russell's problem of the class of all classes that are

feature takes a little longer to explain. Let P be a description of the main components of some problem-situation, and let S be a promising scientific solution for P. Then, typically, S will logically transcend P, 'go beyond' P, have excess content over P. It may even happen that S is strictly inconsistent with P, that part of the solution is to *correct* the problem as previously formulated (as the Newtonian solution corrects the problem: why is the acceleration of all freely falling bodies near the earth's surface *constant?*). In any case, S cannot be computed from a knowledge of P: it has to be invented. Fourth: a proposed solution cannot be verified; but it may survive testing and other kinds of criticism.

I want now to carry over this view of human reason from the domain of theoretical problem-solving into the domain of practical problem-solving. Here, it becomes essential that we make a distinction between merely *reacting* to an external situation in a causally determined way, and *responding* to a problem-situation in a (more or less) rational and resourceful or inventive way.

This distinction is obliterated by determinism. (Priestley dismissed something like it as 'a distinction merely verbal'.[38]) If *all* behaviour is completely determined, we cannot single out certain human actions as having an extra something that lifts them out of the class of causally determined reactions. But I am assuming that determinism has been overthrown.

I concede that there are borderline cases in which this distinction becomes blurred. (I will discuss one such case later.) But the distinction comes into its own in difficult and demanding situations where one man may have the imagination and knowledge to see a possible way out where another man would have been trapped. My idea of human freedom comes essentially to this: a man preserves his autonomy in a threatening situation so long as he continues to respond to it in a resourceful and inventive way of his own.

Before elaborating on that, let me say that I regard freedom as a matter of degree, rather than a yes-no affair. So I will begin by replacing the autonomy/heteronomy dichotomy with a scale ranging

---

not members of themselves will serve as an example. Russell did not manufacture this problem, *he found it*; and when he found it, he at first seriously underestimated it, imputing it to 'some trivial error in my reasoning', Bertrand Russell, *My Philosophical Development* (London: Allen & Unwin, 1959, p. 76).

[38] Op. cit. (see note 18 above), section II (p. 62). Priestley's standard case was that of a child who likes apples and dislikes peaches being offered an apple or a peach. But even here the distinction is not entirely obliterated: an enterprising child might respond inventively to the situation by taking the peach in the hope of swapping it for two apples later.

from full autonomy to full heteronomy. Full autonomy is no doubt unattainable by human beings, even for a Socrates or a Spinoza. Whether it is possible to sink into a state of full heteronomy I would not care to say. I imagine that a case of heroin-addiction may fall not far short of it.

As I see it, a person's position on this scale is a function both of the situation he is in and of the way he is responding to it. Let us look at *situations* first, *responses* to them afterwards.

Some situations threaten one's autonomy, others do not. I say that a situation threatens a person's autonomy if there is a serious risk that he will become a prisoner of it in the sense that what he 'does' ceases to be something that *he* is doing and becomes a series of reactions to external circumstances in which all initiative is lost.

Let us begin with a kind of situation which does *not* threaten the agent's autonomy. Assume that my preferences (moral and otherwise) have not been 'got at' by brain-washing, subliminal advertising, hypnotic suggestion, etc.; and suppose that I find myself in a situation where, given my preferences, there is just one course of action that I obviously ought to take, though the situation leaves open other courses which I might have taken if my preferences had been otherwise. Such *rational determinacy* within an objectively open situation does not entail heteronomy.

The fact that there is much rational determinacy in everyday life has often been used in support of the reconcilability-thesis. In normal circumstances, a person acting in a rationally determinate way acts both *freely* and *predictably*. On the assumption that predictability presupposes causal determination, this would mean that his behaviour is at once *free* and *causally determined*.[39]

But the kind of predictability – I will call it R-predictability – associated with rational determinacy is, of course, very different from the kind of predictability – I will call it C-predictability – associated with causal determinacy. An R-prediction (say, that a party leader will try to placate his left-wing) may say nothing about the physical detail of the predicted man's behaviour; and a C-prediction (say, that after a cerebral commissure a right-handed patient will not verbally identify objects in the left half of his field of vision) may say nothing about the predicted man's future course of action.

Thus we should, in strictness, say that a person acting in a rationally determinate way acts both freely and R-predictably. To get from this to the conclusion that he is at once free and causally determined would require the additional lemma that R-predictability

[39] This and the next two paragraphs were added in response to a suggestion by Alan Musgrave.

implies C-predictability. I argued earlier that, on the contrary, in so far as behaviour is C-predictable it is to that extent not R-predictable. If we can C-predict that a post-hypnotic subject will take off his shoes and place them on the table, then we cannot R-predict that he will do so.

Although it is not essential to my idea of freedom, I may mention that my belief in certain kinds of (partial) physical indeterminacy is matched by a belief in certain kinds of (partial) rational indeterminacy. I am not thinking primarily of cases where the agent has to choose arbitrarily between equally good alternatives; nor of cases where he is pulled in one direction by self-interest and in an opposite direction by duty; nor of cases where he is torn between two moral rules which yield conflicting prescriptions for his present situation; nor of cases where he is under-informed about his situation and uncertain about the outcomes of the possible decisions open to him. I am thinking of certain formal types of situation where the agent's preference-system is consistent and complete,[40] and where the requirement of perfect (or optimal) knowledge is satisfied. It has been the programme of decision theory in general, and of game theory in particular, to work out rules for optimal choice that would render all such situations rationally determinate, however intractable they might seem at first sight. This programme has been pursued with considerable success. But in the course of its pursuit, situational models have been constructed – essentially simple in structure, though they all involve two or more agents – which turn out *not* to be rationally determinate. Or so I have claimed elsewhere.[41] This has the following implication. A military leader, say, in a crisis-situation has a crucial decision to make; how he decides is bound to affect the course of his country's history very seriously. I take it for granted that his decision is not C-predictable: the only way to predict it is by examining his problem-situation with the aim of estimating what would be, from his point of view, the best decision for him to make. But now suppose that his situation approximates one of those rationally indeterminate situational models. In that case there is *no* best decision for him to make. His decision is not R-predictable either. If such cases occur, as I believe they do, we have here an

[40] For the notion of 'completeness' or 'connectedness' see, for example, Amartya K. Sen, *Collective Choice and Social Welfare* (Edinburgh: Oliver & Boyd, 1970) p. 3.

[41] In my 'Imperfect Rationality', *Explanation in the Behavioural Sciences*, ed. Borger & Cioffi (Cambridge University Press, 1970) esp. pp. 197 and 202 f.; and my 'Self-Interest and Morality', *Practical Reason*, ed. Stephan Körner (Oxford: Blackwell, 1974) pp. 67–77.

additional argument against the possibility of scientifically fore-
casting the future course of history.[42]

I turn now to situations that do threaten the individual's autonomy.

A tell-tale sign of the existence of such a situation is this: an on-
looker is in a position successfully to predict an individual's behaviour *without* recourse, whether explicit or implicit, to assumptions
about his values and problem-solving resourcefulness. A troublesome hospital patient is given a tranquillising injection. 'He'll be
more co-operative now', the doctor predicts. (By contrast, there
would have been no suggestion of reduced autonomy if the doctor
had said: 'I told him that there are patients in this ward who are
more ill than he is, and that his behaviour makes it harder for the
nurses to look after them. He took the point and *he'll be more co-
operative now*.')

There are situations where the distinction between rational
response and caused reaction is blurred. In Occupied France during
the last war German S.S. men were in the habit, when a village was
suspected of harbouring a resistance-fighter, of lining up all the men
in front of a machine-gun, and all the women opposite them; the
women were then told that their menfolk would be machine-gunned
unless the outsider was identified. It seems that this method always
worked.

Now one might say that a woman who identifies a resistance-
fighter in such circumstances is responding rationally to her problem-
situation: it is just that she finds herself in a rather stark example of
what Latsis has called a 'single-exit' situation.[43] She does not want
the resistance-fighter to be caught and tortured by the S.S. But still
less does she want her father, brothers and fiancé to be shot.

But I am rather inclined to say that such a terrorised 'response' *is*
a causally induced reaction: the woman is trapped in a situation
which makes her do what the S.S. men require.

A situation may threaten a person's autonomy; whether it actually
impairs his autonomy depends on the nature of his reaction
or response to it. Let us now consider this other side of the matter.

If Houdini were held *incommunicado* in a prison-cell he would
have a thousand and one ideas about how to escape. Even if he did
not actually succeed, he would have retained more autonomy than

---

[42] Additional, that is, to the arguments in Karl R. Popper, *The Poverty of
Historicism* (London: Routledge, 1957).

[43] Spiro J. Latsis, 'Situational Determinism in Economics', *Brit. Jour. Phil.
Science*, vol. 23 (August, 1972) p. 211 and *passim*.

most of us would have, for he would have repeatedly *attacked* his situation with resourceful hypotheses, refusing to give in to it.[44]

I suggested, as an indication of reduced autonomy, the possibility of successfully predicting a man's behaviour on the basis of external circumstances without reference to *him* (or with reference to him only as a human animal and not as a moral person). Let us now consider the converse of this. Is it an indication of maintained autonomy if such an external prediction is refuted by what the agent actually does?

Not if the prediction misfires merely because of a mistake about some external circumstance (as might have happened if that troublesome hospital patient had been inadvertently injected with a stimulant and had become even less co-operative, contrary to the doctor's prediction). Nor is it if the prediction is refuted by behaviour which, though unexpected, is also futile (as when a motorist in a traffic-jam flashes his headlights and blows his horn).

But it may be an indication of maintained autonomy if the prediction is refuted in a more interesting way. Suppose that agent *A* appears, to a competent and informed observer *B*, to be in a grim 'single-exit' situation: *A* can do *X* which will be nasty for him; anything else would be disastrous. So *B* predicts that *A* will do *X*. But then *A* does something else; and when *B* reflects upon what *A* is doing he realises that, although it is something that he, *B*, would never have thought of doing in that situation, it does actually have some chance of succeeding. Suppose, however, that it fails. *B* now makes another 'single-exit' prediction. But *A* again comes up with a surprise move that refutes the prediction and which again has some chance of succeeding . . .

Let us break off the story at that point, with the question of the eventual success or failure of *A*'s series of prediction-refuting moves left open. Whether or not he finally succeeds, *A* has been defying a situation which seemed to an informed observer to have him in its grip, and defying it in inventive and resourceful ways.

---

[44] Of course, trying to escape is not the only way in which a prisoner can try to preserve his autonomy. I have an unbounded admiration for those political prisoners of totalitarian regimes – Alex Weissberg, the pseudonymous F. Beck and W. Godin, Edith Bone, Eugenia Ginzburg, Paul Ignotus, George Paloczi-Horvath, Bela Szasz, and others – who, though they sometimes came near to breaking-point, continued basically to defy the system of lies and terror in which they were caught, hoarded their experiences like misers anxious to let no bit of truth slip away, and – eventually – turned the tables by telling the world, in sharp detail and without bitterness, the truth as they knew it.

7. INTERNAL HETERONOMY

My account is still incomplete. As so far presented, it could be summarised thus. How a man acts in a given situation is a function both of external factors and of internal factors (his preferences and his intellectual inventiveness); and his degree of self-determination is roughly proportional to the relative significance of the internal factors in shaping his response to his situation.

But I believe that it is possible for the internal contribution to be *too* strong, so that there is something pathological about the ensuing behaviour. Our account takes care of cases where a man's autonomy is reduced by external factors; but as it stands it does not yet take care of cases where it is reduced by something within himself.

I can introduce the kind of thing I have in mind with the help of a story which Lorenz tells about a little rodent called a water-shrew.[45] Placed in new surroundings, the shrew moves very slowly, with much sniffing and whiskering, picking out, step by step, an erratic path for itself. On subsequent outings it tries to stick to exactly the same path (if its path crosses itself, the shrew sticks conservatively to the extra detour). Where the shrew is sure of the way, it rushes forward; when it becomes uncertain, it starts sniffing and whiskering again. A time comes when, knowing by heart every detail of the route it originally picked out for itself, it rushes round it at high speed. In the case of Lorenz's water-shrews, the route included two stones. He writes:

> If I moved the stones out of the runway, ... the shrews would jump right up into the air in the place where the stone should have been; they came down with a jarring bump, were obviously disconcerted and started whiskering cautiously right and left, just as they behaved in an unknown environment. And then they did a most interesting thing: they went back the way they had come, carefully feeling their way until they had again got their bearings. Then, facing round again, they tried a second time with a rush and jumped and crashed down exactly as they had done a few seconds before.

Yet, as Lorenz pointed out, they had been able to see the stones perfectly well on their earlier exploratory outgoings. To put it anthropomorphically: it is as if their perceptions had been over-ruled by an idea which had become fixed. (Actually, their behaviour did not, in the end, fulfil my idea of internal heteronomy: they did not

45 Konrad Lorenz, *King Solomon's Ring*, second edition (London: Methuen, 1961) pp. 108–10.

keep on jumping and crashing. The method of trial-and-error re-asserted itself, and they picked out a new path where the stones had been.)

There are famous examples in fiction of lives dominated and eventually destroyed by too strong an idea. In the case of Kirilov in Dostoyevsky's *The Possessed*, the idea by which he is possessed is precisely the idea of destroying himself – to prove his mastery over himself! Adrian Leverkühn in Thomas Mann's *Doctor Faustus* gets the idea of going with a *diseased* prostitute. It seems to me that if he had taken a cool, critical look at it, he would have concluded that that was not a good idea. But no, the idea gets hold of him, with the eventual result that he is destroyed by disease of the brain. I do not think that such cases occur only in fiction. Hume pointed out that a desire for vengeance may so fill a man that it ruins his life.[46]

It seems that something *alien* may lodge itself in a person's mind, like a stranger who insinuates himself into a family and then acquires an increasing ascendancy over it.[47] Trivial examples of this are familiar (the irritating tune that keeps going round in one's head).[48] Sometimes, ideas that obtrude themselves into consciousness are *welcome*, as in the famous cases of mathematical discovery recorded by Gauss, Klein and Poincaré. (In this connection Waismann quoted approvingly Lichtenberg's suggestion that 'One should not say "I think", but rather "it thinks", just as one says "it thunders"', and also Coleridge's remark that 'Thoughts are their own masters.'[49]) However, in the case of these welcome intrusions, the discoverer (recipient?) can soon bring them under rational control by writing them down next morning, objectifying them so that they become amenable to critical scrutiny. One hardly imagines Kirilov, or Lever-kühn, or a man hell-bent on revenge, doing that to the idea that obsessed him.

A possible way of dealing with the latter kind of case would be to

[46] David Hume, *Enquiries*, Appendix ii *ad fin*. (ed. Selby-Bigge, p. 302).

[47] My analogy is inspired by Dostoyevsky's short story, *The Friend of the Family*.

[48] An unusual and alarming example was reported by Newton (in a letter to Locke). Newton had found that, on going into a dark room after looking at the sun in a looking glass, he could revive an image of the sun at will. But after doing this a good many times he found that *he could not make it go away again* for several days; and 'for some months after, the spectrum of the sun began to return as often as I began to meditate upon the phenomenon, even though I lay in bed at midnight with my curtains drawn'. (Quoted in Maurice Cranston, *John Locke* (London: Longmans, 1957) pp. 346–7.)

[49] F. Waismann, *How I See Philosophy*, ed. R. Harré (London: Macmillan, 1968) pp. 196–8.

lay down that autonomy-preservation requires, not only that internal factors should be relatively significant in determining the agent's action, but also that the action should be *successful* from the agent's point of view, or at least should not result in self-injury or self-destruction.

But I have deliberately avoided invoking success as a condition for the preservation of autonomy, and I do not want to resort to it now; for success is often largely a matter of luck.

I prefer to deal with such cases by invoking a main feature of Popper's 'third view' which I have not stressed hitherto. The feature that I *have* stressed is that a promising solution S for a non-trivial problem-situation P will typically be, within certain limits, a free invention which logically transcends P. But this is complemented by the requirement that S should be tested and criticised independently of its adequacy as a solution for P.[50]

Setting aside direct introspective findings, we might characterise an *idée fixe* as an idea that has somehow elevated itself, in someone's mind, to a position where he is psychologically unable to criticise it, so that it is beyond his rational control. (This could be extended to ideas, conscious or otherwise, instilled by hypnotic suggestion, brainwashing, etc., on the supposition that such ideas are unamenable to rational control.) And then we could say that an agent is a victim of some degree of internal heteronomy if there is a component in his decision-scheme[51] which is an *idée fixe* in this sense.

It may be objected that every decision-scheme contains '*idées fixes*' in this sense, namely the agent's preferences; for preferences are not open to rational control: *de gustibus non est disputandum.*

But we are considering the special case where the satisfaction of one particular overriding desire would endanger, or even destroy, the possibility of satisfying other desires. In such cases it may surely be rational to curb the rogue desire.

In any case, since I operate, not with an either/or dichotomy, but with the idea of degrees of autonomy and heteronomy, and since I do not claim that anyone enjoys complete autonomy, I do not need to make exaggerated claims about the extent to which relatively autonomous agents in an open society have the components of their decision-schemes under rational control. It is enough that I can say

[50] In terms of Popper's schema '$P_1 \rightarrow TT \rightarrow EE \rightarrow P_2$' (where P_1 is an initial problem, TT is a tentative theory, EE is error-elimination, and P_2 is the resulting problem), I have been emphasising the relation of TT to P_1 at the expense of its relation to EE.

[51] The idea of a decision-scheme is explained in my 'Imperfect Rationality' (see note 41 above), pp. 206 f.

of, for instance, a man consumed by hatred, that this puts him nearer the heteronomy-end of the scale than he would otherwise be.

8. IMPLICATIONS FOR LIBERALISM

What difference would be made to liberalism if its central principle, as I called it in my opening remarks, were interpreted in accordance with this third view of human freedom?

It would turn into something like the liberalism of J. S. Mill's *On Liberty*, but of a more uncompromising kind. For Mill was there handicapped by his own empiricist philosophy (utilitarianism, determinism, reconcilability-thesis, inductivism) which was inimical in various ways to his libertarian principles; whereas they develop naturally out of the view of freedom and the associated epistemological and metaphysical views (conjecturalism, indeterminism, interactionism) subscribed to here. Or so I will now argue.

Consider first his tergiversations in trying to reconcile libertarianism and utilitarianism.

When an *empiricist* interpretation, as I called it, is put upon the principle that freedom should be maximised, the latter turns into a utilitarian principle: if one is happier doing what one wants to do than doing what one does not want to do, and if being free *is* doing what one wants to do, then the maximisation of freedom would be equivalent to the maximisation of happiness.

Now liberty, as envisaged by Mill, had more to do with such things as truthfulness, rationality, integrity, moral courage and personal independence, than with happiness. Perhaps because he had been stung by Whewell's claim that Benthamism makes it 'a duty to increase the pleasure of pigs',[52] Mill made the famous declaration: 'better to be a human being dissatisfied than a pig satisfied; better to be Socrates dissatisfied than a fool satisfied'.[53] Notoriously, however, instead of breaking with utilitarianism in his defence of liberty, he made a sorry attempt to reconcile them with the help of his distinction between 'higher' and 'lower' pleasures.

Replacing the empiricist interpretation by our interpretation of human freedom does not make liberalism puritanical. Liberalism thus interpreted does not say that because want-satisfaction is

[52] Quoted in John Stuart Mill, *Collected Works*, vol. x, p. 186. Attention is drawn to this pasage by H. B. Acton on p. xiii of the work mentioned in the next note.
[53] J. S. Mill, *Utilitarianism*, chap. 2 (p. 9 in *John Stuart Mill, Utilitarianism, Liberty, Representative Government*, ed. H. B. Acton (London: Dent, 1972)).

something pigs engage in, it is not something that human beings should engage in. But it does say that human beings, unless reduced to a sub-human level, say in a concentration or forced-labour camp or through drug-addiction, have to a greater or lesser degree a distinctive capacity for responding resourcefully, or imaginatively, or inventively, or creatively to situations, and that it is in the exercise of *this* capacity that their peculiarly *human* freedom shows itself. And in the event of a conflict between hedonism and autonomy (for instance, in cases of what I called pleasurable servitude) it comes down squarely against hedonism.

There were other philosophical ideas of Mill's which did not fit in easily with components of his idea of liberty. His determinism (or 'necessitarianism' or 'universal law of causation') did not fit in easily with his principle of individuality. And his inductivist methodology did not fit in easily with his argument for free discussion. (These two philosophical ideas were connected: he regarded the law of causation as an indispensable precondition for his canons of induction.)

According to Mill's principle of individuality, it is better that a person be *active* rather than *passive*, that he fashion his own life rather than let the world choose a plan of life for him. This active/passive dichotomy (or scale?) has a marked resemblance to our autonomy/heteronomy dichotomy (or scale). But given Mill's views on determinism (an issue which he set aside in the opening sentence of *On Liberty*), it is difficult to see how this distinction could ultimately be sustained. The man who 'actively fashions his own life' has been causally predetermined to do what he does just as the passive man has. True, there may be something in a person's present character that causes him to be dissatisfied with his present character and determines him to try to modify it (a point much emphasised by Mill); but the existence of such a disturbing factor will be contingent on prior causal factors.

At one stage Mill had regarded determinism with a kind of horror:

... during the later returns of my dejection, the doctrine of what is called Philosophical Necessity weighed on my existence like an incubus. I felt as if I was scientifically proved to be the helpless slave of antecedent circumstances; as if my character and that of all others had been formed for us by agencies beyond our control ...[54]

I have little doubt that if, in Mill's day, indeterminism had received

[54] *Autobiography*, ed. H. J. Laski (Oxford University Press) p. 143. See note 16 above for a parallel development in Russell's estimate of determinism.

any encouragement from contemporary science, Mill would have eagerly explored this as a possible way out. But it did not; and he was driven instead to what I regard as another sorry attempt to reconcile two antithetical ideas – in this case, the idea of the causal formation, and the idea of the self-formation, of human character.[55]

Mill's excellent argument for liberty of discussion boils down to this: we want to improve and enlarge our understanding of things (including religious, moral and political matters); and the best way to achieve this is to subject currently accepted opinions to searching criticism inspired by rival opinions. This is very much in line with the conjectural-cum-critical rationalism behind our third view. But it is out of line with the account of the advancement of scientific knowledge given in Mill's *Logic*. Mill afterwards claimed 'that my treatise contains...a reduction of the inductive process to strict rules'.[56] But if scientific knowledge can be arrived at by following strict rules, then there is no place for controversy and criticism in science.

9. FREEDOM AND KNOWLEDGE

The empiricist view of freedom does not seem to relate freedom and knowledge in any important way. By contrast, the rationalist view of freedom relates them very intimately. Indeed, for Spinoza the possession of rational knowledge was a necessary and sufficient condition for freedom. What is the relation according to our third view?

The view of knowledge on which this view of freedom is grounded itself ascribes a kind of situation-transcending activity to the scientific innovator. He does not wait passively for nature to obtrude ideas into his mind and to build up natural associations between them. He *attacks* nature with speculative hypotheses; and at the same time he *challenges* accepted scientific doctrines. And when he finds himself in an awkward scientific situation involving refutations and inconsistencies, he may surprise us by the resourceful ingenuity with which he surmounts it.

[55] *Logic*, Book VI, chap. ii. R. P. Anschulz, after quoting the passage referred to in the previous note, comments: 'Nor in spite of much painful pondering did Mill ever succeed in producing a satisfactory solution of the problem. On his premisses, indeed, it is an insoluble problem.' (*The Philosophy of J. S. Mill* (Oxford: Clarendon Press, 1953) p. 172.) I agree with this and also with his subsequent remark: 'In the upshot Mill contrives to retain both these views of human nature [the naturalistic or scientific view and the romantic or self-formative view] by expounding them in different parts of his philosophy.' (Ibid., p. 173.)
[56] *Autobiography*, p. 177.

But we cannot all be scientific innovators. What role is there for curiosity and intelligence and knowledge in the preservation of the freedom of less exceptional people?

Obviously, if a man is in an awkward situation, the better he understands it the more likely he is, other things being equal, to preserve his independence within it.

But is such situational awareness always desirable, even in situations whose outcome is inevitable? If a man has an incurable cancer, say, will it not be better to keep him, perhaps with the help of drugs, in a drowsy and relatively painless ignorance of his true situation?

A man who prefers autonomy to heteronomy will repudiate this suggestion at least in its application to himself. He will prefer to remain in an atmosphere of candour and truthfulness and to go on using his intelligence while he can.[57] One does not give up the maxim *Dare to know!* just when to obey it would actually take a little courage.

So he will face his situation and make certain preparations. But he will not, at least while his mind is still vigorous, succumb to it. There still exists for him a wider world, and his continuing curiosity about it may raise him above the forces that are closing in on him.

In 1634 Galileo was a house-prisoner in Arcetri. He obviously could not have very long to live. He was over seventy, suffering much illness and pain, and in a state of deep depression over the death of his beloved eldest daughter. His sight was deteriorating and he was afflicted by insomnia. But instead of succumbing to it he rose magnificently above this situation, composing during the next two years his greatest book, *Dialogues concerning Two New Sciences.*

[57] There is a moving account of Freud's last days, as he was dying from cancer of the jaw, in Ernest Jones, *Sigmund Freud*, vol. III, pp. 261 f. During his long illness Freud had never taken more than an occasional aspirin, preferring 'to think in torment than not to be able to think clearly'. He took an interest in outside events to the end. When things got too bad ('It is only torture now and it has no longer any sense') he was given, by prior arrangement, a dose of morphia ('Tell Anna') and died peacefully.

12

NATURE, HISTORY AND MORALITY

Shirley Robin Letwin

THE question that I propose to consider is the ghost in modern philosophy. Its step has been heard more distinctly at some times than at others. But it has never rattled its chains so loudly as during the recent popularity of Existentialism. The question is: How is man related to the universe? All philosophers who pride themselves on being modern reject the ancient answer to the question. The most emancipated modern philosophers refuse to hear the question. Nevertheless some answer to this question is presupposed by all philosophy.

I intend to argue that if we reject the ancient answer, the consequences are not so radical as the Existentialists believe but far more radical than many outraged critics of Existentialism recognise. For if we cannot know nature in the ancient sense, we have no ground for knowledge other than history (which must be distinguished from historicism). If we substitute history for nature, we are not, however, obliged to reduce our choices to arbitrary commitments as Existentialists have argued. We are not deprived of all objective grounds for our judgements and we can distinguish, without having to make excuses, between true and false and between right and wrong. But such distinctions cannot be made with the simplicity and security yearned for by philosophers who denounce alchemy and keep looking for the philosopher's stone.

We must begin by seeing what is lost through rejecting the ancient picture of nature. This has been obscured by a misconception of ancient nature fostered by Moore's criticism of naturalist ethics. According to Moore, naturalist ethics declares 'the sole good to consist in some one property of things that exist in time'.[1] This is a

[1] G. E. Moore, *Principia Ethica* (Cambridge, 1968) p. 41.

misrepresentation of ancient naturalist ethics that arises from ignoring what it presupposes, without which the reliance on nature is indeed unintelligible.

The postulate overlooked by Moore was first stated by Anaxagoras when he said that reason is present throughout nature as the cause of its order. Aristotle praised Anaxagoras for being 'like a sober man in contrast with the random talk of his predecessors'[2] because they did search for nature in something like Moore's sense. Thales's discovery that water was the fundamental substance was designed to answer the question: What is the permanent constituent or substratum of nature? This is a very different question from the one that concerned Aristotle or Plato and that made Anaxagoras's suggestion so telling for them. Their question was: Why do things change as they do?

What impressed Plato and Aristotle was that although everything observed by human beings is constantly changing, there appears to be a limit and order to these changes. On the one hand, perishable things have such an insecure hold on their own characteristics that any one of them can at any moment be lost. On the other hand, for all the changes constantly going on, things do not suddenly cease to be, and men appear to have some understanding of what to expect. How there can be a limit and order in the changes that we observe could be explained, Plato and Aristotle concluded, only by the existence of an external ordering spiritual principle. They understood men as beings who are not only subject to this ordering principle, but incorporate it. This active sharing in the ordering principle of the universe is what Plato and Aristotle meant by rationality. It followed that rationality made men capable of understanding nature. The subject of such understanding was not what Moore meant by nature – 'all that has existed, does exist, or will exist in time',[3] but rather, 'the first principles of things', that is, the unchanging order hidden in the changing world of ordinary experience.

It semed absurd to Plato and Aristotle to try to demonstrate that there is a rational cosmic order because, as Aristotle said, that would be attempting to prove 'what is obvious by what is not'.[4] Their concern as philosophers was to disclose the eternal design that constitutes nature.

The notion that nature is an eternal design giving the conclusions to changes in things is regularly described as a teleological view of nature. But promiscuous use of this description has over-

[2] Aristotle, *Metaphysics*, 984b 15.
[3] Moore, op. cit., p. 40.
[4] Aristotle, *Physics*, 193a 5.

looked a crucial distinction between two different sorts of design, one of which cannot provide a ground for human choices.

Any design can explain what comes to be. But designs differ according to whether they necessarily come to be in a fixed manner, or are potentialities that are not necessarily realised in a given manner, if at all. A design that is necessarily executed commands a succession of operations and the means for setting the operations in motion. Such a design may be called a mechanism because the end result can come to be only in a single fashion and cannot fail to occur unless the mechanism is destroyed or deformed. The operations and the outcome may be simple or complex and allow for no variations or for a great deal. But any deviation from what is expected, whether in the result or the mode of operation, must be ascribed to a distortion in or ignorance of the mechanism. In other words, a mechanism is not only a design but also an agency.

If the nature that governs men is a mechanism, men cannot shape their lives but are being shaped by a non-human design to which they are necessarily subject. They may suppose that they are discovering and choosing alternatives but they are really just executing eternal commands more or less subtly disguised. Although knowledge of nature understood as a mechanism provides an eternal, universal, and necessary truth, it cannot account for self-consciousness about such knowledge, for the freedom not to know or act on this truth, or for any contingency. If man is considered part of such a nature, moral choice becomes an illusion. If moral choice is taken to be real, then man must be distinguished from nature.

The reason why the ancient view of nature does not produce this dilemma is that it distinguishes sharply between design and agency. The design of nature on the ancient view could serve as a ground for human judgement because it is an idea, not a mechanism. An idea may not be realised if the agency is lacking. Moreover just how an idea is realised is not necessarily specified. That the realisation of the eternal design in the human world had to differ from that of the non-human world was assumed by Plato and Aristotle because they took rationality to be not just a power to conform to the design in nature but, being man's unique participation in the ordering cosmic principle, a power also to create ideas. They had then to account for different manners of realizing the eternal design.

Explaining how nature is related to the contingent world was more difficult for Plato because he described the first principles of things as Forms. Had he stepped into the sea of nonsense against which Socrates warned and tried to explain in detail the connections between the Forms and the world of appearances, Plato might have reduced the cosmic design to a mechanism. But he avoided this hazard and made it clear that the Forms were to be understood as ideas, not as agencies. The Forms do not determine what happens. In the human world, the concrete conclusions to be drawn from knowledge of the Forms are not fixed for all times and places, but must constantly be decided by the philosopher king. Though Plato tells us nothing about the character of deliberation and excludes some men from deliberating on some subjects, his account of nature as governed by ideas leaves room for deliberation.

Yet at the same time his conception of nature provides a sure criterion of truth. Resolving contradictions in ordinary discourse is the way to truth for Plato not because he had a mystical faith in logic, but because truth for him is knowledge of the rational cosmic order. The coherence of this order has one logical pattern. Therefore an inconsistency in our knowledge is necessarily an imperfectly grasped truth. The procedure of the Platonic dialogue is accordingly governed by the assumption that when the natural order is fully understood, our ideas will be perfectly coherent and therefore true because they will perfectly mirror the rational cosmic order.

Aristotle avoided Plato's difficulty by introducing the concept of a 'final cause' – that for the sake of which things happen. Aristotle could then distinguish the design for what happens from what makes things happen, what happens, and the material to which it happens. The final cause of human life is described by Aristotle as the *summum bonum*. Though regularly translated as happiness, it has nothing to do with the maximum satisfaction of desires which is happiness as Bentham defined it. Aristotle's *summum bonum* is the fulfilment of all the potentialities of human nature. Far from being the satisfaction of desires, it is a criterion for judging desires. The *summum bonum* constitutes an eternal truth compatible with human freedom because whether or not the potentialities it designates are realised depends on human choice. Men have to decide to order their lives by the *summum bonum*, and having done so, they must besides deliberate about what particular choices will fulfil their potentialities. For no specific practical policy can be deduced from the idea of a final cause. It does not dictate a programme; it only indicates considerations that should be taken into account in deliberating. Aristotle therefore considers not only the conditions of persuasion, but also the character of deliberation in the *Rhetoric*, which should be read as part of his *Ethics*.

What makes the idea of a final cause so ingenious is that it allows for a distinction between the human and the non-human realms within a single order of nature. Collingwood wholly mistook

Aristotle's nature when he said that 'no difference was recognised between the way in which an Athenian conceives and obeys the laws of Solon . . . and the way in which inanimate objects conceive and obey those laws of nature to which they are subject'.[5] The contrary is true. The final cause that governs the growth of an acorn resembles the final cause that governs human nature only in so far as both designate the potentialities of that form of being. But whereas an acorn – though its growth may be promoted or stunted by external circumstances – cannot choose whether to become an oak tree, the final cause of human nature, Aristotle makes it plain, is a realisation that must be chosen to be achieved.

But again, as for Plato, the rational cosmic order provides a secure basis for deliberation. There is no logical fallacy in Aristotle's ethics. He did not move from an empirical to a normative principle; he carefully distinguished between statements about what is and about what ought to be. His understanding of the cosmic order made available to him the major premise of a normative argument. The major premise of Aristotle's ethics is the normative principle that we ought to want completely to fulfil the potentialities of our form of being. This normative principle is not demonstrable but implicit in recognizing that there is a rational cosmic order. 'People who seek a "starting point"', Aristotle said, 'seek a reason for things for which no reason can be given, for the starting point of demonstration is not demonstration.'[6] The normative principle from which Aristotle starts is intuitively known with certitude by anyone who reflects on his rationality. This follows from taking rationality to be man's participation in the ordering principle of the universe.

It is impossible to see what gives substance to Aristotle's notion of the 'mean' without referring it to his understanding of nature. Aristotle's 'mean' is not the middle way of muddled minds. The mean is that choice that enables a man to satisfy his potentialities in the right order which he could not do if he sought too much or too little of any single kind of satisfaction. Aristotle could give the notion of fulfilling the potentialities of a human being a genuine content because the potentialities are given by nature in a particular order. That is why Aristotle could speak meaningfully of the 'essence' of man. The Greek word *ousia* that we translate as 'essence' denotes substance, species, true nature, or being, all of which for Aristotle (as for Plato) are one because what anything really is can be known by reference to the cosmic order. Without such reference to a rational cosmic order, it is meaningless to speak of the essence of man except

[5] R. G. Collingwood, *Nature* (Clarendon, 1964) p. 111.
[6] Aristotle, *Metaphysics*, 1011a 12.

in a metaphorical sense. For only knowledge of the governing principle of the universe makes it possible to distinguish the essences of things from their properties or appearances in the contingent world.

The cosmic order, as Aristotle understood it, is a hierarchy of being which ascends from inanimate matter to a pure act of thinking. From this it follows that as a human being is not purely spiritual, he has to attend to acquiring certain material goods but only to the degree that is essential for actualising his spiritual potentialities. Whatever is required to fulfil the potentialities of a man constitutes his natural needs. When nothing lies waste in the soul, the natural needs are fulfilled. There is a natural economy of the soul because there is a hierarchy of being given by the cosmic order. Thus knowledge of a rational cosmic order made it possible for Aristotle to distinguish between 'apparent' desires and 'real' ones, or needs.

If we deny that we can know nature in the ancient sense, we have no natural ground for distinguishing among desires and none of them can be described strictly as a need. The confusions of modern men have arisen from a failure to recognise that access to an eternal universal standard for human activities, without denying that men are free to create and order their desires, can be had only from an understanding of nature that allows us radically to distinguish human beings from rats and rocks. But these confusions are not to be blamed on the scientists who are credited with liberating us from ancient teleological nature. They were well aware of what they destroyed by reducing nature to a mechanism.

Newton elaborated the picture of nature that Copernicus had introduced by emptying nature of all qualities. Whereas Leibniz still described the universe as full of a multitude of changing things directed by final causes, Newton's world was an unchanging set of purely formal mathematical relations. Thus Voltaire remarked that when he left France the world was full, but when he arrived in London, he found it empty. In Newton's physics final causes became obsolete. Still he retained the God inherited from the older understanding of a rational cosmic order. Newton never admitted that gravitational attraction was a physical force, and preferred to say nothing conclusive about its character. He regarded his mechanical explanation of nature as a limited one, and his God had to keep supervising the mechanism He had made. As Leibniz pointed out, Newton's God is an incompetent clockmaker. The result was an inconsistent account of nature. But it had the great virtue of allowing for both a mathematical science of physics and a human world still tied to a nature that had the ancient teleological character.

The modern cosmos was purged of this inconsistency by the end of the eighteenth century in Laplace's *Mécanique Céleste*, which totally banished God from this world. 'I do not need that hypothesis', Laplace replied when Napoleon asked about the place of God. The world clock could now tick on without repairing or rewinding. God was out of a job and the human world was totally severed from nature. Man became a stranger in the universe.

But this divorce of man from nature in modern physics has been pointedly ignored or denied most of all by those modern philosophers who take their bearings by modern science. They assume that they have rejected what Hobbes called those 'insignificant sounds... coined by Schoole-men and pusled Philosophers'[7] and they disdain the ancient dependence on nature. However, they have rarely had the endurance required for achieving the purity to which they aspire. They have softened the rigours of their renunciation in one of the many sordid half-way houses that clutter the slums of modern philosophy. In these half-way houses nature is allowed to enter only in disguise and by the back door. But once admitted, this illicit tenant makes puppets of the slum-dwellers.

Though they chatter on about the mind-body problem, they devote themselves to reducing what they see as the disorder of the human world to the perfect order of empty Newtonian nature. They have tried to discover in the human world the same sort of patterns that Newton had found in moving masses, and, of course, they have succeeded. The patterns produced generally take one of two forms, either evolutionary or structural, and even though they are restricted to organic nature, both are mechanisms.

That sort of evolutionary pattern that has been condemned as 'historicism' describes nature as a series of stages in a mechanical process that takes place over time. Thus Comte and Marx spoke of laws of historical development. But these laws have nothing to do with history which consists of contingent connections between contingent events which are the outcome of human choices. The so-called historicist understands all events as phases of a mechanical process which determines rather than reflects human behaviour. In other words, historicism reduces the human world to a part of nature understood as a mechanism. That this mechanism operates over time does not make it historical.

Historicism has been attacked by two sorts of critics, who, for all their incompatibility and vehemence, also understand the human world as a mechanism. Karl Popper attacks historicism for the scientific impropriety of laws of succession, because science deals

---

[7] Hobbes, *Leviathan* (Clarendon, 1947) p. 30.

only with universally valid laws, limited by conditions not time. Instead Popper proposes that changes in the organic world should be understood as the result of efforts to solve problems by trial and error. All organisms, whether amoebae or men, Popper says, are 'constantly day and night engaged in problem-solving'. The problems are given by a natural necessity to adapt to their environment, that is, to survive. As the objective of any organism's activities is thus given by nature, every activity can be understood as a method of adaptation and graded in terms of its effectiveness for securing survival.

This is what enables Popper to speak of 'lower' and 'higher' functions of language and to conclude that science is the highest human activity. The lower function of language is to express or signal distress so as to 'release or trigger' in other organisms a pattern of behaviour appropriate to avoiding danger. Human beings are higher than the amoebae because they use language also to make arguments. This function is perfected in 'critical discussion,' which has given rise to science, 'the most powerful tool for biological adaptation which has ever emerged in the course of organic evolution'.[8]

Only the attitude to error distinguishes the 'cloud-like trial and error movements' of the amoeba from Einstein's thinking. 'The one really important difference between the method of Einstein and that of the amoeba', Popper tells us, is the 'consciously critical attitude towards his own ideas' that enabled Einstein 'to reject, quickly, hundreds of hypotheses as inadequate....'[9] 'So we can say', Popper concludes, 'that the critical or rational method consists in letting our hypotheses die in our stead: it is a case of exosomatic evolution.' Human rationality then is the capacity to approach solutions 'critically'. It is a more efficient mechanism for survival because it is a 'plastic control' that allows for 'feed-back' and this is what constitutes human freedom for Popper.[10]

This is a radically different understanding of human beings from that of the ancients who supposed that men were capable of inventing an infinity of purposes. Classical nature provided men with a criterion for ordering their purposes; it did not set them problems to solve. The Greeks thought that men were capable of putting a manner of living above survival. Men were not like animals because they could sacrifice everything, even their lives. They could choose

---

[8] K. R. Popper, *Of Clouds and Clocks. An Approach to the Problem of Rationality and the Freedom of Man* (Washington U., St Louis, Missouri, 1965) p. 19.

[9] Ibid., p. 26.   [10] Ibid., pp. 27 and 29.

to die. But for Popper choosing to die is an aberration, as is everything else not directed to survival. Dangerous attempts to climb mountains, or music, can be explained only as by-products of 'the almost excessive abundance of trials and errors upon which the method of trial and error elimination depends'.[11] These by-products may, however, be indirectly useful for recharging tired scientists. In short, for all Popper's talk about freedom and despite his repudiation of determinism, his human beings are just as subject to nature, understood as a mechanism, as the creatures described by historicists.

The very different attack on historicism made by Leo Strauss, who advocates a return to classical nature, suffers from the same affinity with the enemy. Strauss also speaks of 'solving problems' and in a 'universally valid manner'.[12] But his solutions take the form of 'principles of justice' rather than of scientific hypotheses. Unlike the ancients, however, Strauss describes these principles as if they were programmes of action given by nature which anyone who understands nature necessarily accepts. As nature is eternal, and as 'justice' is a programme deduced from nature, any concern for changing circumstances is interpreted by Strauss as a denial of nature. 'There cannot be natural right', he says, 'if all that man could know about right were the problem of right, or if the question of the principles of justice would admit of a variety of mutually exclusive answers, none of which could be proved to be superior to the others.'[13] To suppose that two just men might arrive at contrary answers, as Aristotle does in the *Rhetoric*, is for Strauss tantamount to asserting that justice is unreal. Anyone who denies that the political problem is 'susceptible of a final solution' is, according to Strauss, condemning us to 'blind choice'.[14] In fact, Strauss is defending not ancient nature, but Kantian nature which has a totally different character.

As Kantian nature is not an eternal idea but the fundamental structure of the mind that necessarily determines all reasoning, it is fixed and certain in a manner totally foreign to classical nature. In the Kantian world, moral choice is a matter not of deliberation, but of ratiocination. Kant's man is free in so far as he can will whether to be good. But having willed to be good, his concrete choices must be deduced from first principles. Thus Kant tells us that just as geometry unambiguously defines a triangle, so the science of right can determine 'what every one shall have as his own with mathematical

---

[11] Ibid., pp. 30 f.
[12] Leo Strauss, *Natural Right and History* (U. of Chicago, 1953) p. 24.
[13] Ibid.
[14] Ibid. pp. 35 f.

exactness'.[15] How to regulate relations between men and women is as definite and certain as Newton's laws: 'If a man and a woman have the will to enter on reciprocal enjoyment in accordance with their sexual nature, they must necessarily marry each other; and this necessity is in accordance with the juridical laws of pure reason.'[16] All moral principles, just as Newton's laws, are necessarily true, and logically related to form a system deduced from first principles.

What is currently known as 'Structuralism' is the most recent and popular reformulation of this metaphysical terrorism. But Structuralism has the virtue of making it obvious that the reason for the modern chaos is not the death of God or of nature but the death of history.

The Structuralist, whether he is a linguist, historian, literary critic, or anthropologist, is concerned with discovering what Lévi-Strauss describes as the single 'unconscious structural scheme' that underlies the shifting images of consciousness and the 'chaos of rules and customs'[17] recorded by conventional history. From apparent realities such as language, events, or rules the Structuralist proceeds by transformation to the real unconscious structures. Only economic history therefore receives Lévi-Strauss's blessing because that is 'by and large, the history of unconscious processes'.[18] The 'types of transformations' that Structuralism tries to discover are 'formulas showing the number, magnitude, direction of the convolutions that must be unravelled in order to uncover . . . an ideal homologous relationship between the different structural levels'.[19] We are helped to see that the timelessness of Structuralism does not fundamentally distinguish it from historicism by Lévi-Strauss's pointed acknowledgement of an affinity with Marxism.[20] Even before the advent of Structuralism, he tells us, dialectical materialism had already discovered that the historical world is a chaos asking to be understood in terms of a fixed unconscious reality. For both Marxism and Structuralism, history is but a disguise for a mechanical nature.

That human choices are merely products of a mechanism, whether it takes the form of a process in time or a timeless structure, is the striking revelation brought by the modern hierophants of nature. Unfortunately it has the slight defect of being self-contradictory. For men are being told that they have the power to know

---

[15] I. Kant, *The Philosophy of Law*, trans. W. Hastie (Edinburgh, 1887) p. 49.
[16] Ibid., p. 110.
[17] C. Lévi-Strauss, *Structural Anthropology* (Penguin, 1968) p. 21.
[18] Ibid., p. 23.   [19] Ibid., p. 334.
[20] Ibid., cf. pp. 23 and 333–45.

universal truths about themselves and to know that they know. But the truth that men know reduces them to mechanisms totally devoid of any power to know what they are or to decide how to live. In short, Structuralism and Evolutionism save eternal truth by dispensing with human freedom, that is, human intelligence.

The reverse of this disaster is produced by Sartre's Existentialism which saves human freedom by eliminating any reason for exercising it. History, instead of being absorbed by an all-pervasive fixity, is disintegrated into nothingness. In his major philosophical discourse, Sartre argues that objective discourse is impossible because God does not exist. If there is no God, there is no cosmic design and no guarantee of truth; therefore every idea is as true or false as every other, and every statement can be contradicted. The only truth is that whatever is might not be.

Sartre's concern is to restore our awareness of moral choice. That is why he has emphasised the freedom of men to choose death. He assumes that recognising objectivity is tantamount to denying the concreteness of an act, and thus the moral responsibility of the actor. Sartre's attack would be justified if he had confined it to the 'objectivity' of the modern hierophants of nature who seek, though sometimes unwittingly, to reduce every concrete act to an instance of a universal law, and thus leave no room for moral choice. But Sartre's attempt to defend the reality of moral choice by denying the validity of referring concrete choices to an objective context lands him in nonsense.

He contradicts himself with every word when he says, 'I discover myself suddenly as the one who gives its meaning to the alarm clock, the one who by a signboard forbids himself to walk on a flower bed or on the lawn ... the one finally who makes the values exist in order to determine his action by their demands ... I make my decision concerning them – without justification and without excuse.'[21] If Sartre can identify an alarm clock, a signboard, a flower bed, and a lawn, he has not made but accepted meanings and values given to him in common with his readers. Indeed anyone who bothers to deny that there are objective meanings and values assumes that the words he uses to make that denial will be understood by others. In declaring that only concrete decisions are real and that all appeals to objective standards are fraudulent, he declares himself to be a liar. The only consistent way to deny the reality of all objective standards, which necessarily implies that meaningful discourse is impossible, is that of Cratylus. When he became convinced of the

[21] J.-P. Sartre, *Being and Nothingness* (Methuen, 1969) p. 39.

Heraclitean doctrine that everything was constantly changing, he concluded that as nothing true could be said, he would never again speak and thereafter he only wagged his finger. Anyone who does more than wag his finger assumes that he shares with others a universe of discourse.

Nevertheless Sartre's charge of 'bad faith' against any talk of objective right and wrong or true and false has the merit of drawing attention to the consequences of denying that men can know nature in the ancient sense. If human beings are not part of a rational cosmic order whose governing principle they are capable of knowing, then human beings cannot discover in nature an eternal and necessarily true criterion for judging and ordering their ideas. If they pretend that they can, they are guilty of 'bad faith'. But it does not follow that if men cannot know the rational order of the universe, then they can only make wilful commitments. For they have available to them a universe of objective discourse created neither by God nor by nature, but just by men.

It is a historical universe, whose reality used to be taken for granted even by the ancient Greek philosophers. They never supposed that human beings arrived at truth by confronting nature with blank minds. Plato's philosopher comes to his contemplation of the Forms only after a long period of rigorous instruction in coherent language, about the nature of coherent thought. Moreover the Platonic dialogues get much of their force by references to what particular men with distinctive personalities said and did in the past. For ancient philosophers recognised that rationality is inseparable from memory, in the sense of a purposeful and coherent recollection of ideas, not a random recall of images.

Because human beings can remember and understand their past, they have a history. A man who cannot coherently remember his own history is devoid of a personality. A man who is unaware of what other men have thought and done in the past is a barbarian. Thus the present contempt for history threatens to inundate civilisation with barbarians, and has produced a literature about anonymous bundles of random utterances and gestures that resemble human beings, if at all, only in shape.

The denigration of history reflects a disposition to think in terms of a dichotomy between universal truth and incoherence. If we cannot know nature, the implicit argument runs, then we cannot know universal truth; and if there is no universal truth, there can be no truth at all or only the 'instant certainties' of 'apocalyptic utterances'.[22] Consequently modern men, who are beguiled by these

[22] Cf. J. Shklar, 'Hegel's Phenomenology', *Political Theory* (August, 1973).

blatant alternatives, clutch at a nature that allows for no humanity, or else they wallow self-righteously in a chaos of disjointed thoughts and acts, and cultivate an appreciation of nothingness.

This nothingness is the result of deliberately repudiating all historical orders. Such orders consist of contingent connections between contingent ideas made by men. Therefore Sartre is right when he says, as Hume did before him, that there is no necessity for any of these connections and that they might have been made differently or not at all. But having been made they constitute an objective order. What makes it objective, however, is far from obvious.

It is easiest to recognise the character of historical objectivity in a language, in the narrow sense, such as English or French. Every such language has changed and is expected to go on changing; words alter in meaning, new words or constructions are allowed and old ones dismissed as archaic. Those who speak a language may be aware of alternatives to theirs which they might speak if they chose. Nevertheless, they will have no doubts about whether utterances are meaningful in their language, and they will take it for granted that they cannot alter or question their language without speaking it. They will recognise their language at different times and places, in a variety of accents and dialects, even though they consider certain manners of using their language to be superior to others. In short, they will accept a certain vocabulary, grammar, syntax, idioms, and usage as belonging to their language. This means that they find in their language an independent, coherent, impersonal public identity that they take as given. This constitutes the objectivity of a language, even though it has been made by men over time and is not found in nature. It is therefore a historical objectivity.

That other historical objectivities are more difficult to recognise is not, however, due just to perversity or obtuseness. Two serious kinds of obstacles stand in the way of recognising any historical objectivity.

The first is the lack of a permanent substratum or end to the incessant changes that characterise all historical objectivities. Even in a language, the objectivity rests on stability, not fixity. Stability is preserved because something has always to be taken for granted in order that something else may be altered. And the new is bound up with what remains of the old and thus acquires the maturity of an established form. What is taken for granted may be different each time. More or less may be questioned or changed and nothing is beyond change. But everything cannot be altered at once without abandoning the language. Thus throughout incessant changes a language remains stable.

But stability is difficult to identify and understand even in so obvious a historical objectivity as a language. One cannot master English just by reading a grammar and a word book because the stability of a language depends on a manner of making connections and variations. The man who writes English prose from a dictionary and a grammar is unlikely to produce more than a travesty of English. On the other hand, masters of a language will use words that are not in the dictionaries, and make constructions forbidden by grammarians. And their novelties will be accepted by dictionary makers and grammarians not because a majority of English-speakers vote to accept their innovations, but because those who speak the language gracefully will recognise the innovations to be fitting. Only pedants and *parvenues* in the language will fail to distinguish such novelties from the gaffes of ignorant and insensitive speakers.

If a language cannot be learned from a handbook, it must be learned by apprenticeship to a master of the craft. It should be noticed that the novice is an apprentice, not a disciple, and is only temporarily so until he acquires the skills – not the style – of the master. Still, this introduces the difficulty of identifying those who are truly skilled. The apprentice must start by accepting someone's word not only for what he has to learn but also for whom he should listen to. The identification of a master, whether it is in French, physics, or painting, can only be made by other masters. But there may be periods when the acknowledged masters have a meretricious reputation and debase the standards of their craft. Therefore the apprentice can never be sure that he has found a true master. Still, the continuity of a craft as of a language or science provides a ground for objectivity, and those who know its history can restore criteria that have for a time been lost or distorted.

A judgement of what belongs to a historical objectivity is then a matter of knowledge. It is difficult to distinguish such judgements from personal whims only because, as a historical objectivity is stable rather than unchanging, any understanding of it is bound to be complicated, indefinite, and uncertain. No historical objectivity therefore can be recognised without an effort to dispel ambiguities, though this is more evident and easier to do in some cases than in others. But to suppose that such differences are a ground for ranking historical objectivities as more or less rational or true is a delusion.

This delusion is encouraged by a wish to avoid the second set of obstacles to understanding historical objectivities arising from the fact that there is no limit to their number or variety. As each is a pattern made by men, each will differ according to the purposes that the pattern is meant to serve. The world of historical objectivity is therefore full of diverse patterns. These can be arranged in groups so that we can speak of kinds of knowledge or activities. But any such grouping, however long it persists, must be recognised to be contingent. If no purpose is given by nature, there can be no hierarchy of patterns. Consequently there is no single structure to knowledge and no unity of truth.

If logical principles do not constitute the fundamental cosmic pattern, they are neither more nor less true or noble than patterns of rhyme and metre. Logic is a particular manner of making coherent connections that has over time acquired a certain steadiness recognisable to all those who have become acquainted with it; and poetry is another such manner. Logicians who would reduce all rational activity to resolving contradictions by the canons of one or other system of logic are either assuming, as Russell did for a time, that logical principles are, if not literally Platonic Forms, at least a 'region of absolute necessity to which not only the actual world, but every possible world must conform . . .'.[23] Or else such logicians are what Carlyle called 'sandblind pedants' that resemble 'a pair of spectacles behind which there is no eye'.[24] These 'sandblind pedants' are obsessed by the economy of their symbols and intent on producing 'the leanest results'. They are best dubbed, as William James suggested, 'the knights of the razor', and encouraged to go on a crusade to some remote land.[25]

The delusive infatuation with mathematics and science that now threatens to make barbarians of the learned gets credibility from the observation that it is relatively easy to make judgements about what constitutes a right understanding of scientific laws and mathematical demonstrations. Yet we possess both Euclidean and non-Euclidean geometries and we know that in every science there are aspects of varying degrees of ambiguity. What are called facts are recognitions about which there is relatively little dispute; the wave theory of light, however, is very much in dispute. But the disagreements within physics do not destroy its objectivity any more than the multiplicity of geometries makes the conclusion of a geometric demonstration a matter of personal taste. As the objectivity of science and mathematics is wholly independent of any uncertainty in them, science and mathematics cannot be more objective and therefore superior forms of knowledge just because they are more certain.

There is just as much objectivity in patterns characterised by considerably more uncertainty, such as art. Patrons or creators of

[23] B. Russell, *Philosophical Essays* (London, 1910) p. 82.
[24] T. Carlyle, *Sartor Resartus*, I, X.
[25] Cf. *The Will to Believe*.

art who suppose that they need not take instruction from those who know about how to understand art, whether painting or poetry, and how to distinguish between real and spurious, good and bad art, display the brashness and presumption of the uneducated. Certainly good art is a matter of judgement. But so is good science a matter of judgement. Because in art the judgements are more subtle and ambiguous, and cannot be made fully explicit, it is more difficult to become a master in the arts, and it is easier for charlatans to pass. Nevertheless, judgements about art made by genuine masters are just as objective as those in science.

Conversely, however indisputable scientific laws may be, they are as much a human creation as the resonance of poetic images. The scientist may refuse to hear what the poet says. But he cannot claim a superior rationality for science unless he supposes that his laws or his methods are given by nature and situated at the top of the cosmic order. Science and poetry, logic and painting are all stable manners of making coherent connections and they are familiar and comprehensible to those who have been educated in those patterns. If there is no rational cosmic order, the variety cannot be arranged in a hierarchy. Any attempt to reduce the diversity of human patterns to a unity must be rejected as either arbitrary or as an attempt to reduce history to mechanical nature.

That there can be no unity of truth is extremely vexing to philosophers who want to go around the world without leaving home. In a world of many languages, to understand what is being said, we are obliged to identify the language that is being spoken and to learn how to speak it. As there are no eternally given univocal meanings to utterances, any utterance may acquire a cluster of meanings, and which of these is to be attached to it in any instance will depend on the context that it is designed to serve. We are therefore always obliged to ask what language is being spoken. This is an essential but also the most primitive question to be asked about an utterance. The mark of an educated man is his unself-conscious though meticulous effort to recognise what language is being spoken. If there is no hierarchy of truth descending from the first principles of the universe, no man can be master of all knowledge and no method can be a universal key to truth. There is no alternative to serving an apprenticeship in each language that one proposes to speak.

Finally, apart from the difficulty of understanding and mastering the variety of historical objectivities, we are obliged to accept an even more annoying discomfort – a genuine qualification on their objectivity. The qualification is inescapable because a historical objectivity rests ultimately on agreement. But this should not be confused with the agreement in a coterie of beautiful souls. A coterie defines itself by its rejection of what outsiders take as given, and its insistence on self-consciously considering and sanctioning whatever it accepts. Thus a coterie is constantly and deliberately making its agreement. When it ceases to do so, a coterie ceases to exist.

A historical objectivity, unlike the agreement of a coterie, is not something created here and now. It is not the result of a contract but the unforeseen consequence of performances by men who were thinking of other things. Though it is a perishable historical creation, it is trans-historical. The agreement on which it rests has grown up and been recognised at different places and times. The breadth of the agreement may vary. How long it takes for any historical coherence to acquire a recognisable identity cannot be known. And the difficulty of answering these questions is part of the uncertainty intrinsic to a historical objectivity. What matters is that a historical objectivity is not created by the agreement of those who submit to it; for them it is just as given as if it were a cosmic order. They take it to be given because it has a continuous identity that has been recognised over many generations of men. Thus a historical objectivity has the character of a second nature.

Nevertheless, although a historical objectivity is nothing like the communion of beautiful souls, it does rest ultimately on agreement. We must therefore recognise a grain of truth in the Existentialist talk of commitment.

Take the obligation to keep promises. If we ask why promises should be kept, though we may be given a variety of justifications, at a more abstract level we may find some common ground underlying the variety. If, however, we persist in our questions, we will arrive at a reason for which no justification can be given.

Keeping promises cannot achieve the status of a necessary truth by being connected with a necessity to survive. For then we deprive men of the freedom to choose death and reduce them to organisms subject to a natural mechanism. Moreover, there is no answer on this basis to the man who has flourished by dint of regularly breaking his promises. Nor can we, by referring to survival, condemn the man who lives among people who obey some promises but otherwise use promises to deceive. We can only reject the practice of such men by saying in effect that they are barbarians. The obligation to keep promises rests ultimately on a preference for surviving in a particular manner. This may be formulated in a principle such as, 'Every human being is to be treated as an end never as a means.' To break promises is to manipulate others as means by arousing false expectations. But if we cannot offer a cosmic sanction for this principle, to the man who says, 'I do not choose to regard every human being as an end in himself', we can only declare that this is our understanding of what it is to be a human being. The understanding is a commitment in the sense that we accept it even though there are alternatives to it that we cannot demonstrate to be necessarily false. Talk of rights can obfuscate, elaborate, or embellish, but not explain our commitment to regard every human being as an end in himself.

There is no escaping the point of commitment by arguing that unless we accept certain obligations we land ourselves in irremediable and destructive chaos whether mental or social. A desire to avoid such chaos inspires the recognition of an obligation to avoid contradictions as well as the various formulations of natural law. But neither of these can supply an irrefutable argument against the man who says, 'I prefer irremediable and destructive chaos.' There may be an inconsistency in his thinking which, if pointed out, will lead him to change his mind. But we have no argument that he is rationally obliged to accept against the man who consistently prefers barbarism to civilisation.

The fact that all men suffer pain, can starve and die cannot offer a foundation for moral thinking; it can only indicate conditions that must be taken into account. For an observation that a man is in pain, even if it were beyond doubt, decides nothing. We are still obliged to determine whether to respond and how, whether to understand the suffering as self-indulgence, or as a case of pain that must be endured for the sake of something that the sufferer or observer or both value more than the absence of pain, or as an occasion for offering relief. Civilisation is not built on minimising suffering. The appeal of such apparently worthy and simple objectives has led to the current wreck of moral and intellectual education. For all education requires great effort; it cannot be had without suffering. Pain is intrinsic to any activity of learning and only those who acquire indifference to such pain are capable of learning, just as only those who can endure the pain of risk and turmoil, can truly love. Civilisation consists in learning to distinguish among different reasons and justifications for suffering, to accept some as worthwhile even though exceedingly painful and to dispose of others as cruel and unnecessary.

Even if it were an established fact that men invariably feel 'sympathy' for the sufferings of others, that fact could explain only how men have come to concern themselves with judging such suffering. It cannot provide a universal criterion for such judgements, as Hume pointed out when he stressed the diversity of moral languages, even though he believed that all were founded on the capacity for sympathy. Not even a belief in the sanctity of human life rests on a simple aversion to death. Our belief in the sanctity of human life may entail courting death for ourselves and others, whether as Christian martyrs or as soldiers in a war against barbarians. What we take to be an evil demanding a remedy is not given to us by nature; it is not self-evident; it is our interpretation of what we observe in the light of what we have learned to understand and esteem.

What we learn to regard as suffering deserving relief or indifference is anchored well and truly in our civilisation. But we cannot anchor that civilisation to any cosmic necessity by rational demonstration. Civilisation has been learned by men, not given with or to them. Consequently the shape of civilisation is not fixed and universal and we are obliged to recognise the possibility of an infinite variety in understandings of human life and to commit ourselves to one or the other. What we commit ourselves to is more than any one man or generation can make or even understand and our commitment is displayed in an acceptance, largely if not wholly unselfconscious, of what we have to learn to become civilised. But the foundation of that acceptance and learning has the character of a commitment because there is no demonstrable necessity for it.

An affable cannibal may stop to chat before boiling and the missionary may try to persuade him that men are not for eating. But if he is a sound, stalwart cannibal, not seduced by soft words or frightened by foreign gods, he will after all proceed to the pot. And the missionary can save himself only by killing the cannibal. The cannibal's understanding of men does not include the sanctity of human life and we can offer no rational necessity why it should. A man may knowingly be a cannibal and some are. This is the unpleasant truth hidden in the nonsense about the nothingness that threatens us.

Science is as vulnerable as morality. If we accept a scientific explanation of the precipitation that we call rain, we may confidently say that anyone who expects to produce precipitation by rolling stones is mistaken. Our awareness that we may later find reason to change or modify our views on rain need not prevent us from declaring our statement to be true. But we cannot ultimately justify our view about the uselessness of rolling stones for getting rain other than by declaring a commitment to a particular manner of explaining such phenomena. The stone-rolling rain-maker may be as convinced of the correspondence theory of truth as the knowing observer, only he may choose to judge correspondence differently. He is committed to a wholly different language.

The point of commitment cannot be evaded by saying that we should regard all truth as hypothetical. Of course all historical truth is open to question, but it cannot all be hypothetical. Just the ability to make a statement about hypothetical truth and to be understood rests on the acceptance of certain commitments by both the speaker and his audience, to say nothing of the preference for regarding truth as hypothetical.

Religious faith cannot affect the point of commitment unless God is understood as a final cause, in which case we have returned to the ancient view of nature. But if God is understood in the Christian fashion, as a Creator whose Reason and Will are supreme, we may feel obliged to accept his commands but we cannot claim to understand them without declaring ourselves to be God. Nor can we use religion to dissolve the point of commitment by thinking of God as man's highest good. That way of thinking measures God according to a human standard conceived of by man's self-sufficient reason. God is then reduced to a means found by man for satisfying human needs. Truly religious faith refrains from assimilating God to an idea created by man. Religion unadulterated by the ancient view of nature may serve to reconcile us to the mystery of our commitments. Or it may enable us to believe, without understanding why, that there is a cosmic foundation for our commitments and that the heavens would fall if we betrayed them. But if God is the Creator of all and man cannot know God, religious faith cannot provide us with a rational justification for our commitments. The reflectiveness of Adam and Eve is the consequence of, not the cure for, their disobedience. A readiness to obey God's commands must rest on what Kierkegaard rightly describes as a 'leap'.

In short, once we refuse to understand man as an embodiment of the Reason or the Divinity of the universe, we must admit that it is a delusion to suppose that man can survey everything human from a non-human standpoint beyond history.

But many who are free of this delusion are prone to fall into another that could destroy civilisation. It is totally false to conclude that if our morality rests ultimately on a commitment, that is, on a presupposition taken on faith, then our moral conduct must be irrational and every moral choice can be nothing but a shot in the dark. The commitment to a moral understanding or practice is nothing like the commitments bandied about by Sartre and his legion of destruction. The metaphysical truth that makes the Existentialist talk of commitment seem plausible does not in the least justify the Existentialist picture of moral conduct.

It does not follow from denying a cosmic foundation for morality that there is no way of making objective judgements about what is right and wrong or true and false. Such judgements are possible because civilised men are born into a world full of historical objectivities of which a moral practice or language is one. The predicaments discussed by Sartre do not, as he supposes, demonstrate the absence of such objectivities. On the contrary, his discussion of so-called blind commitments to a moral choice bears witness to the reality of an objective morality. Take the dilemma of the man who has to decide whether to stay to look after his ailing mother or to leave in order to fight for his country. He can recognise these alternatives and find choosing between them difficult only because he had already learned to think in terms of a moral practice in which both care for an ailing mother and defending one's country are recognised to be highly desirable. The only blindness involved in this situation is that of Sartre who is unaware of the moral language he is speaking while denying its existence.

All that Sartre and his like have discovered is – something that educated men regularly used to understand – that commitment to a language cannot determine what we will utter in that language any more than a system of law can eliminate the need to decide how it should be subscribed to in contingent circumstances. Accepting a moral language or practice does not and cannot dictate what practical decisions we ought to make on any particular occasion. But neither are such choices blind commitments. They are made rationally because they are made within the context of a moral practice which provides objective grounds for understanding and choosing alternatives. Concrete practical choices – that Sartre and others indiscriminately and misleadingly describe as 'commitments' – are embedded in an understanding of relevant considerations given by an impersonal moral language.

Even those who reflect on how their moral language differs from others are not restricted to grunts of approval or disapproval, but have available various vocabularies for such discussion. It is only if our allegiance to one moral language rather than another is questioned deeply enough that we must reach a presupposition that has to be taken on faith. But the commitment that lies at the foundation of our morality is a commitment at the most abstract level. It does not detract from the objectivity and rationality of our moral language. It casts no doubt on the grounds of moral choice. It bears only on the ultimate foundation of those grounds, that is, on a philosophical understanding of our moral reasoning.

To most men, however, the foundation for their thinking is not an issue. To accept an objective order one knows does not foreclose all questioning, but the questions may stop short of the point of commitment. And there is no reason to sneer at men who do not press so far. No one is obliged to ask philosophical questions.

For if there is no knowledge of first principles, the philosopher has no special claim to be heard. He loses the pre-eminence given to him by the ancient view and its modern counterfeits. Far from being the fountainhead of all truth, philosophy is rather dependent on other kinds of truth. This does not mean that the philosopher is reduced to inventing and solving crossword puzzles. He assumes that words are meant to convey truth just as the ancient philosophers did. His business is not however to displace historical objectivities, but to explain their presuppositions and character.

This more humble role is unlikely to make the philosopher popular. He cannot offer to replace conventional certainties with superior incontrovertible ones. Nor can he offer the exhilaration of apocalyptic uncertainty. He leaves his audience with the whimsical obligation to stand firmly on certainties that they know to be fragile.

13

ATTITUDES TO NATURE[1]

John Passmore

THE ambiguity of the word 'nature' is so remarkable that I need not remark upon it. Except perhaps to emphasise that this ambiguity – scarcely less apparent, as Aristotle long ago pointed out, in its Greek near-equivalent *physis* – is by no means a merely accidental product of etymological confusions or conflations: it faithfully reflects the hesitancies, the doubts and the uncertainties, with which men have confronted the world around them. For my special purposes, it is enough to say, I shall be using the word 'nature' in one of its narrower senses – so as to include only that which, setting aside the supernatural, is human neither in itself nor in its origins. This is the sense in which neither Sir Christopher Wren nor St Paul's Cathedral forms part of 'nature' and it may be hard to decide whether an oddly shaped flint or a landscape where the trees are evenly spaced is or is not 'natural'. The question I am raising, then, is what our attitudes have been, and ought to be, to nature in this narrow sense of the word, in which it excludes both the human and the artificial. And more narrowly still, I shall be devoting most of my attention to our attitudes towards that part of nature which it lies within man's power to modify and, in particular, towards what Karl Barth calls 'the strange life of beasts and plants which lies around us', a life we can by our actions destroy.

In what respect is animal and plant life 'strange'? The attitudes of human beings to other human beings are themselves variable and

[1] This paper is an attempt to bring together and to reformulate some of the basic philosophical themes in my *Man's Responsibility for Nature* (Duckworth and Charles Scribner, 1974). It should properly be pock-marked with references. Those who are interested will find most of the historical references fully annotated in my book.

complicated; our fellow human beings often act in ways which are, in our eyes, strange. But there are ways of dealing with human beings which fail us when we confront nature. We can argue with human beings, expostulate with them, try to alter their courses by remonstration or by entreaty. No doubt there are human beings of whom this is not true: the hopelessly insane. And just for that reason there has been a tendency to exclude them from humanity, in some societies as supernatural beings, in others as mere animals: old Bedlam was, indeed, a kind of zoo. The psychopath, immune to argument or entreaty, arouses in us a quite peculiar fear and horror. As for artefacts, these admittedly we cannot modify in the ways in which we modify human beings; it is pointless to entreat a building to move out of the way of our car. But we understand them as playing a designed part in a form of human behaviour which we might, in principle, attempt to modify; we look through them to their human makers. When this is not so, when we encounter what clearly seems to be an artefact but cannot guess in what way of life it played a part, we find it, like Stonehenge, 'uncanny'.

'Strange', as Karl Barth uses the word, connotes not only unfamiliar but foreign, alien. (The uneducated find any foreigner 'uncanny' because they cannot communicate with him – to get him to act they have to *push* him like a natural object rather than speak to him.) That nature is thus alien, men have, of course, by no means always recognised. During most of their history they have thought of natural processes as having intentions and as capable of being influenced, exactly in the manner of human beings, by prayer and entreaty – not by way of an anthropomorphically-conceived God but directly, immediately.

For the last two thousand years, however, the Graeco-Christian Western world has entirely rejected this conception of nature. At least, it has done so in its *official* science, technology and philosophy: the ordinary countryman was harder to convince that natural processes cannot have intentions, even when they are not so much as animal. As late as the nineteenth century German foresters thought it only prudent to explain to a tree they were about to fell exactly why it had to be cut down. In Ibsen's *Wild Duck*, Old Ekdal is convinced that the forest will 'seek revenge' for having been too ruthlessly thinned; in Büchner's *Woyzeck* a countryman explains the drowning of a man in a river by telling his companion the river had been seeking a victim for a long time past. (Recall the familiar newspaper metaphor: a dangerous stretch of coast 'claims another victim'.)

Such attitudes, I believe, still exert an influence; in some of the recent ecological literature, the view that nature 'will have its revenge' on mankind for their misdeeds operates as something more than a metaphor, just as old ideas of pollution, sacrilege, *hubris*, are still, in such writings, potent concepts.

The fact remains that the Stoic-Christian tradition has insisted on the absolute uniqueness of man, a uniqueness particularly manifest, according to Christianity, in the fact that he alone, in Karl Barth's words, has been 'addressed by God' and can therefore be saved or damned but also, in the Stoic-Christian tradition as a whole, apparent in his capacity for rational communication. If nature, on that view, is not wholly strange, this is only because it has been created by God for men to use. Animals and plants can for that reason be assimilated, at least in certain respects, to the class of tools, dumb beasts but none the less obedient to men's will. Peter Lombard summed up the traditional Christian view in his *Sentences*: 'As man is made for the sake of God, namely that he may serve him, so is the world made for the sake of man, that it may serve him.' So although nature is 'alien' in so far as it is not rational, it is for orthodoxy neither hostile nor indifferent, appearances to the contrary notwithstanding. Every natural process exists either as an aid to men materially or as a spiritual guide, recalling, as flood or volcano or tempest, their corrupt state.

In this doctrine, which they trace back to the Old Testament, the ecologically-minded critics of Western culture discern the roots of its destructiveness. This is a mistake on two accounts. First, that everything exists to serve man is certainly not the regular teaching of the Old Testament, which constantly insists that, in the words of the Book of Job, God 'causes it to rain on the earth, where no man is; on the wilderness, wherein there is no man; to satisfy the desolate and the waste ground; and to cause the bud of the tender herb to spring forth'. To Paul's rhetorical question: 'Doth God care for oxen?' an Old Testament Jew would have answered 'Yes, of course.' It was the Stoics who took the contrary view. And it is they, under the pretence that it was the Old Testament, who were followed by such influential Christian intellectuals as Origen. Secondly, the doctrine that 'everything is made for man' does not at once entail that man should go forth and transform the world. On the contrary, it was for centuries interpreted in a conservative fashion: God knows best what we need. To attempt to reshape what God has created is a form of presumption, of *hubris*. Sinful corrupt men ought not to attempt to reshape the world in their own image.

After the Crusades, Europe witnessed the development of the 'mechanical arts', as exemplified in the water-wheel, windmills, the

compass, clocks. But these inventions were in many quarters condemned as diabolical. In a wonderful example of Heideggerian
etymology, 'mechanical' was derived from 'moecha', an adulteress.
God, so it was argued, had provided ready-made on earth all it was
proper for men to desire. For them to seek to make their labours less
onerous was to go directly against God's will, by attempting to construct a world which was as if Adam had never sinned.

Yet there is this much truth in the ecological diagnosis: the view
that everything exists to serve man encouraged the development of
a particular way of looking at nature, not as something to respect,
but rather as something to utilise. Nature is in no sense sacred; this
was a point on which Christian theology and Greek cosmology
agreed. God, no doubt, could make particular places or objects
sacred by choosing to take up residence in them, as in Roman Christianity he made sacred the sacrificial bread and wine. But no natural
object was sacred in itself; there was no risk of sacrilege in felling a
tree, or killing an animal. When Bacon set up as his ideal the transformation of nature – or, more accurately, the re-creation of the
Garden of Eden – he had to fight the view that man was too corrupt
to undertake any such task but not the view that nature was too
sacred to be touched. It was man, he pointed out, whom God made
in his own image, not nature.

When Christian apologists see in science and technology the
product of a distinctively Christian civilisation, they are so far right:
Christianity taught men that there was nothing sacrilegious either
in analysing or in modifying nature. But only when Christianity
modified its belief in original sin, only when it became, in practice,
Pelagian could it witness without disapproval, let alone positively
encourage, the attempt to create on earth a new nature, more
suitable to human needs. Locke's vigorous attack on original sin –
explicit in his theological writings, implicit in the *Essay* – formed
part of his task as an under-labourer, clearing away obstacles to
the transformation of nature – and man – by man.

Associated with the Christian concept of nature was a particular
ethical thesis: that no moral considerations bear upon man's relationship to natural objects, except where they happen to be someone
else's property or except where to treat them cruelly or destructively
might encourage corresponding attitudes towards other human
beings. This thesis the Stoics had strongly maintained and it was no
less warmly advocated by Augustine. Jesus, Augustine argues, drove
the devils into swine – innocent though the swine were of any crime
– instead of destroying them, as a lesson to men that they may do as
they like with animals. Not even cruelty to animals, so Aquinas tells

us, is wrong in itself. 'If any passage in Holy Scripture seems to forbid us to be cruel to brute animals that is either . . . lest through
being cruel to animals one becomes cruel to human beings or because
injury to animals leads to the temporal hurt of man.' In other words,
cruelty to animals is wrong only in virtue of its effects on human
beings, as Kant, in this same tradition, still maintained in the final
decades of the eighteenth century. And what is true of cruelty to
animals applies, on this view, even more obviously to our dealings
with other members of the non-human world. Only in Jewish, or
Jewish-inspired, speculation, was the opposite view at all widespread.
The Talmud in several places advocates a more considerate attitude
to nature and when Kant reaffirms the traditional position it is in
opposition to Baumgarten, who had on this question followed the
Talmud.

The question whether it is intrinsically wrong to be cruel to
animals has an importance much greater than at first sight appears:
it is precisely for that reason that philosophers like Kant, humane
though they certainly were, insist that cruelty to animals is wrong
only on the – in fact very dubious – empirical hypothesis that it
encourages cruelty to human beings. For if cruelty to animals is
intrinsically wrong, then it is *not* morally indifferent how men behave towards nature; in at least one case – and then perhaps in
others – man's relationship with nature ought to be governed by
moral considerations which are not reducible to a concern for
purely human interests, to a duty either to others or, as Kant
thought, to oneself.

There is one simple and decisive way of denying that it is wrong
unnecessarily to cause suffering to animals, namely by denying that
animals can in fact suffer. This is the step Descartes took. The philosophy of Descartes represents, in certain respects, the culmination of
the tendency of Graeco-Christian thought to differentiate man from
his fellow-animals. For Descartes denies that animals can so much
as feel, let alone exercise intelligence. (One is forcibly reminded at
this point of the Ciceronian dictum, to which he subscribes, that
there is no doctrine so absurd but that some philosopher has held it.)
All suffering, so his follower Malebranche tells us, is the result of
Adam's sin: animals, as not implicated in that sin, cannot suffer. As
a result of our actions animals do not *really* suffer, they only behave
exactly as if they suffered – a doctrine that some of the Stoics had
also managed to believe. So it is not only wrong to suppose that we
can reason with animals but wrong to suppose, even, that we can
sympathise with them. It is true that this conclusion was reached
at the cost of placing the human body itself within nature, as

something not sacred; what was left outside nature was only consciousness. Yet at the same time the human body was for Descartes unique in being in some way 'united' with consciousness; the human person, conjoining mind and body, could thus be set in total opposition to the non-human world it encounters.

So the Cartesian dualism could be used, and was used, to justify the view that, in his relationships with nature, man was not subject to any moral curbs. Yet at the same time Descartes broke this doctrine loose from its historical association with the view that everything is made for man's use – a view he characterised as 'childish and absurd'. It was, he thought, *obvious* that 'an infinitude of things exist, or did exist, which have never been beheld or comprehended by any man and which have never been of any use to him'. No doubt, man could in fact make use of what he found in nature, and he ought indeed to do so, but nature did not exist as something ready-made for him. Effectively to use it, he had first to transform it. One is not surprised, then, to find Descartes proclaiming that it is man's task 'to make himself master and possessor of nature'; the proper attitude to the world, in his eyes, is exploitative. The paradigmatic case of a material substance is, for Descartes, a piece of wax, the traditional symbol of malleability.

Like Bacon before him he also suggests a particular method of exploitation, what he calls a 'practical philosophy', what we should call a 'science-based technology'. So far as we can make natural processes less 'strange', the assumption is, this is only by first bringing them under concepts which are either inherent in or created by human reason and then using this conceptual grasp to make them work in a manner more conformable with human interests. This is the attitude to nature which has dominated Western science: understanding through laws, transformation through technology.

The philosophy of science associated with this enterprise has been, in certain important respects, Platonic. 'Understanding' has been identified with the discovery of mathematically expressible functional relationships between abstractly-conceived processes and objects. Science, so it is then said, is not about the particular things we see and attempt to cope with in the world around us, except in a rather indirect way. The physics textbook talks about everyday natural objects only in its description of experimental set-ups. And physics is presumed to be science in its ideal form. Rutherford's notorious description of science as 'physics and stamp-collecting' expresses this attitude very precisely; natural history, the direct investigation of nature in a manner which is content to describe qualitative relationships between everyday natural objects and processes, is condemned as mere 'stamp-collecting'. Only a third-rate mind, the presumption is, could devote itself to studying, let us say, the life-history of the whale. To be what Plato calls 'a lover of sights and sounds', to take delight in the flight of birds as such as distinct from the mathematical problems set by that flight, is at once to show oneself an inferior, sensual, being.

Of course, this attitude to nature has always had its critics. Poets like Blake protested against it; painting, before painters, too, were beguiled into pure geometry, drew attention, sensually, to the forms and colours in the world around us. Biologists like John Ray emphasised against Descartes the importance of the multiplicity and diversity of forms of life. But the mainstream of science has been Cartesian-Platonic.

Philosophers, however, were generally unhappy with Cartesian dualism, for reasons which practising scientists found, and still find, it difficult to understand. Descartes, so philosophers argued, had separated consciousness from nature so absolutely that the two could no longer be brought into any relationship with one another. In general, if in very different ways, they reacted against Descartes by trying to maintain that nature was a great deal more human-like than Descartes had been prepared to admit. But they did so, in many cases, at the cost of denying to nature a wholly independent existence, or, at best, by treating independent nature as a sort of 'thing in itself', not as the nature we encounter and try to deal with in our everyday life.

For Berkeley, indeed, the whole of nature is nothing but a vast system of signs, warning and admonishing men. In a different tradition, for Hegel, as for Marx after him, nature in itself is 'negativity'. This does not mean, of course, that it does not exist. But it exists simply in order to be overcome, to be humanised. Man offers it liberty, frees it from its fetters, only by making it human, as he does, to use a favourite example of Hegel's, when he eats plants and flesh. In one way or another, that is, post-Cartesian metaphysicians – with, of course, some notable exceptions – try to maintain that nature is man-centred, even to the extent, in extreme instances, of denying that it so much as exists when man is not perceiving it, thus cutting the ground completely from beneath Descartes's argument against anthropocentrism. Nature is made less 'strange' by being converted into a tool, a language, a secret ally, an aspirant after humanity – or by being denied actuality, except in so far as man cares to bestow actuality upon it. (Remember Hume's reference, although he was not a consistent phenomenalist, to the perceptions 'we choose to dignify' with the name of reality.)

Associated with this attitude to nature is a depreciation of natural beauty as vastly inferior to works of art: the feeling one finds in classical literature and which is still enunciated by Hegel that nature deserves appreciation only when it has been transformed into a farm, a garden, and so has lost its wildness, its strangeness. It was a common theme in Christian thought that the world had been created a perfect globe; nature as we now see it with its mountains and its valleys is a dismal ruin, a melancholy reminder of Adam's sin. Malebranche regretted that nature contains shapes other than the regular solids; the seventeenth-century formal gardener, in the most Augustinian of centuries, did his best to convert nature into such shapes with his pyramidal trees and cubic hedges. The less geometrically-minded Hegelians were no less confident that nature was as it ought to be only when man had transformed it, converting wildernesses into tamed landscapes. Herbert Spencer saw the human task as the conversion of the world into one vast garden.

The two leading traditions in modern Western thought, then, can be put thus: the first, Cartesian in inspiration, that matter is inert, passive, that man's relationship to it is that of an absolute despot, reshaping, reforming, what has in it no inherent powers of resistance, any sort of agency; the second, Hegelian, that nature exists only *in potentia*, as something which it is man's task to help to actualise through art, science, philosophy, technology, converting it into something human, something in which he can feel thoroughly 'at home', in no sense strange or alien to him, a mirror in which he can see his own face. Man, on this second view, *completes* the Universe not simply by living in it, as the Genesis myth suggests, but by actually helping to make it.

It is easy to see from this brief historical excursus why the ecological critics of Western civilization are now pleading for a new religion, a new ethics, a new aesthetics, a new metaphysics. One could readily imagine a sardonic history of Western philosophy which would depict it as a long attempt to allay men's fears, their insecurities, by persuading them that natural processes do not represent any real threat, either because they are completely malleable to human pressures, or because men are ultimately safe in a universe designed to secure their interests – an enterprise which issued in wilder and wilder absurdities in a desperate attempt to deny the obvious facts. This would not be a wholly accurate history of philosophy; even phenomenalism has its merits as the *reductio ad absurdum* of the plausible-looking theory of perception. Philosophy, as we have already suggested, had good reasons for rejecting the Cartesian dualism even if its reasons are less good for replacing it with a new version of anthropocentrism. At the same time, to think of philosophy thus is not an entirely monstrous interpretation; it is quite understandable that philosophy should look like an apologia for anthropocentrism to those who now so urgently emphasise man's responsibility for nature. Western metaphysics and Western ethics have certainly done nothing to discourage, have done a great deal to encourage, the ruthless exploitation of nature, whether they have seen in that exploitation the rightful manipulation of a nature which is wax in man's hands or the humanising of it in a manner which somehow accords with nature's real interests.

As philosophers, of course, we cannot merely acquiesce in the demand for a new metaphysics or a new ethics on the simple ground that the widespread acceptance of the older metaphysics, the older ethics, has encouraged the exploitation of nature – any more than a biologist would acquiesce in the demand for a new biology if that demand were grounded merely on the fact, or alleged fact, that men would be less inclined to act in ecologically destructive ways if they were persuaded that all living things possessed a developed brain. The philosopher is unlikely to be at all satisfied, in particular, with the demand of the primitivist wing of the ecological movement that he should encourage man to revert to the belief that nature is sacred. We are in fact *right* in condemning as superstitious the belief that trees, rivers, volcanoes, can be swayed by arguments; we are *right* in believing that we have found in science ways of understanding their behaviour; we are *right* in regarding civilisation as important and thus far in attempting to transform nature. It is not by abandoning our hard-won tradition of rationality that we shall save ourselves.

We can, however, properly ask ourselves what general conditions any philosophy of nature must fulfil if it is to do justice to the scientific themes of the ecological movement, as distinct from its reactionary, mystical, overtones. Any satisfactory philosophy of nature, we can then say, must recognise:

1. That natural processes go on in their own way, in a manner in-different to human interests and by no means incompatible with man's total disappearance from the face of the earth.

2. When men act on nature, they do not simply modify a par-ticular quality of a particular substance. What they do, rather, is to interact with a system of interactions, setting in process new inter-actions. Just for that reason, there is always a risk that their actions will have consequences which they did not predict.

3. In our attempt to understand nature the discovery of physics-type general laws is often of very limited importance. The

complaint that biology and sociology are inferior because they know no such laws can be reversed, formulated as an argument against an undue emphasis on a Platonic-Cartesian analysis of 'understanding'. When it comes to understanding either biological or social structures, we can then say, what is important is a detailed understanding of very specific circumstances rather than a knowledge of high-level functional relationships. The 'laws' involved are often trite and ill-formulated, serving only as boundaries to what is possible. Whales, to revert to my previous example, must like every other animal, eat and breed; we can describe it, if we like, as a 'biological law' that every animal must ingest food and must have a way of reproducing itself. But these 'laws' leave almost everything of interest about whales still to be discovered.

One could put the general conditions I have laid down by saying that in an important sense the philosopher has to learn to live with the 'strangeness' of nature, with the fact that natural processes are entirely indifferent to our existence and welfare – not *positively* indifferent, of course, but *incapable* of caring about us – and are complex in a way that rules out the possibility of our wholly mastering and transforming them. So expressed, these conclusions sound so trite and obvious that one is almost ashamed to set them out. But, from what has already been said, it will be obvious that they have not been satisfied in most of the traditional philosophies of nature. To that degree it is true, I think, that we do need a 'new metaphysics' which is genuinely not anthropocentric and which takes change and complexity with the seriousness they deserve. It must certainly not think of natural processes either as being dependent upon man for their existence, as infinitely malleable, or as being so constructed as to guarantee the continued survival of human beings and their civilisation.

Such a philosophy of nature, of course, would be by no means entirely new. Its foundations have been laid in the various forms of naturalism. Naturalistic philosophies, however, like the Darwinian biology which lends them support, often attempt to reduce the 'strangeness' of nature – even if they do this by naturalising man rather than by spiritualising nature. That way of using the word 'nature' which I have so far employed is, so many naturalistic philosophers would say, wholly misleading; we should think of 'nature' only as something of which man forms part, not alien to him because he is a full member of it. And, of course, I should agree with the naturalistic philosophers that, in a very important sense of the word 'nature', both man and human artefacts form part of nature: they are subject to natural laws. Nature does not have that *metaphysical* 'strangeness' which Descartes ascribed to it. Both senses of 'nature', however, have a particular role to play; they are important in different types of discussion. Naturalistic philosophers are sometimes tempted into reductionism, tempted into denying that our dealings with our fellow-men differ in any important respect from our dealings with other things, that nature is any 'stranger' than those of our fellow human beings with whom we are not fully acquainted. This is a temptation which has to be resisted. It is not anthropocentric to think of human beings and what they create as having a peculiar value and importance, or to suggest that human beings have unique ways of relating to one another – most notably through their capacity for asserting and denying, but also because, as the existentialists argue, they are unique in their concern for, and about, the future. For many purposes, it is not arbitrary, but essential, to contrast the human with what is not human – with the 'natural' in the limited special sense of the word.

So it will not do to argue, for example, that what has happened in the world is just that man as the dominant species is destroying, in normal biological competition, competitive species, and that to repine at the disappearance of these species is as absurd as it would be to complain that the world no longer contains dinosaurs. It is perfectly true that like any other species men can survive only at the cost of other species. But men can see what is happening: they can observe the disappearance of competing species; they can consider what the effects of that disappearance will be; they can – at least in principle – preserve a species and modify their own behaviour so that it will be less destructive. That in many ways, fundamental ways, men are *not* unique is the starting point for any satisfactory metaphysics. But in other ways they are. A 'new metaphysics', if it is not to falsify the facts, will have to be naturalistic, but not reductionist. The working out of such a metaphysics is, in my judgement, the most important task which lies ahead of philosophy.

What of the contention that the West now needs a new ethics, with responsibility for nature lying at its centre? This, too, is often carried further than I am prepared to follow it. Men need to recognise, it is then suggested, that they 'form a community' with plants, animals, the biosphere, and that every member of that community has rights – including the right to live and the right to be treated with respect. In opposition to any such doctrine, the Stoics long ago argued that civilisation would be quite impossible, that indeed human beings could not even survive, if men were bound to act justly in relation to nature. Primitivists would reverse this argument; since civilization depends upon men acting unjustly towards nature, civilisation ought, they would argue, to be abandoned. Men, so Porphyry for one maintained, ought to reduce their claims to the barest minimum, surviving, under these minimal circumstances, on nothing but the fruits which plants do not need for *their* survival.

Even the fruits a plant does not need, however, may be needed by a variety of micro-organisms; men cannot survive, as I have already suggested, except by being in some degree a predator. As Hume said, it is one thing to maintain that men ought to act *humanely* towards animals, quite another to maintain that they ought to act *justly* towards them. The first of these doctrines rests on no more elaborate assumption than that animals suffer; the second doctrine rests on the much less plausible assumption that animals have claims or interests in a sense which makes the notion of justice applicable to them. Some moral philosophers – Leonard Nelson for one – have taken this view. But I am not convinced that it is appropriate to speak of animals as having 'interests' unless 'interests' are identified with *needs* – and to have needs, as a plant, too, has needs, is by no means the same thing as to have rights. It is one thing to say that it is wrong to treat plants and animals in a certain manner, quite another thing to say that they have a *right* to be treated differently.

No doubt, men, plants, animals, the biosphere, form parts of a single community in the ecological sense of the word; each is dependent upon the others for its continued existence. But this is not the sense of community which generates rights, duties, obligations; men and animals are not involved in a network of responsibilities or a network of mutual concessions. That is why nature, even within a naturalistic philosophy, is still 'strange', alien.

To a not inconsiderable degree, it can be added, very familiar ethical principles are quite strong enough to justify action against ecological despoilers. We do not need the help of a 'new ethics' in order to justify our blaming those who make our rivers into sewers and our air unbreathable, who give birth to children in an over-populated world or – this is a little more disputable – who waste resources which posterity will need. Only where specifically human interests are not so obviously involved does the question of a 'new ethics' so much as arise. Even the preservation of wild species and of wildernesses can largely be defended in a familiar utilitarian fashion.

What has certainly to be dropped, nevertheless, is the Augustinian doctrine that in his dealings with nature man is simply not subject to moral censure, except where specifically human interests arise. Few moral philosophers would now accept that view in its original unrestricted form. It is, indeed, very striking with what unanimity they condemn the older doctrine that cruelty to animals is morally wrong only when it does direct harm to human beings. Their predecessors, they say, were guilty of moral blindness, a blindness with theological origins, in not seeing that it was wrong to cause animals unnecessarily to suffer. The question remains, however, whether moral philosophers are not still to some extent 'morally blind' in their attitudes to nature and especially to those parts of nature which are not sentient and therefore do not suffer.

Certainly, they – and we – have a tendency to restrict such condemnatory moral epithets as vandalism and philistinism to the destruction of property and indifference to works of art. On the face of it, however, the condemnation of vandalism is as applicable to those who damage or destroy the natural as it is to those who damage or destroy artefacts. When, for example, Baumgarten condemns what he calls 'the spirit of destruction' this has as much application to the wilful destruction of natural objects as it does to the wilful destruction of property, or of things likely to be useful to our fellow human beings. The last man on earth would for that reason be blameable were he to end his days in an orgy of destruction, even though his actions could not adversely affect any other human being.

Similarly, a failure to appreciate the natural scene is as serious a human weakness as a failure to appreciate works of art. Once we fully free ourselves from the Augustinian doctrine that nature exists only as something to be used, not enjoyed, the extension of such moral notions as vandalism and philistinism to man's relationship with trees and landscapes will seem as obvious as the extension of the idea of cruelty to man's relationships with animals. It is the great importance of Romanticism that it partly saw this and encouraged us to *look* at nature, to see it otherwise than as a mere instrument. But we do not need to accept the Romantic identification of God with nature in order to accept this way of looking at the world. Indeed, the divinisation of nature, even apart from the philosophical problems it raises, dangerously underestimates the *fragility* of so many natural processes and relationships, a fragility to which the ecological movement has drawn such forcible attention.

In general, if we can bring ourselves fully to admit the independence of nature, the fact that things go on in their own complex ways, we are likely to feel more respect for the ways in which they go on. We are prepared to contemplate them with admiration, to enjoy them sensuously, to study them in their complexity as distinct from looking for simple methods of manipulating them. The suggestion that we *cannot* do this, that, inevitably, so long as we think of nature as 'strange', we cannot, as Hegel thought, take any interest in it or feel any concern for it underestimates the degree to which we can overcome egoism and achieve disinterestedness. The emergence of new moral attitudes to nature is bound up, then, with the emergence of a more realistic philosophy of nature. That is the only adequate foundation for effective ecological concern.

14

HOG IN SLOTH, FOX IN STEALTH: MAN AND BEAST IN MORAL THINKING

John Benson

HUMAN beings find themselves sharing the world with a great variety of other animals. Besides using them in various ways, we think about them and compare ourselves with them, and it is hard to envisage the difference it would make to our understanding of ourselves if they were not there. For one thing we should not have the concept of the human species, and that human beings should be thought of, however theoretically, as all belonging to one species is of momentous importance for morality. The existence of other species might be significant in that way, however, even if we did not pay much attention to them and even if more particular thoughts about or observations of them did not form part of the fabric of our moral thinking. It is with some particular ways in which other species enter our moral thinking and our thinking about morals that I intend to concern myself. There are three of these that I shall discuss: first, the use of animal characters in moral tales, secondly the description of human characteristics in terms of real or supposed analogies with the characteristics of beasts; and thirdly much more briefly the application to human beings of behaviour patterns established in studies of other animals.

There are two common themes that emerge in considering together these rather disparate topics. The first is that they all involve the problem of relating nature and culture. The second is the problem of what constitutes a proper use of human-animal analogies. 'Anthropomorphism' is a term that is commonly used of the ascription to animals of human characteristics, especially mental ones, and usually with the implication that this ascription is unjustifiable.

But it is not clear precisely when it is an error to ascribe human characteristics to animals. After all, Professor Skinner objects to the ascription of thoughts and intentions to men, and denounces that as anthropomorphic. If it is no worse an error to ascribe such things to beasts than to men we can stop worrying about it. But I am not concerned with the problem of behaviouristic analyses of mental concepts, except marginally in connection with my second topic. What I am interested in is the way that anthropomorphism works in different contexts, and in showing that there are contexts in which it is pointless to insist that anthropomorphism is an error. Of equal interest is the opposite of anthropomorphism, namely the ascription of animal characteristics to human beings. For this also the Greeks had a word: theriomorphism.

To get down to business I shall start with the use of animal personages in children's stories. The reason for this is that my interest in theriomorphism stems from having in the past few years read (aloud) a great many children's stories. Animal characters are such a familiar part of one's own growing-up and one's children's that it doesn't naturally occur to one to wonder what is the point. The animals are humanised, their adventures transferable to a human context, so why not just write about human beings? Beatrix Potter provides a good case for consideration. Tom Kitten, Peter Rabbit, Mrs Tiggywinkle and the others are all small animals who are given human character-traits, motives and relationships. The projection is obvious and the point of the stories is that what is related about the characters should be immediately understood as applying to human situations. Peter Rabbit has brothers and sisters, a mother who behaves like a human mother. He gets into scrapes, is rescued, chidden, comforted, and so on. At the same time he and his family live, not in a house, but in a hole in the ground; they eat the sort of food that rabbits eat (though Mrs Rabbit does some cooking too). The scrapes Peter gets into are also a consequence of rabbit-behaviour – eating lettuces in Mr McGregor's garden for example. There is a thorough interpenetration of human and animal worlds.

The obvious point is that Beatrix Potter creates an analogue of the child's social world as a setting for some undidactic pointing of morals. The animals help because they are the sort of attractive small animals that children are fond of. Their tiny clothes and furniture have the same attraction as those of dolls. But that is only a small part of the explanation. More important is the fact that the child-listener is enabled to grasp his own social world in this form, but at the same time be at some distance from it. He can, for example, identify both with Peter Rabbit, and with Mrs Rabbit. That the characters are rabbits (or cats, or mice) facilitates a degree of moral detachment. The child can indulge in making moral judgements of which he is in life the object, and certainly young children seem to delight in expressing shocked disapproval of the naughty behaviour of the characters. It may be that the ability to generalise moral judgements is stimulated by such stories because the child's identification with the characters is less entire than it is in the case of actual child-characters.

The presentation of an objectified moral world could however be done without animals. It might seem that what matters is what is projected, and that there are many different and equally effective recipients of the projection. There are stories whose characters are dolls, for example, or engines. What is missing here is the interpenetration of human and animal worlds that I referred to, and to bring out the significance of this it is instructive to compare Beatrix Potter's stories with those of the Rev. W. Awdry, in which James the Red Engine, Thomas the Tank Engine and the rest play in many ways the same roles as Peter Rabbit and Tom Kitten. There are significant differences however which make one aware that the conversion of railway engines into inhabitants of a social world is brought about by a rather deliberate act of adult imagination. The presence of a jocular uncle entertaining the children with make-believe is obtrusive, and so consequently is the moralising. In Awdry the place of Mrs Rabbit and the other grown-ups is taken by engine drivers and most notably by those pillars of the Protestant Ethic the Fat Controller and the Thin Controller. The engines have no family life; the grown-ups are unrelated and impersonal, capable of indulgence towards an erring engine which shows a serious intention of becoming 'a really useful engine', but in the end officials who have a railway to run. A related point is that the purposes, thoughts and emotions of the engines are merely epiphenomenal. When Thomas the Tank Engine takes it into his head (steam-box?) to go for a jaunt without his driver the author is careful to point out that a careless engine-cleaner must have left the brake off. Awdry is interested in his own kind of realism which requires that every untoward incident should be explicable in a way that will be intelligible to the railway enthusiast. This in no way reduces the anthropomorphism; it merely reminds us with a wink that the author knows what he is up to. The anthropomorphism is in fact complete because the human characteristics are projected onto a screen which is inert. The images it gives back derive no additional significance from being projected. They convey only the message that the author consciously designs.

Beatrix Potter's screen by contrast is not inert. It makes a real difference that the animals she uses have a life of their own which the stories do not forget. The characters rarely do anything that is entirely foreign to the habits of their natural counterparts. The patterns of behaviour they display offer genuine analogies on which to build. This immediately allows of greater subtlety in the moral meanings and allows them to develop with more spontaneity. Rabbits, mice and cats do have a family life. Their young do need to be fed and protected and taught things – for example about the sorts of dangers that are to be avoided by small animals.

One of the most important ways in which this enriches the stories is that it brings into play the relation between nature and culture and intimates the tension between them which is central to the moral experience of the child. This could be illustrated by many examples, but one will suffice. Beatrix Potter's animals sometimes wear clothes and adopt human postures and movements, but not all the time. They are observed, and drawn, with sufficient realism for their reversion to natural behaviour to seem quite unforced. And they are not comfortable in clothes, nor are they naked without them: their wearing clothes corresponds not to a child's wearing clothes, but to a child's wearing its best clothes, in which it must behave with unnatural decorum. The alternation of animals behaving like humans and the same animals being themselves is an effective image of the tension in the child's life between its spontaneous desires and the need to grow into such aspects of culture as being clean, polite and composed.

There is one other subtlety of meaning I want to mention which depends upon the use of animal characters treated with some attention to their natural characteristics. When we use animals in our thinking it is not only the appearance or behaviour of other species that we draw on but also their 'social' relationships with us, a point I shall refer to again later. This is significant in those of Beatrix Potter's stories in which the animals are mice or cats, animals whose family life is not only in certain respects analogous to ours but dependent on ours since it is maintained as part of the human household. The positions of cats and mice are different, in that cats are recognised as a legitimate part of the establishment even if their status is a low one, whereas mice maintain their parallel social life clandestinely, dependent on but barely recognised by the human household. These animals thus provide vehicles for a variety of thoughts and feelings about the relation of the child's world to that of grown-up society.

How much of all this was part of Beatrix Potter's conscious intention I do not know. My point indeed is that just because of the natural analogies and relationships between human and animal, the animal story can make use of a symbolism which generates its own meanings. Animals as metaphors can enable one to say more than is readily said at a more explicit level. Understanding the metaphors is not a matter of being able to translate them, and to express oneself by their means is not a matter of transforming into images meanings which have a prior mental existence in some other conceptual form.

In Beatrix Potter's stories the characters are individual animals not the species to which they belong. This of course is necessary if she is to use animal families as analogues of human families. There is another kind of moral tale in which it is the different species as such that provide the characters, or to be precise indefinite individuals identified only by the species-name. Thus in Aesop the characters are 'a crow', 'a fox', 'a hare' and so on. In Uncle Remus they are Brer Rabbit, Brer Bear and so on. Species characteristics stand in for individual ones in establishing a number of sharply differentiated characters. The sort of behaviour to be expected of each character is predetermined by the stock associations of particular traits with the species used, so the story-teller is saved the time that would be spent in character-description. In Aesop this is used to achieve extreme economy, and to my mind it is only neatness that saves these fables from banality. In Uncle Remus the main gain is uncluttered narrative. Neither kind of tale however is of much interest from the present point of view except as showing in more concentrated form something which is found in our unstudied moral talk, namely the use of the names of animal species as a shorthand way of referring to human character-types, or to particular traits. Among the animals that we associate with undesirable traits are the wolf, the donkey, the worm, the snake and the vulture. The lion, the horse, the lamb and the dove are associated with good traits. A few animals seem to be ambivalent, such as the dog and the fox, and perhaps the monkey.

There seem to be two main forms in which animal-terms appear in evaluative statements. The names of some animals can be used substantivally of human beings, as 'pig', 'wolf', 'ass', 'worm'. Some of the nouns that are used in this way have corresponding adjectives, and though some do not this is probably not significant for the present subject. The second form in which animal terms appear is in phrases of the form 'as ... as a ...': 'as brave as a lion', 'as faithful as a dog', 'as gentle as a dove'. The difference between this form and the first one, in which the term provides a simple epithet which can be applied directly, does seem to be significant. For example, though 'as faithful as a dog' is approving, 'dog' as an unadorned epithet is not complimentary – it implies dirty habits, or obsequiousness. While that is rather a special case, which arises from the ambiguous position of dogs in human society, there is a difference of more general significance. While many animals do provide analogies with virtues or with qualities which are not plainly undesirable, it is hard to think of any that provide simple epithets which are applicable to people in a favourable way. 'He is a lamb' is an expression of affection rather than an appraisal of character. 'He is a lion' is possible, but I have not heard anyone say it. Nor can I find in the *Shorter Oxford Dictionary* any animal term to which a favourable evaluative meaning is ascribed with quotations of recent date. It may be that this is explained by our assumption that we are superior to the beasts, and more readily associate our vices than our virtues with their attributes. By doing so we imply that a vicious quality is *primarily* a characteristic of the animal whose name is used, and simultaneously that the man who is termed a wolf, for example, is made non-human by his ferocity or ruthlessness. The same implicit separation of man and beast would make us shy away from the suggestion that a virtue might belong with as good a right to a beast as to a man. To use a substantive is to suggest a more substantial identity than to use a simile. 'As brave as a lion' simply picks out a point of similarity.

All the same it *does* pick out a point of similarity, and although it is true that one motive for bringing animals into the characterisation of moral qualities is to dissociate certain characteristics from human nature, it is important to consider other motives. Not all the animals we make use of in describing human beings are scapegoats. And I want to suggest that we bring animals in not only, and perhaps not primarily, for the sake of drawing moral boundaries, but also for the sake of understanding. We make the wolf our image of ferocity, the fox our image of cunning not just so that we can express our repudiation of these qualities, but so that we can hold them before our minds. It is because the beast is the concrete representation of a concept that it can be also a vehicle of feelings and attitudes. The animal, or a behaviour pattern which is seen as distinctive of it, provides, in Susanne Langer's phrase, a presentational symbol, which can mediate the formation of the corresponding concept.

To see what force there is in this suggestion it is necessary to reflect for a moment on the nature of such qualities as ferocity, cunning or greed, and what is involved in being able to apply them. What no one I think need find contentious is that they are qualities that manifest themselves in behaviour but which, if a person can truly be said to have them, he has, whether he is currently manifesting them or not. A ferocious man may behave pacifically most of the time without for most of the time being a non-ferocious man. Not every item of a cunning man's behaviour is a manifestation of his cunning. When Aristotle said that a man can be virtuous though asleep he did not want to imply that his sleeping is an exercise of virtue, but simply to point out that he need not be said to lose his virtue every time he goes to sleep.

Our primary way of detecting greed or ferocity is by observing behaviour. It is that commonplace which lends an apparent plausibility to the idea that such qualities can be analysed in terms of the behaviour in which they are manifested. This idea, unlike the commonplace which lends it plausibility, is not all uncontentious. It is in fact untenable, and not only in its behaviourist form. It is untenable as a claim to the effect that 'Smith is greedy' can be translated into a logically equivalent set of statements about Smith's behaviour. But it is also untenable that though not reducible to pieces of behaviour, a quality like greed can nonetheless be defined as a feature of a person such that he will act in such and such ways. (This view is sharply contrasted with behaviourism in that it takes greed to be something other than greedy behaviour, and further in attributing explanatory power to something not publicly observable.)

The reason for saying that both are untenable is that both depend on its being possible to give a list of the kinds of behaviour which are characteristic of the trait. But this cannot be done for we do not know what to include and what to exclude. Of the many individual actions that may be manifestations of greed none will be such that it could be a sign of nothing but greed. Something rather specific, like gobbling the last cake when there are others to come, is obviously something that might be done absent-mindedly, or by someone who was just very hungry, or thinking that no one liked that sort of cake. The list of conditions which would suffice to remove the act from the list of greedy acts can't be completed, consequently we cannot decide whether to include it in that list. A more general tendency to act, such as a disposition to over-eat, may be due to glandular deficiency or worry rather than to greed. So the difficulty does not apply only to isolated acts. Equally there is hardly any act that may not be attributable to greed. A course of slimming which involves heroic efforts of abstinence may be preparation for a bout of gluttony.

To be sure, if one fills in the description of the action in such a way that it is made clear what thoughts and feelings accompany it, what its point is, what it was intended to achieve, and so on, then it may be possible to define the trait by reference to behaviour. But this is tantamount to saying that we can pick out an act as one of the sort that a greedy man would do, if it is of the sort that fits into that pattern of thought feelings and actions which we associate with greed. In other words although greed collects instances – we might well explain what it was by citing typical bits of greedy behaviour – it is the concept of greed that provides us with a rule for selecting the instances.

How, it might be asked, do we ever arrive at the conclusion that a man possesses a character-trait if our only evidence is his behaviour and if we can identify the behaviour as of the sort to constitute evidence only if we know it to be part of a pattern which is constitutive of the trait? The answer is that we do not have to identify individual pieces of behaviour in any final way as manifestations of a trait. Our observations give us ambiguous evidence. The initial observations we make we interpret according to some familiar pattern into which they appear to fit. The more observations we make that are consistent with this the more confident we shall be that our initial identifications were correct.

The conclusion to be drawn is that trait-concepts are quite complex pieces of theoretical apparatus, and to have a proper understanding of any trait it is necessary to be able to use the apparatus. Its complexities are greater than I have suggested so far. Two further sources of complexity deserve to be mentioned because they are partly responsible for the indeterminateness of the relation between traits and the sorts of action which manifest them. One is that what people say, as well as what they do, has to be taken into account, and in two ways. In one way, what people say can improve the situation, help us to interpret action, by telling us what was intended or what feelings accompany action, so giving us access to those elements in a pattern of action which otherwise have to be inferred from outward acts. In another way, speech gives just another set of data that has to be interpreted. For a person's avowed purposes may conceal his real ones, and his avowal of them may therefore be one of the pieces of behaviour which must be conjecturally fitted into a pattern before it is related to an appropriate trait. Thus someone's apparently straightforward expression of concern about my health may be part of a plan to win my confidence so that he can take advantage of me.

The other source of complexity is that traits never come singly. No one is merely vain or merely compassionate or merely self-seeking or merely secretive. Everybody is many things at once. Nor can one suppose that a person's behaviour is divided neatly into the bits that arise from one trait and the bits that arise from others. A good deal

of it may be explicable only on the supposition that it manifests more
than one trait, so that for example the compassion of a very shy
person can only be seen in his actions by someone who sees them as
issuing from someone who is both compassionate and shy. The greed
of a vain man will be manifested in different actions from those of a
greedy and shameless man.

From this hastily surveyed conceptual mountain there is now to be
born a rather inconspicuous mouse. For I have been trying to say
enough to suggest why it is that animal images have a function in
helping us to grasp some of these difficult concepts. The discussion
shows, I think, that it is not possible to acquire these concepts by
building them up out of individual bits of behaviour labelled
'greedy', 'vain', etc. It seems more plausible to suppose that one
begins with relatively simple paradigms which reveal a structure
or pattern, in which, for example, behaviour is related in a straightforward way to purpose and belief. The behaviour of animals provides us with paradigms of this sort, for instance the behaviour of a
predator which stalks, kills and eats its prey. If, focusing on one bit
of this pattern – but as part of the whole – we think of cunning in
terms of the stealth of a stalking fox, we avoid all the kinds of ambiguity I have mentioned. The particular movements – sniffing, lying
low, creeping, running round and so on – can be related to the *prey*;
that they constitute stealth, that is adopting a means of pursuit of
one's end that involves concealment and surprise, is not speculative:
that a particular fox behaves like this is not due to a private fancy of
its own which we might have misinterpreted. This fox does it because it is a functional part of fox-behaviour. Moreover it is pretty
clear that what is at work is a single motivational structure not a behaviour pattern which involves the simultaneous operation of two or
more motives. And finally the structure that we observe could not be
clearer if the animal told us what it was up to, while we avoid any
of the reasons for uncertainty that may arise from having to con-
jecture what the animal is thinking. We can suppose it to think only
what we can read off from its actions.

With regard to the way that animal behaviour can be a help in
our understanding of human behaviour there is a general point,
namely that such a paradigm as that of the predator provides an
elementary instance of purposive behaviour. I would suggest that so
far from its being the case that we attribute purpose to animals only
by analogy with human behaviour, our highly complex concept of
purpose is a refinement of a concept which applies to animal behaviour and to such human behaviour as is of the same elementary
kind. There is good reason to be sceptical of ascriptions to non-

language-using animals of purposes which depend upon the possession of language, but to condemn any attribution of purpose to animals as anthropomorphic is unjustifiable. Over and above this general point, however, it is plausible, I think, to suppose that we may derive particular paradigms of certain traits, such as the ones I have used as examples (cunning, greed, ferocity), from the behaviour of particular species, and regard the more complex manifestations of the trait in humans as approximating to these paradigms. This is a process that can be seen not only in such trite and hallowed examples as I have mentioned so far. Animal behaviour patterns with which we have been made familiar by recent ethological studies have entered into our language, providing us with paradigms which encourage new ways of seeing human behaviour. Two examples. The expression 'pecking-order' testifies to a piece of scientific observation which has led to our seeing certain social rituals and relationships in a new way. Or think of the force of the image of the wolf's gesture of submission, rolling over to expose its vulnerable throat and under-belly, which (to use an inappropriate term) quite unmans its victorious antagonist. This sets off a train of reflection, but it is as a striking instance which can symbolise a general idea that it does so.

Let us stick though to the association of traits with particular species of animal. One reason I suggested why animals provide clear paradigms is that the motivational structures are properties of the species, not of the individual. *This* fox's behaviour is assigned to a particular pattern because we know that this is how *a fox* must behave. One reason why human beings are baffling, and trait-terms difficult to comprehend, is that the traits of an individual human being are not ones that the individual has *qua* human being, nor are his desires only those which he has as an instantiation of the 'needs' of the species. This is one reason why some people are moved to say that man does not have a nature. Interestingly though, we do attribute 'natures' to individuals (though of course existentialists object to this too), and suppose than an individual's behaviour flows from his nature in the way that an animal's behaviour flows from its species-nature. In order to do this we have to be able to see some kind of pattern in the various traits, dispositions, interests, needs, desires and so on that make up his nature. Indeed the point of thinking in this way and the sense of seeing actions as issuing from a nature depend on the possibility of conjecturing at some sort of hierarchy among the salient elements. There may be room for a good deal of looseness. A man's reaction to many contingencies may simply be unpredictable on the basis of his traits. But if his character provides no explanation of his behaviour we have no reason to talk about character, or nature, at all. The simplest case is one in which a single trait, e.g. avarice or greed, is dominant. If we postulate a relatively small number of such single-trait character-types we can classify people according to their degree of approximation to one or more type. If to each character-type we can assign a beast in which we find a paradigm of the trait then the classification of men can borrow from the classification of animal species, the distinctness of each species and its association with a single behaviour pattern providing a means of thinking of human beings as themselves divided into distinct species. Obviously this way of thinking contains a reductive tendency. In Ben Jonson this is exploited for satirical purposes. In *Volpone* the three old men who are waiting to inherit the fortune of the Fox, Volpone, are presented, under the guise of corpse-eating birds, as dominated by a single trait, and the effect is to show the monstrous distortion of human nature that results. In general, however, the association of various traits with different types of individual makes it possible to talk about a complex of traits in a single individual in a concrete way, as though the individual were made up of a number of simpler individuals, between which there are relations of subordination, agreement, disharmony and so on. An individual can be thought of not as a single species but as a menagerie.

I have suggested that the use of animal analogies is comprehensible as an aid to the conceptualisation of certain complex human traits, and as a way of articulating a division of human beings into character-species. I should now like to indicate two sorts of qualification that are necessary. First, I have not wanted to claim that we could not form these concepts if there were no animals that lent themselves to this kind of analogy. We can find in human behaviour straightforward as well as complex examples of particular motivational structures, and these we can and do use as starting points for constructing concepts that can be applied to the complex as well. A pattern is often more readily seen however if it can be shown in a different set of elements. Animals are there, and it is natural that we should use them to point out and refer to patterns in which we are interested. Secondly I have emphasised one kind of association, in which the analogy concerns a motivational pattern. This is because this seems to me the most profound kind of association. But clearly there is a host of other associations which would have to be invoked to explain the bringing in of some of the animals which play a part in our moral language. For example any animal which has a creeping motion may be associated with furtiveness and obsequiousness.

Doves mean gentleness because they are soft and make gentle-sounding noises. The associations here are with aspects of human appearance and behaviour which are expressive of emotion. Another set of associations arises from actual relationships between men and animals. The rat is an enemy of man, and when the term is applied to a man it invokes no very specific behaviour pattern, but primarily transfers to the man the aversion felt to the rat. When the dog is used as a symbol of servility and subordination – as in Pope's inscription for the collar of the Prince Regent's dog (I am his Highness' dog, from Kew/Pray tell me, Sir, whose dog are you?) – it is because of the dog's dependent social position.

The sort of association I have said most about has more than a psychological explanation. I have tried to show that it performs a logical function even if it is one for which animal analogies are not strictly indispensable. This is important for the next part of my argument in which I take up again the idea that animal imagery serves to dissociate from us our own ferocity, greed and cunning. In only a few cases is an animal term applied to a human being on account of a prior attitude to the animal. One of these is the rat, to which we have an attitude of aversion. There is no general justification for interpreting the use of animal symbols as a projection onto animals of qualities which we want to avoid acknowledging in ourselves. I don't of course want to deny that in taking the wolf as our paradigm of ferocity we have in a way done a great injustice to the beast. As Mary Midgley says in her article 'The Concept of Beastliness'[1]: 'We have thought of a wolf always as he appears to the shepherd at the moment of seizing a lamb from the fold' and have neglected his social and family virtues. If this is used to justify cruelty to wolves, or to give us confidence in our superior gentleness, then of course it is monstrous and absurd. To the extent that 'man has always been unwilling to admit his own ferocity, and has tried to deflect attention from it by making animals out more ferocious than they are', it is a good thing to show, as Mary Midgley does in her article, that the instinctive life of animals is 'a much more structured, less chaotic life than people have been accustomed to think'.

However although there is some evidence that the use of animals as symbols of evil has ministered to human complacency, the main support for the view that this is its main motive relies I believe on a fallacious argument: if people identify a species of animal as representing a quality which is evil in men, then the animal is thought to be evil, and indeed an embodiment of evil. 'I am not surprised', says Mrs Midgley, 'that early man disliked wolves – But why did he feel so morally superior?' How does she know that he did? Because a

[1] *Philosophy*, April 1973.

quality thought to be a vice in men is seen by the aid of an analogous quality in an animal it does not follow that it is thought of as a vice in the animal. If the reason for using the animal is that a salient aspect of its behaviour strikingly represents that quality, then when we attribute, for example, wolfishness to a man we are thinking about the man not about wolves. That the aspect of the behaviour of the wolf that is selected falsifies the character of the animal does not matter unless we assume that the analogy is being used to draw inferences, e.g. from the wickedness of wolves to the wickedness of men who behave like them. But it is illegitimate to assume that when someone uses an analogy he is committed to all the inferences that *might* be drawn from it.

The reason why I am taking issue with Mary Midgley is that it seems to me that she rather misguidedly wants to banish the myth and metaphor from our thinking about animals because she thinks that they incorporate distortions in our conception of animal nature and human nature alike. Along with the projection onto animals of evil qualities goes the picture of human instincts and impulses as the beast within. Evil is located in that aspect of ourselves which we share with the beasts. Everything good we suppose to be achieved by reason in the teeth of the beast within which, unless forced to conform to order-imposing reason, would run amok killing, raping, and gorging itself. Mrs Midgley's case for ethology is that it demonstrates that 'Every existing animal species has its *own* nature, its own hierarchy of instincts, in a sense, its own virtues which allow it to live an orderly life.' We need not, then, think of the part of our own nature that we have in common with animals as an evil and chaotic element which must be kept battened down. In spite of our aggression we are adapted by our instincts to social life, not forced into it against our instincts by reason. 'If then there is no Lawless Beast outside man, it seems very strange to conclude that there is one inside him. It would be more natural to say, the beast within us gives us partial order; the business of conceptual thought will only be to complete it.'

My quarrel is certainly not with the thesis expressed in this last quotation. I believe Mrs Midgley makes interesting and largely justified claims for the benefit that moral philosophers can gain from considering the light that ethological studies throw on the nature of human instinct. I am in disagreement with her only about the campaign she conducts against the heritage of folklore about animals and the way that it has spilt over into philosophy. Traditional ideas about animals incorporated into moral thinking do not uniformly present the animal world as chaotic and evil. In Shakespeare, whose tragedies abound in animal imagery, the animal kingdom is itself an image of order which is applied metaphorically to the moral order. When in Macbeth, one bird of prey kills another, and horses 'turned wild in nature' break their stalls, these lawless acts are symbols of the breach Macbeth has made in the moral order. The two realms of order are seen as parts of a single natural order. When Swift wants an image of human nastiness he uses the Yahoos, who resemble no species so much as man, and contrasts them with the orderly horse.

As for the beast within, even here I believe that animal metaphors have not been used to such malign effect as might appear. Plato is cast in the role of first active exponent of the beast within, but the use he makes of animals can be seen, if one is attentive to the need to take his metaphors in their context, to be less discordant than she supposes with the view of man's animal nature that Mrs Midgley thinks we should adopt. It is true that there are passages in which the idea of the soul as tethered to a demanding and rebellious animal is insistent. But not all his beasts are intractable. The auxiliaries in the *Republic* are compared to watchdogs because dogs are both brave and gentle. The dog is not a murderous beast whose nature is changed or held in check by training, but a beast with natural capacities that lend themselves to intelligent direction. To be fit for society it needs to learn the difference between friends and enemies. Part of Plato's point is that the instincts in man do not form a self-regulating and self-adjusting hierarchy. They are not of their nature resistant to order, but they will achieve order only in a person who is capable of reflection, and is aware of being part of a social order. It would be surprising if Plato regarded human instincts as just evil considering that he held human society to be natural to creatures having the needs and talents that human beings have. It will not do to cite as contrary evidence the many-headed beast which Plato invokes in describing the anarchic array of desires in the soul of the democratic personality, for this beast is not intended as an image of the animal nature of just any human being but of the nature of a personality in disintegration. And the fact that it is a composite beast that never was on land or sea preserves Plato from the imputation that he thought that to be morally degenerate is just to become like an animal.

Throughout this discussion I have been defending the use of human-animal analogies and of metaphors drawn from them. That it involves both anthropomorphism and theriomorphism is true, but these transformations and exchanges of similarity between beast and men I have suggested are harmless. Their harmlessness is a result of their empirical innocence. When I have claimed that an analogy helps us to think about human moral characteristics I have not meant that it does so by giving us information of the kind that a psychologist might obtain from interviews, questionnaires and so on, nor that it enables us to come to moral conclusions in the way that empirical evidence about the consequences of certain kinds of behaviour might do. A good analogy helps us to think in the same sort of way that being given a word for some feature of a situation that we could only point to vaguely does. Or in the way that a schematic diagram can enable us to read the composition of a picture that seemed chaotic. An analogy between a human trait and a perceived pattern of animal behaviour can provide an 'image' of what an abstract noun – say 'courage' – refers to. The animal may enter our vocabulary so that 'foxy' just becomes an alternative way of saying 'cunning', but the animal term may still, faintly or strongly, evoke a schematic behaviour pattern which functions in the same way as the composition-diagram.

It becomes appropriate to regard analogies with suspicion when they are offered as informative. For example the theory propounded by Konrad Lorenz, and others following in his footsteps such as Irenäus Eibl-Eibesfeldt, that aggression in human beings is instinctive depends very largely upon observed analogies between behaviour patterns which ethologists already can demonstrate to be genetically determined in non-human species and behaviour patterns in men which are similar in form and function. These analogies are not meant to be seen as surface similarities, illuminating in that they prompt us perhaps to think about the point of some familiar sorts of human behaviour in a new way. (Perhaps academic polemics are a substitute for fist-fighting.) They are meant to support a conclusion about the causal explanation to be given of the human behaviour patterns. Moreover this conclusion, together with others derived in the same way, is used to support views about the way in which it is rational for human beings to behave. It really matters therefore that we should be sure that we are not interpreting the behaviour on the human side of the analogy by means of a metaphor derived from the animal side of it. I confess to a suspicion that this may be happening when the behaviour of people in libraries, keeping a certain distance from one another, or erecting symbolic barriers, is interpreted as an instance of territorial behaviour strictly analogous to the territory-defending behaviour of many other species. (The experiment is cited by Eibl-Eibesfeldt in *Love and Hate*.) It matters equally that we should be sure that we are not interpreting the behaviour on the animal side of the analogy by means of metaphors derived from the human side. There is more than a suspicion that this is going on in the writings of Robert Ardrey, who uses social metaphors freely in describing the group-behaviour of animals and so not surprisingly is able to point to similarities between their behaviour and that of human beings. He really cannot see any difference between an alpha-fish, a silver-back gorilla, and a charismatic political leader.

It is not part of my brief to try to evaluate the analogies presented by ethologists and I have drawn attention to difficulties involved in their use because I hoped that this would throw into relief the contrast between the use of analogy in establishing empirical conclusions and the quite different uses of it which it has been my purpose to describe in the main part of this lecture. Although they are different there is a danger of their being confused, and ethology seems particularly subject to this danger. For it offers information about other species which is fascinating and often surprising, and even if none of its discoveries help to establish anything of scientific value about the human species, it still furnishes the imagination with irresistible metaphors. Different ones however. There are brand-new mythical beasts like the naked ape and the territorial animal. And the familiar non-mythical animals appear with changed metaphorical significance. We must now say 'as harmless as a wolf', 'as cruel as a dove'.

15

CONTRASTING METHODS OF ENVIRONMENTAL PLANNING

Richard Hare

In planning the conduct of his affairs in relation to nature, man is faced with many problems which are so complex and so intermeshed that it is hard to say at first even what kind of problems they are. We are all familiar with the distinction between factual and evaluative questions, and I do not doubt that there is this distinction; but the actual problems with which we are faced are always an amalgam of these two kinds of question. The various methods used by environmental planners are all attempts to separate out this amalgam, as we have to do if we are ever to understand the problems – let alone solve them. I wish in this lecture to give examples of, and appraise, two such methods. I shall draw from this appraisal not only theoretical lessons which may interest the moral philosopher, but also practical lessons which, I am sure, those who try to plan our environment ought to absorb. Though my examples come mostly from urban planning, because that is the kind of planning with whose problems (although only an amateur) I am most familiar, what I have to say will apply also to problems about the countryside. Whether we have to deal with the human nature of the man in the congested street, or the nature of the nature reserves or of the areas of outstanding natural beauty, the word 'nature' may bear slightly different senses, but the problem is still the same: to ascertain the facts about this nature, and then to think how we should conduct ourselves in order to make things better, or at any rate not worse, than they would otherwise be.

Suppose that I am a single person living by myself in a flat, and have decided to remodel my kitchen. I can please myself – questions about other people's interests are unlikely to arise, and in any case let us ignore them. Even in this simple situation it is possible to illustrate some of the pitfalls that practical thinking can fall into. What I have to do, according to the first method that I am going to consider, is to decide upon certain ends or *goals*, and then look for *means* to them. I shall call this way of doing things the *means-end* model. I think you can see its disadvantages. What are the ends that I am setting myself in remodelling the kitchen? It is not difficult to make a list of them: convenience; economy; beauty; hygiene; and so on. But this is going to be of not much use for my purposes, for several reasons. The first is that even if we confine ourselves to one of these ends it may be difficult to say *how much* of the quality in question is required, or even to find a way of measuring how much of it has been provided. This is obviously true of beauty; but even if we take economy, which looks more promising, because we can at least measure how much gas, at what price, it takes to boil a pint of water, we are still in difficulties, because we do not know how small a gas consumption would satisfy us. Similarly with convenience: it is possible to do ergonomic studies – and very useful ones have been done – to determine how many steps or arm-movements are required on a certain layout in order to wash a given collection of dishes. But how many is too many?

However, it is when we come to comparisons and trade-offs between the various desiderata that we are in real trouble. We should need to know how much convenience we are prepared to sacrifice for how much economy, or how much beauty for how much hygiene (for example, if the old copper pans which we keep on the shelf just for show collect the dust and harbour flies, are we going to put up with this because they look so good?). Economists discuss this sort of problem, and help with it up to a point; but the philosophical problems about method remain, and I can illustrate them without doing more than the simplest economics, if any.

One of the things that tend to happen if we use the means-end model is that the goals whose attainment is in some degree measurable, and which can therefore easily be put into cost-benefit calculations, tend to get taken care of, whereas the ones that are not measurable, like beauty, tend to get left out. It may help us to understand the problem if we contrast the means-end model with another model which I am going to call the *trial-design* model. It is the one in fact used by nearly all architects in dealing with their clients, because it is so much more helpful than the means-end model. In this way of doing things, the designer just produces more or less detailed particular designs for the client to look at, all of which he certifies as at least feasible, and attaches perhaps a rough costing to them; and the client then chooses the one that he prefers.

The process of choice is then in its logical aspects very similar to that which I go through when I go to a shop and choose a pair of shoes, except that I cannot actually try on the shoes, but have to choose them from drawings.

This difference is, however, of very great practical consequence. For clients are often not very good at understanding from the drawings what the finished product is going to be like to live with (in our example, what it is going to be like cooking in this kitchen); and some designers are not very good at explaining it to them. However the system can work, and is not in principle different from choosing goods from a mail-order catalogue when you are not allowed to have them on approval.

It is important not to exaggerate the difference between the two models. No doubt even in the trial-design model the designer will have had some idea, obtained by preliminary questioning, of what the client's goals and preferences are; so the alternative designs he produces for the client to choose from are not churned out at random. Knowing the client's preference, he gives him a short list of designs, or in the first instance just one, which he thinks the client will like. A certain amount of means-end reasoning has gone into this process. And even in a means-end system there may be trial-designs produced in the later stages. It may be that in a complete and adequate procedure both models would play a part. But it is still important to distinguish between them, and above all not to think that the means-end model by itself is enough.

I want now to illustrate the important difference between these two models or methods by contrasting two studies in which they are employed, each in a fairly pure form. These are, first, the book *Urban Transportation Planning*, by Roger Creighton,[1] an American traffic engineer, which advocates a certain method in transport planning and illustrates its use in two important studies which his team did for the conurbations of Chicago and Buffalo; and secondly, Sir Colin Buchanan's Edinburgh study published in two books *Alternatives for Edinburgh* and *Edinburgh: the Recommended Plan*.[2]

The first of these books uses the means-end model. Before I go into detail, I must repeat that one of the chief things that all planning procedures have to do, if the thinking is going to be clear and unconfused, is to distinguish questions of fact from questions of value. I am not going in this lecture to try to justify this remark; anybody

[1] R. L. Creighton, *Urban Transportation Planning* (Urbana, 1970).

[2] Colin Buchanan and Partners, Freeman Fox, Wilbur Smith and Associates (Edinburgh, 1971, 1972) (obtainable from Edinburgh Corporation).

who spends much time reading about planning problems cannot help noticing the terrible confusions which result when people think, either that they can answer factual questions by making value-judgements (which we call 'wishful thinking'), or that they can answer evaluative questions by elaborate observation of the facts. It is neither the case that you will make a certain proposed road net-work lead to a certain reduction in traffic in some environmentally sensitive area just by thinking how nice it would be if it did have this result; nor that you can by traffic statistics prove that it is the *best* solution to the problem. You can prove, perhaps, within certain limits of error, that *this* is what the traffic will do when you have built the network; but the public still has to decide what kind of city it prefers to have.

The two methods that I am discussing are essentially two rival ways of separating factual from evaluative judgements. The means-end model used in Creighton's book strikes many people at first as an obvious way of achieving this separation. We incorporate all our value-judgements at the beginning of the planning process into state-ments of what are called 'goals'. Having thus, as it were, put all our values into the machine once for all, we cause the machine to turn out various plans and to evaluate them with reference to these goals, and the 'best' plan will automatically be chosen. This process is re-presented schematically on p. 136 of the book:

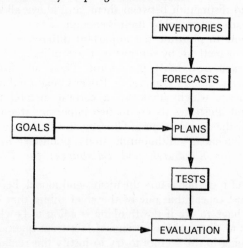

We first make our factual enquiry into the inventories, that is to say into the actual statistics of the present situation: existing road networks, traffic counts on them, the same for rail and other public transport networks, distribution of population and of places of work, and so on. We also check one of these groups of statistics against the other; there are certain reasonably reliable models which allow one to predict the distribution of travel over a network given the distribution, as to places of residence and of work, of the people who are going to use it. So we can test these models for their predictive accuracy by seeing whether, by using them, the existing population- and work-distribution can be made to generate the observed existing traffic flows. All this is common to both the methods I am considering, so I shall not have to repeat it.

So is the step called 'forecasts'. This consists in making predictions, on sociological, economic and other grounds, of the *future* distribution of population and places of work, and thus of the 'desire for travel', in the future, along various lines within the area to be covered by the plan. A date is normally set for which the plan is being made; 20 years is thought to be about the limit of human prescience by existing methods.

The two methods now start to diverge. The Creighton method, having made its inventories and forecasts, requires the determining at this point, once for all, of a number of 'goals'. The approach of the author is well illustrated by this excerpt:

Scientific Method: Objectivity. In great part due to the influence of Carroll, the transportation studies adopted the scientific method as the standard for their work. The features of observation, advancement of hypotheses, and replicability of calculations were considered to be the proper guidelines for all the analysis and development of theory which were done by transportation studies. Although the preparation of plans necessarily included the subjective element of human goals, even this part of the planning operation was treated with extreme objectivity once the list of goals was adopted. And even in selecting goals, attempts were made to deduce goals from an observation of what people actually choose to do. In short, judgement was out and the rules of evidence and demonstration were in as the standards by which decisions were made (p. 146).

In order to fit into this method, the goals have also to be stated in very simple terms, and such that the extent to which they are realised is not only quantifiable, but quantifiable in a way that enables us to compare the realisation of one goal with that of another on a common scale (which in practice has to be that of money). For example, if one goal is saving of time and another saving of lives, we have to find a way of measuring both these benefits in money terms.

The same applies to even more difficult items like the enhancement of the quality of life in cities or the preservation or improvement of their visual quality.

When we come to look at the actual goals listed in Creighton's book, we see how difficult the task is going to be. Eleven are listed (overlapping with one another to some extent):

Safety
Saving time in travel
Reducing operating costs
Increasing efficiency
Mobility
Beauty
Comfort and absence of strain, noise or nuisance
Reducing air pollution
Minimising disruption
Increasing productivity of the economy
Ability to move about without an automobile (pp. 199 ff.)

In the Chicago study in which the author was involved, says Creighton,

> One of the tasks the staff set for itself was to build a formal bridge between goals and plan. *We wanted to be able to prove that the plan we recommended for the Chicago area would be the best.* If the Policy Committee to whom we reported approved our statement of goals and objectives, and our reasoning processes were correct, then they would almost automatically approve the plan, because the one had to follow from the other. The ultimate extension of this idea, of course, would be one in which a computer would be given a statement of goals for a given metropolitan area, together with the facts describing that metropolitan area, and then it would be programmed to produce the best plan for the area automatically. We later achieved this, though only at very small scale (p. 201).

The restrictions on the kinds of goals that the machine can cope with and which I mentioned earlier, lead in practice to the simple omission of goals the extent of whose realisation is not measurable in terms of money. Thus in the two studies taken as examples by Creighton, concerned with Chicago and the environs of Buffalo, only the first four goals which occur in the list I quoted were used in evaluating the alternative plans: safety, reduction of travel time, operating costs and capital costs. The last three of these are easily expressible in money terms; safety is so expressible if we apply to the accident statistics (actual and predicted) the values set upon loss of life, injury and damage to property by the courts, though the basis of such valuations is quite unclear.

The other goals simply get omitted. Economists have tried to find theoretical ways round this difficulty;[3] but in practice a means-end model which insists on prior statement of goals and a mechanical operation of the evaluation process thereafter is almost bound to have this result; and the outcome of such thinking is to be seen in typical American cities. It was also to be seen in the majority report on the third London airport,[4] in which the cost-benefit analyses were expressed in money terms, and everything that was going to be considered had to have a money value set on it – the commission were in difficulties as to whether the value of an irreplaceable Norman church was to be taken as the sum it was insured for.

Is there an alternative? I think there is, and that planners are beginning to use it, although I doubt whether they really yet understand how different the new method is from the old. Perhaps I am exaggerating; perhaps traces of the new kind of thinking are to be found in Creighton's book. On p. 318 we have a trial-design method used:

> The 'modal model' described in the preceding chapter was used in 1966 to test eleven different combinations of transit and highway systems for the Niagara Frontier. These tests were released to the public in December that year, but without recommendation;

and on p. 343 there is another diagram, which ends:

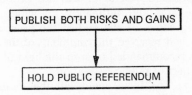

And perhaps traces of the means-end model are to be found in the Buchanan study which I am going to consider in a moment. But I have somewhat schematised the methods in order to make the contrast clearer.

Buchanan's team was called in to report on Edinburgh after a

---

[3] See, e.g., D. L. Munby, 'Faith and Facts: Quantity and Quality', in *Humane Gesellschaft*, ed. T. Rendtorff and A. Rich (Zürich, 1970).

[4] *Commission on the Third London Airport* (the Roskill Commission) (London: H.M.S.O., 1971).

plan proposed by the Corporation had aroused a lot of opposition, because of the very obtrusive character of the new roads proposed in it and the destruction of the environment, especially its visual qualities, that would be entailed. What the team did, after doing the factual analyses and forecasts which, as I said, are common to both the methods, was to prepare in skeleton form a number of different plans (including an adaptation of the one which had caused the fuss), involving different degrees of reliance on public transport, different scales of road expenditure, and different amounts of restriction of access for private cars to the centre. I will not say that goals were not considered at all before the plans were made (as I said, I do not want to exaggerate the break between the two methods or to represent the transition between them as having occurred suddenly). Obviously, in selecting just *these* plans for elaboration and evaluation the team had some idea in mind of what they and the public were after (just as, even in Sir Karl Popper's theory of scientific method,[5] the scientist, though he *may* adopt a hypothesis for testing on a mere hunch, normally has more to go on than that). But Buchanan's study is, so far as I can see, altogether free of the doctrine that goals or ends have to be stated once for all at the beginning, the rest of the evaluation being done mechanically by application of these goals to the facts.

Instead, what the study does is to predict the factual consequences of building each of the schemes in turn, describe these in some detail and in as clear and quantified a way as the nature of the facts allows, and then ask the public (that is, the inhabitants of Edinburgh and their elected representatives) to discuss the various alternatives in the light of these facts, and, ultimately, say which they *prefer*. The crucial evaluation comes at the end of the process, not at the beginning. After it had received the comments of the public, the team then produced a recommended plan in the light of them which was also to be the subject of public evaluation.

This method at one blow avoids all the disadvantages of the previous one. Goals do not have to be tied up in advance. Nothing is in principle presupposed about goals until the time comes to opt for one or another of the plans. The public can just look at the plans and say which it prefers. The point of all the analysis of consequences of the plans is not to *prove* an evaluative conclusion, namely that one of them is the best, as Creighton's method tries to do; it is, rather, to make the ultimate choice as well informed as possible, in that the public will have a clear idea of what it is choos-

---

[5] K. R. Popper, *The Logic of Scientific Discovery* (Vienna, 1934; London, 1959); *Conjectures and Refutations* (London, 1963) chap. 1.

ing between. Therefore, it is not necessary to express all the goals in terms which allow of a financial comparison; they do not have to be commensurable at all, any more than the fit of shoes has to be commensurable with their cost. Thus, Buchanan's team estimated the environmental effects of the various proposals quite independently of the economic cost-benefit analysis. These environmental effects were predicted by working out what volumes of traffic would be present in the various streets. Then these volumes were compared with what is called the 'environmental capacity' of the streets – i.e. the amount of traffic that there can be in the streets without disrupting the environment to more than a certain degree. This degree is measured in terms of the amount of noise, the amount of visual intrusion of vehicles and road structures, and so on. Where precisely the 'environmental capacity' is fixed is of course an evaluative matter. However, the method employed does (for me at any rate) considerably clarify the evaluative process, so that when I come to choose between the plans, I feel that I know much more clearly what I am choosing between. In principle the choice is left to me; nobody is trying to prove anything to me, except that those would be the consequences of the adoption of a certain plan.

The two methods lead to two very different sorts of plans. Buchanan, unlike Creighton, is led, after the public discussion, to propose a plan which requires quite a high degree of restriction of private cars for commuting, with closure of streets in the centre, restriction of some existing and new streets to buses, fairly low road expenditure, and large reliance on public transport. He does not, indeed, go as far as some people would like, and the debate in Edinburgh continues. It is also alleged that the terms of reference which he was given compelled him to concentrate too much on the scheme's effects in the central area of the city, and not enough on those in the suburbs. But at least he has displayed a method which enables the debate to be conducted rationally; and those of us who on the whole share his preferences have a right to insist that those who do not, work out the factual consequences of *their* preferred schemes as conscientiously as he has those of his, and try to convince the public that these consequences would prove in practice more acceptable.

The difference between the outcomes of the two methods is not entirely due to the difference between the methods themselves; but it partly is. Another factor is a greater readiness of the British public than of the American to contemplate restrictions on private cars (due perhaps to our lower degree of motorisation). The second of the two methods, if followed in America, might lead to a choice by the public of solutions involving higher road expenditure and less restriction on private cars than is likely to be acceptable in Edinburgh. And, of course, Edinburgh is an outstandingly beautiful city. Nor do I want to suggest that all Americans adhere to the means-end model in their thinking – even all professional planners.

The means-end model is naturally congenial to the engineer, the trial-design model to the architect. Buchanan is both. Engineers usually get, when they are designing a bridge, a fairly cut-and-dried statement of goals (e.g. that it should have a certain traffic capacity, take a certain maximum load, and cost as little as possible); and they then exercise their science and prove that the design which they recommend is superior in these respects to others. The architect, on the other hand, normally produces sketches and then more worked-out plans of alternative layouts, and the client has to say which he wants. Though I am convinced that the engineer is an indispensable member of the planning team, I am equally convinced that the 'architectural' overall method is the better one.

I have been speaking mainly about urban problems; but what I have said is obviously applicable to all decisions about environmental planning, including those that affect nature in the narrow sense. But these latter problems are likely to bring out, even more than those of city planning, a distinction which I have not yet mentioned. This is the distinction between the work of the architect or the engineer on the one hand and that of the planner on the other. The architect and the engineer are likely to have just one client who is going to choose the final design and pay for its execution. I have been speaking as if this were so in city planning; but it is not. The planner has to satisfy great numbers of 'clients' whose interests are often in conflict.

The difference is not merely a difference in complexity. I started by considering a problem about planning a kitchen. Architectural problems like this could become extremely complex without becoming a battlefield for conflicting interests. Suppose, for example, that some rich landowner is redesigning his entire mansion and perhaps a vast estate too; the problems may then be as complex as a great many planning problems. But provided that the landowner is concerned solely with his own interest, and not at all with the interests of the others affected (he is quite ready, say, to shift a whole village to improve his view, as Lord Harcourt did at Nuneham[6]), he will be able to proceed just as in the 'kitchen' case. He will, that is to say, if he follows the trial-design model, get Vanbrugh

[6] It has been suggested that Oliver Goldsmith's *Deserted Village* is about this eviction; but the text presents obvious difficulties for such a claim.

or Capability Brown to give him some alternative designs and choose between them. He will not have to consult anybody else.

In planning decisions, however, almost by definition, other people are involved and will have, in any democratic system, to be consulted. There are first of all the many different people who are going to live or work in or visit frequently the piece of land whose use is being decided; then there are the neighbours who will live where they are affected by that use; then there are other members of the public who will see it; and those who, though they will not see it, will use, or be affected by the use of, whatever is produced there (gravel for example); and so on.

There are two questions – both of them moral questions – which at once arise when many people are concerned like this. The first is about procedure; what is the most just way of arranging for the decision to be made, so that the interests of all these people get their due consideration, and they have some say in the decision proportionate to their interests? The second is about the substance of the decision arrived at; what makes a decision a just or a right one in such cases?

On the first question: it is obvious that whatever procedure we adopt will be some kind of *political* process. In this it is different from the 'kitchen' case or even the 'mansion' case; the addition of all these different people whose interests have to be considered has made politics inescapable, as it is not for our bachelor who is consulting with his architect. Even in the extreme case of a dictator who just says 'Pull down the old quarter in front of St Peter's and build the Via della Conciliazione instead', this is a political act, and it is only because the *polity* is like that (namely a dictatorship) that he can make the decision and get it executed without taking anybody else's views into consideration. If anybody objects that this is true of the landowner too, I shall not argue the point. At any rate, in normal polities, even some quite undemocratic ones, there has to be some process whereby the interests of different people are taken into account, and the question is (a moral question): Which of these arrangements is most just in the circumstances of a particular society?

The second question would arise even if the first did not. Suppose, again, that there is a dictator; or suppose, less extremely, that a particular person (say the Secretary for the Environment) has the sole decision about some particular issue (for example whether, or on what route, to build the extension of M40 from Oxford to Birmingham). Suppose that *that* is the political procedure which has in fact been adopted. The first question has then been answered, but the second question still has to be answered by this dictator or minister, if he is a moral man and is trying to do the fair or the just thing.

I will only indicate my own view, without arguing for it, about how the second question is to be answered. As it happens, an answer to it is implicit in the theory about the nature and logical properties of the moral concepts which I have worked out in my books. To be prepared to say 'That is the solution which ought to be adopted' is to be prepared to prescribe it for universal adoption in cases just like this. I have argued elsewhere[7] that this way of putting the matter comes to the same thing as two other theories which have had a wide currency: the so-called ideal observer theory and the so-called rational contractor theory – but only in certain of their forms, and in the latter case *not* in the form preferred by its best-known advocate, Professor Rawls. Certain forms of utilitarianism lead to the same conclusions, as do certain interpretations of the Kantian doctrine and of the Christian injunction to do unto others as we want them to do to us. So the method which I am advocating ought to have the support of a fairly wide spectrum of philosophers.

What it comes to is this. If I am prescribing universally for all situations just like this one, I shall be prescribing for situations in which I myself occupy the roles of all the persons affected by the decision. If you like to dramatise the method, you can adopt C. I. Lewis's device of imagining that I am going to occupy, *seriatim*, the positions of all these people in identical corresponding situations.[8] If I do this, I am bound to accord equal weight to the equal interests of each individual affected (and of course the weight will vary according to the degree to which they are affected).

So then, the first thing that the person making the decision has to do is to find out, by factual enquiry, how various alternative decisions *will* affect the interests of the various parties. And this question is divisible into two elements. He has first to find out (as precisely as needs be) what will happen if one decision or the other is taken. This includes questions like: how many aircraft will use the proposed airport; how much noise they will make and over what areas; how many passengers will travel by them, and how far they will travel, and by what means, to reach the airport; how much land and how many buildings of what sorts will be taken over or destroyed; how much the whole thing will cost; how much the passengers will have to pay in transport costs; and so on. And secondly he has to find out how

---

[7] *Philosophy and Public Affairs* i (1972), repr. in *War and Moral Responsibility*, ed. M. Cohen *et al.* (Princeton, 1974) pp. 47 ff.; *Ar. Soc.* lxxii (1972/3); *Ph.Q.* xxiii (1973).

[8] C. I. Lewis, *Analysis of Knowledge and Valuation* (La Salle, 1946) p. 547.

all these facts will affect people's interests: the people whose homes will be destroyed or disturbed; the people who travel by air; the people who send freight by air or use it the other end; the people who pay taxes which are used to finance the construction; and so on. The facts here are facts about the desires and likes or dislikes of these people: how much they mind what is being done to them, or how much they appreciate what is done for them. It must be emphasized that facts about people's likes and dislikes are still facts, although to have a certain like or dislike is not to state any fact. From these facts, we can get conclusions about what the people's interests are.

One of the arguments for 'participation' and for democratic ways of deciding questions about planning is that they automatically give those concerned a certain voice, so that they can make known how they think their interests are affected. But a procedure may be procedurally just, or be accepted as being so, but still not achieve a just solution to the substantial problem. This is because people (usually because they lack foresight) do not always use the procedure wisely in even their own interests. Shopkeepers have in the past often opposed the creation of pedestrian precincts or the building of by-passes to their towns, in the mistaken belief that this would result in loss of trade. Actually, when this is done, it seems usually to improve trade, because people like shopping where they are not disturbed by traffic. So if you had tried to follow procedural justice by giving traders a big voice commensurate with the extent to which their interests are affected, they would have actually used this voice to bring about a decision (the maintenance of the *status quo*) which was against their interest. The same applies to members of the general public, who may object to certain features of planning schemes as against their interest simply because they are unable to foresee or visualize the actual effects of the schemes.

Another objection is that it is extraordinarily difficult by democratic procedures to ensure that people get a say in proportion to the degree to which their interests are affected. In theory, the people who are going to suffer most will howl the loudest, so that if we had an instrument for measuring in decibels the loudness of howls, *and* people were always the best judges of their own interests, and if posterity could howl, we could use this instrument as a just procedural means of ensuring justice in the result. But in fact it may be the people who are best organized, or who have most money, who succeed in making the most noise, and the resulting political pressures may be an extremely imperfect reflection of the degree to which people's interests are actually going to be affected. For these two reasons (ignorance, and the imperfection of the participatory process) there is almost bound to have to be a certain amount of paternalism in these decisions if they are going to be just ones; one can do one's best to bring the facts before the public and to get those whose corns will be trodden on the hardest to make the most noise, and the rest to pipe down a bit; but probably someone in the machine will have always to be looking after the interests of those who lack the knowledge, or the power, to stand up for their own real interests.

It is at this point that both the uses and the limitations of cost-benefit analysis (about which Professor Self will be speaking with greater authority than I can) are most clearly revealed. In the cases considered previously, in which one person only was concerned in the choice of a design (the 'kitchen' case, for example) there was no need for cost-benefit analysis at all; when the client was fully apprised of the factual consequences of adopting each of the different designs, he could just choose. There was no need to express the alternatives in terms of costs or benefits measured by some common scale (for example money). We compared the choice with that of shoes at a shoe shop; in order to choose rationally between pairs of shoes at different prices one does not have to *price* the value to oneself of good fit, smart appearance, etc., although one may show *by one's choice* what monetary value one attaches to these qualities. The monetary value thus derived is a *deduction from* the choice made, not an *aid to making* the choice rationally.

But where many people are affected, as in most planning decisions, there is the problem of balancing their interests fairly against one another. So it looks as if it might help to work out the costs and benefits to all the parties on some common scale and thus make the adjudication fairly. One would then not be imposing a cost on one person unless a greater benefit was thereby secured to another; and thus one would be maximising utility. Alternatively, if one were an adherent of some non-utilitarian system of distributive justice, one would seek to distribute costs and benefits in some other way considered just. Any of these processes, however, depends on knowing what value, on a common scale, each of the individuals affected attaches to the 'costs' and 'benefits' in question. And this, as before, can only be a *deduction from* the choices which are made,[9] or which

---

[9] Cf. p. 146 of Creighton's book, cited above p. 285. On the general question see Amartya Sen, *Collective Choice and Human Welfare* (London, 1972). Obviously much more needs to be said than I have been able to say about the uses and pitfalls of cost-benefit analysis. In this lecture I wish merely to claim that the trial-design method is less dependent on it than the means-end method, and not that the former can dispense with it altogether

it is predicted would be made, by these individuals. Cost-benefit analysis can therefore not be a substitute for making these choices. It can never altogether take the place of voting and other political procedures or of selective purchase and other economic procedures. We can observe how people do vote, what they do buy, whether they go by car or bus when travelling from A to B, and so on, and thus make inductive inferences about what choices they and people like them *would* make in relevantly similar circumstances. But they have to do the initial choosing.

The element of paternalism, therefore, which I said is inevitably involved in planning if the ill-informed are to be protected from making choices which they will regret, is of a very limited sort. It consists in predicting what choices the ill-informed would make if they were more fully informed. For example, it might be legitimate, if the planner could get away with it politically, and if he were sure of his facts, for him to make the traffic-free shopping precinct referred to in my earlier example; if in the end the shopkeepers and the public liked it, he would have been proved right even if he went against their wishes at the time. But it is not open to the planner to dictate to them what they *shall* like or dislike or choose or reject; he can only make more or less hazardous predictions about what they *will* like or *would* choose, and an item can appear as a 'cost' or a 'benefit' in his calculations only on the basis of these predictions. And, if the public were much better informed than it is about the consequences of different planning policies, participation and democratic voting would be a better means of choosing policies than bureaucratic direction. If, therefore, the public wants not to be paternalised, it has to some extent to learn (or at least learn from) the planner's predictive skills. Even so, however, there are difficulties, familiar to political theorists, but beyond the scope of this lecture, about whether distributively just solutions are likely to be arrived at by democratic processes however well oiled.

Let us, however, suppose that the two kinds of facts that I mentioned (about the consequences of planning decisions and about how these will affect people's interests) have been ascertained. We have

---

when more than one person's interest is involved. However, the inevitable crudities in practice of cost-benefit analysis make it a virtue of the trial-design method that it at least allows the preference-ordering of solutions by an individual to be made without recourse to it. When it comes to converting these individual preference-orderings into a collective choice, some kind of cost-benefit analysis may be the only way of balancing them fairly against one another. But this is too big a topic for the present lecture.

then a number of trial designs, each of them accompanied by an array of these two kinds of facts. The decision has, however, still to be taken. It does not follow logically from these facts. If a dictator were interested only in the glory of his national airline or, more commendably, in the preservation of the countryside just as it is, and so made his decision regardless of all the other factors, we should not be able to fault his logic. However, if he, or if the people who are making the decision, ask what they can prescribe universally for situations just like this, they are bound, as I said, to give equal weight to the equal interests of all those affected, and so will choose a solution that does the best for those interests taken as a whole. And this is what planners should do.

I wish to contrast this essentially utilitarian solution, which is that adopted by the best planners, with the sort of solution that is likely to get adopted if we follow some less adequate methods. They are nearly all less adequate for the same reason, which is that they have taken a highly selective view of the facts. But this can be for a number of different reasons. First we have those who, obsessed with the need to be scientific, take into account only those facts which can be measured. I have said enough about them already. On the other hand we have those who take a selective view of the facts for entirely non-scientific (e.g. for political) reasons, and ignore, for example, economic factors. I know people whose views on planning all stem from a pathological hatred of the motor car (sometimes because it is anachronistically taken to represent middle-class values), and others who are led to the opposite extreme by an insane love of this useful but dangerous machine. It is the one-sided character of most of what most people say about planning and conservation that makes me despair of our getting many wise decisions.

What is the philosophical interest in all this? First of all, it is an excellent illustration of the necessity for understanding ethical theory, if we are going to think rationally about our practical moral problems. I have mentioned, and I hope exemplified, the usefulness of carefully distinguishing factual from evaluative questions. The most harmful theorists of all are those who say (without producing any good arguments) that this cannot be done and that therefore we are condemned to argue endlessly in terms which bend as we use them, reducing the discussion of these issues to a contest between rhetoricians. If we can separate out the questions of fact from the others, we can at least obtain reliable answers to *them*. But when we have done this, we then have to resist the seductions of the second most dangerous set of theorists – those who say that since only facts are 'objective', and values are merely 'subjective', there can still be no rational process for deciding questions of value, which all questions of planning to some extent are.

I have tried to explain to you how, having separated out the two kinds of questions, it is possible to use our knowledge of the facts in order to present ourselves with an informed choice between possible solutions. If only one party is affected by the choice, then that is all there is to be said, and his choice, if fully informed, is as rational as it could be. But if many people are affected, as in planning decisions they are, we need also a rational means of adjudicating between their interests; and this, I have claimed, ethical theory can supply. The difficulty remains of finding a political procedure which will make this rational adjudication possible; but since this difficulty takes us into the heart of all the as yet unsolved problems of political philosophy, I will not now embark on a discussion of it.

16

TECHNIQUES AND VALUES IN POLICY DECISIONS

Peter Self

INTRODUCTION

INCREASING use is made of techniques which are supposed to make policy decisions more 'rational'. Rather little attention, however, has been paid to the relation between these techniques and (a) the logic of choice, (b) the political process, (c) value judgements and assumptions. This short paper will investigate these questions in relation to a particularly fashionable technique, that of cost-benefit analysis.

The theoretical basis of cost-benefit analysis as an economic tool rests in welfare economics, but CBA (as I will call it for convenience) is frequently used in a very pragmatic way. At a minimum CBA recommends no more than listing in a systematic way the expected 'costs' and 'benefits' of a decision. This can be done in a wholly non-economic manner (perhaps substituting 'drawbacks' and 'advantages') or one side of the equation only is quantified – for example, costs are often measured in economic terms but benefits not. However, the technical thrust of CBA is towards measuring in some economic sense as many factors as possible, so as to put them on a consistent basis. Often, however, there is not much attention to the design of the relevant policy framework, and it thus becomes necessary to infer the political and normative assumptions of this kind of analysis.

I have no space here to go far into the interesting question as to how far the various techniques of quantification which the economists use are grounded in political and normative beliefs or ideologies. Nor can I deal with the main types of decision-making model and their relation to values, a question Mr Hare considers in his paper and which relates in an interesting way to CBA and planning.

These matters are examined in my forthcoming book, *The Econo-crats and the Policy Process*. Instead I want to look first at the claims which CBA can make to improve policy-making (such a justification is very necessary, because economic quantification itself does not explain what or whose costs and benefits are relevant to a decision, nor why they should be taken into account). Secondly, I will con-sider how CBA deals or could deal with questions of justice and welfare as politically understood. Finally, I want to contrast the methods of policy-making that seem to be implicit in an idealised version of CBA and in an alternative approach which I will label 'consensus planning'.

ECONOMIC TECHNIQUES AND THE POLITICAL PROCESS

Welfare economics which underlies CBA is rooted in respect for the freely articulated wants or preferences of individuals. Individuals are assumed to receive varying amounts of satisfaction or 'utility' from their consumption of goods, but it is now usually accepted that these utilities cannot be directly known or inspected but only inferred from the free choice of individuals exercised under appropriate conditions. Whether or not individuals do choose so as to maximise their satis-faction, the economist can reasonably argue that there is no better way of knowing what would please them and perhaps add that experiences are not worth having if they are not freely chosen.

The essence of CBA is to apply the concept of consumer choice in a properly working market to a much broader range of policy situa-tions. The usefulness of the market model is that, given certain assumptions, it provides a precise measurement of my preference for one good against another good, for example, butter against bacon. It is just this precision which is absent in the political expression of policy choices. But what if the extent of my preferences for achieving or preventing certain results, for example, protecting a bird sanc-tuary or reducing traffic noise or getting free public transport, can be somehow inferred or ascertained and converted into a common scale of measurement? If such things are possible, Peter Hall will be justified in his prophecy that for the first time CBA opens up the prospect of a rational science of policy evaluation.[1]

It is easy to see the limitations of the political process as a means of ascertaining individual preferences. A vote at a periodic election is a very crude instrument for this purpose indeed; usually it can do no more than contribute to the choice as to which political leaders

[1] P. Hall, *Labour's New Frontiers* (London, 1964).

(themselves subject to various influences and advice) are to make the actual decisions. A rational voter has to pack a great number of specific judgements into a single act. Suppose voting on specific issues (referenda) to be introduced, the limitations still remain formidable; in particular (a) many voters from ignorance, apathy and other reasons will not address themselves to the actual issue and (b) the interests of voters in any issue vary considerably, some being hardly concerned, others closely involved or involved in several different capacities.

The first of these limitations is not in principle soluble through the conception of an individual preference function, because an individual cannot be made to exercise choice; if he doesn't do so and his interests are in consequence adversely affected, he can be said perhaps to deserve the result. The second limitation, however, might be partly overcome if some means existed for estimating the extent to which a policy choice would confer gains or penalties upon sets of individuals. Such tests will relate to aggregated bundles of wants or preferences and not to the way in which a particular individual might resolve his own conflict of interests or inclinations if he were able to do so. By contrast a political referendum does enable each individual to produce an integrated verdict if he chooses to do so, despite the other considerable limitations of this device.

It follows that the proper unit of accounting in such cases may be asserted to be not the individual as such, but the bundle of wants which a group of individuals happen to share in varying degrees. Thus bundle of wants may be tentatively described as an interest. Logically and ideally, a cost-benefit analysis will reveal the anticipated costs and benefits of a decision as they affect all relevant interests. For example, the costs and benefits of various airport locations will be attributed to such groups as air travellers, displaced householders, country lovers, etc.; and each group can be further sub-divided – for example, country lovers include bird watchers and possibly bird watchers could be sub-divided. Each of these interests should ideally be measured as the sum of the intensity of individual wants, which (again ideally) would be based upon some consistent test of the individual's willingness-to-pay (WTP) to achieve or to avoid the result in question. There is, of course, the problem that in ordinary parlance the individual can only pay what he can afford so that a theory is needed for discovering what 'spending-power' is available for making public policy choices. It is hard to find such a theory.

This economic approach to the articulation of interests offers an interesting parallel to political treatment of the same subject through the formation of 'interest groups'. For example, the AA claims to speak for various individuals in their capacities as motorists (and not of course in other capacities), and may be prepared to offer its opinion about the effects of some decision upon the 'aggregated preference function' of motorists although not in that language. Two differences between the economic and political methods of assessing interests may be mentioned:

(a) The political method works spontaneously, the economic one must be contrived. Only those interests which appear on the scene can enter into a political decision (although 'latent' or 'potential' interests may be included if recognised by a political leader or influential official). Thus the political recognition of interests is self-activating. However, the economic method logically requires explicit decisions as to *which* interests are to be judged relevant, *how* these interests are to be structured, *how far* forward in space or time the analysis is to be pushed, etc. Economic principles themselves do not help here because (as the theorists usually recognise) any decision has a virtual infinity of ripple effects upon some individual preferences. Nor are these questions unimportant, since the way that interests are structured has a considerable effect upon the outcome of the analysis, one that may often be more crucial than the choice of methods of quantification. In practice CBA usually deals with this problem by not asking too many questions. The analysts either rely upon 'common-sense' judgements, or else they follow guidelines set by the political process.

(b) On the other hand, it may be said that economic analysis should be much more 'objective' than the political process. Interest groups make extravagant claims and may not accurately represent the preferences of their supposed clients. By contrast CBA has no axe to grind and is trying to measure the intensity of individual wants in as objective a way as possible. Of course, the problems of measurement (both theoretical and practical) are extremely formidable, but at least they need not be defects of intentional bias. Against this it might be argued that interest groups are only one element in the total political process, and that if this whole process is adequately 'democratic' (a question needing much more exploration), its results will in fact achieve a better correspondence with the wants of individuals than economic analysis could even in principle manage. It is fair to say though that probably the best case for CBA is as a check upon interest group claims within a general policy framework.

JUSTICE AND WELFARE: POLITICAL OR ECONOMIC?

In the political process individuals and groups do not simply advance their wants as if these were self-validating. They express these wants as claims and counter-claims, and the claims that are in fact made reflect certain notions of justice and propriety. Political argument represents a continuous dialogue about the importance and legitimacy of the various claims, which in a democratic and pluralist society are continuously modified and adapted to take account of competing claims. For these reasons the political meaning of 'interest' is more flexible and slippery than the economic definition which we have just considered.

The difference does not rest upon any simple dichotomy between self-regarding and other-regarding attitudes. An individual's preference function as measured by economic analysis can perfectly well be altruistic. For example, I may value the pleasure which a beautiful landscape gives to others even though I cannot visit it myself, and I may be prepared to make some sacrifice to preserve it for others which might (at least in principle) be measured by economics. Conversely much of the political argument which goes on about justice is well known to be rhetoric and humbug. It may plausibly be said that, whatever the political talk about justice, the big battalions still get their way.

The differences then seem to concern process and language rather than any fundamental contrast of normative assumptions. But we must look more closely at this point. The political process, at any rate in modern democracies, appears to be guided by two very generalised sets of norms which are often in opposition:

(a) Respect for existing rights, which are generally given much more weight than a calculus of individual wants would seem to warrant. An example is the importance attached to wage or income differentials in so far as these are politically or organisationally determined. The differentials are changed only slowly, if at all. Such results cannot be justified by economic tests of utility whether these are applied to consumers or producers. To the extent that wages are responsive to consumers' demands they will respond flexibly to shifting patterns of taste or to shortages or to shifts in technical efficiency. But if the utility of workers is in question, it would seem plausible that the narrowing or abolition of a differential would confer more satisfaction upon poorer workers than would be removed from richer ones. This produces a familiar problem of welfare economics: whose interests – producers' or consumers' – are to be preferred? But in any event the only Utilitarian argument in defence of existing rights is an appeal to the close association alleged by some to exist between happiness and established expectations.

(b) Conversely, political argument shows respect for claims grounded in 'basic needs'. Contrary to the market-place, the wants of individuals are not accorded an equal political credit. Political dialogue confers more credit upon primary wants such as food, shelter and employment than upon secondary wants such as cars or holidays; more upon serious tastes such as education or music than frivolous ones such as drinking or gambling; and more upon the wants of the lowly than of the successful, so long at least as the former are sufficiently basic and sober.

How are these questions dealt with in CBA? They are certainly not simply disregarded, as can be seen from the very large part in the literature of welfare economics that is played by theories of distribution. But on close inspection these theories dissolve into ambiguities or contradictions which appear to reflect alternative political ideologies.

Classical welfare economics holds that consumers' satisfactions will be maximised in perfectly functioning markets (we must leave aside the meaning of 'perfectly functioning'), subject to there being an 'optimum' distribution of incomes. If there is not then the correct course is to redistribute incomes through taxation and subsidies, but not to interfere with how consumers spend their incomes. Unfortunately, the theory is silent as to how much redistribution is desirable, although the apparently reasonable assumption that the poor man's last penny gives him more satisfaction than the rich man gets from his creates a bias in favour of redistribution. These difficulties have led economists often to separate the two issues: to evaluate changes by their effect upon total wealth or assumed well-being (the 'efficiency principle') and to leave problems of distribution to be dealt with separately – if at all.

As CBA seeks to extend economic measurement into a broader range of phenomena this separation of the issues becomes still less adequate. For example, the Roskill Commission put a notional price upon the time absorbed in travelling, and it became natural to ask whether a rich man's time was worth more than a poor man's, an Englishman's than a foreigner's, and so on. The more conservative economists stuck to the 'efficiency' criterion; the more radical ones

urged that 'weights' should be applied to the various interests
according to norms of social justice, but the Commission felt unable
to use the suggestion.

A final twist to theories of distribution is provided by one of the
canons of welfare economics, the Pareto principle, which holds that
a change is worth making only if it leaves at least someone better-off
and no one worse off. Applied literally this is a profoundly conservative doctrine, reminiscent of natural rights (which is why CBA does
not usually apply it literally). For example, the householders who
told the Roskill research team (perhaps quite truthfully) that no sum
of money would compensate them for the loss of their homes were,
on the Pareto principle, putting a veto on this and perhaps any other
project.

This brief discussion illustrates some of the difficulties about the
differences between economic and political ways of thinking about
the nature of 'interests'. Welfare economics starts usually by assuming a perfectly functioning market so organised as to reflect
accurately the varying intensity of each consumer's wants. But this
model is subject to two assumptions, (a) that the distribution of incomes is satisfactory or anyhow, the best that is possible and (b) that
the content of consumers' wants is a matter of indifference (as
Bentham put it, 'quantity of pleasure' [e.g. utility] 'being equal,
pushball is as good as poetry'.

Now these assumptions *may* plausibly be regarded as ethically
valid within the context of those transactions that should properly
be left to the operation of the market. This is particularly true of the
second assumption – why should the consumer not spend his money
as he chooses, and which he supposes to yield him the most satisfaction, subject to certain limitations (which most economists would
accept) that are imposed by legal and moral prohibitions? And as
far as distribution of income is concerned, a rough-and-ready remedy
can be sought for inequity through the tax and subsidy methods
already noticed (although this may pose a choice between the
'efficiency' criterion of maximising total wealth and distributive
theories either of justice or of satisfaction).

But a critical question – for both politics and economics – is how
far resources should be managed through the market and how far
through public action. When welfare economics crosses the hazy
boundary between these sectors that is traditionally assumed to exist,
and seeks to apply its measuring-rod to as wide a spectrum of individual wants as it can, then political issues patently cannot be denied.
But how shall they be treated?

Curiously, welfare as politically understood is the most neglected

subject of welfare economics, because of its traditional indifference
to the *content* of individual wants, which may be 'basic' or
secondary, selfish or altruistic, capable of purely (or primarily)
private enjoyment or depending closely upon shared experience
– all with no difference to the logical status of the want. If
this position is maintained then economics cannot enter into the
debates about 'rights' and 'justice' which are the lifeblood of
politics, and the economic approach to the definition of 'interest'
would (if understood) command little support. For no politician
would admit that the sum of individual wants for bingo should be
given preference (if it proved to be larger) over the sum of individual
wants for health or education or defence. Nor could they agree to
'reckon' the price of a Norman church at its fire insurance policy or
at some better test of people's willingness-to-pay to preserve the
church. The Roskill Commission gave up its attempt to measure such
items in the face of much criticism, and also abandoned its initial,
still more ambitious attempt to put a price upon the loss of community life (as experienced of course by individuals) which the
demolition of a village would produce.

Now doubtless, as already noted, there is hypocrisy or double
standards in political and popular protestations on such matters.
After all, churches and villages are demolished even though a sum
of money would often suffice to shift the development in question to
another site; and the resources spent upon bingo are not shifted to
the Health Service. Still the language of politics is not simply hypo-
critical. It points to social standards or values which play some part –
no doubt an erratic one – in relating wants to ideas of rights, justice,
welfare and the good life.

Some welfare economists, as we have seen, accept the need, indeed
are often spurred by radical consciences, to get in on this debate.
They accept the case for 'weighting' values as between rich and
poor individuals. Once this is conceded, why should one not weight
also (as politicians pretend or try to do) for different kinds of want,
allocating a larger weight to those wants that are socially more useful
or defensible? No doubt it could be done. But to move along this
path perhaps does more credit to the hearts than the heads of the
economists. The difficulty is to know what really is being achieved
by translating into technical language differences of political and
ethical opinion, and by assigning to those differences a greater degree
of precision than their essentially flexible and argumentative character would seem to permit.

Other economists take a different road out. Utilising the Pareto
principle, as I have suggested, they stress the high economic price

which an individual can reasonably place upon some of his subjective experiences; as used by Mishan[2] this approach can build up
to a powerful defence of individual rights against the impact of
technological and economic expansion. But once again the argument
is in its essence political rather than economic. Indeed the argument
that very large (or even infinite) sums in compensation are due to
adversely affected individuals perhaps shows the hollowness of this
way of arguing an essentially ethical and political case; for many
who would accept the wrongness of destroying a village for the sake
of a motorway would also regard it as irrelevant or even wrong to
offer a vast financial compensation to those displaced.

Mishan's analysis appears to ignore normal ethical judgements.
He interprets the Pareto principle as requiring that a person shall
receive enough compensation for him to 'continue to feel as well
off' as he was before some adverse effect. But if, for example, I have
to move from a home and community which I have lived in all my
life, is there any sum of money which in itself will make me feel as
well off as before? (I might, of course, feel *more* content for different
reasons.) A very large sum will doubtless make me feel wealthier than
ever before, but a subjective state of experiencing wealth cannot be
compared with a subjective state of enjoying a given way of life,
except in the tangential sense that injury to the latter calls in justice
for compensation. But what compensation is just and what (if anything) will make me as content as before are different questions
which cannot be given the same answer.

Moreover the welfare economist who is prepared to appeal to
subjective valuation as a basis for compensation is treading a road
which is highly ambivalent in political terms. The critics of technological intrusion into private life will not necessarily (or indeed
probably) support the defence of a rich ex-urban enclave against the
claims of factory workers in urgent need of housing. Political theories
of justice and welfare can make the distinction without too much
difficulty. But a Pareto-based compensation theory of the sort being
discussed has to recognise the equally possible existence of a large
'consumers' surplus' in both types of case; or in other words, it is
logically biased towards the rights of all existing incumbents. This
theory then seems to mirror the stress often laid upon existing or
'established' rights in political debate; but to do so much more
extremely than political argument which is more open to counter-
claims relating to criteria of justice and welfare.

[2] E. J. Mishan, *Cost-Benefit Analysis* (London, 1971), Parts 2 and 3 and
Chap. 46 (from which quotation is taken). See also Mishan, *The Costs of
Economic Growth* (London, 1967).

Of course, one could modify this application of the Pareto principle by arguing that subjective evaluation by an individual of his expected loss is an arbitrary and unrealistic procedure, and can be meaningful only if there is an actual (as opposed to a notional) bargain being struck. In my view this is certainly so, in which case market prices become the appropriate guide for determining how much 'worse off' anyone is made in money terms. It will still be conceded that individuals may suffer a considerable loss of contentment as well, but this is just the loss for which in ordinary parlance money cannot compensate.

The case for nonetheless making a special monetary compensation arises in those cases where compulsion is being exercised or where evidence of market price does not exist; but compensation in such cases can only be based upon rough social norms of justice, such as the familiar idea that the compulsory acquisition of a dwelling should be compensated at, say, market price + 25 per cent. It is instructive that the Roskill survey team, after finding that some householders put the loss of their houses at infinity, fixed an arbitrary sum instead and conducted a straw poll to see whether ordinary opinion regarded the figure as reasonable. This exercise conceded that there was no 'right' price to be found in such cases other than some rough sum which might be defended (but could also be attacked) in terms of ordinary social norms. The Pareto principle then comes to depend closely for its application upon law and public opinion.

Why should welfare economists then get any credit for translating political issues into their own esoteric language? Our answer might be that if these 'translations' were exceptions to a generally objective process of measurement they might be tolerated as such; but they are much more than this. A deeper reason may be that economics is assumed to possess a single normative yardstick (such as consumers' welfare) which is lacking in politics. A little reflection shows this belief to be unfounded. The real reason, I suppose, is that few people know what CBA is about.

ECONOMICS, PLANNING AND HUMAN NATURE

It is interesting to compare the theories of policy-making which appear to underlie CBA with some alternative model of policy-making, and to ask what each assumes about the nature of man in society. Necessarily the exercise is somewhat speculative.

I have described CBA as the tool of a theory of economic populism. In an ideal model CBA is seeking to register the actual wants or preferences of individuals, and to convert these where possible to a standardised form of accounting, usually expressed in notional monetary terms, which permits the aggregation and subtraction of the raw material of individual wants. This has obvious attractions. It appears to be rational in that quantitative differences are substituted for qualitative ones; in fact, some exponents of the art deny rationality to any other method of making policies. The fallacy of this belief cannot be demonstrated here.

At the same time CBA offers an alternative of sorts to the obvious limitations of political populism and to the claims of political interest groups. Its claims here to objectivity depend upon how political values, such as those concerned with justice and welfare, are translated into economic analysis. If the analyst attempts to remain neutral on these points, as some do, he is left with a welter of alternative assumptions which he is wont to describe as 'sensitivity analysis'. The net result if honestly carried through is in almost every case an inconclusive analysis (if as is often said there are cases where almost any plausible combination of value assumptions would produce the same result, I suspect that this result would be obtainable by much simpler methods). But if the analyst accepts one of the various sets of values that are linked with welfare economics, he is at the same time holding a political position. He may be none the worse for that but it would be better to come into the open. The more mundane probability is that a cost benefit analysis will be organisationally biased. In this usual form it becomes a way of translating organisational claims into technical language. Whether anyone gains, once opponents do the same thing, is a moot point.

But CBA has other interesting tendencies. It is logically biased towards the greatest possible disaggregation of interests which are then recombined in the final analysis. In this way greater precision can be given to the ascertainment of wants. It is biased again towards projecting present preferences (or observable trends in those preferences) into the future; for what more reliable, or anyhow more democratic, methods are available? This prevents the analyst from allowing for situations and problems which the individuals being observed or interrogated cannot foresee; but, he may ask, who has such foresight? Then again CBA is biased ideally, like all economic reasoning, towards extending the range of the analysis as far as possible, with results that, of necessity, are increasingly speculative. Finally, CBA does not in principle have much respect for tradition or history – if the incidence and intensity of individual wants change (and this may happen frequently) the equation ideally should be recalculated.

We can present an alternative style of policy-making which may be loosely described as 'consensus planning'. Though democratic it is more authoritarian than CBA in the sense that it works through goals set by political leaders and other opinion leaders such as spokesmen for interest groups. It depends upon the construction of successive and related forums of generalised agreement or 'consensus'. It allows a considerable place to professional influence over the integration and application of policy goals. It is a historically grounded process in the sense that goals or standards once authoritatively established are not lightly revoked, and that policies build upon precedents.

The report of the Roskill Commission reflected the philosophy of cost-benefit analysis, even though the logical and political implications of the exercise were very weakly understood by the men who signed it. By contrast the minority report of Buchanan reflected the philosophy of consensus planning, albeit that Buchanan may have stretched the doctrine of professional interpretation beyond defensible limits. His rejection of any inland site for the airport was based upon the premise that the evolution of post-war planning policies, as well as a more recent movement of public opinion, pointed unequivocally in that direction – an interpretation of policy-making that was clearly open to question.[3]

What light does all this throw upon man in society? The 'planning' approach is prone to see the needs of man and society in integrated terms, whereas CBA proceeds through a successive differentiation of competing group and individual wants. There are echoes here of familiar divisions between idealist and individualist schools of thought or between modern structural functionalism and the logicians of individual choice (the 'sociologists' and 'economists' of Brian Barry's book).[4] Only as often happens the wires get crossed. The economic school may underplay the role of social norms, but it does not substitute for them a competitive struggle in the manner of either Bentley or Lasswell. It seeks rather the design of a perfect political market, where (just as in the perfect economic market) competing wants can be harmoniously reconciled with the aid of the analyst's skill. But the resulting picture of human nature and values that would emerge is left completely open-ended. There are no norms allowed for that could guide the articulation of wants, except to the extent that certain legal and ethical restrictions are admitted as unavoidable constraints. Some economists allow themselves the luxury of speculation whether certain 'costs' – for example that of

[3] *Report of the Commission on the Third London Airport* (London: H.M.S.O., 1971) (the Roskill Report).
[4] Brian M. Barry, *Sociologists, Economists and Democracy* (London, 1970).

putting up with a tiresome neighbour – are admissible in principle into cost-benefit equations, and Arrow suggests that second-order judgements may be needed to deal with cases of this kind.

Consider the way in which Ebenezer Howard[5] argued for new towns compared with the approach of cost-benefit analysis. Howard had two relevant beliefs or assumptions:

(1) that all men had similar likes and dislikes about certain things; for example they wanted a 'reasonable' range of social facilities and job opportunities close at hand, but they disliked crowded areas or long journeys;

(2) that men needed or anyhow benefited from certain opportunities such as frequent access to the countryside, and participation in community life.

On both tests he claimed that new towns were preferable to either big cities or rural areas because they achieved most of the virtues of each of these alternatives without the drawbacks.

A cost-benefit analyst would regard this as naïve. He would not start from the assumption that men had similar tastes, since they might be very different, and he would reject the Aristotelian character of Howard's second assumption. He would be more sympathetic, however, to Howard's contention about increasing returns following upon economies of scale and diminishing returns resulting from indirect congestion costs. This would be a way of saying that, to the extent that similar likes and dislikes can be posited, these can best be realised under given technological and other conditions in settlements of a given size.

This approach recognises the necessity of 'averaging' but the average emerges from the estimation of wants under given conditions, it is not based upon any norm. Of course, CBA must recognise that social norms influence individual preferences; only this influence is excluded from the analysis and certainly is not allowed to be a substitute for it.

By contrast what I have called 'consensus planning' is guided by a large number of social norms which play a subtle and often unconscious part in the processes of political and professional evaluation. Moreover consensus planning is guided also by certain general beliefs about the 'public interest' or 'common good' which are not usually inspected very closely – perhaps because to do so would uncover the often conflicting norms or values which have been built into the chosen policy. Policy-making moves in small jumps; once a

[5] Ebenezer Howard, *Garden Cities of Tomorrow* (London, 1902; new edition, 1946).

new measure has been introduced it is not likely to be set aside unless specific disadvantage to a considerable number of people can be convincingly demonstrated. For example, the London green belt has become an accepted element of 'consensus planning'. It might emerge badly from a cost-benefit analysis of who wins and who loses from its existence.

And this brings me to a crucial and final point. If we want to make out a brief for CBA we have to use a very modified version of the technique as an instrument of policy criticism, not as a positive instrument for decision or arbitration. It cannot be the latter because there is no authoritative way of defining and evaluating the 'interests' involved in a decision. But this is not the end of the matter because it certainly is the case that public action places an 'implicit price' upon all sorts of things that are not normally bought or sold. This implicit price is the resource cost that government is prepared to pay to achieve or to avoid some result. There are all sorts of problems about the measurement of resource costs, but at least respectable attempts can be made; and it is always worth trying to know costs even if we cannot measure the benefits in economic terms. If CBA supposes that it can measure these benefits in an independent and value-free way it becomes foolish; but if it is used simply to question the rationale of implicit prices and to point to *apparent* inconsistencies among these prices, it can become a useful tool of social criticism.

I emphasise the word *tool* because CBA must be powered by an enquiry into social values which cannot easily be derived, and is best not derived, from any normative theory of economics. Take a good field for such applications – the National Health Service. In principle the availability of NHS treatment is determined by only one criterion, that of medical need. Unfortunately resources are quite inadequate to provide all the treatment which this criterion properly requires. Other criteria are therefore introduced, which include various professional and ethical rules for determining the more urgent cases and 'fair share' principles for allocating any increase of resources among the various branches of medicine. Now cost-effective studies appear to show that there are considerable differences in the costs of preventive and curative treatment even between different branches of the same illness such as cancer. It would appear that the total amount of suffering might be appreciably reduced through a switch of resources within the NHS. But should the analysis stop here? On Utilitarian grounds one might also argue, for example, for concentrating cures upon those patients who have the best prospects of an adequate recovery and/or the longest life expectations. At each point the economic calculations become grounds for action only on the basis of a succession of normative positions, each of which can be opposed by other normative positions. It so happens that in this case Utilitarian philosophy has a powerful cutting edge when fuelled by economic data, but CBA has no more than a loose and somewhat ambivalent relationship with Utilitarian philosophy (this is an interesting field of discussion in itself).

When governments show themselves willing to spend a large sum upon 'saving amenities' in one context and very little in another, or will seemingly pay much more to avoid one type of accident than they will another, an interesting field of enquiry is opened up. But the most that can be done by CBA is to ask why outcomes are by implication so variously valued.

INDEX